ALWAYS THE YOUNG STRANGERS

BY CARL SANDBURG

ABRAHAM LINCOLN: THE PRAIRIE YEARS
  (*Two Volumes*), 1926
ABRAHAM LINCOLN: THE WAR YEARS (*Four Volumes*), 1939
ABRAHAM LINCOLN: THE PRAIRIE YEARS AND THE WAR YEARS
  (*One-Volume Edition*), 1954*
THE CHICAGO RACE RIOTS, 1919
THE AMERICAN SONGBAG, 1927*
STEICHEN THE PHOTOGRAPHER, 1929
POTATO FACE, 1930
MARY LINCOLN: WIFE AND WIDOW
  (*documented by Paul M. Angle*), 1932
STORM OVER THE LAND, 1942
HOME FRONT MEMO, 1943
THE PHOTOGRAPHS OF ABRAHAM LINCOLN
  (*with Frederick H. Meserve*), 1944
LINCOLN COLLECTOR: THE STORY OF THE
  OLIVER R. BARRETT LINCOLN COLLECTION, 1949
ALWAYS THE YOUNG STRANGERS, 1953*
THE SANDBURG RANGE, 1957
THE LETTERS OF CARL SANDBURG
  (*edited by Herbert Mitgang*), 1968

Novel
REMEMBRANCE ROCK, 1948*

Poetry
CHICAGO POEMS, 1916
CORNHUSKERS, 1918
SMOKE AND STEEL, 1920
SLABS OF THE SUNBURNT WEST, 1922
SELECTED POEMS (*edited by Rebecca West*), 1926
GOOD MORNING, AMERICA, 1928
THE PEOPLE, YES, 1936*
COMPLETE POEMS, 1950
HARVEST POEMS: 1910–1960, 1960*
HONEY AND SALT, 1963
THE COMPLETE POEMS OF CARL SANDBURG, 1970
BREATHING TOKENS, 1978

For Young Folks
ROOTABAGA STORIES, 1922
ROOTABAGA PIGEONS, 1923
ABE LINCOLN GROWS UP, 1928
EARLY MOON, 1930
PRAIRIE–TOWN BOY, 1955
WIND SONG, 1960
THE SANDBURG TREASURY, 1970
THE WEDDING PROCESSION OF THE RAG DOLL AND
  THE BROOM HANDLE AND WHO WAS IN IT, 1978
RAINBOWS ARE MADE, 1982

*Available in a Harvest/HBJ paperback edition

CARL SANDBURG

★ ★ ★ ★ ★

ALWAYS
THE
YOUNG
STRANGERS

A HARVEST/ HBJ BOOK

HARCOURT BRACE JOVANOVICH, PUBLISHERS

San Diego   New York   London

Library of Congress Cataloging-in-Publication Data
Always the young strangers/Carl Sandburg.
p.   cm.
Includes index.
ISBN 0-15-604765-9
1. Sandburg, Carl, 1878–1967—Biography—Youth. 2. Poets,
American—20th century—Biography. I. Title
PS3537.A618Z464   1991
811' .52—dc20   91-28099

TO MARY, MART, AND ESTHER

CONTENTS

SCROLL

Memory is when you look back
and the answers float in
to who? what? when? where?

The members who were there then
are repeated on a screen
are recalled on a scroll
are moved in a miniature drama,
are collected and recollected
for actions, speeches, silences,
set forth by images of the mind
and made in a mingling mist
to do again and to do over
precisely what they did do once—
this is memory—
sometimes slurred and blurred—
this is remembering—
sometimes wrecking the images
and proceeding again to reconstruct
what happened and how,
the many little involved answers
to who? what? when? where?
and more involved than any
     how? how?

—From Carl Sandburg, COMPLETE POEMS

ALWAYS THE YOUNG STRANGERS

All I can give you now is broken-face gargoyles.
All I can give you now is a double gorilla head with two fish mouths
and four eagle eyes hooked on a street wall, spouting water and
looking two ways to the ends of the street for the new people, the
young strangers, coming, coming, always coming

It is early.
I shall yet be footloose.

BROKEN-FACE GARGOYLES

★

ONE

★

Man-Child

★

A big unseen bell goes "Bong!" Knots come loose, long-woven bonds break from their folds and clutches. "It is my time now," says the mother while tugs and struggles in her womb say, "My time too has come." There is a tearing asunder of every last hold and bond, the violence of leaving the nine-month home to enter a second and vastly larger home. In the mother and the child the crashes and explosions go on, a series leading to the final expulsion. Not till then can there be a birth certificate, a name and a christening, a savage small mouth tugging at pink nipples.

Many have written and spoken it, "I was born—*why?*" Seeking the answer in brief, some have summarized it, "I was born because my father and mother met and exercised between them an ancient act of passion, love, and generation."

In my case the announcement came, *"Det är en pojke,"* the Swedish for "It is a boy," and so definitely not, *"Det är en flicka."* The first baby, some three years earlier, was my sister Mary. They wanted a boy. I was a welcome man-child.

I was born on a cornhusk mattress. Until I was past ten or more years, when we became a family of nine persons, I remember the mattresses were bedticking filled with cornhusks. And as we all slept well on cornhusks and never knew the feel of feather beds till far later years, we were in favor of what we had. Of the slats on which the mattress rested, we sometimes murmured. One would break, then another, till finally the mattress crashed to the floor—and we were suspicious of the new slats.

I was born a little after midnight, my mother told me. A Swedish midwife had been at hand early in the evening. She cut the umbilical cord, tended to the afterbirth, did her responsible duties, and was praised for her skill. This was in a three-room frame house on Third Street, the second house east of the Chicago, Burlington & Quincy Railroad tracks, in Galesburg, Illinois. The date was January 6, 1878. Exactly one year later on January 6 Joseph Medill Patterson was born. Exactly one hundred years earlier on January 6 Thomas Lincoln, the father of Abraham Lincoln, was born. And the coincidences of these births don't mean a thing except that the odd facts stick in the mind even though they prove nothing.

The midwife stayed two days, doing the needful, cooking and cleaning, seeing to my father's breakfast before he left to start swinging hammer and sledge at the C.B.&Q. blacksmith shop at seven in the morning. After those two days my mother was up and around, doing a washing, cutting and sewing diapers. Some of my diapers she made from Pillsbury Best Flour sacks. When the later babies came I saw her cut and hem the Pillsbury sacks in which came a white flour. Often we children heard from the father and mother, "In the old country we had *white* bread only at Easter and Christmas. Here in America we have *white* bread every day in the year!"

Of the house where I was born I remember nothing. I sucked at my mother's breasts there, had hundreds of changes of diapers and took healthy spankings there yet memory is a blank on those routine affairs. My sister Mary once pointed at the cradle in later years and said, "When they took me out they put him in." And a year and a half later they took me out to put Mart in. The cradle stood on three legs at each end, and mother told Mary that father made the cradle with his own hands. Mary said too that before I was three I ran away from home one afternoon and mother sent her to the C.B.&Q. shops and she brought father home from the shop and he found me a few blocks away going nowhere in particular.

We moved to another three-room one-story house, this on the north side of South Street, three doors west of Pearl Street. Here I wore dresses and watched my father spade a garden and plant and dig potatoes and carrots. I can never forget the feel of potatoes and carrots as my fingers brushed the black loam off them and I threw them into the baskets. Here we had the mare Dolly—a small bay, old, fat and slow—kept in a shed at the end of the lot. It was ten or fifteen dollars my father paid for Dolly, selling her after a year or two—for ten or fifteen dollars.

Dolly pulled us in a four-wheeled, two-seater wagon out from the town streets and houses to where we saw for the first time the open country, rolling prairie and timber, miles of zigzag rail fences, fields of corn and oats, cows, sheep, and horses feeding in pastures. Grazing animals in the open had wonder for me then and will always have.

We were fairly regular at Swedish Lutheran Church services, though about once a month of a Sunday morning father would throw the harness on old Dolly and the word was, "We are going to the Kranses." Out seven miles near a small coal-mine crossroads with a post office named Soperville, on a thirty-acre farm, lived John and his wife Lena Krans, Lena a cousin of my mother. Those four Swedish-born Americans had warm kinship. Their faces lighted on seeing each other. The Swedish language was hurled back and forth, too swift for us children to be sure what they were saying. When they talked of the steerage trip from Sweden, six to ten weeks on a sailing ship, their food only the black bread and cheese and baloney they brought along, we children couldn't quite follow it though we knew it was rugged going. The Kranses were the nearest kinfolk we had in America except for one family in Galesburg. Their talk ran warm and pleasant. They were strong for work, liked it, and talked it in those years of their thirties. Devoted Lutherans, convinced and complete Republicans, they couldn't argue religion or politics.

Here was a wooden barn with a dirt floor, three horses, four cows driven to and from the near-by pasture night and morning. Here we saw hands at udders, milk streaming into pails, pails carried up a slope to the house thirty yards away. There the cellar had a clean, hard dirt floor and plank shelves with a long line of crocks into which the milk was poured. We saw the yellow cream at the top of the crocks and once saw cream churned into butter. For the first

time we drank milk from cows we saw give the milk. For the first
time we ate fried eggs having seen the hens that laid the eggs.

Riding home from the Kranses I usually fell asleep and was laid
on the wagon bottom and awakened when we reached home in
Galesburg.

My father was a "black Swede," his hair straight and black, his
eyes black with a hint of brown, eyes rather deep-set in the bone,
and the skin crinkled with his smile or laugh. He was somewhat
below medium height, weighing about a hundred and forty-eight,
well muscled, the skin of his chest showing a pale white against
the grime when his collar was turned down. No sports interested
him, though he did make a genuine sport of work that needed to be
done. He was at the C.B.&Q. blacksmith shop, rated as "a helper,"
the year round, with no vacations, leaving home at six forty-five in
the morning, walking to arrive at the Q. shop at seven, never late,
mauling away at engine and car parts till twelve noon. He walked
home, ate the noon "dinner," walked back to the shop to begin work
at one and go on till the six o'clock whistle. Then he stood sledge
alongside anvil and walked home.

His hands thick with calluses, he was strictly "a horny-handed
son of toil." It would take him ten or fifteen minutes to get the soot
and grime off hands, face, and neck. He poured the cistern rain
water from a tin pail into a tin basin on a washstand, twice throwing
the used water into a tin pail on the floor before the final delicious
rinsing at a third basin of the water that had run off the roof into
the cistern. The calluses inside his hands were intricate with hollows
and fissures. To dig out the black grit from the deep cracks took
longer than any part of the washing. Even then there were black
lines of smudge that failed to come out. Then came supper and often
his favorite meat, pork chops fried well done. In late spring, summer,
and early fall, he would often work in the garden till after dark,
more than one night in October picking tomatoes and digging po-
tatoes by the light of a moon. In the colder months he always found
something to fix or improve in walls, floors, chairs, tables, the stove,
the coal shed, the cistern, the pump. He liked to sew patches on his
jeans pants or his work coat, having his own strong thread and large
needle for replacing lost buttons. In those early years he read a

weekly paper from Chicago, *Hemlandet*, the Swedish for Homeland. Regularly he or the mother read aloud, to each other and the children, from the Swedish Bible.

And the mother, young Clara Mathilda Anderson who had married my father, what was she like? She had fair hair, between blond and brown—the color of oat straw just before the sun tans it—eyes light-blue, the skin white as fresh linen by candlelight, the mouth for smiling. She had ten smiles for us to one from our father. Her nose was recessive, retroussé, not snub. Her full and rich white breasts—how can I forget them, having seen the babies one by one, year on year, nursing at them, having seen her leave the washtub to take up a crying child and feed it and go back to the washtub? She was five feet five inches in height, weighing perhaps one hundred and forty, tireless muscles on her bones, tireless about her housework. She did the cooking, washing, sewing, bedmaking, and housecleaning for the family of nine persons. At six o'clock in the morning she was up to get breakfast for her man, later breakfast for the children, and meals for all again at noon and at evening. Always there were clothes to be patched, the boys sometimes wearing out a third seat of trousers and having the other kids hollering, when the shirttail stuck out, "There's a letter in the post office for you!" As we got into long pants, the knees always needed patching. Playing marbles in the spring, wrestling, and scuffling, we wore holes at the knees of pants, going bare at the knees till "Mama" patched them. That was always our name for her when we spoke to her or of her in the family circle. The father always called her "Clara," spoken in Swedish as "Klawrah."

Two memories of the little South Street house stand clear. On a Sunday John Krans and his wife drove into town. They went to Lutheran church services with my father and mother and drove back to our house for a dinner of fried chicken, mashed potatoes, and gravy. I, still wearing dresses and about three years old, stood at the back door and watched John Krans snap a halter to the bit of one of the horses and tie the halter to the pump. Then Mr. Krans came into the house, gave me a pat on the head, and began talking with the folks. I stood watching that team of farm work horses, well-matched iron-grays hitched to a farmer's light market wagon. Then it hap-

pened. On a sudden impulse that I couldn't explain afterward, I ran
out to the pump, got my hands on the halter and pulled it loose. I
climbed up a wheel and got myself onto the seat. I had the reins
in my hands—oh glory! I was going to call "Giddap" to the horses.
Then my father and Mr. Krans came rushing out of the house. They
had me hauled down from that wagon in a flash. Then came a scold-
ing and reproaches. I was ashamed because I couldn't explain. I felt
guilty of doing something terribly foolish. The horses were facing
the garden, which was no place to take a pleasant Sunday drive. I
had never driven Dolly. My father had at no time offered me the
reins, though I recalled I had asked him once and he had said we
would wait till I was older. I have done many silly things in my life,
and often taken incalculable risks, but none so suddenly on impulse
and unaware of the danger.

The second memory is of late summer. South Street was dusty.
The black dirt had been ground fine by wheels and horseshoes over
many days of dry weather. My bare feet liked the feel of the street
dust. I was standing in the middle of the street. Along the wooden
sidewalk across the street from our house came a Negro woman
known as Mammy Lewis. She was the first woman of black skin I
had ever seen and a few days before I had heard neighbor boys older
than I hooting at her. Now she was walking along with long slow
steps, looking straight ahead. Standing there with bare feet in street
dust, I poked my head toward Mammy Lewis and called in my
loudest jeering child voice "Nigger! Nigger! Nigger!" Mammy
Lewis, a servant woman of good reputation, as I later came to know
well, stopped and turned slowly to see who could be so mean and
low as to cry like that at her on a sunny summer morning. We were
about twenty feet apart. I could see her eyes glisten. I heard her
voice, a marvelously deep harsh contralto. And she was saying words
that came slow and clear and made me know her dignity and her
righteous anger. She was saying, "I'll get a pair of scissors and cut
your ears off!" I heard her. I believed her. I picked up my feet and
scampered breathless into our house and clutched my mother's
skirts and more than half expected to see Mammy Lewis come
through the door with the promised scissors. That morning I didn't
dare tell my mother what had happened, though later I managed to

get it told. She gave me a talk in Swedish. What I had done was bad manners, was not Christian, and I should look out about following the ways of the older neighbor boys. Sweetly and softly she could say, "*Var en snäll pojke*" (Be a good boy).

When I was about four we moved two blocks over to Berrien Street and a ten-room house with a long roomy third-story garret running the length of the house, a four-room cellar having floors in the two front rooms. A two-compartment privy had a henhouse back of it. The lot was three times the size of the South Street place, had a big garden with several gooseberry bushes, a front yard with five tall soft-maple trees, a picket fence, a brick sidewalk, and a ditch in front. It was really two houses and lots. Over the front door a small tin sign read "Aetna Fire Insurance Company" to show that the house was insured, and two sign numbers said that we lived at 622 and 624 East Berrien Street. Here the emigrant Swede August Sandburg set himself up, with due humility and constant anxiety, as a landlord. The two east rooms of the first floor, along with the two cellar rooms under them, were rented to different families across the years, never vacant for more than a day or two, while the large upstairs east rooms always had a renter.

My father wrote no letters. He did no writing at all. He had never learned to write. When his father and mother died in Sweden his schooling had only taught him to read and he earned some kind of a living as a chore boy in a distillery. He became a teamster at the distillery, finally laying by enough money to buy steerage passage to America, to "the new country where there was a better chance." Arriving at the port of New York, Swedes who had kinfolk at Herkimer, New York, sent him to a job in a cheese factory there. After a few months at cheese-making he read a letter from a cousin, Magnus Holmes, in Galesburg, Illinois, who wrote that the chances were all good in Galesburg. Magnus Holmes ought to know. He had been in Galesburg for many years. Holmes had a face with likeness to my father's, their faces more alike than is common among brothers. Holmes voted for Lincoln, but refused to answer Lincoln's call for troops. He had left Sweden to keep out of military service. He hated war and had a conscience about it. As his daughter Lily told me more than once, "He wouldn't argue with anyone about it, simply wouldn't talk, except to say to his wife and children that he couldn't take a hand in killing men." So on account of Holmes hating military service and leaving Sweden early, to end up at work in a C.B.&Q. Railroad shop, he was there to advise a newcomer cousin to come on West and get a job. The first job my father had was on the Q. railroad with a construction gang at a dollar a day. They lived in bunk cars, cooked their own meals, did their own washing, worked six days a week, ten hours a day.

My father had respect and affection for his cousin Magnus Holmes, and it lasted. Holmes was older by fifteen years. He had become well Americanized when August Sandburg arrived at Holmes' house in Galesburg in the early 1870's. The older cousin had been in Galesburg more than fifteen years. The men he worked with on the job were mostly Irish and English, and he and Mrs. Holmes learned English so well that they made it the one language spoken in their house. Their four sons never learned to speak Swedish. Their daughter Lily learned her Swedish speech by going one summer to the Swedish Lutheran parish school kept in a barnlike building west of the church. "One summer of my keeping company with the Lutherans and having them teach me was enough for my father," Lily told me. "He was a steady member of the Swedish Methodist Church and if I had joined the Lutherans he would have taken my head off." Lily told it just so.

The interesting fact was that a Swedish emigrant and his wife learned the language of the new country so well before the children began coming that four of the five children never learned Swedish and the one who did learned it outside the home. In the Sandburg family the first three children, Mary, Carl August, and Martin Godfrey, learned their Swedish fairly well, and the two boys, Emil and Fred, and the two girls, Esther and Martha, who came later knew that *mjölk* was milk but they couldn't count to six in Swedish.

I am sure that while I was still in dresses, not yet in my first pair of pants, I used only Swedish words and sentences to tell what I was wanting. I would say, "*Ja vill ha vatten*" (I want a drink of water) or "*Ja är varm*" (I am warm) or "*Ja är kall*" (I am cold).

I said *far* (pronounced "fawr") before I learned the word

"father"—and *"mor"* (pronounced "moor") before I learned to say "mother."

The English words for things to eat and wear, *mjölk* (milk), *bröd* (bread), *sko* (shoe), *strumpor* (stockings) my little tongue picked up after I was out of dresses. There was an early day when I looked out of a window in the South Street house and saw the ground white and more of the white coming down and my mother nodded toward it and said with a smile, *"Snö."* It was the first snow I ever saw with a name to it. There was the first time I saw drops of water streaking down from high up somewhere and splashing and shining as it dripped and ran from trees, bushes, and the house roof. I heard then from my mother the word *regn.*

I can remember my father saying, *"Nu ska vi spela"* (Now shall we play) and throwing me into the air and catching me as I came down. He would put me eight or ten feet from him, stoop low and call to me, *"Spring fort nu."* And so I learned three Swedish words meaning "Now run fast." My mother would lay me down saying, *"Sov nu, sov min pojke,"* and I came to know she meant I should shut my eyes and let something soft and cozy come over me. The time came when I could say each of those words and I knew they meant, "Sleep now, sleep my boy."

The word *skratta* came early. I was saying *skratta* sooner than I said "laugh." They mean the same but I have always felt that *"skratta"* (pronounced "skrah-tah") comes out of the mouth with more of a funny twist than the English word "laugh." So with the word *gråta.* Early I heard from mother and father, *"Du ska inte gråta,"* or *"Gråt inte"* or *"Varför gråter ni?"* meaning, "You should not cry" or "Why do you cry?" I may have been bawling with tears running down my face because I was hungry or a safety pin had come loose and was sticking me. I may have been learning to walk and fell when stumbling and heard the words *"Varför gråter ni?"* (Why do you cry?). Ever since then the word *gråta* to me means "weep" rather than "cry"—it is a word you sort of grind and gnash when you say it.

Early a spoon of pea soup or a piece of fried egg would be held toward me with the word *"smaka"* (pronounced "smawkah") meaning "smack of it" or "taste it." Early too when face and hands were dirty I would hear, "*Vaska dig*," meaning "Wash yourself." Early my nose had to be blown and I learned to call for "*en näsduk*," meaning "a nosecloth" or handkerchief.

When the Kranses or Holmeses came there would be talk about different relatives. I heard the word *farfar* (and found it meant father's father) and *farmor* (meaning father's mother). Your *morfar* is your mother's father and your *mormor* is your mother's mother. These words seemed so queer to me when I first heard them that I had a feeling I wouldn't understand them. I was surprised at how easy I got them into my head. When one day I asked my mother if her mother's mother's mother was her *mormormor*, she told me to run along and play with my new two-wheeled wagon.

I would guess there were two or three hundred words I learned in Swedish before I learned them in English. I believe one thing that has happened to me in the world of language other millions of good American citizens have known. There are words we no longer use. Those words belong to the language of a foreign country. In a way you might call them "lost words." We use them and say them over sometimes when talking with those who like us feel something warm and cozy about those words because we knew them so well in our earliest years.

Among the younger church members later there were grumblings and mutterings. "Why must we listen to sermons in Swedish when we don't know what the words mean and we can't understand what the preacher is telling us?" After a time there were occasional sermons in English, and changes went on in many churches till all the preaching was in English. This didn't come easy for gray-bearded old-timers who could remember when they sat in their pews two hours with their ears drinking in the beloved syllables of the speech of *hemlandet*, the homeland that still had its hold over them.

From Magnus Holmes, August Sandburg learned many simple and important English words he needed. And this cousin explained where to go and what papers to sign in order to become an American citizen and voter. For years the Holmeses came to the Sandburgs for Thanksgiving dinner and the Sandburgs went to the Holmeses on New Year's Day. Once in our house on Thanksgiving I heard Mr. Holmes give a talk on the Declaration of Independence and then make clear to my father the Constitution of the United States. The one time later that I heard my father refer to the Constitution was when he said, "The Civil War was a fight so they could put it in the Constitution no man could have slaves."

Magnus Holmes bought a used lumberyard office on South near Seminary, had it moved on rollers pulled by horses to a vacant lot he owned next to his home. This he fixed over into a house to rent. I am sure that when my father bought the Berrien Street house he had talked over with his cousin the advantages of having enough rooms so you could rent them and have cash coming in every month from renters. And when August Sandburg went in for buying a quarter section of land away out in Pawnee County, Kansas, he was keeping pace with his cousin, who had bought a quarter section near Holdrege, Nebraska.

Though Mr. Holmes spoke to his cousin as "August" and August usually called him "Magnus." we children and our mother always spoke to him as "Mister Holmes." We gave him no nickname and it pleased us and came natural to always call him "Mister Holmes."

We heard about his quarter section of land out in Nebraska, taxes to pay on it every year, and Frank Holmes, the twenty-year-old son at last saying, "Papa, why can't I go out there and make a farm on that land?" So Frank went out there, built him a sod house, plowed the smooth bare prairie, not a tree in sight, raised corn and fed cattle and hogs. The third year of "batching it," he wrote letters home about how lonely he was. His sister Lily had graduated from high school and had a certificate she could teach school. She offered to go out and keep Frank company and show the Nebraska children how to read, write, and figure. Frank wrote back that sister Lily couldn't come on any too soon, he was that lonesome. Lily packed her best clothes, took a morning train, saying to the folks, "I'll be in Nebraska tomorrow afternoon and I haven't forgotten my teacher's certificate." The school district board said she could teach if she didn't mind a sod house for a school. She said she believed the children in Nebraska could learn to read and write in a house built of brick. stone, wood, or sod. They told her the pay would be twenty-five dollars a month and the school year six months. She said that in Illinois plenty of the country schoolteachers were getting exactly twenty-five dollars a month and sometimes they weren't worth that. At this both Lily, the new teacher, and the board members took a laugh. She found the sod schoolhouse clean and warm, the pupils well behaved and ready to learn, the stove burning coal and corn-cobs—and corn, when the price of corn went too low. The floor was of dirt packed down hard and the pupils sat on long benches facing long board tables.

"After six months of teaching," Lily told me, "the board gave me an order for one hundred and fifty dollars. I found it couldn't be cashed right away. I gave it to Frank and he traded it for a wind-mill and at last had a regular water supply. He had dug one well and then another till there were four holes in the ground that had gone dry on him. You had to go deep to get water for your cows and steers." On going into some of the sod houses, Lily was surprised and pleased to find them floored and the walls plastered. Most of the settlers around and about were Swedes talking Swedish and Frank was glad to have his sister to talk English with.

Lily joined the Swedish Methodist Church, telling them that was her church back in Illinois. She attended services regularly. Also she attended several square dances. The church deacons heard of it and checked up on it. The deacons and the minister took action. They were against dances, whether square or round. "And they cut me off from the membership," Lily told me. When she came back to Galesburg she joined the American Methodist Church and a few years later it was the minister of that church, the Reverend Charles H. Blodgett, who united her in marriage to Albert Harpman. I was delivering milk to the Blodgett house and often saw there and on the streets a red-haired, stockily built boy in short pants with thick strong legs. I knew he was Tom Blodgett, the minister's son, but I didn't know that he would become Chairman of the Board and President of the American Chicle Company, Chairman of the Board and President of the American Writing Paper Corporation, a director of the Wilbur-Suchard Chocolate Company, and one of the fathers of the girl Sue Shard whose face is familiar to fanciers of chocolate almond bars.

Lily Holmes liked to tell of her father's talk about driving into the country to see some Swedish friends and at North Creek of passing through the Barefoot Nation. That was the name given to a huddle of shanties where Irish laborers lived with their families. "Everybody runs barefoot," said Mr. Holmes. "The little houses have no windows. *They bring the daylight into the houses in sacks.*"

"The Barefoot Nation" in time was shortened to "Barefoot," and if you had no shoes you said you were going barefoot to Barefoot. My rich-hearted Irish friend and comrade William P. ("Wiz") Brown told me that shoes and shoe leather cost more good money than some families at Barefoot could afford. There were families with only one pair of shoes, and whoever on Sundays and holidays was the first to get out of bed jumped into that one pair of shoes. In one family, said Wiz, there was a young fellow who was sweet on a girl over at Henderson Grove. And one Sunday and holiday after another he was too slow getting out of bed, so he walked barefoot to see his girl. Henderson Grove people saw him coming and said, "He's from the Barefoot Nation over there on North Creek." When I asked Wiz about the houses with no windows and bringing in daylight in sacks, he said, "That's a joke they had in Ireland a thousand years ago." When I asked John Krans about carrying in daylight by the sackful he said, "I heard that in Sweden when I was a boy."

Magnus Holmes was my father's close friend and adviser over many years. He arrived in Galesburg by rail in 1854, the first year the C.B.&Q. reached Galesburg, and joined a gang that built a bridge over the Rock River. He was nineteen. Had he stayed two years longer in Sweden he would have had to serve two years in the Swedish army. His father, Lars Holm, spent all his years after he was twenty-one serving in the Swedish army, till he was retired. Lars Holm went by the name of Lars Sturm when stationed at a place named Sturm, and when they stationed him at a garrison named Holm, he changed his name to Holm. And Magnus Holm, the son of Lars Holm, had seen army life close up, didn't want to be a soldier, and at nineteen skipped Sweden, took steerage passage for the port of New York on a sailing vessel that buffeted stormy seas for ten weeks and, blown out of its course, landed at Quebec.

Magnus Holm reached Albany, took the Erie Canal to Buffalo and railroads to Chicago and Galesburg. There in Galesburg he kept his

name of Magnus and changed his name of Holm to Holmes because
Holm sounded Swedish and Holmes sounded English. He worked
with a railroad construction gang out of Hannibal, Missouri. At a
Methodist camp meeting he fell in love with a Swedish girl. She was
a housemaid living with a family that kept slaves. She moved from
Hannibal to Galesburg, and Holmes used to call on her when she
worked at the Ladies' Dormitory of Lombard College and he had a
job in the Q. blacksmith shop forging and hammering bolts. He
was interested that she was not merely good-looking and handy as
a cook but that she owned a book she was reading, a translation of
Faust.

They went to the Knox College campus the afternoon of October
7, 1858, and stood for three hours in a sour and cold northwest wind,
in a crowd of twenty thousand, listening to the famous debate be-
tween Abraham Lincoln and Stephen Douglas. They were married,
and fifty years later, in the year of 1908, the fiftieth anniversary of
the debate, they sat on the speakers' platform alongside a few others
who had heard Lincoln and Douglas that October day. They looked
out from the west wall of the college on a crowd of twenty-five
thousand. They saw near them on the platform Mrs. Henry R.
Sanderson, at whose home Lincoln had been entertained. They heard
William H. Taft, Republican nominee for President of the United
States, and other speakers, including former Vice-President of the
United States Adlai E. Stevenson and Robert Douglas, a grandson
of the man who debated with Lincoln.

I was away from Galesburg when Magnus Holmes died, and it
was twenty-three years after the 1908 ceremonial that I saw Mrs.
Magnus Holmes in Owatonna, Minnesota, at the home of her daugh-
ter Lily. The girl who met Magnus Holmes in slavery days at
Hannibal, Missouri, lay bedfast at ninety-one years of age, smiling
brightly and talking with a clear mind of old days when my father
arrived at their house and took advice from Mr. Holmes, and remem-
bering that when my father worked on a construction gang he often
spent Saturday nights and Sunday at their house. Her daughter Lily
wasn't absolutely sure she remembered clearly that August Sand-
burg's father and Magnus Holmes' father were brothers. The
mother's quick answer came: "Yes, they were brothers and we

called their sons cousins." And the aged woman tried to recollect whether she had ever heard what August Sandburg's father did for a living, what he worked at, whether he had a trade, what kind of a peasant on the Swedish land he had been. She could only remember that this grandfather of mine, on my father's side, my *farfar*, had died much earlier than his brother Lars Sturm who changed his name to Lars Holm. And the aged woman and her daughter both recalled Magnus Holmes saying that having served in a garrison town named Sturm, he was not sure but that Lars Sturm had had some other surname than Sturm before he went into the army. My guess would be that the surname was Danielson, because once when I asked my mother if August Sandburg's name had been Johnson before he changed to Sandburg, my mother said positively that his name had been August Danielson.

So there we are. I may be a Sturm, but to the best of my belief I am a Danielson come to judgment. I don't wonder genealogy is a racket and the genealogy room at the Library of Congress is always packed with pedigree-seekers. Once on a train from Fort Worth, Texas, to Denver, Colorado, I had long talks with an oil man who had hit a gusher and was riding high, flush with money. He told of his wife with aristocratic hopes having their ancestral branches examined and charted by a journeyman genealogist. He chuckled as he told it. "And would you believe it? It turned out we had horse thieves on both sides of the family!" He liked it. He was that kind of an American. He knew that if you get too familiar with the closet skeletons of your numerous incalculable ancestors you're going to run into some black sheep and more than one stinker you'd like to forget. I may yet go to Sweden and mull around in church records of births, weddings, deaths, and learn whether I am a Sturm or a Danielson. For the sound of it I would prefer the name of Sturm. I have never met a Sturm and I shall look with curiosity at any Sturm I meet. The name Sturm could be woven into a song to be strummed on a guitar. I could hear the greeting in Linköping, "*Hur mår Herr Sturm?*" meaning, "How are you, Mister Sturm?" The betting, however, is that it will turn out Danielson.

What kind of a clean wholesome *flicka* did this grandfather Danielson (?) of mine pick for a wife? They died early and my orphaned father August Danielson (?) went to work instead of to school, having just enough schooling to learn to read. What was it came along and swept away both the father and mother of my father? Did they both fade out about the same time? Could it have been Asiatic cholera, in those years making its devastations in Europe and America, and which took away Carl Holm, a brother of Magnus, and others whose names sprinkle the records? And if I got the answers to all these questions, then what? Would the answers serve anything more than to gratify a mild curiosity? Isn't there a case to be made out for the man who pointed out a verity in saying, "I don't know who my ancestors were but we've been descending for a long time"?

*

TWO

*

The House on Berrien Street

*

In the house at 622-24 East Berrien Street I was to live growing, formative years from 1882 to 1899, from dresses to short pants to long pants, from a babbler with bibs to a grown young man. In that house came babies across ten years, the bright companionable boy Emil, the vague younger one Fred, the beautiful girl Esther and her plain and modest sister Martha.

I was six years old on the October night I walked holding my father's hand from home to Seminary Street near South. It was the first time I saw politics run hot in the blood of men. Hundreds of men were standing in line, two by two. The line ran farther than my eyes could see. The sidewalk edges were black with people waiting to see the march begin. My father had told me it was "a Republican rally" and would be good to see. The men standing in line two by two were Republicans. Each man had a pole over his shoulder. At the end of the pole swung a lighted torch. I had never seen one torch in my life, and now of a sudden I saw hundreds of torches in a straight line in the middle of Seminary Street. Over his shoulders each man had a red, white, and blue oilskin cape. Drippings from the kerosene lamp of the torch fell on the oilskin.

We walked north and came to the men carrying flambeaus. When the order was given they put their lips to a pipe that ran high over their heads. When twenty of them blew into their pipes it sent up into the air from those pipe ends twenty tongues of fire three or four feet high, spreading and weaving like twenty big flowers

31

of fire. I had never seen one flambeau before, and now to see twenty of them blaze up at once was a wonder. When the long red and yellow tongues slowed down and flickered out, the darkness was darker and I hoped they would soon blaze up again. I would not forget the word "flambeau" I heard that night for the first time.

We walked farther north to the brass band heading the procession. In front of them and leading them as they turned into Main Street was a tall man in yellow pants with a red coat and a red-velvet hat nearly as tall as I was. He had a stick with a big gold ball on the end and with this stick he motioned the parade how to make the turn. West on Main Street went the brass band marching and blowing horns and pounding drums.

On a Main Street corner we watched the parade go by. Every man marching was a Republican. By marching he was showing the Democrats he was a Republican. My father explained that to me. I heard the marching men call and holler to people along the sidewalks. What they called and hollered most often was "Hurrah for Blaine!" or "Blaine for President!" Sometimes a hundred of them would be keeping time with their feet to the words, "Blaine, Blaine, James G. Blaine." I had heard that Blaine was a man far away somewhere and he was the man the Republicans wanted for President. And the President was the head of the country, the highest man of all, and you couldn't go higher than to be President of the country.

I heard a man on the sidewalk yell out, "Hurrah for Cleveland!" Right away came howls from the procession, "And a rope to hang him!" I asked my father about it and he said, "Cleveland is a Democrat. He is against Blaine."

On the way home I asked my father more questions. Most of his answers were short. He gave me the idea that Republicans are good men and Democrats are either bad men, or good men gone wrong, or sort of dumb. I wondered if someday I would march with a torch. Maybe I might even have a flambeau someday and blow into a pipe and watch a line of fire go up and up and wriggle into a big fire flower. And I had a feeling that Cleveland was an ugly man, ugly as you could think of, and if the Republicans got a rope and hanged him I wouldn't be sorry. Nobody had ever explained to me exactly how you hang a man, but if hanging was what the Republicans wanted for Cleveland then I was for it. I was a young Republican, a six-year-old Republican.

A few months later came the election. I was told that Grover Cleveland, instead of being hanged, had been elected President of the United States. And when Cleveland named a new postmaster for Galesburg it was William Twohig. He lived only two blocks from us in a plain frame house and we called him Billy Twohig. In his back yard he had a sand pile. When my father had bricklaying to do he sent me with a wheelbarrow over to Billy Twohig's for ten cents' worth of sand. I mixed this sand with ten or fifteen cents' worth of lime that I had carried in a paper bag from Bogue's lumber-yard next to the Q. depot. I poured water over the sand and lime as I shoved a hoe back and forth to mix the mortar. I liked the smoky fume that came up from the lime. And on these trips to Billy Twohig's house I met him and came to know him. He was fair in his dealings and I thought he was a pretty good man even though he was a Democrat, even though the ugly Grover Cleveland had named him the Galesburg postmaster and boss of all the mail carriers. My father too liked Billy Twohig. It was so mixed up in my head about the Republicans and the Democrats that I didn't ask my father any questions about it.

A few years later I heard Republicans marching and singing, "We'll hang Grover Cleveland to a sour apple tree," men and boys keeping step to, "Dead cats and rotten cats are good enough for Democrats." And it stayed with me, the story that a lean, ragged man came to the White House lawn and got down on his hands and knees and was chewing at the grass. President Cleveland from a front window saw the man and asked, "What are you doing?" When the man said, "I'm hungry and have to eat grass," Cleveland told him, "Why don't you go around to the back yard where the grass is longer?" I was suspicious it might have happened.

A story had come out that Cleveland was the father of a baby by a woman named Maria he wasn't married to. And there was a rhyme that some Democrats liked to say for the Republicans after Cleveland was elected:

> Hurray for Maria,
> Hurray for the kid.
> I voted for Cleveland
> And I'm dam glad I did.

I was seven and a half years old when General Ulysses S. Grant died and I went to his funeral. He had died somewhere away far off from Galesburg, I didn't hear where. And they didn't bring his body to Galesburg. But Main Street stores closed for the afternoon and the Q. shops and the Brown Cornplanter Works and Frost's foundry shut down for the afternoon. A parade began at the Q. depot on Seminary Street and moved to Main Street, turned west, and marched to the Public Square. They said it was the longest parade Galesburg had ever seen.

The five long blocks of Main Street sidewalks from Seminary to the Square, on both sides of the street, were crowded with people. It was a hot July afternoon in 1885. My father had been pushed and squeezed and had done some pushing and squeezing himself till at last we stood about three or four feet from the curb in front of the big O. T. Johnson dry-goods store. It was good they had made me put on shoes and stockings, because the way I got tramped on would have been worse if I had been barefoot. I tried to see the parade looking between the legs of men ahead of me but all I saw was more legs of more men. I pulled my father's hand and blubbered, "I can't see! I can't see!"

My father lifted me up, stuck his head between my legs, and there I sat straddle of him, and only a giant could see the parade better than I could. There was a marshal of the parade on a skittish sorrel horse with a shiny bridle and with brass buttons, each bigger than a silver dollar, on the saddle. The marshal rode at the head of the parade and made people know they ought not to get in the way of the parade. Then came two rows of policemen with nickel-plated stars shining on their blue coats. Each had a belt with a club hanging from it and they marched with straight faces as though they could take care of any trouble that might come up. Then came a fife-and-drum corps. It seemed the pounding noise they made was shaking the buildings and I took a better grip on my father's hat to make sure I wouldn't fall off. Then came a long line of men dressed like they might be going to church on Sunday, keeping their faces straight like they were in church, marching four in a row.

The Galesburg Marine Band marched past, men walking and their mouths blowing into their horns as they walked. One man had a big horn that seemed to be wrapped around him and I was puzzled how he got into it. They had on blue coats and pants and the stripe down the sides of the pants was either red or yellow and looked pretty. Their music was slow and sad. General Grant was dead and this was part of his funeral and the music should be sad. It was only twenty years since the war ended and General Grant was the greatest general in the war and they wanted to show they were sad because he was dead. That was the feeling I had and I could see there were many others had this same feeling. Marching past came men wearing dark-blue coats and big black hats tied round with a little cord of what looked like gold with a knot and a little tassel. They were the G.A.R., the Grand Army of the Republic, and I heard that some of these men had seen General Grant and had been in the war with him and could tell how he looked on a horse and what made him a great general. Eight or ten of these G.A.R. men walked along the sides of a long black box on some kind of a black car pulled by eight black horses. The body of General Grant wasn't in the box, but somewhere far away General Grant was being buried in a box like this one. I could see everybody around was more quiet when this part of the parade passed.

I remember one or two cannon came past with six or eight horses pulling them. The Negro Silver Cornet Band marched. Their music too was slow and sad. I saw them with the only black faces from the beginning to the end of the parade, and as they passed I saw faces of men and women light up though they didn't smile. I had heard from my father and Mr. Holmes that the war where Grant was the big general was a war for the black people to be free. I didn't quite understand what it was for people to be not free, to be whipped and worked hard and bought and sold like horses. There was nothing like it in Galesburg or Knox County. But whatever it was it was terrible, and men would shake their heads talking about it. So there was something people liked about seeing the black men with their horns playing sad music because General Grant, who had helped them get free, was dead.

A big flag was swinging high over the man carrying it. The end of the pole holding the flag came to some kind of a pocket the man had in a belt around his middle. It looked heavy to carry and I could see the sweat rolling on the puffed-out cheeks of the chunky man carrying a flag that went away high over him.

The parade was different from other parades I had seen. I had seen a circus parade and people on the sidewalks laughing and hollering at the clowns and elephants and wild animals in cages. I had seen the Republican rally parade with torchlights, and the Democrats on the sidewalks hooted the Republicans marching and the Republicans hooted back. But in this General Grant funeral parade there was no laughing, no hooting, and the men marching had straight faces and so did the people on the sidewalks. Except the two bands and the fife-and-drum corps and the sound of feet and horse hoofs and wheels on the street stones, you couldn't hear much of anything. Even the slow sad music the bands played seemed quiet. I had heard those bands play "Yankee Doodle" and "Pop Goes the Weasel" and they made you feel like running and hollering. I didn't see any boys running or hollering. What three or four boys and girls I saw stood still in their foot tracks watching the parade go past. They shifted their feet a little when the marshal's horse acted skittish as though it might run up on a sidewalk full of people. The children stood with straight faces like the old folks. They knew, like I did, that it was a day that meant something.

I remember how hard I tried to think about what the war was and what General Grant did that made him the greatest general of all. I heard that he had been the President, the head man of the government in Washington. And now since he was dead and somewhere far away they were laying him in a coffin in the cold ground, he would never come back to be a great general in a war again and he would never be President and head man of the government in Washington again. I heard too that he was one of the high men of the Republican party and the Republicans would miss him. I heard too that there were some Democrats who had been in the war with General Grant and they liked the way he did things and the way he treated them and these Democrats were sorry along with the Republicans.

My father kept his hands on my feet and legs and I think the only smile I saw while the parade was passing was once when my father turned his face up toward me and felt good over the way he had fixed it so I could see the parade.

It was nearly like being in church the way people kept still and never smiled while the parade passed. But it wasn't like being in church to look at a pretty girl in a pink dress near us. She was about my size. She stood on the sidewalk edge, maybe three feet in front of my father and me. She looked puzzled when she saw me away up there high over her and straddling my father's neck and shoulders. Then she went on looking at the parade. Several times I took my eyes off the parade and watched what she was doing. Her right hand would go down somewhere and come up and put something in her mouth and I could see her mouth working. Then I saw what she was putting in her mouth—peanuts! I couldn't see her hands shelling the peanuts but that was what she was doing. While the parade was passing she must have chewed and swallowed half a five-cent sack, maybe a whole sack, of peanuts. Two or three times she turned her head and I caught her looking up to see if I was where she saw me the last time, as if I might fall off and if I did she didn't want to miss it. She went right on chewing peanuts while she looked at me. And when she turned her head back to see the parade I could see her jaws working and her hand going down for more peanuts to shell and put in her mouth. She had a pretty face and her pink dress seemed to go with her face. The parade was about half over when I said to myself I would watch the parade and not let her bother me. When the parade was nearly over I did sneak a look toward her, and when she caught me watching her jaws wagging I made an ugly face at her. I never saw her again.

My father let me down from his neck and shoulders. We walked along Main Street among thousands of people. And now you could see a smile once in a while and boys snickering and bumping each other. We walked home. I could see it was a day that meant some-

thing to my father but he didn't tell me. In some store windows I
noticed pictures of General Grant with black cloth hung around
them. I couldn't see where he looked so different from other men I
had seen with whiskers over the whole face and the hairs cut close.
He didn't look much different from Mr. Grubb, the Lombard pro-
fessor who lived across the street from us and every morning milked
his cow before going to the college. And then I said to myself that
even though Professor Grubb's face was nearly exactly like General
Grant's face, if he should die there wouldn't be any such parade as
we had seen for General Grant. I went to bed that night saying I
hoped sometime I would know more about the war, about the black
people made free, about Grant the general and what it was like to
be President and the head man of the government in Washington.
When the face of the pretty girl chewing peanuts came back to me
for half a minute I gave her an ugly look. Later her face came back
again and she gave me an ugly look. And I was so tired I went to
sleep without making any kind of a face back at her.

The ten-room house on Berrien Street was a challenge to August
Sandburg. He couldn't see himself paying—or wasting—money for
repairs. He became a carpenter, a bricklayer, a house painter, a
paperhanger, a cabinetmaker, a truck gardener, a handyman restless
and dissatisfied unless there was something to fix or improve on the
property he owned or was paying for. What he made or fixed with
his hands wasn't always finished perfectly smooth and correct—but
it would do, it would serve. I was his helper, his chore boy, my
brother Mart later throwing in. When the roof needed shingling I
went up the ladder bringing him shingles. When a pump was ailing
he let me down on a rope to put on a new leather sucker. When a
cistern had its yearly cleaning I was let down barelegged to shovel
mud and silt into the bucket he drew up with a rope. A chair or
table getting wobbly, my father brought it down to his cellar work-
bench and had me holding a kerosene lamp to light him while he
chiseled, fitted, mortised, and hammered. I might after supper have
taken my place at the kitchen table to read J. T. Headley's *Napoleon
and His Marshals*, from the Seventh Ward school library. And I
might be saying to my father, "It's a good book and I want to know

about Napoleon," but he would say, "Sholly (Charlie), you let
Napoleon go for tonight and hold de lamp for me."

Though I had been solemnly christened, with holy water sprinkled
on my infant head, by the name of Carl August Sandberg, some-
where in the first year or two of school I decided to use the name
Charles instead of Carl. I am not sure now just why I did this. It
could have been I had a feeling the name Carl would mean one more
Poor Swede Boy while the name Charles filled the mouth full and
had 'em guessing. There were important men lived and died named
Charles and I hadn't yet heard of Carl the Twelfth of Sweden and
other Carls who were pretty good. Also it was at a session of Mary,
Mart, and myself about this time that we decided from then on to
write "burg" instead of "berg" in our surname.

Those two letters *ch* bothered many a Swede boy trying to
Americanize himself. In our third-grade Sheldon's school reader was
a story titled "Charlie's Chickens," about a boy named Charlie who
planted feathers and expected a crop of chickens. One after another,
Swede boys Johnson, Nelson, Bostrom, and Hillstrom stood up to
read the story out loud so as to learn how to speak and pronounce.
One after another they blurted out "Sharlie's Shickens." The teacher
would ask for it again, herself pronouncing it distinctly correct.
But from Johnson and Nelson it came out again, "Sharlie's Shickens"
and from Bostrom and Hillstrom, "Sharlie's Shickens" and the good
and patient teacher gave it up. In my seat I laughed inside myself
because I had picked the name Charles and had a noble and correct
way to fill my mouth with it.

In the cellar next to my father's workbench we had a pile of
boards, slats, shingles, where we cut kindling for starting fires in
the coal stove. I was working one evening on some knotty pine lum-
ber pieces. I was using a large knife that my father had made at the
blacksmith shop and he had put a wonderfully sharp edge on the
heavy blade. I was more than interested in what fine thin kindlings I
could cut with that knife. It was such fun that I worked faster than
I ever had at that little job. I suddenly came to know I was working
too fast as I whanged the knife blade across the forefinger of my
left hand, just back of the lower knuckle. The blood gushed from
the cut and I ran upstairs leaving a trail of blood drops on the stairs

and floors. My mother helped me wash it and wrap and tie a piece of clean cloth around the unlucky finger. A scar came that is still there, nearly halfway around the finger. My mother came near crying and kept saying, "Oh Sharlie, it is too too bad. Don't take it hard. It will be better. It is too bad." The father looked on with a glowering face and kept saying, "Why don't you *see* what you are doing, Sholly? Why don't you be *careful?*" He had further remarks in Swedish about my dumb way with sharp-edged tools, returning to an English sentence he sometimes used, "I be clear, I be clear," his way of saying, "I declare, I declare." I was a *dumskalle,* a numbskull. I'm sure he knew it was a good finger, that I came near amputating it, and that I had more pain than fun out of it. I am also sure he didn't know that his angry advice was given in a tone and manner as though I was in the habit of slashing my fingers with sharp knives and considered it good fun and I must learn to stop playing such jokes on my fingers. The idea came to me to lay the main blame on him for making so heavy a blade and sharpening it to a keen edge. The idea no sooner came than I forgot it.

Monday was Washday. When I was strong enough to carry a pail of water I went out the kitchen door, down eight steps of the back stairway, eight more steps to the cistern, where I lifted the cover and let down a bucket and filled the pail. After enough trips to the cistern there would be water for two washtubs, one tub with warm water and a washboard for soaping and rubbing, the other with cold water for rinsing the clothes and running them through the attached wringer. On summer and vacation Mondays I often turned the wringer while my mother fed the clothes into it. On many winter Mondays I carried the basket of clothes out to the back-yard clothesline. In a blowing wind I pressed wooden clothespins to fasten bedsheets, shirts, drawers, handkerchiefs, stockings, and diapers on the rope clothesline. Often I found the clothes left in the basket had frozen stiff. Coaxing those frozen pieces of cloth to go around the rope for a wooden pin to be fastened over them was a winter sport with a challenge to your wit and numb fingers in Illinois zero weather, with sometimes a wild northwest wind knocking a shirt stiff as a board against your head. I remember more than once taking a basket into the kitchen for the clothes to thaw out while my fingers thawed out.

After the wash was hung three or four children would climb on the kitchen table. Mama threw soapy water on the floor and scrubbed and mopped while we played we were on an island or on a housetop floating down a river. After supper or the next morning I would go out and pile the frozen clothes high into a basket and bring them into the house. The noon dinner and the evening supper on Monday, never failing for years, were boiled herring and boiled potatoes, *sill och potatis*, for generations a simple classic menu of which they said with straight faces, "This is what makes the Swedes so strong."

On the highest shelf of the pantry Mama kept her latest bake of cookies or freshly fried doughnuts. On her leaving the room to be gone five or ten minutes, we would climb a chair and with a long reach get our fingers on cookies or doughnuts or the little bag of sugar lumps and run to the cellar or some other room for sweet eating. She usually saw later that there had been thieves in her pantry and she called us thieves and tried to be stern with a severe face, but generally a half-smile broke through. She was not a natural scold. When she had to scold it didn't come easy, whereas the father in a dark mood about something broken or lost could cut loose with moans and reproaches and come out of it sort of refreshed and sanctified.

Mama saw to it when we had been too long without a bath—she half filled a washtub with warm water, gave us soap, and told us to scrub. There would be the months we boys went swimming and didn't need the home baths. There would be the winter weeks of bitter cold when a bath once a month might be considered right. The three sisters would clear out of the kitchen while Mart and I took our washtub bath. Then we would go to bed and the girls would take over.

Mama watched carefully the cellar corner where the cabbage heads were piled in October so that in part of the winter there would be slaw and boiled cabbage. About early-frost time she would buy several bushels of green tomatoes at ten cents a bushel and put up preserves for bread spread and jars of chowchow and piccalilli.

If we forgot, she reminded Mart and me in February of the garden and frozen ground where we could pound, dig, and rassle out one or two bushels of parsnips. She saw us peeling raw turnips, enjoying them, and said, "They are good for you." For fun we ate raw potatoes to show her we could do it and she said they would be better fried or boiled. We told her that on the way to school we had scraped grains from the floor of a railroad wheat car and had fun chewing and tasting raw wheat. She said the wheat might not be clean and having done it once, that was enough.

In a triangle closet under the stairs from the first floor to the cellar in winter months Papa used to keep, when he could afford it, a barrel of apples, Baldwins or Winesaps. He put a lock on the door and hid the key. He had seen that when a barrel of apples stood where everyone could get at it, we would soon be at the barrel bottom. He would have put a board over the gap above the door had he known what Mart and I were doing. Over the door by hard wriggling our boy bodies could squeeze through and drop down and we could get at the apple barrel. We took two apples at a time and only every other day. What we stole wasn't noticed and we said, "Stealing two apples isn't really stealing," and "When two of us steal two apples and divide them, that's only stealing one apple apiece and stealing one apple isn't really stealing, it's snooking."

One week when I was perhaps eight years old my howling could be heard, and at times with no letup I moaned and yelled through a whole hour. In the joint of the left knee there was a grinding devilish pain. I remember sitting at the top of the stairs to the second story, my voice going "Ai! ai! ai!" changing in spells to the Swedish equivalent "Ack ack ack!" and howling, "Why do I have to have this? Why does God punish me like this? Is this what happens to you when you go to hell?" A doctor call would have cost a dollar and a half. Over on Day Street on the west side between Mulberry and South, in a house set far back from the sidewalk, with hollyhocks, lilacs, and ivy, lived a hermit with a long gray beard. He walked slow and had quiet on his face. He made a liniment that you rubbed where there was pain and he said it would help. On the third day of my howling, mother bought a half-dollar bottle of this liniment. It was dark brown and had a powerful stink to it. Mother told me, "They say it is good for horses and people." I rubbed my left knee with it, rubbing hard as if to punish the wicked knee. The pain had already eased on the third day and I believe it might have gone away even without the liniment. Yet maybe the liniment helped. Never again has that knee joint acted up wicked. It could be that it is afraid I will again rub it with the hermit liniment that was made of things the hermit kept a secret. I found that I had a soft spot in my heart for the hermit and when I met him on the street I told him his liniment had fixed me up all right and he took my right hand and shook it and called me "Little man."

Our renters never made trouble except once. They always paid on time and there were no quarrels or fights, no fool noises. The Hockenberrys from Kentucky were the first I remember. Living with them was a cousin, Susie Hough, a short, sturdy woman with smiles that won us all. She sang "The Spanish Cavalier" so many times that I began singing it.

They moved and there came the Danielsons, man and wife with one baby, two more arriving in our house. They had been over from Sweden only a year or so. We saw Mrs. Danielson grow pale and weak and it was said that the housework and the babies were too heavy for her. Mr. Danielson was the slow-thinking Swedish peasant. He had picked up the word "certainly," and if you had so much as a two-minute talk with him he would say, "Suttonly, suttonly," and if the talk went on another minute or two he would be saying, "Suttonly, suttonly."

The night policeman, Frank Peterson, with his wife and baby had the three upstairs rooms for two years. We felt, of course, that we were strictly respectable and law-abiding citizens to have a policeman living in our house. Officer Peterson made a good showing, was put on the day force, and promoted to something like Assistant City Marshal. He was a heavy, round-faced man with a light-brown mustache and a voice that could ring out. When we played two-old-cat below the second floor where he was sleeping in the daytime and we were yelling like Kickapoo Indians, we could hear him when he called through the open window for us to either shut up or go away. We stayed but we shut up.

After the Petersons came the Smalleys from a town in the Ozarks. They arrived with two wagons and teams of horses. Mr. Smalley got work as a tailor. He was a man of dignity, with a lean face and a mustache like Senator John J. Ingalls of Kansas, who wrote the famous poem on "Opportunity." He was a widower with two sons who hauled coal from mines near Galesburg. The younger son gave me something to remember him by. I was sitting with other boys in the little pasture near by in late October around a fire. We were talking and it was like most any other night. Out of the dark suddenly came the younger Smalley and he was crying that I had said something about him. He swung a leaded slung shot on my head, then turned and ran. It wasn't a knockout but it was a bruise that took weeks to heal and it left a bump that was years in going away. For a long time I could reach up and feel that bump on the top of my head. I couldn't remember anything I had said about the Smalley boy that he could take as mean or insulting. He was raised in a corner of Missouri or Arkansas where they feud and take the law in their own hands. When I spoke to my father about going into "a fair fist fight" with the boy, who was about my age and size, my father said we had better forget it. The Smalleys moved soon after and when I would run my hand along the top of my head I would remember they had been with us a year or two. They were the only renters who made us trouble.

Joe Elser came to our house with a carpenter's tool chest on one shoulder. His bed, three chairs, a bureau, and a stove had arrived by wagon. He moved into the two upstairs east rooms, reached by the outside wooden stairs, the coalbin under the stairs. Here Joe Elser lived three or four years, our tenant and our upstairs neighbor.

He didn't drink hard liquor, wine, or beer. He didn't smoke tobacco or chew it. He didn't go to church on Sunday or to prayer meeting on Wednesday evening or to religious services of any kind. He didn't have any newspapers delivered to him though he bought one sometimes on the street. He didn't have any books in his rooms and didn't take any from the Public Library. He did his own cooking, made his breakfast, fixed a box for his noon meal where he was working, came back to his rooms at night and fixed his supper. He never complained about weather, politics, religion, diseases, ailments. We never knew him to be sick a day or an hour. "What's wrong with the country," I heard him say, "if I can't fix it I don't bother my mind about it. If I get a headache I just say nothin an try to get along with it."

Joe Elser was tall, strong, spare of build, and we saw him several times with his tool chest on one shoulder carrying it as though he liked it. His face and hair were grayish and his mustache close-trimmed—he didn't care for the long curling kind.

Many a winter night Mart and I went up to see him. He always made us welcome. He could smile and talk with a bright face as though we were a couple of nephews he liked. We began calling him "Uncle Joe" and he enjoyed that. He never referred to his being lonely in any way. The more we came to know him we couldn't have believed he had anything sad in his loneliness. He hinted that for years he had had to put up with company that was hard to take and now it was pleasant to live by himself.

What Mart and I heard from him about how and where he used to live wasn't much. He gave the name of the Illinois town not far off where he had been. And though Mart and I wanted to mind our own business and didn't want to be nosy, we did get around one night to asking him if he was a regular bachelor or whether he had sometime been married. There was a hurt look on his face. His lips pressed tight and his eyes had trouble in them. He waited a little and then said, "Oh, I had a wife and the time came when I had to quit her for keeps." That was all. He didn't go on from there. How and why he had quit her for keeps we knew could go on into a long story. We could see from his face it wouldn't be easy for him to tell what had happened that made his living alone now comfortable, with a peace in the day and the night that he hadn't had for years. Years later Mart met some folks who had known Joe's wife and they said, "She ragged and nagged him, just a natural-born scold. He stood it for years and then one day walked out of the house with his tool chest on his shoulder and her standing in the doorway crying and yelling at the top of her voice." And these folks hadn't heard whether there was a divorce or whether Joe ever saw her again. Nor did he ever tell Mart and me or any of our folks about what kind of a separation it was. At no time did we see or hear of any woman calling on him or of his hunting any women around the town. He washed his own shirts, drawers, undershirts, handkerchiefs, socks, and we saw him hang them on the back-yard washline. He darned his socks, sewed patches on his pants, swept and scrubbed the floors, and kept his rooms neat and shipshape. We heard him say, "I like to have things in good order."

Joe Elser was in his early fifties when we knew him. He never hurried. In any work he was doing he seemed to have a knack for the next motion after the one now. We would come up to his kitchen after our supper and he would be setting his table with its oilcloth cover, bringing a steak, chops, or fish, with potatoes and a vegetable or two. He would set chairs for us at the table, then step to the oven and bring out a fresh-baked pie. He would cut the pie and put a quarter of it on my plate and another quarter on Mart's plate. He was proud of the pies he could bake. So were Mart and I. We told him we had never tasted such good pie and it was the truth and he believed us and his face had a quiet shine on it as he watched us eat and grin. His favorites and ours were peach and cherry pies though for a change we liked apple, mince, custard, and currant.

Joe had fairly regular work as a carpenter across the year. He went to bed at ten o'clock at night, was up at six in the morning, made his breakfast and was on the job at seven, an hour off at noon, then at work till six in the evening—a ten-hour day. Sometimes on account of weather or a foundation not finished on a house, he would have days off for sharpening tools and making repairs and washing bedsheets and pillowcases.

Mother said we were going up too often and too early to eat his pies. "You should leave him some pie for himself," she said. And when we came up to see him finished with supper and washing the dishes, we would talk about this and that. Then he would get out a couple of flatirons, hand us a hammer apiece, and bring out a canvas sack of black walnuts, hickory nuts, or hazelnuts. And while he joined us in cracking and eating nuts—though we always ate more than he—he did most of the talking. We asked him to go on and on.

Joe Elser had been in The War. There was only one war then a

man could have been in, the war over the Union and the slaves. Joe
had had near four years of it. He went in as a private and came out
as a private. He had been in battles. He would take stove wood and
kindling, put one piece on the floor "where they were lined up"
and another "where we stood." Then he would change the wood
pieces to show "where they came at us" and "where we counter-
charged." He had heard bullets flying and seen men fall and he named
the places. He had never been wounded, "but once I had malarial
fever bad for six weeks." He didn't make himself out any kind of a
hero. "You enlisted and then you took what come." The eating was
mostly "sowbelly and beans, though sometimes in enemy territory
we had rich living on cattle we took and butchered and sometimes
there was a sight of pigs and chickens we caught and roasted and
fried." They had knapsacks and haversacks at first and threw them
away and put everything into a blanket roll. On the march, over the
left shoulder went the blanket roll and on the right shoulder the
rifle—and a cartridge belt around the middle.

This or that was "issued." Uniforms, shoes, socks, rations, they
were issued. You didn't need to buy anything, but if you wanted
something special there was the "sutler," who followed the army
and set up a store where the army stopped. "The army issued us
bricks we made soup of. The bricks were made of dried vegetables
with meat. You put 'em in hot water over a fire and they melted and
you had your thick soup, which was a nice thin stew."

He had learned the army cuss words and dirty talk. "Cussin,"
he said, "is good for some men. It's like opening a blister or lettin
pus out from a sore. I used to be good at cussin. Time came I said
it was no help. So I quit."

As Uncle Joe rambled along in what he remembered he would
tell what came to his mind, things that interested him as he looked
back, some things that he might never have talked about since they
happened. Suddenly one night he was saying that sometimes the boys
got hard up for women. "There was a stretch of woods next to our
camp. And a fellow comes back from that woods and tells me the
boys had a woman over there. I went to see. What I came to was a
crowd of fellows around one woman layin on the ground. They
told me over seventy of the boys had had her—a dollar apiece. They

shoved me toward her where she lay on the ground. I thought she looked nearly give out. I wouldn't try to tell you what she looked like. I don't believe to this day that more than seventy men had had her. I pushed my way out and went back to camp. I could hardly believe what I had seen. I guess if I had been a drinkin man I would have taken on some of the corn liquor the boys was passin around and joined in with them."

Joe had been looking back and remembering and talking exactly what came back to him. I was fifteen, Mart a year and a half younger. Suddenly he smiled with a quizzical look on his face, his eyes crinkling, as if saying to himself, "Maybe I shouldn't have told that to these young boys. But it came to my mind and I told it just like it happened."

After three or four years Joe Elser moved away from our house and we lost track of him. I like to think about him. I don't get tired of trying to remember what he was like. Out of what he had he made a pretty good life of it. He had his carpenter's wage of two dollars a day and thirty dollars a month pension from the government and he could have gone to the saloons, to shows and concerts. He could have bought bright fancy clothes to wear. He could have hired his washing and ironing done. But he did none of these things. He liked his regular eight hours sleep and was a good sleeper. He liked his work and took pride in being a good carpenter—his saw, plane, hammer and nails, they had each a use and he knew how. He was temperate and never talked about temperance. He did cooking and washing as if saying, "This is my kind of fun." He was lonely and prized his loneliness. The point could be made, "He had only himself to worry about," which could be answered, "So he didn't worry." Joe Elser never showed any signs of being afraid. He learned somehow to get along without being afraid of what is or of what is to come.

"Papa" we called the father to his face and to Mama. To Mart and me he was "the Old Man" though the mother was never "the Old Woman." We were a little superior about him. We didn't really rate him for what he had. We had something of the smart-aleck Young America, an element that seems to have been on hand in every American generation past and present. The Old Man lived sober, was known to all who knew him as a hard worker who always paid his debts on time, never failed to keep a bargain, never got into fights and fool quarrels, a "peaceable citizen and neighbor," earning a strict and unquestionable name for that peculiar thing termed Honesty. "He gets to work on time, he works hard, his word is good, and you can count on him," I heard the grocer Will Olson say one time. He warned us to never run on Main Street: "Thieves steal and run and you might be taken for a thief."

Payments he owed on the big house he had bought were a load on his mind. So were the payments on the first quarter section of land he bought in far-western Kansas. He sold this land at some kind of profit and bought another quarter section. For several years those one hundred and sixty acres of land out there in Pawnee County, near the county seat Larned, haunted the whole family. I came to know by heart the numbers of the range and the township, because once a year I would write for him the letter to the County Treasurer of Pawnee County, enclosing a postal money order for that year's taxes. To write that letter the Old Man would hand me a pencil he prized. Just why he had that pencil around, his personal pencil, we never knew definitely. He may have been secretly practicing on shaping letters and numbers—though I doubt it. We knew merely that the pencil cost twenty-five cents, that the lead was purple and indelible. The Old Man called it "indebible." He liked it that you couldn't erase what you wrote.

And why were we all haunted by that Kansas farm land? Because Papa talked vaguely about leaving Galesburg and trying his hands on that land way out there. Folders with pictures came from railroads and speculators, showing what bumper crops of wheat and corn, even of pears and apples, could be raised there. Then came the crash, the Panic of 1893 and the Hard Times. We heard how corn went to ten cents a bushel in Kansas. We read of Kansas farmers burning corn for fuel. Kansas land went down in price. What the Old Man sold his farm for I never heard, whether at a loss or a profit. He had bought it for about three dollars an acre and neither the profit nor the loss could have been heavy. But we quit our family discussions about whether a man is more independent working for a railroad or taking his chances as a farmer. "Independent"—we learned that word. The farmer never starves, he can live on what he raises, he is his own boss, he can't be fired from his job, he is "independent" —so ran the points in our child minds.

A panic, people running to the banks to find the banks closed, men out of work, charity balls where those who had plenty of plenty danced for the benefit of those who had plenty of nothing. A cartoon had a high lady, in décolleté and furs, meeting at her carriage a ragged tramp holding his hand out and hearing from her, "Why you are absurd. I have been dancing for you all night!" Coxey's Army in the news for months, men out of work marching on Washington to ask Congress to get them work. And the Panic, the Hard Times, definitely reached Galesburg. Except for watchmen, the railroad shopmen went from a ten-hour day to a four-hour day, the checks on payday less than half what they were used to.

We learned to eat bread spread with lard sprinkled with salt, and we liked it. We growing children would have preferred butter or butterine, but we found we could favor the flavor of clean white lard. When lard was short we put molasses or sorghum on the bread, which was not so good, though the Old Man smiled and said it was like old days with the construction gang in the bunk car. We were lucky in our garden giving a bumper crop of potatoes. The land laughed with spuds. As Mart and I helped the Old Man dig potatoes and carry the bushel baskets into the cellar, we saw him do the only writing of his we had ever witnessed. For each bushel brought in he would chalk on a ceiling rafter a straight vertical line. When there were four verticals he would cross with a diagonal line, meaning we had five more bushels, by golly.

A little co-operative of neighbors sprang up. They borrowed a horse and wagon and hauled to town a hog from John Krans, a hog bought below the market price then, "the price near nothing," laughed Krans. Two lots away from us, outdoors in front of a small barn, I first saw a hog killing. I carried home a bucket of blood from which Mama made a tasty "blood pudding." Mart and I hustled home with a ham and hog sections from which we had across the weeks that winter pork chops, pork loins, side meat, spareribs, cracklings, sowbelly, pig's knuckles, lard for frying and for bread spread. The butchering was a drama to us kids. In open daylight of a winter day we saw the hog knocked in the head for its last squeal, the carcass scalded and the hair scraped off, the disembowling, the hacking with axes and cleavers, and at the finish what we all had seen often hung on hooks in the meat markets.

There was a note of doom and fate about the big railroad whistle in those Hard Times months. For years we had heard it at seven in the morning, at twelve noon, and at one and six o'clock in the afternoon. Now it blew at eight in the morning and twelve noon only. It was the Hard Times Clock saying, "Be careful, watch your pennies, wait and hope!"

We learned about "slack" that winter, screenings of coal with no lumps, much cheaper than regular soft coal or bituminous. Into our small heating stove in the kitchen we would shovel it and then keep watch on it, breaking its cinder formations with a poker. If not carefully tended there would be clinkers too large to pass through the grate below; then with poker and shovel we would bring up the clinker and put it in its special galvanized iron bucket.

On the west side of the house were stairs and a porch floor that made the roof of our coalbin. I learned to stoop going through that door to the coalbin. I learned to stoop swinging a hammer breaking big lumps into little lumps so they would fit into the coalhod and the stove door. I learned like millions of other boys how to carry the hod up the stairs and set it by the stove and wait for the later word, "Charlie, the coal is gone." Hands covered with coal dust, nose and ears filled with the fine coal dust, I felt I was earning my board and keep.

I would have thought my fate a hard one if I hadn't been reading the *Youth's Companion* with its stories about miners and breaker boys who didn't have it so good as I had it. They worked all day and came out with black faces and the coal dust in layers. One winter week I rigged up a small tin can, fastened it to my cap, and went into the dark coalbin playing it was a mine and I had a head lamp like a regular miner.

The little door opened out, not in. When there was snow it had to be shoveled away so the door could swing out. When the weather was cold I had to have mittens, and the yarn would slip along the

hammer and shovel handles and on the handrail up the stairs when
there was snow or ice. I made the same trip hundreds of times from
the stove where the empty coalhod stood, through one door into a
small hall, through another door out onto the porch, then down the
stairs and around to the bin door, repeating in reverse the same trip
back to the stove. And they were a help—the stories by C. A. Ste-
phens and others about men sleeping in snow and tramping through
wilderness with heavy packs on their backs. I was no boy hero of the
late 1880's and the early 1890's, but it helped sometimes for me to
play a game in my own mind and to imagine I was a heroic struggler
amid continuous and monotonous obstacles of circumstance.

The kitchen was the only room really heated during the cold
months. The second-floor bedrooms got what heat went through a
door and up the stairs. No heat reached the third-floor garret where
Mart and I slept. But we enjoyed, on a winter below-zero night,
standing by the warm kitchen stove, stripping to our underwear
and then dashing up two floors and getting under the quilts and
snuggling into the cornhusks before Old Mister Zero Fahrenheit
could tag us.

The kitchen at first was heated by a stove with lids. With a lifter
you lifted a lid, poked the coal around with a poker, raised the
coalhod, and poured in fresh coal. At the stove end was a small
oblong tank holding water warmed by the hot coals. At first we
children called this, as Papa and Mama did, "the rissywarn." Later
we learned it was a reservoir—rez-er-vwahr—a French word, but we
went on calling it "rissywarn" out of habit. Later this cookstove
went to the cellar, where it served on washdays during the warmer
months of the year. Improvements then modern came to the kitchen
—a gasoline stove for cooking, and a heating stove with an isinglass
door and an ashpan at the bottom. Was it a thousand times or two
thousand I pulled out that ashpan and opened the door to the back
hall, then the back door to the back porch and went down the steps
to the ends of the potato rows, where I dumped one more pan of
ashes on the honorable Ashpile? Then back to the steps, up and
through two doors, and again I placed the very essential ashpan into
the stove bottom. Often I would open the isinglass door and with a
poker bring out clinkers clogging the grate and drop them into the

ashpan. It could be that if I should stand before St. Peter at the Gate and he should ask, "What good deeds did you ever do on earth?" I would answer, "For years on years when I was a boy I carried out the stove ashes of a house at 622 East Berrien Street, Galesburg, Knox County, Illinois."

The kitchen was fifteen feet long and twelve wide, and what with cupboard and pantry, sink, gasoline stove and heating stove, a table, and eight chairs, with a baby high chair, any passageway was narrow. There we were, a family of, at one time, nine persons in that one room, a kitchen, a dining room, a study room, a playroom, a workshop. We saw the mother mix flour and knead dough, roll and pat it, put it in the oven, and bring out the brown loaves of bread. We saw her wash and iron while the father during Hard Times cut leather and pegged half-soles on our shoes. We saw coats and trousers patched and socks and stockings darned. We saw our father cut boy's hair with the family scissors. As a haircut it was somewhat ragged-edged but it saved the barber's two bits.

Every day or two it would be Mart or me holding a coffee mill between the knees and turning the grinder with the hand, making Arbuckle's XXX coffee ready for Mama's coffeepot. From day to day the fresh-ground coffee would be added to what was in the pot, and it might be three or four days before the grounds were thrown out and we had strictly fresh coffee. We popped corn with lard in the pan, made taffy and greased our hands to "pull" the taffy. We put a flatiron bottom up on the knees, and with a hammer cracked hazelnuts and walnuts we had picked and carried home in October. We made cocked hats cut and shaped out of newspapers. We wrote and made drawings on brown grocery wrapping paper. We went to the cellar for the kerosene can and filled the lamp after trimming the wick. We scratched a blue sulphur match and waited till the blue light was gone and the yellow blaze came. Then we ran this light along the wick and the lamp was lit and we put on the chimney. We coughed up phlegm and eased it into the coalhod next to the stove. We blew our noses into cotton handkerchiefs and tried to forget boys called them "snotrags."

We tried a cat or two, but it took up too much room and got in the way of the eighteen feet of nine persons. Papa was looking on the bright side of things when one day he said Mama could buy a canary and a cage. As it hung high over our heads it didn't get in our way. The canary stayed a year or two but the babies were coming along and each of them was plenty of a pet to look after. In such a room as our kitchen you come to know each other. Your elbows get in each other's faces and hair. You learn to mind your own business or there is trouble.

The pump in the back yard was wooden and had a wooden handle. I became part of the pump and the pump became part of me. When I hated and cursed the pump I took it back afterward and said I was sorry. I came to like it for all its faults. When I scolded it and snarled at it, it never answered back. The pump went on doing what it had to do while I did what I had to do.

The pump stood about fifteen steps from the foot of the stairs going down from the back door of the house. I took an empty galvanized iron pail from the side of the kitchen sink, opened the door to the back hall, opened the back door, and went down the stairs and then to the pump. I set the pail under the pump spout, put my two hands on the pump handle, pushed the handle down, pulled the handle up, and went on pumping till water poured out of the spout and filled the pail. Then I carried the pail to the back stairs, up the stairs to the back door, the hall, the kitchen door, and the kitchen sink. I did this a thousand times, at least, or it could have been two or three thousand times. Others did this same chore but I was counted the oldest boy, the handy strong boy who was called on. What we brought into the house was "fresh water," or in Swedish *friskt vatten*. In the warm months water standing in a pail an hour or two didn't taste good and the call was for fresh water, the father saying, "*Friskt vatten, Sholly.*"

In a summer dry spell when the pump handle came up light and loose, pulling up no water, I knew the water was low at the bottom of the well and the pump needed "priming." I would go back to the kitchen and get a pail of cistern rain water, pouring it down to the leather sucker and the tubing. Then I would push and pull at the pump handle till at last the pump spout was running glad and free and saying, "Here is your water!" And on hot sweltering summer days when butter melted and stayed melted in the kitchen, mother would put it in a small tin pail, tie a doubled grocery string to the handle, and I would lift the cover of the well platform and let the butter down to become cool and hard again. There were people in town who had iceboxes in their kitchens, and when they wanted ice they hung a yellow card on the house front and the ice wagon stopped and the iceman with his tongs clamping a cake of ice came lugging and sweating to lift the icebox top and drop the ice in. Our house was not in the icebox class.

There were winter mornings when my hands in mittens went around the pump handle and I pushed and pulled and couldn't budge it. They would be watching from the kitchen window. They saw me skipping back to the kitchen. They were ready with a pail of hot water. I poured this down the pump, sometimes ran back to the kitchen for a second pail of hot water. After the pump was thawed out I pumped and carried in two pails of water to last the family till the next morning, when again we thawed out the pump. And this, of course, meant carrying in extra pails of water from the cistern, where there was no pump and you let down your galvanized iron pail and broke the thin ice and pulled the pail up with a rope. I got acquainted with the difference between a fresh-water well and a rain-water cistern.

Three or four times it happened I would push and pull at the pump handle and no water came. Papa looked it over and said it needed a new sucker. He cut leather and shaped a new sucker. He let me down into the well on a rope, told me what to do, and stood looking down telling me more what to do. I was glad when he pulled me up and we could say the pump was fixed and the new sucker worked. It was a good pump, and whenever it didn't work it had a good excuse and you couldn't blame it.

Old folks and young saw the Front Room change and take on style in the Berrien Street house. Larger than the kitchen, it spoke for itself its own importance. The kitchen seemed to say, "I stand for use and service, I am absolutely necessary and you can't get along without me." The Front Room said as definitely, "I represent the higher dignity of human life and when you come in here you look to your manners. I may not be as necessary as the kitchen, but I am important just because I am not absolutely necessary."

The kitchen chairs were entirely of wood and often had scratches and dents and the paint worn and scraped off. The Front Room chairs wore a smooth varnish and we were ashamed of any nick on the brown dignified wood. The seats of these chairs were a woven wicker—they were easier to sit in than the kitchen chairs. One year a haircloth sofa arrived for the east wall and the next year a center table with fluted curved legs and a marble top. Still another year and on that marble top reposed a Family Bible, too heavy to be lifted and read. You opened it and turned the pages and read it where it lay on the marble top. The covers were thick boards of black and on the front cover the letters shone in gilt: "Holy Bible." On the board covers were indentations, embossments, entablatures, plains, mountains, and valleys that our child fingers could rove. On a page with a border of scrolls in gilt were lines for writing in the weddings, births, deaths. All the pages from Genesis to Revelation were in two columns and the type, the letters, big and black, unmistakable Holy Writ. For that Bible Papa paid six dollars and a half. And he must have felt rich and freehearted when he paid six-fifty for another Family Bible just like ours and gave it to the Krans family as a Christmas present to show he loved them.

The Front Room kerosene lamp had a slender table to itself and like no kitchen lamp had a white shade over the chimney. Then along about the year sister Mary graduated from high school came the Parlor Organ, though we never went so far as to call our Front Room a parlor. Your feet pressed pedals connecting with reeds producing sound. The man who sold it to us came with its delivery, showed where to put your feet, sat up to the keyboard playing "Fisher Maiden" so we knew that music could be coaxed from it. Before long Mary could play chords on it and she and Minnie Eastberg practiced till they could sing a duet "In the Starlight," which they gave at a Lutheran church sociable. A few times we caught Papa hunting out chords on the organ and smiling to us as though we had caught him doing something not useful.

In the kitchen and the upstairs bedrooms the floors were bare, with here and there a nailhead sticking up a quarter-inch and polished bright by our shoes and feet. In the Front Room, though, we laid a carpet that was plain, yet it was a Carpet. I helped drive tacks into its edges against the wall. I helped put a layer of straw under it and enjoyed how smooth and soft it felt when I walked over it. In a spring housecleaning about every two years we took up the carpet, carried it outdoors, beat the dust out of it, then put it down again in the Front Room with fresh straw under it and using the same tacks to hold it down.

The Front Room had no stove. In winter it could be made fairly comfortable by keeping open the doors to the kitchen and firing the kitchen stove red-hot. When Mary entertained her "fellows" and the doors were closed they managed to get along on the haircloth sofa.

There came to the Front Room its bookcase. Mart was having his first year in high school and was taking "manual training." He sawed and planed and joined up a four-shelf bookcase. What with our textbooks and the ten-cent paper-covered books I had been buying, the bookshelves filled up and we could say to visitors, "This is our library. Have you read any good books lately?"

On the center table next to the Bible was a big book with red-plush covers and fancy nickel work on the front cover, our Photograph Album. Our fingers locked and unlocked its metal clasps. We could see how Papa and Mama looked about the time they got married. When visitors came they looked through the Album and we told them who was who. You couldn't eat the Album nor wear it. You couldn't say it was useful, and you couldn't get along without it. The Album was something extra. It was one of the things we had in mind when we said, "We're not rich—but we're not poor!"

THREE

Judgment Day

Except for the Swedish Lutheran Church and the Republican Party my father belonged to no organization, no societies, clubs, leagues, orders, nothing except a Mutual Loan Association. He had friends or acquaintances among Masons, Woodmen, Knights of Pythias, but he didn't join any of them. Once for a few weeks, in the cow pasture where us kids played ball, a tent went up and the Seventh Day Adventists held meetings. He went several times, listened to their preaching and was half converted. At the dinner and supper table he would say they had something—but he stayed a Lutheran. There was a deep streak of reverence in him. It did not go so far as saying grace at the table. But it was there in his solemn face, in his voice usually grave, never singing, and only rarely telling any joke or speaking with a light mind. Occasionally he read a half-hour by himself in a small Swedish-language Bible.

One of the most vivid early memories of my life is that first home Bible. It was the first book that dawned on my mind as a book, as a thing made of paper and on the paper black marks your eye could pick off from the page and you could say the words that lay there on the paper. This wonder, I would guess, came into my life when I was four years old. It was in the third house, the Berrien Street house, in the second-floor southwest corner room, the bedroom of my father and mother. It was winter, cold outside, and winds howling. Mary and I heard father by the light of a small kerosene lamp read a chapter. What he read I have forgotten and couldn't have remembered the next day because I didn't understand it. But I recall several times that week going to where that Book lay on top of a bureau. And I opened it and turned pages and held it near a window and had my wondering about how those black marks on white paper could be words your eyes would pick off into words your tongue would speak.

Certain words I had heard my father read stayed with me, *Gud* meaning "God," or *evangelium* meaning "gospel." I asked my mother to point out those words for me so my eyes would know how spoken words look when fastened down in black on white paper. She put her finger on those words and I had a dim beginning of learning to read, a hazy understanding. I took comfort in mother saying it would be clear to me when I started school and learned to read.

I remember out of my earliest years at the First Lutheran Church a man moving with others along an aisle after services and a woman with a nod of her head toward this man and a whisper to my mother, "Klocka Yonson." The man had a face with a hurt and half-scared look on it. I asked my mother about him going home and she said that a few years back they were raising money for a new church bell, *klocka* in Swedish, and this Johnson had held out money he had collected. So whenever he passed by now there would be the nods and whispers, "Klocka Yonson."

The Swedish Lutheran Synod of the United States met in Galesburg, some of the delegates workingmen and farmers. Local church members opened their homes to them. Our delegate was a Nebraska farmer. We looked at him, studied him, watched and listened for his every word. We children had never seen anybody from far-off Nebraska. We had heard of Nebraska. It was Nebraska land that Magnus Holmes owned, and his son Frank, out there farming it, lived in a sod house. We liked our Nebraska delegate, if only to look at. He had a muffler of thin black whiskers from ear to ear; he never scraped the razor over his throat. His thin lips made a straight wide line. His eyes were black and had a peculiar blink when he spoke. His hair was black, almost blue-black. He was taller than our father and both had the same stoop of shoulders that came from bending over at work. The delegate and my father and mother hurled the Swedish language back and forth in a way beyond us

youngsters to follow. And for this particular week we said a bless-
ing on the food on the table and mother brought out a sacred white
linen table spread from Sweden.

The end of the week came and the last Sunday the delegate was
to stay with us. We were all there at the church for the sermon
given by the Reverend Carl A. Beckman, who had a high reputation
in the Synod. He had come to us a couple of years before, a young
graduate of Augustana College, with a melodious sonorous voice,
a rounded cherubic face of strange dignity, his head set on strong
shoulders, a fair creamy skin, waves of curly auburn hair flowing
back from his forehead.

I had more than respect for Pastor Beckman. I looked at him with
curiosity and awe. He was the first author my eyes gazed on. In
the Swedish Lutheran newspaper published at Rock Island, Illinois,
I saw printed every week a column signed "C.A.B." This was written
by our church minister. I was told that he would sit at a table
among his books in the house next to the church. He would dip
a pen into an ink bottle and write on sheets of paper. Friends of
ours had seen him at this work. Then he would fold the sheets into
an envelope and mail them to Rock Island and it all would come
back to him and to us printed in the weekly newspaper and at the
bottom of it the letters "C.A.B." Everybody knew who "C.A.B."
was and liked it better than if he signed "Carl A. Beckman." The
initials looked mysterious and we were in on the mystery. Here was
a writer whose writing was printed, the first such writer I had ever
seen. What he wrote was mostly too much for my little noggin. I
could get sentences and single words here and there. When I met
the word *smör* I knew he meant butter and *himmel* was heaven and
helvete was hell.

In his preaching, however, I could often get the main line of his
argument. I had awe and reverence for him, an adoration for his
gifts and strengths. Along with this I had misgivings. I believed he
was trying to scare me, and I didn't want to be scared. He gave me
the same feeling I had earlier when I believed the crash of thunder
and the spitforks of lightning in the sky were the Wrath of God
warning and threatening us.

For this Sabbath the pastor had chosen a sermon on Judgment

Day. He delivered a massive and simple picture of that Day when all of the living and all of the awakened dead summoned from their graves should stand for judgment. As they passed before the judgment throne they heard their fates. Here would be a husband sent one way and his wife the other. Here would be one brother sent to the Gate of Heaven and another to eternal fire. There would be families torn apart. Not until this final day would it be known who had been truly faithful and acceptable and who had been faithless and banished. But all of the wicked and all of the unbelievers, they would go to their punishment, and it would not be for a day, a month, a year—nor ten nor twenty years like a convict going to Joliet—the punishment would be everlasting, forever and ever, *från evighet till evighet*, from eternity to eternity. There would be on that day the wailing of wives going one way and husbands the other, the sobbing of sweethearts and chums, sisters and brothers, separated never to meet again. The delegates to the Synod, the members of the church, sat very sober and quiet. Here and there I saw a handkerchief lifted to a face and at points the short muffled sob of some woman trying to hold down a personal grief. She was afraid perhaps that a dear one, a man, a child, a brother or sister, would be torn from her, never again to be heard or seen by her, sent to endless hellfire.

I have no memory of a congregation after a sermon walking out with such sober and subdued faces, with such searching looks into each other's faces. I'm not sure that I got the full drift and meaning of the sermon. The main points of it were given with such stress— the promise of Hell was made so many times and in such different ways, the bitterness of the parting of friends and relatives was made with so profound and real a sorrow from the preacher—that I am quite sure I got the message from the pulpit as most of the listeners did.

I might have missed some of the spoken word because of an attraction that always took my mind off part of the sermon. High on the slanted ceiling of the interior was a set of mural paintings. No one ever happened to tell me who was the artist but I give him my thanks and personal salutations whether or not he and I go different ways on Judgment Day. I have forgotten all but two of those murals. On one I could see Moses, with his long flowing majestic beard. He was coming down from Mount Sinai. In his hands were the stone tablets. On those tablets were the Ten Commandments I had early learned to recite in Sunday-school class. "Thou shalt not steal" and "Thou shalt not bear false witness" and "Thou shalt not kill" were the three of the ten that struck deepest in my mind, even though I had stolen apples and turnips from the baskets in front of grocery stores, and even though I had joined with other boys in making a distinction between a falsehood, a lie, and what was "just a little fib." Nevertheless my Moses up there on that mural was against bad people, and he was a fighter for the right and somehow if his Ten Commandments could be put to work and nobody stole, nobody lied, nobody killed, the world would be different and better. Of so much I was sure in my nine-year-old mind.

I had my boyish questions while looking at Moses coming down Sinai. I wondered how it would be to talk with God like Moses had done. Were the tablets handed him with the Commandments already cut in stone? Or did he cut the stones and then chisel the Commandments one by one? If so, how long had it taken him? And how did people get along without the Commandments before Moses brought them down—and did they know right from wrong unless they had Commandments? And there were two Sundays straight I found myself asking why there wasn't among the Swedes or the Irish some grand fellow like Moses who could go up a mountain and talk with God and come down with Ten Commandments.

The other mural that held me and that I talked with across a kind of silence gave us Elijah moving up to Heaven in a chariot of fire. There was a theme for a painter! There was a thing to paint and reach the heart of a boy! My memory doesn't serve as to whether the chariot had horses, like in the circus hippodromes I had seen after carrying water for the elephants. But it was all one piece. A chariot wrapped in yellow and red flame was taking him away from this miserable and wicked world where we live. He had lived a good life, a life so especially good that God said he was wanted up higher. So God provided a chariot and wrapped it in fire and told Elijah to get on it and come home. I knew enough to know that the painter wanted us to see Elijah and the chariot as it was seen by those who saw him leave the earth and go on high. I had seen big kites on the ground and had seen them go high in the sky where they didn't look as big as they had on the ground. So I would sometimes wonder how Elijah and that chariot looked to those on the ground watching it. They must have seen it grow smaller and smaller till it was a speck and after a while they couldn't see it.

On one Sunday morning when the sermon seemed to be the same I had heard sometime the year before I got to wondering how it would have been if God had brought Elijah up higher by using a balloon instead of a chariot. I had seen a balloon ascension that week, a man in pink and blue tights swinging on a trapeze and after a while letting himself down in a parachute, landing safe in a cornfield near town. I thought about this two Sundays and decided a chariot of fire, blazing in a wild streak till it was out of sight, was better than any balloon. So long as I live I will remember that mural on the south slant of the ceiling of that wooden frame church holding eight hundred people in wooden-backed pews. Twice in later years I recall having been asked a sudden question, "What would you rather do than anything else if you could have your wish?" And both times I had to answer right off, "Go up in a chariot of fire like Elijah."

On this Sunday when we were honored with the Synod delegates, I may have communed somewhat with my favorite murals and I may have studied the faces of the delegates from all over the United States. Yet I am sure I heard the high spots of that sermon. It had drama. The preacher wanted to be at his best and in speaking to the leaders of his church from coast to coast, he wanted to surpass himself and did.

We walked home, the mother and father with the delegate from Nebraska between them, we children following. We reached home and Mama flourished around and in no time we were eating at the table in the room that was both kitchen and dining room. On the white linen table spread were set before us fried chicken with mashed potatoes, watermelon pickles, a dish made of dried apples, prunes, and raisins with sauce known to the Swedes as *fruktsoppa* (fruit soup), lemonade, cookies, and coffee. It was a serious dinner. In the evening the delegate was taking a train for Nebraska. A long ways off was Nebraska and we would probably never see each other again—on this earth—in this world. So ran the talk. And we loved him, or if not that, we had all come to like him. He was "one of us."

Slowly and not suddenly the talk shifted to the sermon of the day. Slowly the talk got around to where the preacher had so solemnly told us nobody knows for sure who will be among the saved on that Last Day. It might be you, it might be him or me. There would be loved ones separated, some going to the blessed happiness of Heaven, others to the everlasting fire.

And then, not slowly but suddenly, every one at the table was in tears. Down our cheeks the tears ran and we looked at each other. It had never happened before in our house. We had seen the mother crying once or twice and us children blubbering plenty of times. But never the father. This was the first time we had seen tears in his eyes and running down his face. And alongside him was the hard and rugged homesteader, the delegate from Nebraska, likewise in silence, sorrow, and tears. We children looked out of the corners of our eyes. Nobody was either ashamed or proud. Our friend was going away. Since the next Synod would meet somewhere else than Galesburg and since we would never get as far West as Nebraska to see him, our best chance of seeing him again would be in Heaven. But had we not heard that loved ones would be torn apart on that Last Day? My feeling one moment was that my mother looked at my father and believed it was no certainty that he and she would not be separated on that Last Day—no one could tell till then. The matter of the faithful and the faithless would not be cleared up till that Last Day. So we wept, in unison we wept. Slowly we gulped and choked down the sorrow that had come suddenly, the sorrow that arose out of that mystery of what the judgment will be on us in the Last Day.

Evening came. The delegate from Nebraska shook hands with us children and the mother, giving a bright smile from his straight-lined thin lips and his blinking black eyes. Our father joined in with a rich smile. Then he walked to the C.B. & Q. depot with the delegate and said good-by or rather *adjö* in Swedish. We didn't hear whether the delegate reached Nebraska. He was the kind of Swede who doesn't bother with writing letters—and they are not a few.

Sixty years passed and at an Augustana College commencement I met Carl Lund of Fergus Falls, Minnesota. I happened to tell him of interesting Swedes I had known, including the delegate from Nebraska who stayed at our house. Carl Lund talked it over with his brother, Torsten Lund, a professor in the School of Education at the University of California, a long-time friend of mine. They looked up the delegates for the year of the Synod and, wrote Torsten to me, "Sure enough that year our Uncle Axel Gustafson was the delegate. He wore a full beard and it undoubtedly was coal-black in those days. Uncle Axel was an unusual man. He and auntie had twelve children. Of these twelve, three are preachers today, Cousin Oscar in Alexandria, Minnesota, Cousin Carl in San Diego, California, and Cousin Martin I think in Chicago." In looking back I am sure that in the week we saw Delegate Axel Gustafson at our house we would have thought it gay and reckless Swedish humor if Mr. Gustafson had suddenly and quietly said, "We are going to have twelve children in our Nebraska home and three of the boys will become Lutheran ministers of the gospel." We would have laughed and he would have laughed with us at a wild guess and a bright wish half-spoken as a prayer.

I was ten years old. It was March 1888. I saw for the first time a face in a coffin. I had seen the lips speaking. I had heard the words that came from the mouth. I had seen the blue of the eyes when they were open. I had noticed changes come on the face, added flesh and small lines of care at the mouth and forehead. I looked at the still right hand where it lay crossed over the left hand. This was the right hand that wrote for the church paper and signed "C.A.B." for Carl A. Beckman, Pastor of the First Swedish Lutheran Church. He had died after not quite three years of being the pastor.

The pews couldn't hold all the people who wanted to get in for the funeral services. Many came from far away. He had made a name as a great preacher. Many loved him, his voice and his sermons. Here and there were men and women you could tell had been crying or were trying to hold back from crying.

I walked down an aisle with a hand in my father's hand. When we came to the coffin in front of the pulpit I stood and looked at the face and the right hand. I wanted to stay for a longer look. There was for me a dark wonder about this body that would never again stand in the near-by pulpit where I had heard him a hundred times, about the lips that would never again shape words reaching the flock of which he was the shepherd. Above the still face were the auburn or bronze curls of hair flowing back from the forehead. I would have stayed longer but my father pulled me along to make room for others in a long line.

As we moved along I looked up at the mural painting on the slanted ceiling—Elijah in a chariot of fire going straight away from the earth for his welcome into Heaven. I remembered the sermon about Judgment Day. I tried to picture Carl A. Beckman's body in its grave, waiting and ready for that Last Day. I worked on the question of why death should come to this great man, this rare voice, when he was only beginning his ministry, when so many who loved him spoke their deep wishes and honest prayers that he might live on more years in building the church.

So the church began its hunt for someone to take the place of Pastor Beckman. We heard different preachers filling the pulpit. We heard one young preacher fresh from Augustana College over at Rock Island, the Reverend Carl A. Nyblad (in Swedish they say it "Nee-blawd"). He was a face and figure to look at. Seeing him once you couldn't forget him. Some said he had "a spiritual look" on his face. Others couldn't see it. I remember I sat in a pew and watched him and listened to him and I said, "He looks like a preacher and he has learned a lot of words but what he says doesn't get to me like it did with Pastor Beckman. He is a little stuck on himself and he likes his own voice and his own looks."

Nyblad was a handsome man. You looked twice to see more of him and whether there was more back of him being handsome. He was near six feet high and his head looked extra big on his shoulders and he could hold his head high. He was blue-eyed, straight-nosed, and his medium-sized mouth had curves at the lip ends. I heard girls say he had "such sweet lips." Back from high on his forehead ran a tall shock of light hair, blondish and wavy and combed back in a sweeping, curly pompadour. I heard one Berrien Street girl say, "He's a lady-killer all right."

Nyblad made friends. There were people liked him. They believed he would make a good minister for the church. The talk ran that the church officers would probably elect him to be the new minister.

Then the storm broke. From Rock Island came the news. A maid in a house where Nyblad had lived was going to file a bastardy suit against Nyblad. A baby had come. She was ready to swear that the father of her child was Carl A. Nyblad.

Church officers and leaders let it be known they couldn't think of Nyblad for the new minister. Nyblad called on his friends to meet with him. My father went to some of the meetings. So did our old neighbor, the carpenter contractor Victor Larson, father of my schoolmate "Husky" Larson. The parents of my neighbors and schoolmates Emil Nelson, Bob Eberstein, and Axel and Fritz Johnson, they were all joining up with Nyblad to break away from the First Swedish Lutheran Church and make a new church of their own.

Nyblad named his new church the Elim Church, "Elim" meaning a refuge in the desert. His members believed he was innocent of the bastardy charge. Some believed there was jealousy and church politics back of the Rock Island woman charging that Nyblad was the father of her baby. I came around to thinking that maybe the old folks were right and there were mean people doing Nyblad wrong.

The Elim Church meetings first were held in a hall at South Broad Street on the Public Square. I had been to Salvation Army meetings and political rallies in the hall. It was a low-ceilinged battered place for worship, Danny Flynn's and other saloons only five or six doors away, no stained-glass windows, no murals of Elijah and Moses on the ceiling, no grand pipe-organ music like in the big church we had broken away from.

In a few months the money was raised to begin a new church building. The ground was broken and the basement built at Kellogg and Ferris, the southeast corner, three or four blocks from the church where we used to go. Now services began in this basement with its low ceiling and damp air. During his first year of preaching I didn't see that Pastor Nyblad was improving. You might have thought he was shook up in his mind and soul about what he had been through and what a fine lot of good Swedes there were standing by him in his trouble. But I couldn't think why he should give such attention in sermons to the Salvation Army (*Frälsnings Armén* in Swedish) unless it was that he was afraid the Salvation Army might take away from him some of the Swedes who had stood by him. There had been some members dropping away. And it could be that Nyblad had heard of one or two taking to the Salvation Army. I couldn't think of any other reason for his using a whole hour to slam-bang the Salvation Army as a cheat and a fraud and making himself out a cleaner Christian than they.

I could see changes in Nyblad's face and body. He was getting more fleshy. A paunch came on him, enough so you could notice it. He wasn't working himself to the bone, that was clear. His face said, "I'm eating regular and the going is good." Whatever there was of "a spiritual look" that some people saw when he first came to town was gone. It came over me that he was lazy, and worse yet, proud. They were very plain Swedes who had walked out of the old church to show they believed in him, no rich men in the walk out. On Berrien Street in our block and the next block were four families who had joined with Nyblad—and did he ever visit one of their homes and make like they were brothers in Christ? Not so you could notice it. He liked his comfort, liked taking it easy.

In the Knox County Courthouse there was a trial us kids went to. The housemaid, the hired girl, had come on from Rock Island for her suit against Nyblad. We saw her a somewhat large woman, with a fine bust and curves, a face rather pretty. Her language was decent and she had a quiet and serious way of telling her story on the witness stand. One of the boys said, "She don't look like the cheap and easy kind." We heard her swear that Nyblad paid her attentions and kept at her till she gave herself to him. She named the day when they lay together on a carpet in a certain room of the house. "You then and there had sexual intercourse with Carl A. Nyblad?" we heard a lawyer ask and her answer, "Yes." "And you believe that as a result of that sexual intercourse Carl A. Nyblad is the father of your child?" "I am sure of it," came the answer, "for I have known no other man." The case went to the jury. They came in with the verdict for Nyblad, "Not guilty."

Us kids ran out of the courthouse and along the streets, throwing our caps in the air, and yelling, "Nyblad is innocent, Nyblad is free!"

There were people looked at us hollering about Nyblad as though it was some kind of a new game and we were having fun playing Nyblad. One way and another the papers didn't say much about him. The big noise and the fussing had been a thing for the Swedes to settle among themselves, a family fight for others to keep out of. So there was no excitement, no crowd jamming the courtroom. The Elim Church men were out working for money to build the church higher than a basement—and the women had their housework.

I was thirteen years of age when, with seven other boys, I took the sacrament and was confirmed as a member of the Elim Lutheran Church. For weeks we had been training under Nyblad, reciting catechism lessons. At that time I could give easy and offhand the two hundred or more words in answer to the question, *Vad är evangelium?* (What is the Gospel?) One afternoon we were waiting outside the basement church for Nyblad and two of the class were smoking cigarettes when around the corner came Nyblad. He was smoking a cigar. And he gave us a lecture on how bad it was for boys to smoke. If he had smiled once while lecturing us it would have been different. But solemn-faced and holding his cigar in his hand and now and then puffing to keep it lighted, he told us how bad tobacco was for us. He could have said, "Do as I *say* and not as I *do*," with a laugh and we would have joined him and called him a good fellow.

We were still meeting in the basement. Money to build a second floor, with walls and a roof, was slower coming in. Now and then members were dropping away. And Nyblad was no hand at bringing new members in. I didn't follow all of what happened, but the Elim Church membership just seemed to evaporate. And Carl A. Nyblad himself evaporated to Chicago. Among people he left behind were Victor Larson and others who had signed notes, promises to pay money, in connection with the church building. They were left "holding the sack." You would hear, "Nyblad was a stinker to duck out of town like he did." I remember later reading church notices in Chicago newspapers and an occasional item about a church where Nyblad was preaching. All I could be sure of was that whatever he was doing he wasn't working himself to the bone and he was eating regular and could handle his groceries.

My father and mother didn't go back to the old First Swedish
Lutheran Church. They went to services here and there, most often
at the Swedish Methodist Church. They read their Bible. They kept
to a faith that served them to the end.

With the passing of the years I have sometimes wondered what
became of the child the woman claimed Nyblad had fathered. I
would like to see whether the face of the grown child has something
of Nyblad's face. The mother had a hard case to prove. There were
no witnesses but herself and the father, whoever he might have been.

As I look at it, I ask about fate and circumstance. Had the pneu-
monia germ that struck Pastor Beckman been less virulent, he would
have lived. And had he lived there would have been no Nyblad
come to Galesburg and no dissenters and no Elim Church and no
heavy troubles for some pretty good Swedes.

On Seminary two blocks south of Berrien Street an afternoon Sun-
day school drew boys and girls, about a hundred, from Berrien and
other streets. The meetings ran through the fall and winter months.
It was named the Mission and was meant to bring religion to the
young people of that part of town. The frame building, painted
brown and the paint peeling away at the time we were going there,
stood across the street from the Q. machine shop, and next to the
Peoria branch of the Q.

There were classes for toddlers, for grownups, and for in-be-
tweens. The teachers were mostly students from Knox College. The
language was English and the Swedish boys and girls found it an
interesting change from the morning Lutheran Sunday school where
only Swedish was spoken. I was in a class of boys from twelve to fif-
teen. Our teacher was Miss Nellie Stowell, the daughter of a rich
farmer somewhere far away where we had never been. She was good
to look at and boys said, "She's a beaut, ain't she?" I know there
were boys who came to her class mainly just to sit and look at her
fine mouth and to meet her blue eyes and the sweeping long eye-
lashes. She was gracious and earnest, not so prim and pious that we
could poke fun at her after we went away. We felt she had manners
and "class" in the best sense.

I remember one boy who had his own idea about the Prodigal

Son on the afternoon when that story was the lesson for the day. He said that he felt like telling Miss Stowell what was his idea about the Prodigal Son. "It was like his father was rich and had a thousand-acre farm over near Wataga. And the boy got a hold of a lot of his father's money and went to Peoria and spent it on whisky and wine and fast women and fancy jewelry for the fast women. When they had sucked him dry and he was down to his last nickel he hopped a freight for Galesburg and walked to the farm near Wataga. His father saw him comin a long ways off and got into a buggy and rode to meet him and gave him a ride home. Then his father sent word around to all the neighbor farmers and left word at the Wataga post office anybody and everybody was welcome to a big party he was givin for his Prodigal Son. His father had the fattest calf on the farm slaughtered and roasted. And they opened five big barrels of beer and everybody had all the beer they could drink and all the roast beef they could eat besides roast pork from two big hogs they killed. And the father told everybody he was glad his Prodigal Son had came back home and he had promised never to go to Peoria again."

The boy said he came near telling this to Miss Stowell. We agreed with him that it might have worried her. We had seen her one Sunday when Harry Smith, a good-looker of a boy, handy with the girls, had liked very much some Bible verse Miss Stowell read two or three times. With a big smile on his face Harry Smith broke in, "That's out of sight!" He was talking in the latest slang. Anything that hit you as new and wonderful was "out of sight." It was not polite and proper. The way Harry Smith said it made a look of pain come on Miss Stowell's face and her eyes and long eyelashes flashed as she said, "Oh no, Harry, you shouldn't speak that way about a Bible verse." So we were sure that the boy who had his own idea about the Prodigal Son was polite and proper not to tell it to Miss Stowell.

We had good times at the Mission. We put on "entertainments." We rehearsed a program three or four times and then gave it on an evening when grownups and children came to see and hear us. I sang once in a quartet and we gave a Negro spiritual, "Don't Take de Left-hand Road." Once I took the part of a tramp in a one-act play. I walked into a room with a stick over my shoulder and a bundle hung from the stick. That was the way tramps were supposed to look then, though we had never seen in Galesburg a tramp with a stick and a bundle. But the book said to have a stick and a bundle and I had them. I walked in and said I wanted something to eat and the woman sat me in a chair and gave me some imaginary food that I pretended to eat, though I had a real knife and fork for the imaginary meat and potatoes. The woman was a little deaf. When she asked me where I was from I said, "Baltimore" and she said something like, "Did you say you didn't want any more?" The audience laughed, because Baltimore and "want any more" sound a good deal alike even if you are not deaf. Somewhere she had a line asking, "Did you say your name was Plug Ugly from Baltimore?" and the grownups and young ones laughed, some of them because they knew very well that though Charlie Sandburg wasn't anything special for looks, they knew too that he wasn't a plug nor was he ugly and he had never in his life seen Baltimore.

The Demorest Silver Medal Declamation Contest had all of us at the Mission buzzing, coming and going. We had heard of Mr. Demorest. He was a rich man in the East who had made his money getting out a magazine giving women ideas and patterns for dresses. And Mr. Demorest was more than a strict temperance man. He was what they called "a total-abstinence man." He never went into saloons, never drank a drop of strong water himself. He was against saloons and wanted to see every last saloon in America put out of business. So he had thought up his plan for these Demorest medal contests where the young people of any school or neighborhood would speak pieces, declamations against the evil of alcohol. Mr. Demorest sent us each a book. You could go through the book and pick out the piece you wanted to speak in the contest. Every piece, of course, was against the saloon, against the Demon Rum. I picked the shortest piece in the book. As I remember, it was a short editorial from the *Atlanta Constitution*, telling how in Georgia, in Iowa, and in Kansas there were many counties where they had put the saloons out of business and there was more to come and it was a movement that couldn't be stopped. I remember exactly the last line in my piece: "The world moves!" I practiced many ways to say those three words and couldn't decide whether to give it slow and drawn out or fierce and fast like a shot in the dark.

It was all very exciting, because whoever won the silver medal in our contest at the Mission would go into another contest with other silver-medal winners. Then whoever won that contest with other silver-medal winners would get a gold medal. Then the gold-medal winners would go into a contest for a diamond medal. Then if you should go so high as to get a diamond medal you couldn't go higher. We talked about it and agreed that if any of us went so high as to get a diamond medal that would be high enough and we would be satisfied.

The night of the contest came and there was the biggest crowd the Mission had ever seen. There we sat, a row of us on the platform looking at the audience and the audience looking at us and we picked out faces from them and they picked out faces from us. They smiled and we tried not to smile. When there is a silver medal hanging over you, you don't smile, or anyhow we thought you're not expected to.

Four boys and four girls stood up one by one and gave their declamations. About the middle of the program my name was called and the title of my declamation. I walked to the center of the platform feeling good that what I was going to say, what I had to remember, was only half as long as some of the others. I blurted out my opening sentences wondering how it sounded to the people out there, the rows of faces staring at me, and thinking more about *how* I was saying it than *what* I was saying. Near the middle of my declamation I had to stop. I didn't know what was coming next. It was a longer stop than any of the others made that night. I knew my chance for the silver medal was gone. I reached up and around and somehow my mind pulled down what I wanted and I went on co the end and gave "The world moves!" fierce and fast like a shot in the dark and saw more faces laughing than sober.

The judges didn't make us wait long to hear who was the winner. I didn't expect to be excited or proud about whoever got the prize. I knew I had done a little worse than any of the others on the program. But when one of the judges stood up and told who was the winner, there I was, excited and proud. The judge was saying, "It gives us great pleasure to announce that the winner of the Demorest Silver Medal is Miss Mary Sandburg." So I didn't win but the silver medal went to our house and our family, and I went and hugged Mary and then scooted away half-ashamed to be seen hugging anybody before a lot of people.

About this same time a girl up in Appleton, Wisconsin, Miss Edna Ferber, won a Demorest Silver Medal, but she didn't go into a gold-medal contest and neither did Mary and both of them had to go along through life with just those silver medals. Both of them hoped that sometime they would meet a gold-medal winner and after that a diamond-medal winner, but all they ever met were just silver-medal winners.

One of the teachers at the Mission was Miss Ringstrom. She had a class of the older boys and girls. She knew her Bible well and her class liked her explanations. Sometimes members of her class went to her home for meetings. Her home was on a narrow street only one block long where her father owned four or five houses. He was a short thin man with small black eyes and a black beard with curls in it. His own house stood nearly flush with the street, only a few steps from the sidewalk to the long porch. It was a house with plenty of rooms and a big bay window to the south. Mr. Ringstrom himself kept it looking bright with white paint. We passed the house on our way to the Seventh Ward school. We often saw Mr. Ringstrom and we never once saw him smile and we thought he looked at us as though we might be up to something. Sometimes we talked about whether he was a miser. We had heard and read about misers. What any miser had was a hoard. He kept his hoard in a box in a secret place nobody knew but him. The hoard was pieces of gold and he would go to the box and unlock it with a key and then run his fingers around among the gold pieces and then count them and he got an excitement out of handling and counting them. We believed Mr. Ringstrom might not be a miser but he looked something like what we had heard and read about misers.

We were slow learning that Mr. Ringstrom's wife was dead and his only child, his daughter we had seen often at the Mission, had consumption. We learned that he had built the fine house more for her than himself, that he cared about her and tried to give her anything she wished. I once heard her tell others about her playing a silver cornet. She wasn't particularly musical. She was playing the cornet because her doctor had advised her that it would exercise her lungs and make them stronger. When she died some of us boys went to the funeral, saw her face in the coffin deep pale white like it was in life. And we saw her father, stony-faced, not a sign of crying outside. But inside we knew he was crying his heart out. We had learned he was a million miles from being a miser.

The superintendent of the Mission was Reuben K. Stetson, a farm boy, a Knox College student aiming to be a Congregational minister. He was tall and lean and wore a black longtail coat. His mouth was small and his face sprinkled with large freckles. He gave me the idea there was something rusty about him. I liked him. His smile made me feel easy with him. I felt that he was homely about the same way I was homely and we both knew it. I liked him for looking rusty to me and I wouldn't have changed him to not looking rusty. I felt he had a goodness of some kind that was too far off for me. I believed if I was sick or in jail he might come along and would be good to see. I found I was arguing with myself whether I cared to be as good as he was. I did a lot of wondering about how it would be to be as good as he was. I never did get clear on it. I said, "He is what he is and I am what I am and if I try to be what he is instead of what I am—then what?"

Then the Mission began to fade away. We didn't go any more. Others didn't go any more. The place was empty weekdays and Sundays. The old frame building with the brown paint nearly all peeled away was a wreck and a memory. Miss Stowell, Mr. Stetson, Miss Ringstrom, they were ghosts. Yet I could stand in front of it and say this was a place where I had many interesting hours in Bible reading, this was the first place I sang for an audience, acted in a play, and stood up and spoke a declamation for an audience.

The years went by and I always kept a warm feeling about the Mission there across from the Q. machine shop and the tracks of the Q. Peoria branch. I would wonder what had become of Reuben K. Stetson. I would ask Knox people about him and they didn't know. Then came a year when I read an obituary in the *New York*

Times. He had lived into the eighties after a long life as a Congrega-
tional minister in Connecticut. I wondered whether if I had gone to
the funeral and looked at his face in the coffin I would still feel
something rusty about him. I always liked him looking rusty and I
wouldn't have changed him into not looking rusty.

*

FOUR

*

Father and Mother

*

As I look back I have regrets and wishes about my father. I regret that my father had a fear of want, a dread in his blood and brain that "the rainy day" might come and in fair weather he hadn't prepared for it. He aimed to be "a good provider." This fear, this dread, ran too deep in him. It was ingrained. The church was part of it, the economic system too. In present Sweden is no such fear and terror. "The workless," "the luckless," get a chance. I remember in later years how Mart would say with a rippling gust of laughter, "Charlie, do you remember when the Old Man used to be afraid we were all going to starve to death?" Yet I am sure his buying and selling houses and farms as he did had more than an anxiety to protect his family against want. He found he was something of a manager and he came to like the actions and business of good management. Most of his realty investments turned him small profits, excepting the place he was done out of and perhaps the Kansas land he sold after the '93 panic. That land, could he have held it ten years, would have doubled or tripled in value.

He came to have a feeling about private property as such, his word for it "proputty," the second *r* slurred. He liked to use the word, his black eyes blinking and flashing, "I tink dis iss a good piece uh proputty," or "Dat proputty iss a good speckuhlation—it will go up." The word "speculation" came natural to him. He was a speculator, though never a gambler. It was the children brought the first deck of cards into the house to play casino, seven-up,

77

cinch. We heard his kindly advice, "Dat iss de way you start to be gamblers." Had he been a real mean father he would have snatched the deck of cards and thrown it into the stove. He didn't care to learn the cards, hearts and diamonds, clubs and spades; he wasn't interested. Mart and I brought into the house the first pair of dice and were shooting craps for matches and pants buttons when we heard him, "Trow dem away—shame on you learning to gamble." And I can't forget—he let us keep the sinister bones, the galloping ivories we had fun with then and no future harm from.

He liked company and his face was rich with smiles at meeting the Holmeses, the Kranses, and others. He had instincts about work-manship, about being a craftsman. The Berrien Street house had his handprints over hundreds of places, in foundation bricks and mortar, in roof shingles and chimney bricks, in floorboards he had set and nailed, in paper he had hung on walls. Many a night I held rolls of wallpaper for him and he on a stepladder would hand me down a brush to be dipped in a pastepot. He could stand off from the house and look at it and say, "It is mine because my hands are part of it."

Why did my father, with his exceptional manual cleverness and variety of skills, never learn to write? Had he cared to will to write he could have learned to write the letters of all the words he knew. The desire wasn't there. He never cared for books. Life seemed to have enough stories for him without storybooks. In our early child-hood years he read to us from the Swedish Bible but seldom till later years did we see him spend hours or half-hours reading it for companionship or the learning of wisdom from it or any music its verses might have for him. And seldom did he quote from it. He read the weekly *Hemlandet* a half-hour and let it go at that. He seemed to read it for the feel it gave him of Swedes being alive here and there over America and in the "old country." It was still there, the old country. He had gone away from it but they were still breathing and singing over there around Stockholm, Göteborg, Linköping, with their ships and crops, steel and tools. He would probably never see that land again but he would briefly get the feel of it from the weekly newspaper in the homeland language.

When I became a carrier with a "route," delivering the daily

Republican Register, and brought home an "extra" copy, my father
spent little or no time on it. When there was big news the others
gave it to him. The reading habit never got him. He had some kind
of a natural superiority to books. Several times when I had my boy
head in a book he said with no touch of fun in it, "Sholly, you read
too much in de books—what good iss it?" Printed words, written
sentences, had no charm or mystery for him. They were outside of
his needs, prayers, or wishes.

If he had had even a surface desire to write, he could have learned
from his wife or from any of his children with only a few nights
of fooling around with the shaping of letters. At the blacksmith shop
he could take a crude oblong of steel and grind and sharpen it into a
fine blade which he fitted into a wooden handle he had carved, thus
making a knife he designed, this being more important to him than
reading in books about knives. He could install an iron sink and fit
the drainpipes for it or replace a broken door hinge or lock or put
in a windowpane and smooth the putty secure or pull out a crum-
bling part of a brick foundation and lay in new brick and mortar
into a fairly finished piece of masonry work. He never hungered to
write, never felt the need for it. He was the type of "illiterate" you
can meet occasionally in the journals of Thoreau and Emerson; each
had curiosity about and respect for certain neighbors who managed
to live well enough without reading or writing. Julia Peterkin told
me years later of her great friend "Aunt Venner" who had helped
bring her into life and then nurse her. Julia sat at a table near a large
window with an outlook of pines and live oak, writing *Scarlet Sister
Mary*. Venner came by and asked, "What you doin, honey?" "Writ-
ing." Then Venner, very softly, "Look out duh window, honey,
dere's writin!"

The mother had ways and habits quite different from the father.
Though she seldom kissed the children, she often gave a pat on the
cheek or on the head along with a beaming smile, which the father
almost never did. I used to think that when he had an impulse to
praise me for holding a kerosene lamp two hours to light him on a
carpentry repair job, he checked the impulse, having decided that I
would believe I was worth more than I was. Later it came clear to
me that he had no such impulse. He was doing his work and I was

doing mine and when we were through we were through and there was no call for words unless about something gone wrong. He could no more speak praise than he could sing. When we were visiting friends or kin such as the Holmeses or the Kranses he could tell what he was doing or had done since he last saw them, but it didn't come natural to him to say he was good or he was fine and dandy about what he was doing. He seemed to be guided by the proverb "Self-praise stinks."

The mother, however, couldn't keep from saying nice things when we did well at anything. Whether it was schoolwork or learning the catechism or hanging out sheets and shirts on a cold winter day, she would speak thanks or say I was a good boy. She could give a sudden pinch on an arm with her strong right hand and those pinches and what few slaps she gave me were fair. I deserved them and never held it against her as I did the powerful side fist of my father. Both were earnest persons, though the mother would often laugh at our childish pranks and fooling while the father would keep a straight face or scowl.

We knew he was taking life in hard ways. As the years passed there came by slow growth layers of muscle making a hump on his right shoulder. He was day on day swinging sledges and hammers on hot iron on an anvil. We knew him for a strong man who could hold up his end on a piece of work, but we saw him many an evening come home after the ten-hour day, his shirt soaked with sweat, and he had no word nor murmur though he looked fagged and worn. After washing he would slump into a chair as though now every bone and muscle in his body could be glad and easy. When a muscle was sore he would rub it with camphor oil. When his stomach was out of order he would take two or three drops of camphor in a spoon of coffee. When he had a cold he would give himself camphor smells from a bottle. At times when we had lump sugar he would eat a lump with two or three drops of camphor to add flavor. He carried plug tobacco for years but I never once saw him take a chew and spit brown. Once on washday when a plug dropped from his trousers, I said to the mother, "Papa chews tobacco." And soberly, with a tender light in her eyes, she said, "When the work goes hard it is a help to him."

Mama always on washday took from off the third finger of the left hand her wedding ring of eighteen-karat gold, a plain and simple band. "My hand is better for washing, with the ring off," she said. She placed it high on a cupboard shelf. The washing done, the ring came back on her hand. Only on Blue Monday did that ring come off. It was a token of a true love that lasted, never went on the rocks for all the storms that shook it. Her man could scold and rage, his deep passionate baritone crying out over some waste of money, some breakage or spoilage, a door left open, a broken jug and molasses or sorghum making a mess, a plaything carelessly smashed, a chair gone bust. He would blame the children and then Mama for not training or watching the children. Her cue was to say nothing. Let him go from room to room, upstairs and down, and usually in ten minutes he had worn off his anger. There were two or three times he brandished a fist as though he might let go a sidewise blow to her head. Yet it was only a threat and we never saw him strike her. Had her anger ever run like his it could have been a hell of a home sweet home. He had picked the right woman—for him.

Once on a night of rain and high wind I was sent with a pail to get a quart of milk at Dahlin's a block and a half away. I took along an umbrella. I went into the Dahlin cowshed and Mr. Dahlin measured a quart of milk into my pail. I started home in a wild downpour, pail in one hand, the raised and quivering umbrella in the other hand. I had nearly reached home when a fast twister of wind turned the umbrella inside out and away from my hand. I picked it up and ran to the house. What I got from my father was a hard slam on the side of the head and some furious words about an umbrella costing money that didn't come easy. Mama spoke gently and stepped between us. That was one of the few times he laid a mean hand on me. The hurt of the blow was easier to take than his bitter words of blame.

What other few times he let me have it I probably needed the smack I got. Once was when I had promised I would do something about the potato bugs. They were thick on the leaves. I was to take a pail and with a stick knock the bugs off the plants into the pail and then burn the bugs. Instead I went to the pasture near by and played two-old-cat in the morning and choose-up in the afternoon.

Papa came home. Papa saw the potato rows, plants swarming with striped bugs eating holes in the leaves. I heard from Papa's strong right hand that evening and warm words before and after. The next day I picked two buckets of potato bugs and two weeks later another bucketful. I had learned that lesson.

Papa didn't need the lesson from one of our school readers where a farmer and his wife went to town, finished their marketing, and went to a famous lawyer for any advice he might choose to give them. He wrote it on a paper he sealed in an envelope they were to open when they arrived home. They paid him a small fee and drove home late in the afternoon. They opened the envelope and read the advice: "Never put off till tomorrow what you can do today." The farmer and his wife looked at the sky, saw no sign of rain. Yet they got out in the field and worked till past dark getting their cut and dried hay stacked. The next day came heavy rain and the farmer and his wife were glad they hadn't put off till tomorrow what could be done today like some of their unlucky neighbors whose hay was spoiled.

Mama's wedding ring was never lost—was always on that finger as placed there with pledges years ago. It was a sign and seal of something that ran deep and held fast between the two of them. They had chosen each other as partners. How they happened to meet I heard only from my mother. I had asked her how they came to marry and she said, "I was working in a hotel in Bushnell [Illinois], making the beds and helping in the kitchen. He came to Bushnell with the railroad gang. He came to the hotel and saw me and we talked and he said he wanted to marry me. I saw it was my chance and soon went to Galesburg and the Reverend Lindahl married us and we started housekeeping." A smile spread over her face half-bashful and a bright light came to her blue eyes as she said, "I saw it was my chance." She was saying this at least twenty years after the wedding and there had been hard work always, tough luck at times, seven children of whom two had died on the same day—and she had not one regret that she had jumped at her "chance" when she saw it. One sheet of paper kept as sacred over the years was a certificate signed by S. P. A. Lindahl that on the 7th day of August, A.D. 1874, in Galesburg they "were united in marriage by me."

They were mates. I am sure they had sweet and wild nights together as bedfellows. They had strengths from clean living, hard work, and tough peasant ancestors. They were a couple and their coupling was both earthy and sacramental to them. Across the many passing years they slept in the same bed, even when the babies came. When the midwife had left after her two or three days of attendance, the husband was the night nurse performing the needful for his wife. There were at times smiles exchanged between them that at the moment I didn't understand but later read as having the secret meanings of lovers who had pleasured each other last night.

Their kisses were a private affair. Never once on leaving to go to work, nor on coming in the door at home from work, did I see him kiss her. He made the long trip to Pawnee County in western Kansas to look at land he decided to buy, riding coaches and eating from a basket of home-cooked food, returning home after five days to enter the door with a smile but no kiss, not even a handshake for wife or children. He could pick up a child and throw it toward the ceiling and catch it coming down. But a pat on head or cheek for a child, this we never saw from him. I was later to hear a laughing Swede say, "The Swedes don't slobber over each other like the French and the Italians."

The four-letter words touching sex or defecation Mart and I learned—but not at home. Where the Old Man worked he heard those words day in and day out, most often with a rough mockery at the sex act, at mismatings, at blunders among bedfellows. I am sure he learned all the four-letter words but I never heard him use one of them. It was the same with profanity. The first "goddams" in our house were from Mart and me. We had picked them up away from home, and we met instant rebuke. Among the mother's few friends she could find time to visit with, there was no slattern or strumpet talk. They were hard-working thrifty housewives whose strict everyday duties wouldn't allow them time for sin or dalliance. Like most regular members of the Swedish Lutheran Holy Evangelical Church, they omitted the dirty words and the oaths because it was a habit and a custom among them and it didn't come natural to say them. We of the second and third generation were something else again. We were sure the father and mother in a house on Knox

Street never used bad language. They had two small boys in dresses, tots who had just learned to talk. And those two little babblers would look up at us and say, "doddam" and "tunnybits." They wanted us to know they could say those explosive words they had heard big strong men using, even though their tongues fumbled in saying them.

There were the rare occasions when my father called on the Supreme Being. I batted a ball that smashed a windowpane and he faced me with a sharp cry, "Good God all mind to!" his version of "Good God Almighty!" He was no storyteller. The only story I recall hearing from him was nearly off color. A greenhorn fresh from Sweden was sent to the Commercial Union, a grocery at Main and Seminary run by Swedes. By mistake he went to a grocery where they didn't speak Swedish. He called for *ost*, meaning "cheese." They couldn't make out what he wanted. As he began repeating "*Ost! Ost!*" (pronounced "oost") they thought him a queer fish and a comic. After more of his howling "*Ost!*" they shooed him toward a door. There with his hand on a doorknob he gave them one final insulting blast, an ancient Swedish phrase, "*Kyss mej i röva*," meaning "Kiss my behind," the word *kyss* pronounced "shees." The Americans sprang to it, showed him just the cheese he wanted, and he brought home what he was sent for and said he had to fight for it.

Some peasants sing and some don't. The nearest to a folk song I heard my father and mother sing was the one and only "Gubbah Noah" (Old Man Noah), the verses written by the poet Bellmann. Of the many fine old-time Swedish folk songs, I heard none from the Swedes I grew up with. Nor did I hear of any Swede in Knox County who was supposed to know Swedish folk songs, the sort of a fellow that ballad hunters seek. My mother would hum vague tunes gently at her housework occasionally but no songs, and the father neither sang nor hummed at any time except in church joining in the hymns. Yet he loved music. He bought a cheap accordion and worked out one tune that he played over and over. It was probably a song or dance tune heard in the old country. He never met with other accordion players to pass the time and learn new tunes. His accordion was a private affair. He would play it alone, and if

Mama or the children came near and listened he would give a happy smile to them as if to say, "Of course I'm not a musician, but what little I can coax out of this box is interesting and somewhat sweet to me and I hope you find it the same."

With the passing years and added chores, house repairs and payments due on debts, he let his accordion lay and after a time never touched it. When on Decoration Day or at some public celebration the Galesburg Marine Band and the Negro Silver Cornet Band performed, his face would light with smiles, and more than once he gave his musically critical opinion that the Negroes played better, "more loud and clear and you get the tune better." He had no such habit as the mother, who would repeat remembered parts of sermons or Bible verses, saying them with rhythm. He and the mother seemed to find rewards from listening to long sermons. I never heard them say the preacher went on too long.

For three or four years a blind Negro with an accordion came to town for a few days and gave out with music at the corner of Main and Kellogg, near a poolroom. He had ballads, sad songs and glad, and always my father had time for this fellow. One payday night he listened a half-hour, turning to me once in a while with smiles to see if I likewise appreciated good music and songs. The Jesse James song my father had heard the previous year and wanted it again. His hand went into his pocket and came out with a nickel. He looked with real respect at the nickel, then walked up, dropped it in the tin cup, and asked if we could have "de Yesse Yames song." Again the next year I saw him drop into the tin cup five cents in United States coin of the realm in payment for a sheer personal delight of no practical and material use whatsoever. Later when I learned the song and brought it home and sang it for him, he was only mildly interested, didn't ask me to sing it twice. I tried to figure it out and the nearest I could come to it was that if I had been blind and a Negro instead of a Swede and sung it with an accordion he would have given me a nickel and had me sing it twice a week. Also, of course, my voice was still near a tender boy soprano while the blind man sang in a gravel baritone.

Out of her young years in Sweden the mother had one folk tale about a man whose wife nagged him and often called him a louse. One Sunday morning he told her the next time she called him a louse he would drag her to the millpond, throw her in by the hair of her head, and watch her drown. She cried out, "You louse you! You louse!" He dragged her to the millpond, swung her around by the hair of her head, and threw her into the water. She went under once and came up to sputter at him, "You louse you!" A second time she came up to cry "Louse!" The third and last time came up only the fingers of one hand snipping two fingernails as though crushing a louse between them.

Another she told was about a boy named Sven who had a pet pig and they stood in front of a palace. Sven told the pig to go into the palace. "The floors are spotted with gold—big paintings on the walls, silver dishes and boxes of jewels." The pig went in, stayed a while, and came out. Sven asked, "Did you see the gold spotting the floors, the paintings, the silver dishes and boxes of jewels?" "I didn't see anything," said the pig. "I went everywhere rooting around and at last I came to the kitchen and there was a swill barrel and I rooted around in that but it wasn't a very nice swill. I have had better swill."

Two yarns told by Swedes outside our circle I brought home to father and mother and they said they were nonsense not worth telling. A wild boy was dying and his sisters said, "When you are in the coffin would you like us to put in your hands a Bible?" "No, just put in my hands a big pan of those hot pancakes I always liked." At the Gate of Heaven St. Peter said, "We know about you and you can't come in." "I'm not asking to come in to stay. I only want to give these hot pancakes to the children in Heaven." St. Peter went to the Lord and the Lord said, "Let him in if it is the wish of his heart to give his pancakes to the children on the golden streets." St. Peter let the wild boy in and a few days later St. Peter said, "Have you given the pancakes to the children as you promised?" "Yes, every last one of them." "Then it's time for you to be going. You said you only wanted to stay long enough to give away the pancakes." "I'll go when I'm good and ready." Again St. Peter went to the Lord and the Lord hesitated and said slowly, "We must not act too soon. I ask you, good St. Peter, to search in the highways and byways of Heaven and find *a lawyer* who will consider what is to be done." St. Peter began a search but nowhere, not anywhere, among all the crowded and happy corners of Heaven could St. Peter find a lawyer.

This other I had from Swedes who had brought it from Sweden made more of a hit with Papa and Mama, for they knew people from the province of Skåne who spoke Swedish with a peculiar nasal twang of the vowels. St. Peter came to the Lord one day and said that in looking down to the earth he had seen two figures in the province of Skåne in a terrible fight trying to kill each other. The Lord asked Peter to go down and stop the fight. St. Peter arrived and the two fighters turned on him and hit at him so savagely that Peter swung his sword and cut off their heads. On reporting this to the Lord, Peter was told to go down again to Skåne and put the heads back where they belonged. Peter went down to Skåne and looking more closely saw that he had cut off the head of a Skåne fighting man and the other head was that of the Devil himself. Peter hurried to put the heads back. But Peter in his hurry made the mistake of putting the head of the Devil on the Skåne man. "And that is the reason," the story ends, "why the people of Skåne have ever since had a little of the Devil in them."

When Mart or I thumbed the nose and wiggled the fingers, we heard from mother, "You be careful. If the wind changes, your thumb will stick there and you can't get it loose." We half believed it. And she warned when one of us stuck out his tongue, "If the wind changes your face will stay like that." This too we half believed.

Never in my time did my father go into any one of the town's dozen saloons. He just naturally couldn't have been a barfly. They were not his kind with their foolery and wasting of time. But he did have his alcohol. When the first of the cold winter days came he would buy a pint of raw grain alcohol. We saw him at the table two or three times a week putting a spoon or two of the "firewater" in a cup of black coffee. He sipped it slow and smacked with satisfaction and looked pleasant about it. The bottle would last him over the winter and into the first warm days of spring. Then no more of the bottle. Not until next December would we see his bottle again. He was a temperate man, strictly, could take it or leave it. He had peculiar wisdom about booze. He walked through toils and ordeals of the kind that have driven men to drink and forgetfulness, carelessness, and death.

Many famous singers, minstrels, plays, and players came to town and the Old Man never went once. He had work at home or he sat in quiet resting his bones after his ten hours of service dedicated to the C.B.&Q. He was of the Puritan type in that he never swore and he went to church regularly, read his Bible, believed in hard work, paid his bills and debts, and followed the Pilgrim rule, "Make no long stays at the table." Furthermore, he got into no fights, didn't quarrel with neighbors, smiled to us when on payday night he came home with the bag of candy always given by the grocer to those who paid the monthly bill. At home he did us all wrong at times, storming around and looking for faults, but outside the home I can say in truth he did no man any wrong.

In a certain pinch he would have been a dangerous man. But the pinch didn't happen. Into the upper drawer of the bureau on which his Bible lay, Mart and I sometimes took a peep. Then we would reach in and take out two slung shots the Old Man had made—an iron slug with a cord through a hole—a heavy lead slug fastened to a small rope. One of these we had seen him put in his hip pocket when going downtown to cash his paycheck. Had any robber tried to get his payday money there would have been fighting for fair. "The pay car is in today" was the word passed around, and each man went to the pay car and got an envelope with his name and his paycheck, which he cashed, usually at the grocery.

We never knew him to carry the other article in his top bureau drawer. He had picked up somewhere a small brass one-shot pistol—a weapon we handled with care, for it was loaded in case of a night prowler showing up. Of course there were times in that bedroom when the hackneyed scene could have been re-enacted, the wife waking the husband and saying there was a burglar in the house and the husband, "We'll keep still and if he finds anything we'll take it away from him."

And of the mother, it wouldn't be correct or decent to say, "She put up with him." She did, but there was more than that. She knew his trials and burdens better than we children did. We heard her among other women at times speaking of "my man." She had pride in him for the way he struggled barehanded for his wages, for his anxiety in his homemaking, for the religion they had together and "the All-seeing God" they spoke of and worshiped together. Had women then had the ballot I'm sure she would have gone right along with him as a Republican. Yet curiously enough I doubt that I ever heard her say a word on politics. When later I got to reading newspapers and books and going to campaign meetings of all parties and argued politics with my father, she kept quiet as an eel swimming in oil.

On two occasions she argued with him and defended herself against his charge of wasting money. It happened one morning when he was away at his job, a bright summer day and mother doing a wash in the cellar, rubbing the soaped clothes on a washboard. I came in to see a well-dressed man talking to her. She had quit washing and was listening to him. He was showing her a sample of a book. Here were the covers and here were sample pages—the real book was five times bigger. Mama's face and blue eyes were shining. She was interested. He was saying that education is important. And how do you get education? Through books, the right kind of books. Now this book was no trash affair. It was a *Cyclopaedia of Important Facts of the World*. You have this book around and the children can't help reading it. They will find here the facts about the great battles of the world, how many people live in Illinois or California or Sweden, the national debt, the Washington Monument and how many feet high it is, the names of all the Presidents of the United States. Knowledge—that is what counts when your children go out in the world—knowledge! "The more they learn the more they earn!"

Mother was a little dazed by now. He was speaking her own mind as to education and knowledge. The Old Man would have been scowling and shaking his head. The mother was more than interested. She took the sample and turned pages. She looked down into my face. Would I like the book? I brightened as best I could and said yes in several ways. She signed her name for the book. She had the required seventy-five cents ten days later when the man came with the book. I hugged it. I sunk myself in its many facts and felt proud here was a book of our own that I didn't have to take back to the school library or the Public Library. I read a thousand facts and remembered perhaps a hundred, though I still can't say how many feet high is the Washington Monument. But I was proud of my mother. She had eagerness about books. She would have read many shelves of books if she could have found the time.

About this *Cyclopaedia* the father grumbled—a waste of money, let the children get "eddication" in the schools. It was later he made a real fuss. This time I was there again when the book agent came, not the same man, but well dressed and polite, handy with his tongue, like the first one. His book was three times bigger than the *Cyclopaedia*, bigger pages, two columns to the page, many pictures, *A History of the World and Its Great Events*—nothing less—with special attention to the famous battles of all time. I liked the feel of the sample and the look of the pictures. Mother again looked down into my face. She was not quite so bright, not so sure, as the last time. But I was surer I would like this book. It had all kinds of fighting in it. I said we ought to have it. Mother signed again. This time it was a dollar and a half. That was more than a day's pay of my father. But mother signed and had the money when the book came two weeks later.

I won't go into the scene the Old Man made when he saw the book and heard the price paid. He stormed and hurled reproaches and cried aloud we were heading for the Knoxville poorhouse. "*I hela min tid*"—in all my time. "*Gud bevara*"—God help us. It was a sorrow and a shame. If it ever happened again he didn't know what he would do. It was a real grief with him. It ended mother's listening to book agents.

The book was too fancy-written, but I read most of it, and parts of it several times. Were there ever greater sporting events than the battles of Thermopylae and Marathon? Then there was Rome and Carthage in a death grip and Carthage wiped out, and Charlemagne, Nelson at Trafalgar, Napoleon in a string of battles ending at Waterloo with Wellington the winner, Washington at Yorktown, Grant at Vicksburg—and between times I would scuttle down for another hod of coal or hang out more clothes or pull my wagon of Sunday newspapers over the Fifth and Seventh wards for fifty or sixty cents of real United States money.

The mother had visions and hopes. She could say with a lighted face, "We will hope for the best," as I bent my head over *A History of the World and Its Great Events*. The Old Man would stand over me saying, "Wat good iss dat book, Sholly?" And I had no answer. I didn't like his saying such a thing. But I had some dim realization too that he had in mind mortgages on which payments must be made. In his way he was as good as any of the Greeks at Thermopylae or any of the Swedes fighting with Gustavus Adolphus in the Thirty Years' War—but at the time I didn't know that, and I was a long time learning it.

At the west side door one winter day at the noon hour came a knocking. I opened the door and saw a tall man with stooped shoulders, an open face, and a worn shabby overcoat. The first words he said were, "Ay am saling Svedish buks" (I am selling Swedish books). There it was, a frank confession from an open face. If he had said "I am selling books," I would have told him we had all the books we were buying for the time being and father was home and it would do no good to show him books and try to make him buy a book because his mind was set and it would bother him to ask him to look at a book. Then I would have closed the door and he would have been on his way. But what he said was, "I am selling *Swedish* books." I told him to wait. I left the door open, went in where my father was eating herring and potatoes, it being Monday washday, and I said to him, "There is a Swede standin in the cold out there and he says he's sellin Swedish books. What shall I tell him?" My father raised his black eyebrows and asked, "Hass he had dinner?" I said he looked thin and hungry but he didn't say whether he had had dinner. My father said, "Ask him to come in and eat *sill och potatis*." I hurried out to our now shivering caller and asked him to have *sill och potatis*. His eyes shone and he said, "*Tack så mycket*" (Thanks so much) and came in and ate a square meal and made a hit with my father, saying in Swedish that he was just a poor Swede Lutheran doing the best he could to get along selling books till he could get a better job. He showed the five or six books he had in a gripsack, all of them religious, and my father picked out a paper-covered one and dug into his jeans and paid a half-dollar for the book. The visiting Swede then offered to pay a quarter for the meal he had eaten. But my father gave him one of his rare smiles and said he couldn't take money for our *sill och potatis*, shook hands with the visitor, said *"Gud välsingne dej"* (God bless you), and started for the Q. shops. So it seemed you could still sell a book at our house if it was Swedish and you were a cold and hungry Swede.

At Christmas the Old Man brought home and gave to each of us a five-cent bag of candy, a large five-cent orange, and some present like a toy, a knife, or a muffler. And we knew it was a Hard Times Christmas when the father gave us each only a five-cent bag of candy, a large five-cent orange, and a long sad look. We honored the oranges by eating all the insides, pulp and peelings.

It was early to bed on Christmas Eve and everybody up at four-thirty in the morning for Julotta services in church at five o'clock. I remember walking one Christmas morning with my hand in my father's hand. It was on Chambers Street near Mulberry and opposite the old Acme Mill. I had been reading in the books about stars and I had this early morning been taking a look now and then up at a sky of clear stars. And at this place where a driveway went out onto Chambers Street, I turned my face up toward my father's and said, pointing with the loose hand, "You know, some of those stars are millions of miles away." And my father, without looking down toward me, gave a sniff, as though I was a funny little fellow, and said, "We won't bodder about dat now, Sholly." For several blocks neither of us said a word and I felt, while still holding his hand, that there were millions of empty miles between us.

What would the mother have said? After smiling softly to me probably these exact words, which I heard often from her: "It is an interesting world we live in—full of the wonders God has made for us to think about."

With her the speaking of English became easier and more correct with each year, whereas the father didn't seem to care about improving his accent. Early the mother pronounced it "Sholly," which later became "Sharlie" and still later the correct "Charlie," while the Old Man stuck to "Sholly, do dis" and "Sholly, do dat." She learned to pronounce "is" as "iz" and "has" as "haz" while with him it stayed "iss" and "hass." He said "de" for "the," "wenlup" for "envelope," "Hotty do" for "How do you do?" "yelly clay" for "yellow clay," "rellroad" for "railroad," "Gilsburg" for "Galesburg," "Sveden" for "Sweden," "helty" for "healthy." But he had his syllables perfectly correct in most of the important words he spoke, such as house, pump, water, money, tariff, politics, C.B.&Q., Republican, Democrat, America, Blaine, McKinley, sick, hammer, lamp, kerosene, good morning. Anyone who couldn't get what he was saying was either dumb or not listening. He invented a phrase of his own for scolding Mart and me. When he said, "*Du strubbel*," we knew he meant "You stupid" and he was probably correct. He would impress us about a scheme he believed impossible to work out, "You could not do dat if you wass de Czar of all de Russias."

Mama spoke in hushed tone about the Universalists. I was eight or nine years old when I asked her about them. She shook her head with a grave face. She gave her ideas about the Universalists in two short sentences, "They say there is no hell" and "They believe in dancing in church." On the first point I found out she was correct and the Universalists were saying there is no hell. On the second point I learned that she had been listening to gabmouths. I came to see later that most of the preachers in town spoke from their pulpits against dancing, either square or round, while the Universalists said little or nothing about dancing, either in church or out, claiming only that since there is no hell you couldn't dance your way to hell. I didn't know what to make of it. My mother had a large love heart and wide compassion, and her two brief and absolute points about the Universalists had me looking at Universalists with suspicion. I had a vague notion that maybe there ought to be a hell and there might be something wrong about people who said positively there is no hell.

The only dancing I had seen was out at Highland Park on the Fourth of July where there was a fiddler and a man who called "Circle right and left," "Salute your partners," "Do see do," and the dancers went weaving in and out. They were plain people having fun out of their dancing. I walked away saying to myself, "Maybe what they are doing is a sin and a wrong and they will all go to hell for their dancing. My mother and father have never danced. I didn't see any Lutherans or Methodists dancing today that I know of. Maybe they are right. I hope it will come more clear to me."

That is the nearest I can come to the hazy thought and feeling I had about hell and dancing when I was eight or nine years of age.

Health and strength are gifts my father and mother had. I remember no time that either of them went off their feet and had to go to bed sick. What headaches, toothaches, or "shooting pains" they had they got along with somehow on their feet or in a chair. Occasionally father would take a footbath and sit long soaking his feet. When you swing a heavy hammer and strike blows on hot iron there is a recoil the feet have to take. There were washdays when the mother had a facial neuralgia. One comfort against it that she took was to pour a cup of hot coffee, dip a sugar lump in it, and nibble at the sugar with an occasional sip of coffee.

She had picked up the word "gloomy" and liked to use it, with a long stress on the *oo*, drawing it out. When a fall or winter day came damp with dark clouds and slow rain we would expect her to say, "It is a gloooomy day." She held bread to be sacred. If at table or around the room one of us dropped bread or meat, we were taught to pick it up, clean it as best we could, and eat it. Mama had been brought up to save food when it was plenty against the time it might be scarce. She would say in a tone of holiness, "It is a sin to throw away bread."

The finest smile I remember on my father's face came with the family at the eating table, with a baby in a high chair. He would walk the first fingers of his right hand toward the baby. He would walk them straight and the next time zigzag. At the finish of this finger walk he would gently poke the baby in the breast or under the chin with a forefinger. He had fun, playfulness, and drollery in him, but he preferred his sober and solemn moods. Another smile of his I remember had pride in it, and he wasn't often proud. He had a small hammer he had brought over from Sweden. More than once, as I watched him handling that hammer, I heard him say as his hand stroked it, "Ah! dat iss Svedish steel!" He didn't explain how and why he believed the Swedes made the best steel in the world. As a blacksmith he knew his iron and steel. And it pleased him that of all his tools this particular one was made in Sweden and he could caress it and say with a smile on his face and in his voice, "Ah! dat iss Svedish steel!"

Often when pushing a plane or driving a hard hammer blow, his lips drew away so that all his upper and lower front teeth were flashing to make a terrific fighting face. He looked as though he could kill or smash anyone or anything against him. At first I was terrorized that he might turn on me and I was ready to run. When I got used to it I laughed at him, but I didn't let him see me laughing. When I look back at my father and some of his quirks I think of the Kansas woman whose father was Swedish-born. She made a trip to Sweden and came back to tell her Kansas folks and friends, "I used to think my father was queer but now I know he was just Swedish."

When Papa shaved he did it at the kitchen sink before a small looking glass. We children couldn't help watching him stick his brush in a basin of warm water dipped from the "rissywarn," push his brush in a gilt-edged mug and make a lather he spread over his face. A serious father with lather over cheeks, chin, and neck looks less serious to his small children. Then the sound of the scraping razor mowing down the three days' growth of whiskers, the blade taking off every hair in its path, this had a comic wonder for us little ones. At the rare times he cut himself and the blood came he didn't like it that we were looking on. He reached for a lump of alum, stopped the blood flow, and went on scraping. He couldn't shave without making faces at himself. His upper and lower lips drew back from the front teeth and to us he almost seemed to be saying to his face in the mirror, "Do you see these teeth? If you don't look out I'll tear you to pieces with these teeth!" There were times when he did this that his face took on so fearful and threatening a look that we couldn't see it as funny and we were a little scared.

We saw his razor travel over the cheeks, the chin, the upper lip, along below the jaws, everywhere except a limited area exactly under his chin. There he left a tuft of hair, a small bunch of whiskers, his personal and independent goatee. At intervals over a few weeks we would see him take scissors and trim this three- or four-inch beard down to two inches. He seemed to be saying to people, "You may not notice that I have a beard but nevertheless if you look twice you will see it is there." He didn't hide any part of his fine strong face with whiskers and he didn't care for the muffler of hair around the neck and throat that some men preferred. He designed that tuft of hair under his chin as a sign and token, it seemed, that even though he was not a Somebody he was not a Nobody and neither the Q. railroad nor the Moneylenders to whom he was paying ten per cent on his loans could smother his personality. He wanted whiskers different from everybody else's and had them, and he kept them small enough so no one could say they were flagrant with pride and vanity as is so often a case with beards that proclaim, "If you merely look at the growth and trim of the hair on my face you will at once be aware that I am Somebody."

Our father didn't mind Mart and me singing the popular song that ended each verse, "With the little bunch of whiskers on his chin." His cousin Magnus Holmes put his personal facial signature in just enough of sideburns so you would notice them framing his fine nose and mouth. That was when I was seeing Mr. Holmes in the 1880's and 1890's. A photograph of him in the early 1860's, however, shows him with thick black lilacs beginning at the ear bottoms and flowing toward a clean-shaven chin.

I saw Mr. Holmes often in his churchgoing Prinz Albert coat, its square corners nearly reaching his knees. His daughter Lily told me that once on a passenger train a woman asked him, "Are you a minister?" and he replied with his candid smile, "No, I am just a blacksmith." He wore stand-up collars, corners turned down. Our father was more reserved in style, wearing a black sack coat, always black, never once venturing on brown or blue. He wore a lay-down paper collar which kept clean for three or four Sundays and was then thrown away and a fresh one taken from the box holding a dozen costing a quarter of a dollar. Under the lay-down collar he tucked the ends of a black bow tie. Mother starched and ironed his shirt bosom immaculate and near bulletproof in stiffness.

But the paper collar saved her a lot of washing and ironing. When it first came into use in the 1850's it had caused a furore. Poisonous properties were attributed to the paper used in the collars. Washerwomen rebelled because they saw their income diminishing. Starch manufacturers estimated their probable loss of sales. Society looked on it as vulgar and as a sign of poverty. But all this commotion only served to advertise the new product and the paper collar quickly caught on because of its convenience.

I saw father on Sunday mornings taking a quiet satisfaction in putting through holes of the shirt bosom a pair of flat round studs of genuine gold. If anyone should make the guess that his collar was paper they could look down the shirt bosom and see the gleam of real gold. He carried in the lower left-hand vest pocket a large silver watch, later in derision referred to as a "turnip." From the watch to a vest buttonhole ran a chain of gold links. In an upper vest pocket he carried his "indebible" pencil and Mart said he did it in case he should meet someone who wanted to do some writing and he could say, "Here iss a pencil." He never started for church without having brushed his hat and shined his shoes spick-and-span. I suppose I go back in memory to these details to show that my habits as a sloven did not come from a careless father. In an early photograph of him, taken about the time I was born, he didn't yet have the gold studs, and he wore a gay figured bow tie, the ends tucked under the collar.

The ten-hour workday six days a week, with eight hours of sleep at night, left my father about four hours out of twenty-four to do what he, as a free person in a free country, wanted to do. We saw him guard and hoard those four hours, being careful to waste no hour. Had his workday been eight hours, he would have had twelve hours more in a week to do the things he wanted to do, things his personality craved. There was no yearly vacation. From 1876 to 1904, August Sandburg walked from his home to the same Q. black-smith shop six days a week for a ten-hour workday. On an eight-hour workday he would have had in those years many days amounting to two or three years of time for work of his own choice, for rest, for play and talk with his children and friends, for his accordion and his Bible. In those added two hours a day across those years his personality would have reached out and down and up, would have struck deeper roots in the good earth and sent higher branches toward the blue sky.

In his earlier years on the job he stood and walked erect. He had willing arms and hands that could lift, dig, push, and pound and take it as fun. In the garden, at house repairs, he enjoyed hard work. For toil and heavy labor of his own choosing he had a passion. This was less so as the years passed. He worked slower. If I hurled myself at a chore of potato digging or roof shingling so as to be sooner at

my reading or games, he would say in a father-to-son voice, "Take
your time, Sholly, take your time." He had learned pace, timing. Yet
the muscles on his right shoulder grew more and more into a distinct
hump. His back and torso bent and bowed had no longer the fine
proportions they once had. Part of this wear and tear on his body
came from the way he drove himself after his ten-hour workday. On
his own time he didn't spare himself. He was trying to be a house-
owner and a man free from debt. In his earlier years he reveled and
luxuriated in his strength and how he could hold on and stick it out
on a piece of work that he couldn't afford to have done by an outside
carpenter, painter, bricklayer. The first years on the Berrien Street
place he spent long evenings and night hours spading away in the
garden, spading by the starlight falling over Berrien Street. Later
he saw he was giving too much labor and time for what it paid; from
a block and a half away Andrew Hagstrom came with a plow and
team and did the job in two hours for one dollar.

"Hard work never hurt anybody," we heard from him many a
time. Of his own ten-hour workday he didn't complain. Nor did he
take an interest in millions of other workingmen doing their ten-
hour stretch or more daily. He heard vaguely of the Eight Hour
Movement, with its slogan, "Eight hours for work, eight hours for
sleep, eight hours for recreation and education." He was a steady Re-
publican Party man and a good Lutheran and didn't find other or-
ganizations or movements worth his time. The A.P.A. came, the
fiercely anti-Catholic American Protective Association, and he went
to none of their many largely attended meetings. Of the fellow
Swedes, of the Irish and Germans with whom he worked, he never
spoke as though they bothered him in any way. None of them got
under his skin and gave him trouble that he would mention at home.
The shopmen called him "Gus" and Gus had a name for holding up
his end of a piece of work. He referred to Jack Fowler, the black-
smith to whom he was the helper, as "my partner." Fowler was a six-
footer and a heavyweight, with a round head and a cherubic pink
face, a beef-eating Englishman, someone like him having been the
model for the cartoon figure of John Bull.

I was ten years old when the strike of the railroad engineers hit
Galesburg, a division point. The slogan of the strikers was a take-off

on the letters C.B.&Q., "Come Boys and Quit Railroading." How or why I was completely against the railroad, I don't know. The boys I ran with, the striking engineers whom I knew to speak to, the wild and furious talk against "scabs," hit deep in me. I was a partisan. I could see only one side to the dispute though my little head did no thinking and had no accurate information about what lay behind the crying and shooting. There was shooting. One engineer was shot to death, the strikers claimed by "a Pinkerton hired by the railroad to kill." On our way to school we passed the place in the street where they said the engineer dropped to the sidewalk, his blood turned dry and rusty on the wooden boards—and we cursed this and that.

As the strike dragged on, some engineers went back to their jobs, the places of others being filled by firemen. A row of houses on a new street was built off Mulberry Street east of Chambers, most of the houses occupied by firemen who had taken the places of strikers. It was named Cottage Avenue but for years the strike sympathizers called it "Scab Alley." Also in the course of a few years the C.B.&Q. railroad did recognize the Brotherhood of Railway Engineers, did sign a contract with them, and among the brotherhood members were men at whose doorsteps on Cottage Avenue alias Scab Alley I later delivered newspapers and milk.

And why was I all for the strikers and against the railroad? It could be that I knew some good men among the strikers and they were human and I liked them, whereas the Q. railroad was a big unhuman Something that refused to recognize and deal with the engineers who in all weathers took their locomotives out along the rails hoping to pull through without a collision or a slide down an embankment. I was a little ten-year-old partisan. I took a kind of joy in the complete justice of the cause of the strikers. I spoke of it to my mother. She said, "It is one of those mixed-up things. I wouldn't talk about it if I was you. Be careful you don't talk about it to Papa. It worries him." So I didn't say a word to Papa about the fighting engineers. And I didn't hear him say a word about it to anybody. He didn't like quarrels and this one had brought fist and club fighting to Galesburg and one good engineer laid low.

Two weeks that can't be forgotten my father served as a juror. They were two baffling and solemn weeks we saw him live through.

Baffling because something went on inside of him that had never been there before—solemn because there wasn't one smile seen on his face and he carried heavy loads of responsibility. He was an American Citizen, reporting every day at the big three-story stone courthouse of Knox County, State of Illinois. Lawyers asked him his name, as if it could be important. Lawyers asked him in one case whether he had any prejudice against Negroes. His prejudices, what he liked or didn't like, now counted. What went on in his mind and heart seemed important to lawyers on both sides, to the accused on trial, to the judge on the bench, to the witnesses and the spectators. When all the evidence was in he was one of "twelve good men and true" who would vote. If he believed there was "a reasonable doubt" he would so vote in the jury room where no one was allowed but the members of the jury. August Sandburg heard language slung around that he had never heard before. He felt complimented that they expected him to understand the long words the lawyers spoke to the jury and the court. It made him solemn to think that they believed he might understand half their jargon.

In one case a Negro was charged with grand larceny. I forget how the evidence against him ran. It had been presented on a Friday and Saturday and the speeches of the lawyers to the jury were to come on Monday. On the Sunday before that Monday we saw our father a shaken man. He didn't do any odd jobs around the house, didn't go here and there and putter as he liked to do. He walked back and forth and talked to mother about the case or he sat quiet with a troubled face. He had made up his mind. He had "a reasonable doubt." He kept asking, "Wat iss right? Wat iss fair?"

He couldn't see how on the face of the evidence he could vote to send the Negro to the Joliet penitentiary for several years. He had heard others of the jury saying it looked bad for the Negro. He had heard others who were doubtful like himself. There might be a stormy time in the jury room when they came to voting. And there was a stormy time. There were jury members who kept saying, "We ought to make an example of this nigger." The wrangling, as I recall, went on all of Tuesday, and it was late in the night when the jury brought in a verdict of acquittal. At home we were pleased when the two weeks were over and Papa could go back to the Q. blacksmith shop and sometimes show a smile. It was plain that he appreciated the county government summoning him to hear matters of justice threshed out beyond a reasonable doubt—but he didn't want any more Sundays of walking back and forth and asking, "Wat iss right? Wat iss fair?"

FIVE

The Sleeping Mortgage

Andy Hoover was a grocer on the west side of the Public Square, his store a few doors north of Main Street and near the Union Hotel. He had a sandy beard and I had seen him handling the baskets of apples, onions, and potatoes at the front of his store. He had a daughter Anna who later became public librarian, and I saw her often, admired her apple-blossom face framed in black hair and joined with those who praised her ability and charm as a librarian.

In November 1883, my father bought from Andy and Sarah Hoover Lot 8 in Congers subdivision on South Street west of Pearl, receiving a quitclaim deed from the Hoovers, the consideration stated as $100. Now August Sandburg owned Lot 8; he had paid for it, had a quitclaim deed to it, and he had no more payments to make on it. Such was the understanding he had with Andy Hoover and those who made out the papers.

Five years and three months went by and in that time the father felt serene in a quiet pride that he was the owner of a property he had earned while working as a blacksmith "helper" for the Q. railroad at fourteen cents an hour, with a paycheck of about thirty-five dollars a month, watching the nickels and dimes from day to day. We heard him speak of it as "a nice piece uh proputty."

He came home from the shop one evening in February 1889, and Mama handed him an envelope she had opened. She wasn't sure what to make of it. He took it, ran his eyes over it, and he wasn't sure what to make of it. He laid it by, washed the shop grime and soot off his hands and face, and ate his supper, looking a little worried and saying to mother that after supper they would read again the paper that had come in the mail and they would see what they could make of it reading it together. They went over it by themselves, the two of them together, their faces sober and very alive. We children could see it was none of our business and we didn't try to listen.

The next day Mama told us something seemed to be wrong about the South Street property and Papa was going to see lawyers. We saw him taking time off from his job and losing wages, a thing he hated to do. In his Sunday black suit, white shirt, white collar, and black bow tie, he was having a day off. And several times in the weeks that came he had other days off, his head down often, his mouth sad with the lips moving to tighten, his eyes sometimes blinking and peering as though trying to see through things going on beyond our kitchen and eating table. He told mother and she told us there was going to be a trial. He would go to court and testify and there was no telling how the case would come out. "Something new has come up that he never expected about the South Street property," she said, "and we must all do the best we can by him, for it is the hardest worry he has ever had and he is going through a terrible trouble. He says it looks like they are trying to take the property away from him and he can't tell what will happen and we can only hope for the best."

At the trial Papa was shown a paper, a mortgage on Lot 8. He swore that until this day in court his eyes had never seen it. He swore too that he had never heard there was such a paper, that no one had ever told him of this document written, signed, and dated years before he came to America. He saw the name of William C. Grant on this document of such awful importance to him, and the name was new to him. He must have puzzled about what kind of a man was William C. Grant. It didn't comfort him any that Grant was dead. He wished that Grant could be alive, to do what he was doing while alive.

The mortgage was given to William C. Grant August 10, 1869, nineteen and a half years before. During the five years and three months that the father believed he was the owner of Lot 8, the living Mr. Grant had sent no word or notice of any kind to him of the

mortgage and that payment of interest was due. The first August
Sandburg knew of Grant was that Grant was dead and Jennie A.
Grant, executrix of the last will of William C. Grant, had entered
two suits, one against August Sandburg to foreclose on his Lot 8, and
one against an Ericson family to foreclose on their Sublot 18. The
1869 mortgage was given to Grant as security for two promissory
notes of the same date, each for $556.40, in all $1112.80 applying to
the Sandburg Lot 8 and the Ericson Sublot 18. You could count the
nineteen and a half years one by one back to the year 1869 and
there was no year, no month or day, when William C. Grant was
of record as wanting payment of interest on the mortgage he held.
All those long years the mortgage was either lost, hidden, forgotten
and neglected, or regarded as worthless. Now it had come into open
daylight, brought into an action at law, with an old rule applying,
"The best witness is a written paper." There it lay on a table or passed
from hand to hand, August Sandburg fixing his eyes on it and mut-
tering to himself, "*Gud bevara!*" (God help me!) The paper was a
witness, but beyond what was printed and written on it you couldn't
get a word out of it. You couldn't ask it why it had stayed hidden.
But clear as the light of day it was that if William C. Grant had lived
another six months, letting interest payments pass, the mortgage
would have been outlawed by the statute of limitations, and become
worthless, dead. So the grim fact staring at August Sandburg was a
mortgage come alive because William C. Grant had died.

August Sandburg swore that when he bought the property in 1883,
Andy Hoover told him his title was clear and there was no mortgage
on it. The chances are Andy Hoover didn't know there was a mort-
gage on it because during the years he owned the property there was
no call on him to pay interest.

The lawyers for August Sandburg and the Ericsons were Forrest
F. Cooke, later mayor of Galesburg, and George W. Thompson, later
a circuit judge. They claimed that in their opinion the mortgage was
already outlawed by the statute of limitations and that the negligence,
the "laches" and delays, the concealment by silence of the mortgage,
the utter failure to ask for payments due of interest on the mortgage,
constituted irresponsible action that nullified claims for payment of
the mortgage and the interest. They pointed out, too, that August

Sandburg had made improvements and spent $1100 on the property. Nevertheless the court, Judge Glenn presiding, granted judgment so that under the compulsion of law on June 8, 1889, August Sandburg laid on the line a borrowed $807.24 to redeem the mortgage of $556.40 and to pay every last nickel and copper of the interest, $250.84.

Probably there was quoted *Caveat emptor*, Latin for "Let the buyer beware," along with "Ignorance of the law excuses no one." A Swedish emigrant blacksmith "helper" earning a dollar and forty cents a day should beware when buying real estate, and if he is ignorant of the law that doesn't excuse him. Can any degree of guilt attach to those who by their pleas and actions laid all blame, penalties, and exactions on a workingman trying by hard work and thrift to own a house and lot in free America?

It could be that William C. Grant—who across nineteen years and more never once revealed the existence of the mortgage by pressing for payment of interest—if we could dig him up from the grave where his bones have moldered and have him speak, might say with a laugh, "I wrote it off as a bad debt and clean forgot about it." Of his wife or daughter, Jennie A. Grant, who found the long-hidden and never-mentioned mortgage, we seem to know only that she put it in the hands of her lawyers and left it with them and their fees came out of the $807.24 wrung from the horny hands of August Sandburg. In a practical matter of finance and law a mortgage foreclosure gives music only in the melody of the money it brings. Lawsuit winners don't pay courtesy calls on losers and we didn't expect Jennie A. Grant, peace to her ashes, to look in on us. Neither of us was disappointed. She was to us a name and number that faded into a green mist and a faint echo of nothing to remember as music or color or a light of dawn and hope.

William C. Grant, her father or husband, whichever he was, will always interest me. He was an odd duck. Could he have had a habit of saying, "Sometimes when I look at a mortgage I say I'll let it sleep and see what'll happen"? Or he could have been a careless cheerful man saying, "I've seen men worrying over their mortgages to where you could say it was their mortgages killed 'em." Or he could have been sentimental about a friend to whom he loaned over a thousand dollars, taking promissory notes and a mortgage as security for the notes and saying to his friend over a glass of beer, "I'll put that mortgage where it won't bother you as long as you and I live."

Could that document, that elegantly devised instrument "with no alterations and erasures," have talked to itself as it lay lone and neglected for nineteen and a half years, it might have said, "I get no attention now but some day I will come into daylight and raise holy hell."

When August Sandburg was put on as a witness I am sure he had the feelings of a man accused. Here plain as daylight was a mortgage on his property and he hadn't paid the mortgage nor any interest on it, and the question was "What have you got to say for yourself?" And all he could do was to swear by the most high and holy Almighty God that till then he had never seen the mortgage nor heard of it. He saw them looking at him as though they believed he was a man who paid his honest debts, but how could he be so careless as not to have the seller of the property sign that he, the seller, would take on any such obligation as a mortgage that might come to view in the future? Somewhere there had been blundering and he seemed to be the main blunderer—he could read that on some faces. A careful man, the carefulest man I have ever known, now it was on their faces that he had been careless, had gone along too sure and easy when he should have been slow and watchful. He was not a criminal but he was some kind of a culprit brought to judgment. He had nothing of the actor in him, couldn't put on a bold front, had never practiced at the role of the accused or wronged, and the moment came, I am sure, when his dark and worn heart told him, "I stand mute—and I will pay—what you ask I will pay." There can be moments of assumptions against a man when the only recourse is an armor of silence.

We didn't hear who were there of the codefendant Ericsons. He may have looked toward one of them with the comfort that an Ericson had been as careless as August Sandburg, and he could say, "If I was stupid and dumb so were they. I have company." But that would have been the easy way and more likely he said, "They suffer a wrong done and I suffer with them." He would have had the Swedish words for such a point of conscience.

We were five children in the house at this time in 1889, Emil and Esther too young to understand, but Mary, Mart, and I heard from the mother what the Old Man told her about the case. To us children he said no word about it. We noticed that on the Sunday after the trial he didn't look at the garden nor work at fixing anything nor go to church nor play his accordion. At dinner he looked at a nice spread of food and ate almost nothing. All that day his face was glum with a sad look on it and at times he shook his head in a silence where he couldn't find words, the lips tightening and then parting as though a curse might come from them. He sat for hours at a west window of the kitchen in a wooden chair with no armrests, looking straight ahead to the east wall, dropping his eyes to the floor, then again looking straight ahead at the east wall.

The personal humiliation he could take, not having a high pride from which to fall, never having been braggart or show-off. But where you couldn't figure who had robbed you and the name of the robber was Circumstance, if it was in your heart to have violent revenge you couldn't go out with a gun and shoot Circumstance in the shape of a Sleeping Mortgage. And how inexorable was the Law— with no slightest extenuations, no moderation of payments and penalties, every reckonable dollar of mortgage and interest to be paid, neither blame nor responsibility resting on the owner of the Sleeping Mortgage. This was part of the turmoil in his mind and heart, I am sure. Added to this was the loan at eight per cent from the Mechanics Building and Loan Association of the eight hundred dollars with which mortgage and interest were paid. Now besides his old debts he had a new one. He could study about how soon with a family of seven and a paycheck of thirty-five dollars a month he could wipe out this fresh debt load of eight hundred dollars. He had a right that Sunday to sit quiet in a chair and stare at a blank wall, dropping his eyes to the floor, and again staring at the wall—instead of raving and tearing his hair and calling his curses on men and Circumstance.

He could have let the bitterness of the wrong gnaw at his heart and slow him down in work and hope—but it didn't. He must have said to himself, "I'll not talk about it and the best thing to do is forget it." At the eating table or at work with any of us, at no time did he

talk about it or make any distant reference to it. What we heard of
the case then was from what he told mother and she told us.

We noticed a new word come into his talk. "Sharp" was the word.
He had picked it up among lawyers or friends. In handling a deal in
money or property a man must be "sharp." He would refer to this
man or that lawyer as "sharp." He would raise his eyebrows and slit
his eyes as he looked into your face and spoke the word "sharp." His
face had this and other more shaded expressions out of what he had
been through with the Law.

To my old friend Wilson Henderson, Superintendent of Public
Welfare in Knox County, I am grateful for the research he made a
few months before his death in 1951 to clarify details that had been
vague about this tragic incident in my father's life that cast a shadow
over his home and family. We saw the father going through a change.
After the days when he was seeing his lawyers and going to court,
wearing his Sunday clothes on weekdays, he went ahead in his ten-
hour day, six days a week, at the Q. shop, definitely more thrifty
and saving, saying once, "I am a steady man," with the emphasis on
"steady." The change that came in him was that a certain warmth of
kindliness, an ease, a laughter and merriment that formerly came
not often came now less often. A degree of trust that he had had in
mankind was shadowed into something else. Where he had been
somewhat free and easy he aimed now to be "sharp." His faith in
God, his belief in the church and regular attendance at services, this
seemed but slightly changed. You couldn't say he hardened his heart
to his family, his friends, and the world, though you could say that
every soft spot in his heart had become less soft. He could raise his
eyebrows and slit his eyes with a searching look. He had learned it
from the Sleeping Mortgage.

SIX

School Days

The day came when I started off for the Fourth Ward school, four blocks from our house, at Mulberry and Allens Avenue. But first came vaccination. We were sorry for the kid whose vaccination "didn't take" so he had to have his arm scraped again. Kids made bets on who had the biggest vaccination scar.

In the "primary room" I learned the letters of the alphabet and how with letters you can spell words. We had a thin book with a green cover called a Primer. The one piece in it I remember was about a ladies' tea party. A lady pours tea into a cup for another lady and asks her in three words, "Sugar in it?" And the lady holding the cup of tea answers in the same three words, "Sugar in it." Miss Flora A. Ward, our teacher, had us read that question and the answer. One boy and then another got up and slid straight through the question and the answer in the same tone of voice. You couldn't tell by how they said it which was the question or which the answer. The uptake in the question "Sugar in it?" like asking about something and whether you want it we gave exactly like the answer "Sugar in it" where you mean you'll take what you're asked if you want it. You couldn't tell the first lady from the second; we spoke the question like it was an answer. We believed that whoever wrote the Primer was a silly. If the question had been "Would you like sugar?" and the answer "Yes, I'll take sugar," we would have read it out loud like it was a question and an answer. None of us Swede boys had ever drunk tea and we had never been to a tea party. If it had been a Swedish *Kaffekalas* and the question was three words, *"Socker i kaffet?"* (Sugar in coffee?) and the answer *"Ja, tack"* (Yes, thanks) we would have sailed through it. Miss Ward did her best with us and after she had asked "Sugar in it?" and given the answer "Sugar in it" about forty times we began to understand that one tea-party lady was asking and another answering. I wonder if year after year Miss Ward had the same trouble with sugar in it and sugar in it. She stayed on teaching more than thirty years. Because she unlocked secrets of the alphabet for me I am thankful to her.

The next year our block on Berrien Street was moved over into the Seventh Ward and we had to walk six blocks more to school. I was in Margaret Mullen's room. Miss Mullen was strict but I liked her. We called her Miss Mullen to her face and Maggie Mullen away from her. She was a personable brunette, an Irish Catholic, kindly and competent. She stayed five years teaching and I heard she became a nun. In Miss Mullen's room I learned more about the numbers from one to ten and how they can slide and slip away from you. I respected numbers because you could work so many changes with them and when you were good with them they came out like you wanted.

From the book *Word Study* we recited in class and we learned that when you open your mouth and talk what comes out is words and every word has a right way to say it and a wrong way. We learned that when people don't talk proper it's because they haven't learned the proper words and if you're going to be polite you have to learn the polite words. Here it came clear that any language is a lot of words and if you know the words you know the language.

We wrote spelling and arithmetic lessons on slates with slate pencils. A slate filled up with writing on both sides and we took a wet sponge or rag, wiped off the writing, and had a clean slate. Some boys spit on their slates and wiped them dry on their sleeves. Along about the third or fourth grade we quit slates for paper. One boy said he didn't like the change because he couldn't spit on the paper and wipe off the writing. We bought penny or nickel tablets. At our house we saved a few pennies and nickels a year by using the wrapping paper from the grocery or the butcher shop.

Under Miss Mullen I got straightened out about the earth. I had been going along with the idea that the earth is flat. I had been here and there a few miles out from Galesburg and I had never noticed the earth was anything but flat. What few times I had heard older people or preachers say "the round world" or "the globe" I didn't ask questions. Now I had a geography and it said that men had sailed around this ball, the earth. These men on sailing ships had started west and kept sailing west and after weeks or months of sailing west they came back to the same place they started from—and if the earth was flat, if it wasn't a ball, how could that be? I had never seen any ships or any ocean but I believed the book. I made the picture in my mind many times, how if you watch a ship sailing out to sea away from you, after a while you can't see the sides and hull of the ship and only the sails are in sight. Little by little they go out of sight and there is no sign of a ship. Then I would put myself on the ship and watch the land fade out of sight. This was the first sailing I did on the Illinois prairie.

Then came a couple of stunners. The book said an axis runs through the globe and at one end is the North Pole and at the other end the South Pole and the globe turns on this axis every twenty-four hours. We get daylight when the globe is turned toward the sun and it's night where any side of the earth is not getting the sun. When it's daylight in Galesburg it's nighttime in China on the other side of the globe. Other boys like myself went to bed at night saying, "Now the sun is shining in China the other side of the earth." We liked the equator, that belt around the outside center of the earth and how it's warm for the people there because they get more sun. We wondered whether we would like to be Eskimos up near the North Pole where they have daylight six months straight and then it's night the next six months. Summer we had because the sun was near, and winter because the sun moved off farther. I hugged my geography and called it the best book yet. It made me read the sky and the weather as though they were books.

In our reader was a piece about a stonemason. He was one of a gang of workmen who had finished building a water tower. They had pulled down all the ropes and he was left alone up on top of the tower and there didn't seem to be any way for him to get down. Nobody had an idea. Then from the crowd down below his wife cupped her hands and called to him, "Unravel your sock, John!" She was a smart woman, the only one with an idea. John unraveled his sock, let the yarn down and pulled up a cord. With the cord he pulled up a rope and slid down the rope to his wife, who hugged him and said, "Bless you, John." What the class had fun with was cupping our hands around our mouths and calling to someone away up there, "Unravel your sock, John!" Some called it clear and loud so John could have heard it. Others called it so fast John wouldn't have known what they were saying. Others were afraid how their voices might sound and they wouldn't have reached John.

One month Miss Mullen marked me "Poor" where it said "Deportment" on the Report Card we took home to show how we were doing. That was the month having the day that I passed a piece of paper to the boy across the aisle from me, Conrad Byloff. Con later became a boilermaker in the Q. shop, still later first lieutenant in Company C of the 6th Illinois Volunteers in 1898, an able and beloved officer. I remember the six words I wrote on that little paper. How or why I came to write them I can't remember. Miss Mullen saw me pass the paper to Conrad. And she was not slow about stepping from her platform and taking the paper into her hands. She read it and among the six words she read was one of the notorious and shameful four-letter words. Maybe I wanted to see how the word would look when spelled out. It was the first time I ever wrote it. Miss Mullen read it. She gave me a stern look. She had the kind of a good face I didn't like to get a stern look from. Already I wished I hadn't done what I did. Again and again I wished I hadn't done it as I took my punishment. I was kept after school. I stood at a blackboard and wrote. I covered a long blackboard with my writing. Over and over, two hundred times, I wrote the sentence, "Trifles make perfection and perfection is no trifle." That was the last of my scribbling notes to hand across the aisle to anybody.

In the fourth-grade room on the second floor we met Miss Marian Nelson, gray-haired like a mother and boys too flip about calling her "Mammy" Nelson. Here we recited "Olea of Castile." The verses ran on about Olea in a battle, Olea the head fighter for Castile. The enemy came on and on and time after time they had Olea near wornout. But he kept coming back and in the end he won. At the end of each verse, in the blood and the dust of the fighting you could hear his cry, "O-le-a for Cas-tile!" We tried to give it like we were big strong men with hair on our chests, fighting ten against one. Miss Nelson could give it better than we could but it didn't sound like hard bloody fighting. The trouble was with the poem. We didn't believe the half of it. It didn't shake us up like John L. Sullivan knocking out Jake Kilrain. We left Miss Nelson's room and she took on a new lot of boys and girls. For thirty-six years she went on with a fresh lot of kid faces every year.

The fifth-grade teacher was Lizzie Slattery, tall like Queen Elizabeth in the pictures, with a grand head of bright soft wavy red hair. You never got tired of those big waves of red hair sweeping back from her forehead. One boy said, "With that hair you could flag a Q. passenger train on a dark night." She had pink skin and eyes a reddish brown nearly pink. In our class was a sister of hers, an albino. When you see an albino girl of your own age every school day, you come to feel she might be a sister or cousin of yours and she is what God made her the same as you are what God made you. Her pink eyes and skin, her hair a snow-white with a dandelion-yellow mixed in, you could look at her and say, "If there could be five or six more like you in the Seventh Ward we wouldn't look at you as so special. You are the only one we have ever seen and there isn't another we know of in Galesburg or Knox County. You'll excuse us for sneaking looks at you when you're not looking. There are times you seem to be a flower there is no name for."

We read "The Burial of Sir John Moore" and we could see them moving quiet and burying him on a dark night. "Not a drum was heard, not a funeral note / As his corse to the rampart we hurried." You could march to it and speak in whispers. Here I began reading two books in the school library. What time I could steal from lessons I turned the pages of Champlin's *Young Folks' Cyclopaedia of Persons and Places*, and *Young Folks' Cyclopaedia of Common Things*. I didn't know there were so many famous persons and what they were famous for. I knew "ice" and "glass" when I saw them and "gas" when I smelled it and I had heard about "chloroform," but the cyclopedia made them come closer.

One Friday afternoon in winter I took home the first volume of

John S. C. Abbot's *The History of Napoleon Bonaparte*, and most of
Saturday and Sunday I sat in an overcoat at the north window of our
third-floor garret and read through the book. The next week I did
the same with the second volume. For one thing, I wanted to see how
I would feel after reading a thick two-volume book. And then I had
heard about Napoleon so often I wanted to see what kind of a fighter
he was. I found I had my doubts about Mr. Abbot because on page
after page he would say that an English writer, Allison, made out
that Napoleon did this or that and Mr. Abbot would go on and
show that Napoleon did no such thing and it was Allison who was
wrong. But I got a picture in my mind of what Napoleon was like
and I buckled a leather strap around my middle, ran where the strap
would hold it a sword I whittled from a lath, and walked from gar-
ret to cellar and back giving orders to my marshals like Napoleon
would give them. It was forty years before I met anybody who had
read those two volumes on Napoleon. I met Charlie Erwin and he had
read Abbot and we talked about it. I had never read a review of the
book. Erwin had read Ralph Waldo Emerson's comment and quoted:
"It seems to teach that Napoleon's great object was to establish in
benighted Europe our New England system of Sunday schools."

The sixth grade came and Miss Lottie Goldquist, Swedish mixed
with Yankee, a little woman without a lazy bone in her body. They
said she had "git up and git." She lived near the Knox campus and
walked from her home a mile and back to it a mile every day what-
ever the weather. One of her favorite words was "ed-u-ca-tion," and
she said you could never get enough of it. "If you have knowledge
and ambition, you can go far," she would say, "but you should re-
member that character and principles are just as important as knowl-
edge and ambition." On fall and spring afternoons she took the
classes for a walk into the country. We picked wild flowers and
learned their names. We swung hammers into rocks and she explained
to us about fossils. She would bring back "specimens" new to her and
later tell us about the leaf prints in rocks we broke.

We read Gray's "Elegy in a Country Churchyard." I learned it by
heart and never forgot five or six of the verses. They had a music that
stayed with me and was many a time a comfort. Miss Goldquist kept
at us about getting "the reading habit," saying, "You don't know

what good friends books can be till you try them, till you try many of them." I read a row of history books by Jacob Abbott and John S. C. Abbot, J. T. Headley's *Napoleon and His Marshals* and *Washington and His Generals*. I found Thomas W. Knox's *Boy Travellers* in different countries a little dry and not up to Hezekiah Butterworth's *Zigzag Journeys* over the world. Even when I was older I liked rambling from one country to another with good old Hezekiah Butterworth.

Best of all was the American history series by Charles Carleton Coffin. *The Boys of '76* I read three or four times and some chapters a dozen times. The book made me feel I could have been a boy in the days of George Washington and watched him on a horse, a good rider sitting easy and straight, at the head of a line of ragged soldiers with shotguns. I could see Paul Revere on a horse riding wild and stopping at farmhouses to holler the British were coming. I could see old curly-headed Israel Putnam, the Connecticut farmer, as the book told it:

"Let 'em have it!" shouted Old Put, and we sent a lot of redskins head over heels into the lake. . . . A few days later . . . the French and Indians ambushed us. We sprung behind trees and fought like tigers. Putnam shot four Indians . . . one of the Frenchmen seized Roger's gun, and the other was about to stab him, when Put up with his gun and split the fellow's head open.

I met General Nathanael Greene and watched him fight and in the nick of time draw off his soldiers and fade away and then come back when the time was right to win. He was a whiz at retreating and then, when the enemy didn't expect him, making a comeback and crippling the enemy or breaking him. There were nights I rolled up in a blanket and slept alongside Marion the Swamp Fox in the marshes of South Carolina. I read about Lord North, the British Head Minister running the war. I saw a picture of the fathead and agreed with another boy, "I could cut the guts out of him."

The pictures in *The Boys of '76* had me going through the book just for the pictures. Who it was drew the pictures was as good for the book as Charles Carleton Coffin, the author. I looked on the title page for his name under Charles Carleton Coffin and all it said was

ILLUSTRATED. Who made the pictures you couldn't find out any-where. It was like you would read a program for a concert and two people were going to sing a duet but only one of the singers had his name on the program and they forgot who was the other singer.

I was thankful to Mr. Coffin for other books like *Old Times in the Colonies*. You were right there with those people building their own huts and cabins, clearing timbers, putting their wooden plows to new land and plowing around the stumps while keeping an eye on their shotguns ready for the Indians. In *The Story of Liberty* he tried to tell what went on over in Europe that sent people heading across the ocean to America. You learned about "tyrants" and "tyranny" and people slaughtered in fights and wars about religion, how your head came off if they caught you for "heresy," which was where you didn't see God and Jesus the same way as those who cut your head off. You could see that Mr. Coffin put the edge against the Catholics and he didn't like the Catholics. I wasn't surprised years later to hear that *The Story of Liberty* no good Catholic would read because it was on a list the Pope and the high men of the Catholic Church had made, a list they called the Index Expurgatorius. How the book got into the Seventh Ward school library with such good Catholics as Miss Mullen and Miss Slattery teaching there I wouldn't know. Maybe they didn't read the Index Expurgatorius, or maybe it was a later time the book got on the blacklist.

When I took home Mr. Coffin's *The Boys of '61* and two or three more on the Civil War I found they were dry and stupid compared with *The Boys of '76* and his earlier books. I couldn't understand this because I read that Mr. Coffin had been a war correspondent in the Civil War, went with the armies and was on the spot when some of the hottest battles were fought. When he wrote about a war he had seen with his own eyes his pen stumbled and fumbled and it wasn't worth reading. I puzzled over this. I said, "It was a bigger war in '61 than '76 and maybe so big he couldn't get his head around it. Or maybe following the armies he got sick of the war, so disgusted with it that when he started writing about it he tried to hide his disgust but it got into his book without his knowing it."

Every boy except the dumbest read those two books by James Otis, *Toby Tyler: or, Ten Weeks with a Circus* and *Tim and Tip; or, The*

Adventures of a Boy and a Dog. The books were ragged, dog-eared, thumb-and-finger-dirtied, and here and there a pencil had written, "Good" or "Gee whiz." We talked about what happened in those books and how we would like it to happen to us and whether any of us might go along with a one-ring circus to see what would happen. We read *Huckleberry Finn* and *Tom Sawyer* by Mark Twain but they didn't get the hold on us then that other books did. They seemed to be for a later time. It was the same way with the novels of Charles Dickens. In one of our readers, though, was a little piece by Dickens, "A Child's Dream of a Star," and some of us thought it was the best piece in the book though others argued for "The Death of Little Nell."

The biggest and strongest boy in Lottie Goldquist's room was Stephen (Steve) O'Connor. Only he wasn't a boy, he was nineteen or twenty and a full-grown man. He belonged to an Irish family in a house near the Narrow Gauge roundhouse and he had worked for the Q. as a section hand. He didn't say much to the rest of us. He was long, weighed maybe one hundred and eighty pounds, and his heavy hips and flanks bulged around in his seat and at his desk so we half expected the wood to crash. He was stoop-shouldered and all muscle, had a face that kept the same look all the time. In the schoolyard he stood around and watched the boys play or looked past us. No one dared to think of any two or three boys who would take on Steve in a tussle or a fight. Miss Goldquist worked hard with him one day over the word "character" in a reader. He had read a sentence good and proper till he came to that word and spoke it "char-*rack*-ter." After five or six repeats Miss Goldquist had him softening the "rack" and putting the accent on the first syllable. He was a specimen out of Ireland, out of the people who have worked the land of Ireland for hundreds of years and lived on potatoes and hope.

Miss Goldquist wanted us to know about Eugene Field. We could feel close to him, she said, because he had been a student across the tracks at Knox College. She said England might have Shakespeare and Milton, New England might have Longfellow and Holmes, but Illinois and the Corn Belt had Eugene Field. She read "Little Boy Blue" to us and said it was as good as Longfellow's "The Wreck of the Hesperus," though in a different style. When later I carried a newspaper route I read often the "Sharps and Flats" column of Field in the *Chicago Daily News* and liked him when he was serious or funny. There were years whenever Galesburg put on a concert or a benefit where soloists sang, the program always had "Little Boy Blue" as a song. In school-recitation programs there had to be some boy or girl hitting off "Little Boy Blue."

Miss Goldquist's favorite of all poems was Longfellow's "The Psalm of Life." She was earnest and the poem was earnest. "Tell me not in mournful numbers / Life is but an empty dream!" "She can be strict," we would say, and we meant "strict." But we meant too that most of the time she was smiling and cheerful. For thirty-six years and two months she went on walking a mile and back every day to the school where she met her children smiling and cheerful. For three or four years I went on reciting to myself some of the verses of "The Psalm of Life" that for me had music and hope, thankful to Lottie Goldquist and Mr. Longfellow. Many years later I still believed Longfellow was correct in writing "things are not what they seem."

We had a first book in physiology and then one or two more. Here we saw how the human body looks inside. The outsides were pulled back, in the pictures, so we could see where the stomach is, the lungs and the liver, the ribs and the bowels. I learned years afterward that the book was stupid and didn't do right by us because it didn't tell us anything about taking care of the bowels. We were supposed to learn that from the old folks or the doctors or from reading the almanacs free at any drugstore, the same almanacs us kids put on all the doorsteps in town. But the physiology books did tell us about al-co-hol, how whisky and rum and gin have alcohol in them and in every bottle of beer there is alcohol. The way you get to be a drunkard is by first drinking a little and then more and more. After a while you have to have so much of it every day that you spend most of your wages for drink and you get careless about your work and you lose your job and your family goes hungry and ragged because you are a drunkard.

We saw what happens to a drunkard's stomach and how that stomach looks when the drunkard has delirium tremens or is close to it. One book had charts showing how alcohol makes the stomach lining change in color from pink and clean to a rotten-radish red with blobs of stinking black and purple and a few rust spots. We knew five or six drunkards and we supposed this was going on in their stomachs. The book said so and the teachers said the book was true and it was a State Law we must study the book. We walked on Prairie Street, Boone's Avenue, and the Public Square and the smell of the saloons was enough to tell us of alcohol eating away at stomach linings like rats in a corncrib.

I had been brought up among people who didn't warn you about pouring liquor into a hole in your face. The Kranses, the Holmeses, and the Swedish Lutherans we knew kept away from beer, wine, and whisky if only for the cost of it, for the money it wasted that they could spend for things they liked better. When on a cold winter night Papa took down his pint bottle of pure grain alcohol and poured a small spoon or two of it into a cup of black coffee, we enjoyed the big smile on his face. We knew that pint bottle would be finished that winter and there wouldn't be another till the next winter. We were not afraid that the inside of his stomach was going to change to a raw rotten-radish color with rust spots.

I heard railroad engineers talk about "the booze." They warned each other, "Better lay off the stuff if you want to bring your train through." There had been wrecks, not many but a few, where it came out that the engineer had got into his cab with "a few drinks in him" and "his head wasn't clear." When reports came to the Q. offices that an engineer was seen in saloons too often, it was held against him and they warned him.

The Catholic Total Abstinence Society, with my friend Wiz Brown one of the leaders, was busy among young people. I heard Wiz say, "A barbershop is a safer place than a saloon because after one haircut you don't ask for another one right away." The Good Templars, the Epworth League, and the Christian Endeavor societies of the churches had their members pledged to never touch a drop. In the Junior Christian Endeavor Society of the Seminary Street Mission I signed a pledge to never drink "intoxicating liquors." A Main Street candymaker didn't mean it to be a trick when he sold us big chocolate drops for a penny apiece. You put one in your mouth and when it melted what you tasted was like nothing ever before—it was sweet with a nice funny little burn to it. It was sweet Jamaica rum. One preacher stopped in a sermon to say that the chocolate drops were "an insidious menace to the young children and young people." We were getting a taste for alcohol and starting on the path of the drunkard to his grave. Soon the candymaker told us he wasn't selling any more of those chocolate drops with the sweet funny little burn as they melted in your mouth.

Two houses east of us on Berrien Street lived the only two Swedes we knew who were drunkards, Gus Moody and his father. They slept and did their own cooking in a damp cellar where the water crept up over the boards when rains came heavy in the spring. Several times we saw the father and the son coming home, leaning against each other, steadying each other. When one of them seemed nearly ready to fall to the sidewalk the other held him up. Once we saw them stop and stand looking at the house where they lived. They were not sure this was the place but after a while they decided to go in. They didn't speak to anybody along the street. They didn't pick fights nor make trouble for neighbors. Their clothes were plain and neat and when us kids sneaked a look through their cellar windows we saw they kept their place clean and in good order.

Gus Moody was medium height and well built, with a light mustache and light hair. When sober he walked straight and you could see strength in his arms and shoulders. The father was slender, with stooped shoulders, a mustache, and a thick brown chin beard. They had jobs at ditch-digging for gas mains. They were gone sometimes two or three weeks, away with a railroad construction gang. There would be weeks they didn't have work and we saw them more often come home drunk. The wife of the father, the mother of Gus Moody, had died a few years before. I heard a man say, "She was a pretty good woman. She couldn't keep them from drinking but they didn't get drunk so often when she was keeping house for them. She thought all the world of Gus."

I cannot forget Gus Moody and his father coming along that street and helping each other get home. I cannot forget that us kids smiled and snickered at those two drunks. We half wished when one of them nearly fell to the sidewalk that he had gone down sprawling and we could watch him try to get up. We didn't stop to think that if it was a father or a brother of ours we would have been crying and wringing our hands.

When I heard an evangelist pounding the pulpit and crying, "The saloon is a curse and robs the workingman of his wages and breaks down his manhood," I thought of the Moodys. When I turned the color charts in the physiology book and saw the drunkard's stomach changing from a healthy and clean pink to a rotten-radish red and stinking black and purple with rust spots, I thought of the Moodys. And I joined the other boys and laughed to the tune of "I Found a Horseshoe":

> I got a jag on,
> I got a jag on,
> I got it down in Danny Flynn's saloon.
> The beer it was rusty,
> The beer it was dusty,
> I got it down in Danny Flynn's saloon.

The father and son moved away from their cellar home and we didn't hear what became of them. A family with three children moved in. One of the children died and there was a funeral with an undertaker and a preacher. I was asked to be a pallbearer with three other boys. We took the handles of the white casket and carried it to the hearse and at the cemetery from the hearse to the grave. It was the only time in my life that I was a pallbearer.

On the cinder-covered Seventh Ward schoolyard at the fifteen-minute "recess" at half-past ten in the morning there was room for all the gangs of little kids and big bucks to play their own games or stand and look on. We played tag games, hornaway, crack-the-whip, leapfrog, follow-the-leader. In winter we snowballed each other and once, seeing a man on the other side of the street in a high plug hat, we ran into the street and kept at him till a snowball knocked the hat off his head. We scooted back to the schoolyard expecting him to go to the teachers and have some of us "expelled." But he picked up his hat and walked on looking back and ready to duck his head. We played two-old-cat till a ball knocked out a windowpane and the teachers said that would be enough of that. There were boys wearing leather boots with a copper plate over the toes so they could kick anything and not wear out leather. We invited them to kick us and then ran. When a boy wore brand-new shoes we took turns at spitting on the bright new leather.

A high wooden fence ran back from the school building to keep the boys and girls apart at recess. There were boys cut holes in the fence or knocked out knotholes to peek through. And what they saw was the same girls they saw in class or after school. The girls wore button shoes that came over the ankles and so did the boys, and everyone had at home a buttonhook or two to bring the button through the buttonhole. The girls on their side had a water pump and we on our side had a pump. Each pump had a tin cup. When you wanted a drink you pumped a cup of water. Everybody drank from the same cup. If there was a crowd at the pump some boys would cup their hands for water to be pumped in and then drink from their hands.

In the schoolroom when you had to go out you raised your right hand with two fingers up till you got the teacher's eye and she would nod her head and you would go out. If you were caught whispering a second or third time, you might be called up to stand in one place on the teacher's platform with your back to the class and nothing to look at except a dumb blackboard. Or you might get sent to the Wardroom to stand with only a lot of hats, caps, and overcoats to talk to. If you whittled or carved initials on the wood of your seat or desk you would be kept after school. You would watch the other boys go out to run and have fun while you listened to what the teacher had to tell you about how if all the boys used their knives like you did then after a while seats and desks would be whittled away.

Some boys liked to spit on a piece of paper, roll and wad it into a ball, throw it at the head of a boy or a girl. After making his throw the boy would stick his face between the covers of a book and make out he was studying and learning. A boy was sent home with a note from the teacher when he brought a peashooter to school and sent a pea straight to the nose of a pretty girl he claimed had "sassed" him. One boy in warm May weather brought a crawfish to the schoolroom and put it in the desk of a girl he wanted to tease. The girl and the teacher couldn't guess who had done it. Two weeks later when the girl opened her desk she saw a live frog blinking at her. The teacher and the girl asked questions here and there and they found out there was only one boy in the room who had a name for being handy with birds, bugs, crawfish, and frogs. The teacher kept the boy after school. She liked him and this was the first time he had done things out of the way and against the rules. It came to where he said with a big grin that he had done it. She sent him home with a note asking his mother to come to the school. The mother came and promised the boy wouldn't do it again. And he didn't.

Later I was on a milk wagon and my boss told me to collect a bill that a customer had run up. He said they would have to pay or get no more milk from us. The woman of the house said her husband, a teamster, had gone to a store and would be back in a few minutes with the money for the bill. While I was waiting, her big strong boy came home from the Seventh Ward school and said the teacher had "suspended" him. The father came in about then and the boy said he didn't like the way the teacher talked to him, "so I hit her." Then came language I hadn't expected. The mother said to the boy, "Roy, you're an ornery little rat but you're all right with me even if the teacher did suspend you," and turning to her husband, "I wouldn't care if he had tore every dud off her." She was a dangerous woman bringing up a dangerous boy. They paid their bill, moved West a few months later, and I didn't hear what became of them.

Many of the boys and girls went in for autograph albums. When they asked me I wrote:

> When you are old and cannot see
> Put on your specs and think of me.

Or I wrote an old-time rhyme:

> Count that day lost whose low descending sun
> Views from thy hand no worthy action done.

I had learned these lines from reading autograph albums. The first was supposed to be funny, and the second serious, earnest.

Once a ring of boys stood around a little fellow calling him "Ah-ah." When I asked why I was told, "He had to leave the room this morning and he said to the teacher, 'I have to ah-ah.'" There are nicknames that make a picture like a funny drawing. A girl was called "Squaremouth." Her mouth wasn't a funny nor an ugly mouth, and it wasn't actually square but it wasn't strictly round. "Here comes Squaremouth," a boy would say. If it reached her there was something about it that the boy could well be ashamed of. Another girl had a long neck she could be quick about turning. Someone nicknamed her "Rubberneck," and the boys called that name at her. She was a decent, quiet girl who couldn't help the neck she was born with but the smart alecks took it as fun to blabber a nickname at her about the neck God gave her.

A Swede boy was named Sigfrid. When he was two feet high he said his name was "Siffry." That was as near as he could get to saying Sigfrid. But from then on, when he was five feet and higher, we went on calling him Siffry. He had a brother named Ernest whose Swede mother always called "Arnest." And the boys hearing his mother call him Arnest never called him anything but Arnest.

One or two of the boys were called "Skinny" or "Fats" on account of that's what they were. There was one "Freckles," and one "Wart," and a couple of "Reds," and a round-shouldered boy called "Humpy." A neighbor of Humpy said that he had served a year in the state reform school at Pontiac but most of the boys didn't know about it. He was a fast ballplayer and had whistling tricks none of us could imitate. We saw no signs of his having been in a school where they try to teach boy thieves stealing doesn't pay.

One of the girls, Nellie Newton, had a head of bright red hair. Someone nicknamed her "Moonlight" and it fitted her like a poem. She smiled when we called her Moonlight.

A boy eleven years old the boys nicknamed "Fits" and thought it smart to call him Fits. At recess in the schoolyard he might be walking around or standing still but all of a sudden his head would be thrown back and his eyes turned up showing mostly the whites of the eyes. Then his eyelashes would come down over his eyes and move back up again and he would blink and roll his eyeballs. If anyone said anything he didn't hear it. He just stood in his foot tracks and didn't see or hear anything going on around him. It was a spell, a sickness, though it didn't give him any pain. He would come out of it and be himself again. He was fair in his classes, kept quiet, went by himself, had a good face. The nearest I came to a fight in the schoolyard was one day when a fellow about my size blurted out "Hello, Fits" and I slapped him a stinger on the mouth. I didn't like his mouth. The bell rang for us to go into the schoolrooms. He said he was going to fight it out with me. After school one day he put a chip on his shoulder and dared me to knock it off, which I did and he didn't start fighting. Then I put the chip on my shoulder and he knocked it off and I didn't start fighting. One way and another we never did get to our fight. It seemed "one was scared and the other dasn't."

I remember only one fight where I bloodied another boy's nose. What we fought about I can't remember. We were friends before and after the fight. His mother brought him to our house, showed my mother the bloody nose, and my mother said she would talk to me about it and see that it didn't happen again. And it didn't.

Once a week came to the school a man in a dark suit of clothes, a stiff stand-up collar, and a black necktie. He had a smooth curled mustache and thin sideburns down to the ear bottoms. You could tell he kept his sideburns thin because he didn't care for the side whiskers that stuck out and the boys called "lilacs." He would step to a blackboard with a piece of chalk and write the fanciest writing we had ever seen, "Spencerian script," every curve and loop of the letters perfect. We tried to write like him but we couldn't come near him. This was Mr. Bridge, George Howard Bridge. Besides going to the grade schools and teaching "penmanship," he was teaching bookkeeping in the high school and had charge of manual training. Boys under him learned to use saws, planes, chisels, augers and gimlets, turning lathes. Each year a boy could make something useful to take home and they made chairs, tables, bookcases, hatracks, writing desks, and so on. Mr. Bridge had given much time after school hours, when he didn't have to, to keep this going. He wasn't just a fancy writer with a piece of chalk. He was a woodworker who knew how and we listened to him. We didn't care how he wore his sideburns.

Once a week came Mr. Housel in a light-gray suit of clothes, his coat having tails. When he sat down he parted the coattails so he wouldn't be sitting on them. He was the town's first public-school music teacher. He would pull from a pocket what seemed to be a whistle, put the end of it to his lips, and blow. What came out was always the same sound and we saw his lips stretch out and he blew from his throat and lungs the same sound that came out of what seemed to be a whistle. He called it a "pitch pipe." He was blowing "do," saying it like "dough," and it is the first bottom note in the scale of music when you are singing. He didn't sound "do" loud nor soft but just between loud and soft. He made me feel I wouldn't be afraid to sound "do" like him. After he started at "do" and went on up through re, mi, fa, sol, la, si, do, we felt like following him. At first we laughed at his pursing lips, but we came to love him. We had a music book with songs in it, and he took us through the music book. He was one of those teachers I was thankful for. He could part his coattails and sit down between them and purse his lips and that was all right with me. He would leave our room and we could see him going into another room to pull out the pitch pipe and sound "do" there.

We saw the superintendent of the city schools, W. L. Steele, the head man over all the teachers, when he came to the Seventh Ward school two or three times. He had a dark-red mustache, no hair on his chin, and dark-red side whiskers that stood out from his jaws and drooped down below his shoulders, regular "lilacs," bigger than you see in the pictures of General Burnside in the history books. He wore boots to his knees and the pants pulled down over them. I don't remember that he talked to us or if he did what he said. I remember clear what happened one morning. I didn't know what the boy had done but Miss Slattery called him up to the platform where Mr. Steele had been sitting. And Mr. Steele stepped off the platform with a thick brass-edged ruler in one hand. He told the boy to hold out his hand. The boy did. Mr. Steele brought the ruler down flat on the boy's hand. It was a stinger. The boy dropped his hand and wriggled with his arm and shook the hand. Mr. Steele said, "Put out your hand." The boy did and Mr. Steele let him have another stinger. Maybe the boy had it coming to him. But if the boy had done something terribly wrong to be hit and shamed that way before the whole room Mr. Steele should have let the forty boys and girls looking on know what it was for. I can't be sure now what I saw on Mr. Steele's face. Maybe he was trying to be cool and calm, what the teachers call "self-possessed." His face was like the Law, like the Ten Commandments, like the Old Testament, except for his eyes. What I caught in the flash of his eyes made me think he wasn't sorry he was doing what he believed he had to do. He made a great name for what he did for the schools of Galesburg. Maybe I was wrong about him though I'm sure I wasn't wrong that he or Miss Slattery should have made it clear to the roomful of boys and girls why this particular boy was being slammed on his right hand and shamed. I should have gone out of my way and asked the boy what they had against him and how his hand was doing but I didn't.

Mr. Murdoch came to Miss Mullen's room once, George A. Murdoch, a short Scotchman with mustache and goatee. His talk wasn't long and he told us that education would count in life's struggles. He was a member of the Board of Education and he was the first man to talk loud and straight that every public school ought to have a United States flag. He kept it up till every school in Galesburg had a flag of its own. He was part of what was going on over the country. The *Youth's Companion* magazine in 1889 offered a "premium" to each of the forty-two states in the Union for the best essay on "The Influence of the United States Flag When Floated over a Public School Building." Miss Lizzie Hazzard of the Galesburg High School won for the State of Illinois.

Mr. Murdoch had a shoe store on Main Street near the Square. He was straight in his dealings. He was well thought of. He had a name for being honest and we believed he had plenty of customers and was doing a good business. It didn't sit easy with people when they heard one day that the Murdoch shoe store had "gone bankrupt." One boy quoted his father saying that if you're going to run a store and make it pay you have to give all your time to it and Mr. Murdoch had given too much of his time for "the good of the city" and not enough time to his own business. Another boy quoted his mother, "Mr. Murdoch has a big heart, a good heart, and a poor head for business." I tried to figure it out that Mr. Murdoch giving his time to better schools and flags for the schools maybe had some idea that his business was slipping but he would take chances of going broke rather than not work for "the good of the city." I didn't hear what happened to him after his big trouble. I was seeing many troubles and had some of my own. A song came along, "Never trouble trouble till trouble troubles you." I hoped I could.

An ad in a mail-order paper said by sending a dollar you could join "the only secret society in America for boys who love their country" and you would get a button with the letters C.M.A. on it to wear in your coat lapel. It would be a secret known only to you and other members what C.M.A. stood for. Besides you would get a ritual, a monthly magazine, a password, a grip, and a certificate with your name enscrolled on it, "suitable for framing and placing on the wall of your room." I sent them a one-dollar money order. Back came a packet by mail and first I put the C.M.A. button in my coat lapel, having read that the letters meant "Coming Men of America." The password you spoke in secret to other members was "The future is ours" and the grip was two fingers full-length along the wrist of another member. The certificate with my name enscrolled on it was so fancy I didn't dare frame it. Now when I went out on the streets and met men wearing secret-society buttons in their coat lapels, I could say, "I belong to one, too." I guessed that each one of them, like myself, had sworn and signed a pledge to obey the Constitution of the United States. I wore the C.M.A. button a few times and tried to act like the member of a secret society when I was asked what the letters stood for. As I never met another member I couldn't use the grip or the password, and a feeling came that the secret C.M.A. wasn't so very secret after all. I burned the ritual first and then put in the stove the certificate with my name enscrolled on it.

The next secret society I joined was years later, a lodge of the Patriots of America. William H. ("Coin") Harvey came to town and twenty of us heard him in a second-floor hall on Main just east of Seminary. Coin Harvey said that the big bankers of America in conspiracy with the Bank of England had put the country on the gold standard and made money scarce and poverty everywhere. The country, he explained, could only be saved from its enemies by a secret order of men pledged to keep watch and in time take over the United States Government and run it for the people. Harvey wasn't clear about what you do, first, second, and third, to capture the United States Government, and then, fourth, fifth, and sixth, how you would run it for the people, though of course first of all there would be "the free and unlimited coinage of silver." He was a tall man with a brown mustache, a flat voice, and a face not solemn or sad but just plain serious. We stood up and repeated after him a pledge, three or four Populists and the rest radical free-silver Democrats. Harvey left town, the lodge held two more meetings in a smaller hall, and at a third meeting of four members in a cigar store it was decided that Harvey's scheme was too big to work out and the country would have to be saved some other way.

Coin Harvey wasn't a faker. He fooled himself more than he fooled others. He believed in his gospel of money and politics and for years tried to get people to rally around him and save the American Republic before it rotted and crashed because of the plots and greed of American bankers leagued with the Bank of England. He stayed serious. What fun he had was in being serious. I drifted out of the Patriots of America and the Coming Men of America and have never since joined any secret society.

Going to the Seventh Ward school I would leave home, turn a corner south on Pearl, and pick up the Larson brothers, Husky and Al, and near them the Johnson brothers, Fritz and "Bullhead," and on Knox Street another block would be "Muff" Rosenberg. We were Swedes and Lutherans. On Pearl Street near the Narrow Gauge roundhouse or over on Seminary Street we might meet a bunch of Catholic boys going to their school. We said "Hello" to some of them and they said "Hello" back, usually with smiles. We might be thinking, "Our public school isn't good enough for them. They have to have their own school where they learn things different from what we learn." And we were not clear as to what they might be thinking about us. We were both clear that something or other came between us and set us apart. But nobody called any names and there was no fighting of a kind we had heard and read about between Protestants and Catholics. We had in our school Catholic teachers and a few Catholic boys and girls. We heard there was a fuss among the older people about Bible reading in the schools and we left it to the grownups to settle among themselves.

We had played ball with Irish Catholic boys and gone swimming with them in the Old Brick and they had tricks and ways we liked. They were the same as us in taking themselves as "neither rich nor poor," the children of workingmen. One point we noticed when we went swimming. The Irish Catholic boy took off every last stitch of his clothes before going into the water except for a cord around his neck with something hanging from it. We heard it called a scapular. It connected somehow with his being a Catholic, we didn't hear how or why, but it was sacred and special and Swedish Lutherans didn't have it and couldn't have it.

Few boys in the schoolyard belonged to "the ragtag and bobtail" and few dressed any way fancy. Very little fun was poked at any of them because of their clothes. One good-looking boy with a handsome smile was Harry Smith, living on Berrien Street a block from our house. He had a birthmark on his neck that ran up into his black hair and made a two-inch streak of white hair in the black. It was noticed as odd and out of the way and not because it made any difference with his good looks and rich smile. Another boy would eat black dirt from any spot of clean dirt if other boys would pay him two cents. That was his price for eating dirt. We didn't believe anyone could eat dirt till we stood around and watched him do it.

The detective-story books of those school days were mostly Old Cap Collier at a nickel apiece. We bought them, read them, and traded with each other. We read them in the schoolroom holding them behind a geography. But soon I went back to Champlin's *Young Folks' Cyclopaedia of Persons and Places*. Later came Nick Carter and his sidekick Chick, keener than Old Cap Collier. Either of them tied and gagged in a dark cellar we knew would bust loose and find his way out to trap the robbers or murderers. I divided my time between *The Boys of '76* and Nick Carter and Chick. The year came, though, when I decided that detective stories were mostly tricks. When it came to crime to read about, the Chicago morning papers had the real thing. In the nickel-apiece murders that we hid behind our geographies the police and the Law always tracked down the murderer and saw him hanged if he hadn't already been shot by the police while trying to escape. But in the real-life crimes in the Chicago papers the police couldn't always find the murderer, and if they did the jury might not convict him and if the jury did send him to Joliet he might get a second trial and go free. That hap-

pened in a wild and crazy murder case that had Chicago and Illinois
talking and puzzling for years.

Away out on the northwest side of Chicago where houses were
few and the prairie lonesome there was found a bloody trunk. And
in a catch basin, jammed and crumpled, was the naked body of a
man with his skull crushed. Many days had gone by since he was
reported missing. He was Dr. Cronin, last seen when someone called
for him on the night of May 4, 1889, in front of the Windsor Thea-
tre, to see a patient. The man who called for him drove a white
horse. Every man who had a white horse was under suspicion till
he could show where he was on the night of May 4. It came out
that Dr. Cronin was a leader in a camp of the Clan-na-Gael fighters
for the freedom of Ireland, that there was an "inner circle" in the
camp who were against Dr. Cronin and what he stood for. In Irish
secret societies whispers grew into stories and more and more calls
for the police to solve the murder and find the man who drove the
white horse on the night of May 4, 1889. The police asked hundreds
of men. "Where were you on the night of May 4?" It got to where
any man reading the newspapers expected the police to ask him
where he was on that night. On the streets and streetcars instead of
saying, "Good morning" men asked with a grin "Where were you
on the night of May 4?" Us kids asked it in Galesburg.

After many weeks five men went to trial and saloonkeeper Big
Dan Coughlin and two others were convicted and sentenced to the
Joliet penitentiary for life. Big Dan served part of his life sentence
and then his "influence" got him a new trial. Some witnesses who
had testified against him had died or moved away or couldn't be
found. Things proved clear in the first trial now were not so clear
and the jury voted Big Dan a free man. It was different from the
cases of Old Cap Collier and Nick Carter. Big Dan lived on. There
were lawyers who could use him. He was handy at passing money
to jurymen to get them to vote "right." He was accused of jury
bribing but they couldn't convict him. His lawyer friend Alexander
Sullivan had been accused of having a hand in the murder of Dr.
Cronin, went free in a hurry on "habeas corpus," later was put on
trial for jury bribing, and wriggled out free. What they call "justice"
was one thing in the detective stories we bought and dirtied and

traded, and in the Chicago newspapers it was something else. We found that out when for years we read many columns in those newspapers about the ins and outs of the Cronin case. Anybody bothered what to talk about brought up the Cronin case, the naked body in the catch basin with the skull crushed, the white horse, the men convicted, the new trial, and Big Dan and Alexander Sullivan walking the streets of Chicago "cool as you please" and smooth and oily at handing money to jurymen more interested in money than "justice."

Of course we got education out of the Cronin murder and the first and second trials. We learned that in time of peace, and no war on, men can kill a man not for money but because the man stands for something they hate and they want him out of the way. We learned that juries can be fixed, that if a convicted man waits a few years and gets a second trial there may be important witnesses who have died or moved away or somehow can't be found. We learned that crime and politics are tangled with each other, that law and justice sometimes can be a monkey business with a bad smell. We learned things we didn't hear about in the Seventh Ward school and we never read about them in the detective stories of those days. We learned that if you see a white horse he may be hauling a good doctor to his death and the last one you would blame would be the white horse.

Another case in Chicago a few years earlier had us kids and all Galesburg stirred up. We heard about it, read about it, and talked about it, from May 5 on through every day of that year of 1886. On the night of May 4, a police captain marched one hundred and eighty of his men to a meeting on the Haymarket, where the captain lifted his club toward a speaker on a wagon and said, "In the name of the people of the State of Illinois I command you to disperse." Then came a crash like a bolt of wild thunder. Someone had thrown a dynamite bomb straight where the policemen stood thickest. When it was all over seven policemen were dead.

Then came the murder trial of eight men and we saw in the Chicago papers black-and-white drawings of their faces and they looked exactly like what we expected, hard, mean, slimy faces. We saw pictures of the twelve men on the jury and they looked like what we expected, nice, honest, decent faces. We learned the word for the men on trial, anarchists, and they hated the rich and called policemen "bloodhounds." They were not regular people and they didn't belong to the human race, for they seemed more like slimy animals who prowl, sneak, and kill in the dark. This I believed along with millions of other people reading and talking about the trial. I didn't meet or hear of anyone in our town who didn't so believe then, at that time.

The trial dragged on and the case went to higher courts and the governor of Illinois, and two of the eight men were sentenced for life, one for fifteen years, and five to be hanged on November 11, 1887. I was nine years old, nearly ten, when we were let out of the Seventh Ward school at three-thirty on the afternoon of November 11, 1887. Us kids had been asking and were still asking what would happen. In a world where there could be anarchists doing the things that anarchists do, who could tell what would happen next? We had heard about the crowds and mobs who swarmed around the courtroom when the trial was on. We knew that the jurymen leaving the courtroom were guarded by policemen with hands on their revolvers and sharp eyes for any bomb thrower. And the wild news had come to us on the day before that one of the anarchists, a bomb maker, had somehow got, probably from a woman fascinated by him who visited his cell, what he told her he wanted. It was a "fulminating cap" that exploded dynamite. He had put it in his mouth, bit his teeth into it, and blown part of his head off. There was one, we said, that wouldn't have to be hanged. He was out of this world and that was something. We talked like that.

We walked from school that afternoon of November 11 a block and a half south on Seminary Street. On the other side of the street we saw walking fast toward us a railroad man we knew. We heard him call out, as he went on walking fast, to another railroad man about ten feet ahead of us. I can never forget the four words that came from that man across the street. He had the big news of the day and was glad to spread it. The four words were "Well, they hanged 'em!" That was all. The man was more than satisfied, went on walking fast, more than happy. You could tell that by his voice, by the way he sang it out with a glad howl. No need to say more.

Everybody knew what had gone before. The end of the story was "Well, they hanged 'em!"

Something tight in me came loose and it was the same with the other kids. We looked into each other's faces and said, "I'm glad it's over, ain't you?" and, "They had it comin to them and I'm glad they're dead," and, "A lot of people will be glad today, won't they?"

My mother said, "I don't like to tink of all dose men dead wit ropes around deir necks. But dose arnashists are bad people. Satan had his hand in it." My father came home from the shop, had one arm out of a coat sleeve, was shaking his head and saying, "Dose arnashists, dose arnashists." And getting the other arm out of its sleeve, he went on, looking at mother, "Dey killed and so dey ought to be killed." Then turning to Mary, Mart, and me, "Dey killed and so dey ought to be killed."

Among many Swedes the word was "arnashists." Us kids picked it up and passed to each other "arnashists" for anarchists. It was the only thing we had to laugh at in the whole case and we were laughing at the queer twist that could be put on the word.

Five years later I sat in a gallery and heard John Peter Altgeld in a campaign speech in the Opera House. Not a word came from him about the Haymarket bomb and the anarchists. But a few months after he was elected governor he pardoned the three "anarchists" at Joliet and gave out a sixteen-thousand-word message on why he did it. It took me over two hours to give a slow reading to that message in a Chicago newspaper. Parts of it I read more than twice. "The jury which tried the case was a packed jury selected to convict," wrote Altgeld. He named the jurymen who had said in court that they had read about the case and they believed the men on trial were guilty. With the kind of a jury that was picked it was sure beforehand that the men on trial would be found guilty. The governor wrote that the judge threw in questions and remarks before and during the trial showing he believed them guilty before the evidence was in, and instead of a fair trial it was a farce and a mockery of justice. The man who threw the bomb had escaped and there was no evidence to show that he was connected in any way with the men on trial. The police of Chicago had shot and killed strikers, wrote the governor, and they had broken up labor meetings and had beaten many heads bloody—and the man who threw the bomb probably did it on his own for "personal revenge."

I knew as I moved through that sixteen-thousand-word message, crammed with what I now took to be sober facts and truth, that I wasn't the same boy as five years before when I was glad about four men hanged. The feeling grew on me that I had been a little crazy, "off my nut," along with millions of people like myself gone somewhat crazy. I could understand, when I met it later, what was said by Lyman Trumbull, a Chicago lawyer who had been a United States Senator and the floor leader in the Senate in 1865 for important measures Lincoln wanted passed. Trumbull said, "The time will come when mankind will look back upon the execution of the anarchists as we of this day look back upon the burning of the witches in New England." They hanged the witches instead of burning them, yet Trumbull's meaning cannot be mistaken. In Salem and Chicago it was broken necks for the accused with later regrets over what couldn't be undone.

Newspapers howled that Altgeld himself was an anarchist. Police officers and politicians joined in the howling. In their hate they couldn't find names nasty enough to call him. I had seen him and heard him. I leaned toward him, feeling he was no cheap politician. I heard Republicans and Democrats saying, after the pardons, "Altgeld has killed himself in politics. He can never again be elected to a big office." He ran for governor of Illinois and was beaten, ran for mayor of Chicago and was beaten. He had been a millionaire, owned a tall office building in the Loop, and what he owned was swept away, some of it by trickery.

Years later I heard Edgar Lee Masters, who had known Altgeld, saying, "He had violet eyes, strange and quiet violet eyes. They stripped him to the bone, drove him into a terrible loneliness, but I don't believe those who say he died of a broken heart. He had hidden strengths. In his fifty-four years he lived a thousand years. It could be that five hundred years from now his name will stand out like that of Cromwell or William of Orange." Something like that ran Masters' talk. It was a far cry back to that afternoon when I heard those four words in a glad howl, "Well, they hanged 'em!"

I finished the Seventh Ward school. I could feel I was growing up, halfway toward being a man. It was quite a change to walk twice a day to the Grammar School downtown and walk a mile home again. They came from all ends of the town to the Grammar School, many new faces to see and new names to hear, many more boys and girls from the well-off families with better clothes.

The Grammar School stood a short block from the Public Square. Between stood the Old First Church, built more than forty years before by the First Settlers. The long oak beams holding it together had been hauled by horses from miles away and hewn by the axes of old-timers. The benches inside were black walnut. The old building could say, "When I was built this town had only a few hundred people in it and you could walk across the town in three or four minutes to the cornfields and pastures." In a few years they tore down the Old First Church and sold the great oak beams and black-walnut benches as used lumber. They could have moved that fine quaint antique of a building to some vacant lot to stand as a loving memorial to the pioneer founders of the city, but there didn't seem to be enough care, sentiment, or imagination for such action.

Straight across the street from the Grammar School stood the two-story house where Henry R. Sanderson lived. He had been mayor of Galesburg and had a son George, who would later be mayor, and another son "Bay" we liked to watch playing shortstop on the Galesburg team. We used to see Henry R. Sanderson with his long white beard and quiet face. We heard how when he was mayor he had taken Abraham Lincoln into his house as a guest in the year 1858 when Lincoln came to debate with Douglas, how he had helped with towels and warm water for Lincoln to take a bath. Sanderson could tell of Lincoln meeting a man named John T. Barnett in Galesburg and remembering that years back he and Barnett were spear-fishing in the Sangamon River, with Lincoln holding a torch high up so as to keep the light out of his own eyes. And Barnett had called out, "Abe, bring down that torch. You're holding it clear out of Sangamon County." Lincoln pointed at Barnett and said to Mayor Sanderson, "This is the man."

On the next corner south of the Grammar School was the High

School for the older boys and girls going in for algebra, Latin, and English literature. In the big yard across the street to the north the farmers pulled in with their wagons and hayracks to sell hay, straw, vegetables, and farm stuff. Often going to the school I walked to the Q. depot, Seminary to Main and Main to the Public Square, though I didn't know then that that too, in what I saw and heard, was part of my education.

My first teacher in the seventh grade was Miss Carrie Chapin, young, gracious, and respected. She was born in Springfield, Massachusetts, lived there eight years before her family moved to Galesburg. She grew up speaking a New England accent she never lost. She pronounced the word "can't" as "cahnt," "New York" as "Noo Yawk." She said "lawr" for "law," and we liked it. For us it was traveling out of Illinois to hear Massachusetts talk. She never married. For more than thirty-two years after I left her room she went on teaching, retiring to Claremont, California, to die at eighty years of age.

Then came the eighth grade and Miss Frances (Fanny) Hague. Near my desk in Miss Hague's room were the two Colville girls, daughters of Robert Colville, the leading job printer and bookbinder of Galesburg. They were pretty to look at. I tried to look at them without it being seen that my eyes were enjoying them. Ann had carrot-colored hair that framed her brown eyes, freckled face, and thin-lipped mouth. Her sister Blanche had deep-black hair and eyes and her face was what they call ivory-pale, her mouth more full-lipped than Ann's. Both these girls near my desk had legs good to look at and I would take quick looks at them and flash my eyes in a hurry back to the history or geography pages. Near my desk, too, was Bessie Cooke, daughter of Mayor Forrest F. Cooke. She was pretty as any slumberous brunette showgirl and a few years later was picked to be queen of a festival where she rode in a float wearing a crown and trailing white robes. I didn't wave at her but I did say "Hello, Bessie" so nobody could hear. Among our classmates was a comely brown-faced mulatto girl, Alberta Finney, who held her own in classwork and by her ways and manners won a quiet respect from all.

Miss Hague was truly a great teacher and everyone said so. She knew her books and would have loved them whether she taught them or not. She had traveled Europe and could make cities and ruins there come alive for us. The high spot for me under her teaching was *A Brief History of the United States* published by A. S. Barnes & Company, though the title page didn't tell who wrote the book. Parts of it I had read in other books but it was the first book I read that tried to tell the story of our country from the time of the early Indians on through Grant as President. It was stuffy and hifalutin in style, yet it made me see the American Story in new lights. Nearly every page had footnotes with anecdotes that were fascinating, that carried you along better than the main text. That Columbus, after discovering America, was refused the governorship promised him and instead was ordered sent home to Spain in chains, this you read in a footnote in fine type.

Miss Hague knew her history in a big way and often gave color and good sense to stupid pages. The book sized up the American Indian, the Red Man: "He rarely spoke to his wife or children. He would sit on the ground for days, leaning his elbows on his knees in stupid silence. He was crafty and cruel. His word was no protection. False and cunning, he never hesitated to violate a treaty when his passions prompted him to hatred. . . . Unless he can be induced to give up his roving habits, and to cultivate the soil, he is doomed to destruction. It is to be earnestly hoped that the red man may yet be Christianized and taught the arts of industry and peace." To such a passage Miss Hague might add that it wasn't quite fair to the Indians and there were cases where the White Man had done great wrong to the Red Man.

We heard of Father Hennepin and how they named an early canal after him. He knew the Indians in the early days and wrote: "Illinois comes from the Indian *Illini*, signifying a complete, finished and perfect man, imbued with the spirit and bravery of the men of every nation that ever lived." We read that and asked, "Could he be meaning us?"

When I left Miss Hague's room my mind would keep going back to it. I wasn't sure what was education but I was sure that I got a little under her teaching. From then on until several years later, what schooling I got was outside of schools, from reading books, newspapers, and magazines, from watching and listening to many kinds of people and what they were doing and saying. I knocked around in different jobs, learning a little in each of them and learning too in idle days between jobs.

*

SEVEN

*

Along Berrien Street

*

Every day along our Berrien Street block were comings and goings like clockwork. If we saw Mr. Anderson, our next-door neighbor to the west, going in his front gate in the morning with his tin dinner pail, we knew it was ten minutes past seven. He was a night watchman at the Q. and left the shops at seven. If we saw Mr. Seeley in the noon hour walking west, we knew it was a quarter-hour before the one-o'clock Q. whistle. Our father and two or three others would start four or five minutes later. Mr. Seeley liked to walk slow, liked to finish his dinner earlier and take his time going to work.

If we saw a man of slight, wiry build, a light-brown silken beard over his face, his head held high and bent forward peering through spectacles, a small tan valise in one hand, walking east as though his mind was occupied with ideas a million miles from Berrien Street and Galesburg, we knew it was near eight o'clock, when Professor Philip Green Wright would take up a class at Lombard University some six blocks away. We didn't know then that his father was Elizur Wright, a radical and an agitator who had a stormy career as secretary of the American Anti-Slavery Society and who later worked out and compiled the first dependable actuarial tables used by the large life insurance companies. We didn't know that this funny-looking fellow would become a truly Great Man and forty years later I would write the sketch of him for the *Dictionary of American Biography*. As a boy I didn't have the faintest dim gleam of a dream that this professor would in less than ten years become for me a fine and dear friend, a deeply beloved teacher. He walked with queer long steps, stretching his neck to peer away past the next corner. We would imitate his walk and we didn't know in the least that he had streaks of laughter in him and in time to come would write one of the funniest musical comedies ever seen on the local Auditorium stage even though he was a mathematician, an astronomer, a historian, an economist, a poet, a printer and a bookbinder, a genius and a marvel. All we knew then was that his figure and walk were funny and we liked to watch him and it was near eight in the morning.

About fifteen minutes earlier we might see Professor Jon W. Grubb come out of the house across the street from us after he had milked his Jersey cow. He had a stubby close-trimmed beard and looked like General Ulysses S. Grant. He was the registrar and a Latin teacher at Lombard and we were a little suspicious of him because he was a Universalist believing there is no hell.

Three houses to the east of Professor Grubb lived a roundhouse wiper who with a lumpy textile known as "waste" day after day ran his hands over locomotives and groomed them for their next trips, his pay about one dollar and thirty cents a day. We knew it was Friday night and the Knights of Abbadabba were to meet when we saw him walking west in his regalia. A long-tailed blue coat with brass buttons and streaks of color he wore and on his head a long hat flying a plume, a shining white ostrich feather. It could have been some other bird than an ostrich and maybe the plume was pink or green rather than white. But it was dazzling. And as we saw him walking with a quickstep, trying to look military and medieval in his garments of glory, we tittered. We knew his thought: "Why shouldn't a roundhouse wiper, whose hands wiped and wiped away day after day till a locomotive had a shine like that of a blooded racehorse, why shouldn't he snatch a little glory out of this short life we live?" Yet he walked bashful. He hoped he looked like a royal guardsman pacing the pavilion of a palace. He could have had a secret wish that nobody was looking at him or that he was back at the roundhouse in his overalls. He hurried with long steps and had the comfort that soon he would be in the hall where he would see

his solemnly pledged brothers of the secret order in regalia the same
as he was wearing and there would be the ritual and he would know
happiness and human dignity and a mystic satisfaction that the Q.
railroad was not everything in this world.

Next door east of us for a time lived the Bonham family, Mr.
Bonham a Q. engineer. Their boy Ross blinked his eyes a good deal
and wore large spectacles. Some kids thought it smart to call him
"Four Eyes." Ross Bonham, years later, became the mayor of a city
on the West coast. He had a bright smile showing a set of large good
teeth. For a year or two, on every Friday morning Ross' mother
would give him a nickel and send him to Mr. Edwards' store on
Main Street to get the *Family Story Paper*. Mrs. Bonham was a big
woman with a cute round face and a small cherry mouth. She had to
read every week the latest continued story of Laura Jean Libbey.
What Miss Libbey wrote about was love, and as someone said, "love
in great big gobs." There would be a good and beautiful woman
who loved a good and handsome man but there was always a villain
who was dark and handsome and what he was up to with the good
and beautiful woman was wicked and slimy. But in the end he was
"foiled in his dastardly scheme," as Miss Libbey would put it. On a
Friday morning when the *Family Story Paper* arrived in Galesburg,
if the railroad trains were running, Ross Bonham had to run down-
town for that paper and we knew it was no use to ask him to play
till he had brought home that paper. His mother would let the wash-
ing or ironing go till she had taken the paper and read what was
the latest happening to the sweet, true lovers and the cunning, de-
signing villain. In the black-and-white drawings showing the good
and beautiful young woman she always looked the same in story
after story and so did the handsome villain, whose neat curled
mustache never drooped.

When Johnny Watkins came along we knew what was up. He
was a "caller." He carried in a coat pocket a book. He would go up
to a house and knock at the door. Somebody would come to the door
and say, "Oh, it's you." Then the book would be signed by a rail-
road fireman, engineer, conductor, or brakeman. Having signed the
book there was no mistake that he had been "called" to go out on a
certain train at a certain time. If you were "on the extra list," that

meant you had no "regular run" and were glad to sign. If you wanted to get on and move up into promotion, you signed the book. Whatever the weather, you signed. "The little woman" began getting ready bread and meat and a bottle of coffee that soon went cold, to go into a tin pail or a wicker basket, to be handy in the engine cab or the train caboose.

Whatever the weather, the railroad men go when called. They have ways of their own—the railroad men. No two trips alike. Some trips would "scare the living daylights" out of any but a good railroad man. They have to make quick decisions. They expect the unexpected. They try for a good laugh whenever they can get it. They have the gift of humor—they kid each other and have their own slang. I heard an engineer home from a run call to an engineer up in the cab ready for his run, "Anything eatin you today, you old galoot? Do you expect to pull that old rattletrap all the way to Chicago?" "Well," came the smiling drawl, "if she don't go to pieces I think we'll just about make it." Their standard answer to those who asked, "Why did they put this depot so far from town?" was "They wanted it next to the railroad."

Once I heard two firemen after the news of a wreck. "Well, George got his." The other very slowly, "Yeah, made his last run." "Too bad." "Yeah, too bad." "Every fellow got to have his last run sometime." "Yeah—too bad about George." That was all. They went on their ways.

They told about an engineer in a head-on collision who somehow crawled out of a mess of tangled steel. He was sitting in his overalls, bareheaded, blood and coal dust on his face and hands. The wreck master came along and saw him crying, tears running down his face. He told the wreck master he had a few cuts and bruises and then begged for help to find his cap, a new cap on its first trip in an engine cab. He was crying on account of that lost cap.

Then there was the conductor whose train got off the rails and went down an embankment. The conductor crawled from the wreckage without a scratch on him and was cool and handy in doing what could be done till the wreck master arrived. He looked good and sensible to the wreck master till he pulled out a nickel matchsafe and put it to his ear and listened. Soon he put the matchsafe in a pocket and soon again pulled it out and put it to his ear. The wreck master spoke sharp: "What's the matter with you?" And the conductor, still listening to the matchsafe at his ear, answered in a daze as though he might be mesmerized, "My watch has stopped. I can't get it going. I don't know what time it is." The wreck master took the conductor by the shoulders and gave him a shaking that brought him to. Railroad men told it as nothing to laugh at. "You might be the next one to be acting queer when your train goes off the rails."

A broken rail, a flaw in steel, mixed signals, heavy rains and a slide of earth under the roadbed, the ever variable human element where a man has to make decisions and knows either way he is taking a chance—these are a part of railroading, everyday risks calculated and incalculable. I have seen changes made for the safety of the men on the job running trains. I don't remember the year a Federal law went into force, but from that time on no engineer could run his locomotive more than sixteen hours straight. This was the Federal Government stepping in and "regulating" the railroads. And why was the government stepping in and telling these private interests how to run their business? It was simple enough. There had been wreck after wreck and the dead passengers strewn along the railroad right of way—the engineer asleep in his cab after too many hours of continuous duty. The theory in the new law was that any engineer could keep awake sixteen hours, though later that time limit was shortened.

And there came further Federal Government interference. How the fancy of any old-timer gathers around the Link and Pin! At the Santa Fe station in Dodge City, Kansas, you can find (I hope it is still there) in front of the platform a nice garden bed. And amid green grass and flowers there is a memento, a remembrance, you might say. Here is a rusty iron Link. Fitting into it is the coupling Pin. For generations of railroading this was the simple device that held two railroad cars together. The switchman or brakeman gave the engineer the signal, standing away from the cars waving a gloved hand in the daytime, a lantern at night. The engineer would do his best at bumping the cars together gently, softly, neatly. When they bumped, the two links came together. Then the switchman or brakeman would step in between the two cars and drop or shove the pin between the two links. The bumping of the two cars might be gentle and soft and again it might not. Engines and cars are peculiar. The switchman or brakeman between the two cars might have to run along with the moving cars. The coupling pin didn't always behave right about dropping into the two links. Human feet can slip or slide getting out from between two moving cars. There were "accidents," men killed, men crippled, wrangling with Link and Pin.

What could be done about it? The railway brotherhoods for years went to Washington with their answer. For years they got nowhere. They were asking for a Federal law requiring every railroad in the country to put into operation the Westinghouse automatic safety coupler. Where the cars had that device, they bumped together and locked and stayed locked, no need for a switchman or a brakeman to step between the moving cars. Year on year a powerful railroad lobby at Washington fought this law, fought what it would cost them in cash outlay. In the course of time—though too long a time— the brotherhoods, backed by a rising public opinion and their own increasing political strength, saw the required law come for the saving of life and limb.

I have always enjoyed riding up front in a smoking car, in a seat back of the "deadheads," the railroaders going back to the home base. Their talk about each other runs free. I heard an old conductor size up a younger brakeman who carried four pencils sticking up from an outside coat pocket, "He's one of those young fools who thinks the more pencils he carries the more people will think he knows." I heard one deadhead telling another the gist of what they had been saying about a brakeman they named: "He'd make a good fence post—what? If you want to get at his brain, kick him in the ass."

Once I saw a young fireman in overalls take a seat and slouch down easy and comfortable. After a while a brakeman in blue uniform came along and planted himself alongside the fireman. They didn't say anything. The train ran along. The two of them didn't even look at each other. Then the brakeman, looking straight ahead, was saying, "Well, what do you know today?" and kept on looking straight ahead till suddenly he turned and stared the fireman in the face, adding, "For sure." I thought it was a keen and intelligent question, "What do you know today—*for sure?*" I remember the answer. It came slow and honest. The fireman made it plain what he knew that day for sure: "Not a damn thing!" Then they went on into a talk about how much there is of human ignorance. The country was having a presidential campaign, the railway brotherhoods seething with politics and strike agitation, and the fireman slapped his right hand on his overalls as he cried, "You can never tell if the information you get is reliable."

Johnny Watkins with his call book knew these men who ran the trains. He heard them say, as do sailors and soldiers, "If your time has come it's come." Johnny's mother was a widow, their home at Berrien and Chambers. He was "the family support." They were English, his mother having a touch of the London cockney in her speech.

In the two and a half blocks between our house and the railroad yards the Swedes were largest in number, then the "nativeborn," two or three Yankees, two English families, a sprinkling of Irish and Germans, and in the early 1890's a flood of Italians, some thirty men, women, and children in two houses next to the Narrow Gauge railroad tracks. One of the Italians became known as "Banana Joe." He pushed a cart over the town crying, "Bah-nan-oes, five a duz, five a duz," and "oh-*ranj*-eez, oh-*ranj*-eez, frash oh-*ranj*-eez." Later he had his little fruit store and lived in the house where I was born and had his influence in swinging the Italian vote. I came to know those thirty Italians who moved into those two houses near the Q. tracks. I carried a milk can to their doorsteps and into their kitchens and measured out the quarts for them and sold them tickets, green ones for a quart, pink ones for a pint, twenty quarts for a dollar. I saw their bawling brawling strengths, their black-eyed surplus of vitality. They did something to me. They had the color of history. They made me feel I had been to Italy and seen Italians and how Italians live, speak, and bring up children.

We could feel Europe where the Swedes, Germans, Irish, came from, but the trip took six weeks, even three months, and Europe seemed far away. What few men and women had traveled from

Galesburg to Europe and back to Galesburg would be pointed out, "He went to England," "She's been to Germany." We went to stereopticon lectures, with "slides" showing the Holy Land and Rome the Eternal City. Missionaries gave talks on China, what swarming millions of miserable heathen there were, and how it would take time but there was hope someday the Chinese would become a Christian people. An agent one evening got Papa's eyes into a stereoscope with photographs made by a two-eyed camera. What he saw wasn't like you read from a book. He saw the real places—and Papa bought the stereoscope and a dozen of the photographs. My favorite was a big barge on a river at Hamburg, Germany. "So this is a ship," I said, "and this is a river and this is what you would see if you went to Hamburg." To a kid who had never been out of Knox County, Illinois, Hamburg was many weeks' traveling over the wide and crazy Atlantic Ocean. "And Asia," we said, "Asia, that's too far off to think about."

In the warmer months of the year we had welcome visitors along Berrien Street. Four short men—not always the same men, but always short men and deep-chested—would stop in front of every three or four houses. They wore blue double-breasted coats and fancy hats of blue with a little feather in the hatband. Each had a horn, one a big horn that wrapped itself around him. At a nod from the leader they struck up tunes, "*Ach du lieber Augustin,*" "*Die Wacht am Rhein,*" and others. The sound poured out and we liked it, us kids following them for blocks and watching them go to house doors and hold out a hat for any nickel or dime the music might be worth. This was the Little Dutch Band. They were Germans, but "Dutch" and "German" meant the same thing in those days. We had our ideas about them: "What a way to make a living! How different from working for the Q.! Going all over the country, first one town and then another, and making a living by playing sweet music for people!" They were stocky, thick, short men, with heavy brown or blond mustaches. They looked strong and commanded respect. One question us kids never got settled, "Don't they get tired of playing the same tunes over and over?"

And there was the scissors-grinder, usually an Italian, swinging a hand bell, on his back a wooden frame and a grindstone. Here and there his bell would bring out a housewife with her dull scissors and he would slide out from the straps at his shoulders. He had a foot pedal for turning the grindstone and we stood by and watched the stream of firesparks as he put a new edge on the scissor blades. The grinder we saw most often was a sad man with his mouth pulled down. We wondered whether he had some particular sorrow or whether he just hated the whole human race. Never a word from him as once in a while his black eyes roved over us. Not a word to his customer, the good lady with the bad scissors, till he had finished the grinding and handed her the scissors with a dark grunt, "Tenna cent."

Only once came the man with the bear. A gang of us kids gathered around him in front of the Olson grocery at Berrien and Chambers. It was a gray bear, nearly as tall as the man. He had the bear stand up on his hind legs. Then he waltzed with the bear. It was pretty. We smiled, looked at each other, and turned again to watch the waltzing bear and man. He took off his hat, held it out toward us one by one. Not a nickel or a penny did he get. He had a proposition. The bear would climb a telephone pole if we would rake up ten cents. We were all nearly busted. I had a last nickel and offered it. He shook his head. "No climb pole for a nickel." I had a knife in my pocket and another knife at home. I showed him the knife, a battered two-bit knife. He smiled, nodded, took the knife, led the bear to the telephone pole. We saw the bear put his paws around that pole and go up halfway and look down as if halfway was enough. But the man scolded him and his paws took new holds and he went on up to the top. At the word from the man he came down faster than he had gone up. The man led his bear away. We watched him as far as Seminary Street, where he turned toward the Q. depot.

Of course the handbill peddlers came to Berrien Street as to every other street in the town. Us kids often were the bill peddlers, if we were lucky enough to get the work. The man who hired us at twenty-five cents a day would start us at eight o'clock in the morning and keep us going till six in the evening, running a crew of six or eight of us. He had a wagon and would give us another armful of bills when we ran out. Into every house of the city, rich and poor, veranda and shanty, we put a handbill, on the doorstep, the porch, or if the day was windy under a doormat with part of it sticking out, or around the doorknob or into a latch. What was our message? What did the handbill say? It said in big and little letters that Hood's Sarsaparilla or Ayer's Sarsaparilla or Doctor Munyon's Specific Remedies would cure you of anything that ailed you. We had our hand in giving the town a blizzard of useless information.

In early years we watched the lamplighter come along before the dusk of evening. He carried a small ladder he would set against the lamppost. And we liked to see him climb up, swing open a glass door to the glass case holding a gas burner. One hand would reach inside and turn on the gas. Then he pulled that hand out and another hand holding a lighted taper put the flame to the escaping gas. Then the lamplighter having lighted the lamp climbed down, and with one hand holding the ladder on a shoulder and the other hand holding the taper he moved on from the corner of Pearl and Berrien to the corner of Day and Berrien, a block east. We followed him to see whether he would go through the same motions at Day and Berrien as he had at Pearl and Berrien. And we were a little disappointed to see him go through exactly the same motions. We decided that if we went on following him, all we would see would be those same motions. So we went home. We appreciated his public services, of course. We knew well enough that on the nights when there was neither moonlight nor starlight those lamps helped people to find the way home and to pick out the right house to go into.

Then came the electric lights, one arc lamp at every second corner, exactly spang in the center of the four street crossings, high enough so a man driving a load of hay couldn't reach up and touch the globe where inside the light seemed to ooze and crackle without burning. The lamplighter was gone. We missed him. Away over in a power house we were told one man stood at a switch, pulled it, and every light in the town went on. We didn't know who the man was that pulled the switch. We imagined him looking out over the town and seeing the streets beginning to get dark and him saying as he laid his hand on the switch to pull it, "Let there be light!" Then he looked out and saw there was light and called it good.

We knew the time the lights were to go on. We would stand

under an arc lamp and the instant it lighted we would look toward other lights two blocks east and west coming on the same split second. We half expected we would catch some corner late in getting lighted but that never happened.

In our early years every house and lot in our block and the near-by blocks had a fence in front, on the sides, and a back-yard fence. There were picket fences in front of some houses, every picket sharp-pointed, not easy to climb over. There were picket fences without sharp points to the pickets. There were horizontal board fences and if you were delivering newspapers or milk it saved steps to climb over the fence instead of going as far as the gate. There were many kinds of gates. There were gates where you lifted a wooden bar to get in, gates where you raised a hasp out of a staple. There were gates left open because the hinges or fastenings had come loose and were out of order. There were fences where the gate had come loose and been taken away. On several mornings after Halloween I saw gates hanging from telephone poles, a gate lost and lonesome on a maple-tree branch, gates thrown on the roofs of sheds and privies, gates laid on front doorsteps to say a Halloween good morning to their owners. There was no telling whose gate on that morning would be gone, though usually the gate taken away already had one or both hinges loose. And where a privy was tipped over it was usually a grudge job. The wild boys who did it had their reasons for hating the owner.

Then slowly and little by little the fences and gates were taken away. The front-yard fences went first, then the side and back-yard fences. It began on the North Side on such streets as North Broad and North Prairie where the rich and the well-to-do had their homes and well-kept lawns. One theory of why the fences and gates came and vanished goes back to the early days when people, rich and poor, kept horses, cows, pigs, chickens. These animals were always straying. And if you didn't have your house and yard fenced they would stray into your place and forage and trample your garden, hogs rooting and snousling among your potatoes and carrots. As the roving livestock became fewer and the North Side set the style of tearing fences away and doing without them, the rest of the town slowly followed. The year came when we tore down our front-yard fence and burned it for kindling wood, saving good boards for repair jobs. But the side and back-yard fences stayed the seventeen years we lived at that place.

Of the two gateposts I distinctly remember the east one. I was running away from two other boys, had turned my head to look back at them, and suddenly crashed my forehead and right eyebrow into a mean corner of that gatepost, resulting in a gash and a bruise so I had a "shanty" over the right eye for a week or two. And I remember the "shanty," even though the gateposts and the fence are gone and where they stood is nothing in their place.

In the back yard my favorite weed was the burr-dock. For many years I cut them down and rooted them out with a hoe and I couldn't hate them when they came back. I always let a few near the fence go on growing. I liked the changing blue and purple of the burrs slowly turning to brown. I liked to pick enough brown burrs to shape into a ball the size of a baseball. When I went away from home and met the burr-dock anywhere I would say, "Well, I know you, we've met before, we're old friends."

On one payday night and again on a Saturday night Mart and I saw and heard a Swede who lived a few blocks beyond us walking in the middle of Berrien Street, no narrow sidewalks for him. He was a little tipsy and not exactly walking in a straight line. We stopped to watch him. He saw us and stopped in his tracks and leaned forward, sticking his head toward us. Then came his yell, a fierce and clear-toned yell, one of the wildest I have ever heard. His Swedish syllables cut the air and there was no mistaking them: "*Ah du Cat-o-lika fan!*" (Ugh you Catholic devil). It was as though his fuddled mind saw us as Catholics and his upbringing taught him to spit and spew on all Catholics as children of the Devil. He meant it to be terrifying and followed it with low rumbling growls of threats of some kind that we couldn't make out. Then went on and we followed at thirty yards. We saw him stoop and peer toward some trees that threw queer shadows from the Day Street electric light. Here again he gave his piercing cry that had a touch of terror in it. Mart and I practiced at imitating him. And we found that when we gave it full-voiced some of the people who laughed at it were laughing because they were at least a little scared. I have often thought that if the soldiers of the armies of Gustavus Adolphus, fighting Catholics in Germany during the Thirty Years War, had anything like our own "Rebel yell" of the Confederate armies, they yelled something like our Swedish neighbor on a payday night in the middle of Berrien Street.

There was only one house on the west side of Pearl Street between Berrien and Brooks. It was a small frame house with a basement having windows. We passed the house hundreds of times going to school. I didn't remember people going into the house or coming out. I didn't hear who lived there. No one seemed to know or care who lived there. The house and the doors and windows said nothing, like other houses we passed. Yet one morning that house took on meaning and what it said was dark and strange and like nothing else us kids had ever heard of happening in the Seventh Ward or the Fourth Ward or the city of Galesburg. Two or three people we met on Berrien or Pearl street one morning told us the same thing in about the same words. Pointing toward the house they said, "A young fellow hanged himself in the basement there last night." Going home from school in the afternoon we saw black crape on the front door. And one way and another that was all we knew. We supposed there was a funeral and the police and a coroner asked questions in the house. But we didn't hear the name of the young fellow who had hanged himself nor anything about his folks, how many there were and what they said about why he hanged himself. What few questions we asked our own home folks didn't bring any real answers. The people in that house had moved in and lived quiet and minded their own business, whatever it was.

Morning and afternoon when we passed the house we didn't see anybody going in or coming out nor any faces at the windows. Us kids talked about it, "How do you go at it if you want to hang yourself?" We asked why the young fellow wanted to take his life and there were different answers: "Maybe he was just sick of living and wanted to quit," or "Maybe he was out of a job and ashamed to be so useless," or "If he had a girl promised to marry him and she married another fellow he might have thought she would feel sorry and mean to hear he hanged himself," or "Nobody knows why a suicide does it."

We had heard the word "suicide" but it was far off and we hadn't done any thinking about it. Now we did try to get our heads around it. We were sure that hanging is the worst way to step out of life and the next worst is to drink a bottle of carbolic acid. "You can shoot yourself and it's all over in half a second," said one, and another, "You can drown yourself in no time or jump from a high window to a brick sidewalk and it's all over." I can't remember the bright kid who came up with his idea: "On a cold winter night and snow on the ground you can slip and fall down between the rails in front of the C.B.&Q. Fast Mail train and have the whole town guessing whether you're a suicide or an accident." We didn't get clear on what kind of a rope is best if you want to hang yourself nor how tight you should pull the rope around your neck nor how high a box or chair you should make the jump from. One kid said, "I heard that the second you jump off the box or chair you begin to strangle." Others asked, "How long do you strangle?" and brought one kid answering, "My father says if you make the right kind of a jump you break your neck and there ain't any strangling. But if you make your jump wrong you might be a long time strangling."

After a few days we quit our talk about the suicide. We did more talking and asking questions than we heard from any of the grownups. "Better to forget it," said my mother. But I couldn't forget it. With the rest of the kids I quit talking about it but over and over when I passed that house I would be saying, "Why did he do it? God, why did he do it?" What was it that came into his mind and made it dark? How did the idea of hanging himself come to him? What was he saying to himself when he hunted for a rope and found the rope he wanted? What were his last thoughts when he fastened the noose around his neck? Did he say something like, "This world is a heavy and terrible trouble and I'll be glad when I'm out of it"? The same questions would keep running through my head for weeks on weeks when I passed that house. Then after a while as I came near the house I wouldn't let my mind work on those questions and I would pass the little frame house with a queer blur in my head. The

time had come when I knew it was just sad and useless to try to
answer those dark and awful questions. I had decided, "Away deep
inside of himself he believed he was doing what was right and he
wasn't afraid to meet his God and Maker." And of course·I did a
little thinking, not much but a little, on whether sometime my mind
might go dark and I would slip and fall between the rails where the
C.B.&Q. Fast Mail comes rushing and roaring.

There was a row of buildings running west from Chambers Street
on the north side of Berrien. Every one of those buildings has its
curious memories that stick in the mind. What I remember so often
seems trifling and meaningless yet it sticks, faces and places that will
be there so long as I keep what might be called "my right mind." On
the corner stood the wooden grocery building with its sign "Swan
H. Olson & Bro." Swan had a red chin beard, always neatly trimmed,
waited on customers quietly and politely. He had arrived from
Sweden in 1854, twenty years old, worked on Knox County farms,
and in 1862 enlisted as a private in Company A of the 102d Illinois
Volunteer Infantry, fought in the Atlanta campaign, marched with
Sherman to the sea, across the Carolinas and on up to Washington
for the Grand Review. Not until later years when I studied the
marches and campaigns in which Swan Olson served did I come to a
full respect for him. He was a foot soldier whose feet had taken him
more than two thousand miles. He had been in wild and bloody
battles, had waded creeks and rivers and marched in heavy rains day
after day carrying rifle and blanket roll—but you couldn't tell it by
seeing him measuring a quart of cranberries for Mrs. Nelson or hang-
ing out a stockfish in front of the store on a winter morning to let
the Swedes know their favorite holiday sea food had arrived. His
brother William, with the most elegantly spreading and curled red
mustache in the Seventh Ward, was more of a talker than Swan.
Both of the brothers hung their coats in the back of the store and
put on black sleeves up to the elbows, keeping their cuffs clean when
they dipped into coffee sacks or dusty bins. Like all grocers then,
they fastened strong wire screens over the tops of apple baskets. At
times it did happen that one or two boys would watch inside the
store and when the two Olson brothers were busy with customers

they would signal a boy outside who worked the wire screen loose and ran off with as many apples as his pockets and his hat would hold.

I was six or seven years old when I learned a lesson about dealings at the Olson store or any store. After Will Olson had wrapped what I was sent for, I handed him the book mother had given me and told him, "Put it on the book." He wrote in the book and handed it back to me. Then I asked how much would be a stick of licorice that caught my eye. "Five cents," said Will Olson and I said, "Put it on the book," and handing him the book saw him write in it. Until then I had never bought anything for more than a penny. Occasionally a penny had strayed into my hands and I bought with it a single stick of gum or candy. Now I had found a way to get something for nothing. "Put it on the book." I walked home hoping I would often be sent to the grocery with "the book." When I got home they saw my lips and chin black with licorice and asked about it. I said the grocery man gave me a big stick of licorice. "Did you pay him for it? Where did you get the money?" "I told him to put it on the book." It was then I heard that the book was for the family, and not for me to be a mean little pig. My mother gave me a slap on the chin and mouth that I had coming to me and told me, "Go and wash your dirty face," and saying further that if it happened again I would get a licking I would remember. I had learned what it meant to say, "Put it on the book," if it was the Sandburg family account book that could be carried in a man's hip pocket. On the Q. payday my father would take the book to the Olson store and they would figure up what he owed them for the past month's groceries. After he paid them and they wrote in the book that he had paid they would give him a sack of candy for the children at home and a five-cent cigar for himself. He smoked an inch or two of the cigar each Sunday and it lasted him till the next payday, when he got another cigar. The only smoking he ever did was these payday cigars. He couldn't waste them, so he smoked them.

There was one year somewhere in the early 1890's that the Olson store had rows and piles of wooden pails out in front, on the street. They were filled with red jelly and were sold as jelly at the lowest prices ever heard of for jelly. Our family along with many others bought a pail of this jelly. It tasted a little like regular Concord grape jelly but it didn't sit so good in the stomach. There were people had headaches and stomach troubles from eating what those pails held. It was made in factories and had no fruit juice and was more poison than real honest jelly. The Olsons quit handling it and people talked about it as scandalous that it could be sold. The Olsons were sorry it happened. They didn't know the jelly was poisoned. It was later, under President Theodore Roosevelt, that the Federal Government took action to stop the selling of poisoned food. We traded with the Olsons for many years. They were handy to where we lived and had about as good a stock as any of the other thirty or forty groceries in town.

Will Olson married a Cedarholm girl who had a sister. The sister used to come out for me to pour a quart of milk into a crock. She had a slender and weaving body, a peach-blossom face, and a smile that made a rainy day bright. I always liked pouring milk from my tin quart measure into the crock her gracious hands held.

There was an alley next to the Olsons' wooden building. Then came a one-story brick building where Franz Nelson ran a butcher shop. Here we would stop in and ask Franz when he was going to do some butchering. We liked to go with him to the slaughterhouse southeast of town, watch him knock a sledge into the head of a steer or stick a knife into the neck of a hog. At first we shivered at seeing the blood gushing from the slit in the hog's throat—then we got used to it. We helped at bringing water and carrying things to Franz and he gave us calf or beef liver to take home. We watched him handling customers, sawing bones, cutting steaks and chops on a tree-trunk chopping block, wrapping meat in brown paper and tying a string around it making a package for the customer to carry home. When there was liver at hand and a customer asked, "How about a piece of liver?" Franz would hand over liver without charge. He was free-handed with us boys when it came to baloney. We cut what we wanted and stood around eating it, liver sausage being a favorite, though we sometimes tried our teeth on dried beef. Sawdust covered the floor and was swept out twice a week. The place had a half-pleasant stink of its own—we could smell the air working on the flesh of dead animals.

Years before the Franz Nelson place was built our family began its trading farther west on Berrien, where a building faced the Q. yards and a sign read: "Hartel & Secker: Meat Market." This was two and a half blocks from our home and in all seasons of the year hundreds of times I walked those blocks and never once forgot whether I was going for pork chops or round steak or "a ten-cent soup bone." And whether it was the short, lightweight, blond Mr. Hartel or the heavy and thick-set black-haired Mr. Secker, he would cut a two- or three-inch piece of baloney and hand it to me with a sober German face as though he was thinking about something else.

Next to the Franz Nelson butcher shop, in the same brick building on Berrien Street, was our favorite hangout, the Julius Schulz cigar shop. In the front room were a wide aisle and two glass show-cases filled with Schulz-made cigars and a line of pipes and smoking tobaccos. Mr. Schulz we didn't see often. He was out drumming up trade, a busy man selling his cigars to local stores and saloons, and taking trains to near-by towns. He made quite a name for his cigar "Private Stock," meaning if you bought only one or a box it was your stock and it was private. There was talk too about how different men had different private stocks, one railroad-man customer saying, with a wink, "Some of 'em like to have cigars or whisky on the side and some like a woman." Mr. Schulz was medium-sized, wore a heavy brown mustache and matching it a brown suit and a brown derby, a gold watch chain on his brown vest. He would come into the store, look over his account books, fill a valise with samples, and go away without a word or a look at us kids whether there were two, five, or six of us hanging around. Once when he came and left in a hurry, looking worried, one of the boys said, "He's a hustler. To keep a business goin you gotta hustle." We all liked Mr. Schulz. He didn't know our names nor bother to speak to us. But summer or winter he let us hang around and gab and sing and use his place for a kind of clubroom. We respected him because he never threw us out, which, as we said sometimes, he had a right to.

The back room was the main hangout. There sat "Nig" Bohnenber-ger, whose folks spoke German but he hadn't learned it. "They got to calling me Nig because I'm dark-complected," said Nig. He read the papers and while he rolled cigars and licked the wrappers he told what was wrong with the country and the town. He had a hawk nose, a pale face, a thin body, and a mind that was always thinking things over. And telling it to us kids, he often ended what he said with, "Of that I can tell you I'm pos-i-tive." He liked to be positive and we liked him being pos-i-tive. We saw him in coughing spells and saw him slowly fade away from consumption. One boy came from Nig's funeral saying, "He looked so natural in the coffin I couldn't keep from crying." Nig could have said, "I always welcomed you boys and I never mistreated one of you and I tried to act to you like I was a good teacher."

I remember the tobacco smell of that cigar shop as clear as I remember the meat smell next door. Here was a stove in winter and open windows in summer. Here came the boys in the between-times of work and play. In warmer weather on nights and Sundays when the cigar store was closed, we met on the sidewalk in front. Here we sang. There was tall, skinny, bony John Hultgren, a Swede boy who worked in the Boyer broom factory, and chubby, cheek-puffed, bright-eyed John Kerrigan, an Irish lad learning the plumber's trade under his father—both of them tenors. There was Willis ("Bohunk") Calkins and myself who were fair at baritone and bass. This quartet could give "In the Evening by the Moonlight," "Swanee River," "Carry Me Back to Old Virginia," "I Found a Horseshoe"—and we said we were good and when Al Field's Minstrels came to town they ought to hear us. Kerrigan would give a solo line, "As I was goin down the valley for to pray," and we would chime in, "Down on the old camp ground" and Kerrigan with smiling Irish eyes, "I met old Satan on my way," and all together, "Down on the old camp ground," and so on till Satan's hash was settled. Kerrigan had been working with plumbers who sang at their work and he could give all the verses of "Little Annie Rooney" and follow with "She Is the Sunshine of Paradise Alley" and other songs of the day. "Here," he'd say with twinkling eyes, "is the latest hit," and let us have every verse. Bohunk a couple of nights brought his banjo. From him we heard about the slave girl Nelly Gray who was taken far away from her old Kentucky shore "and I'll never see my darling any more."

One morning about nine o'clock I drifted into the Schulz store to find excitement. In the night someone had broken open a back window and taken what change and bills there were in the money drawer, maybe eight or ten dollars. Heavy rain had been falling all night. The thief, it was said, probably counted on few people being on the street and they would be hurrying through the rain and not stop to look in on the store. We had been reading Old Cap Collier and Nick Carter and we tried sleuthing for clews. We hoped to find something the thief had dropped that would tell who he was. But it seemed he hadn't dropped anything. There was more mud on the floor from his shoes when he stepped in from the window and then less and less mud on a line toward the money drawer—but not a clew!

Soon came a short man with quiet eyes and a fine black mustache. He wore a blue suit of clothes, a star on his coat. We knew him but had never seen him working on a case. He was Marshal Hinman, chief of police, and had with him one of his best uniformed policemen to help him solve the case. We watched them work and we saw that inside the store they didn't find any more clews than us kids did. Then they stepped out the back door and went to work on what we had missed. There in the black mud were shoe tracks. You could see exactly the size and shape of the shoe soles of the thief. Marshal Hinman studied the shoe tracks. His face was sober and earnest as he looked down into the mud. I was thinking, "Now I'm not reading about how you hunt down a criminal. I'm watching a real man hunter at work."

The marshal called for some cardboard and was handed an empty shoe box. The marshal took the top of the box, pulled a knife from his pocket, and laying the shoe-box top over a shoe track in the mud he cut the cardboard to the shape of the thief's shoe sole. Then we saw the marshal crouching again over another shoe track. He was slow and patient, I noticed, like all good sleuths and man hunters. His knife cut the shoe-box bottom to the shape of another shoe track in the mud. It dawned on me like a flash what he was doing. The first cardboard he cut was the left shoe and the second one was the right shoe of the thief. After this was over he studied the tracks some more and went inside the store again. Unless his keen eyes had caught some clew he wasn't telling us about, we could see that all he had to work on was to find some man whose shoes were the same

left and right sizes as his cardboard cuttings. I reasoned to myself
that it wouldn't do for him to stop a thousand people on Main Street
and try his cardboard cuttings on their shoe bottoms. There would
be maybe fifty or a hundred men wearing exactly that size shoe and
it being a rainy night, rain pouring down, they would know where
they had been out of the rain and every one would prove an alibi and
an alibi is where you are when a crime is committed.

We hoped Marshal Hinman would catch the thief. We were curi-
ous about who it could be that would stand in a heavy rain and work
hard to get that back window open for the sake of eight or ten
dollars. We saw the marshal leave after saying, "We haven't got
much to work on but we'll do the best we can." Then time went by
and the years passed and the case was never solved and no one knows
to this day whose feet were in those right and left shoes that made
their tracks in the mud.

From the Schulz store we went sometimes next door west into a
cubbyhole of a house—one room maybe twelve feet by twelve. Here
sat a man with a leather apron and a line of tools and leather in easy
reach. We watched him cut leather for the half-sole of a shoe or a
boot, then fill his mouth with wooden pegs and, taking one peg at a
time from his mouth, he fitted and hammered them into holes he
made with an awl. Or if the customer wanted the half-sole stitched
in, John Swedenborg could do it, carefully waxing the heavy threads
before he stitched. He could glue a patch on or sew it, depending on
what he thought it needed. He liked his work and was steady at it
from eight o'clock in the morning till six in the evening. We looked
in on him more often in the winter when his little place with its coal
stove was cozy.

He was a long man with stooped shoulders, with a good face
when quiet, and burning eyes and trembling lips when he spoke.
Always John spoke to us the same lesson, keeping silence only when
his mouth was filled with wooden pegs. I learned later the word for
John. He was a Zealot. His zeal ran in every drop of his blood.

So many times we heard him say, "I have Yesus in my heart. Yesus
is with me all the time. I pray to my Yesus in the daytime and in the
nighttime. You boys will never go wrong if you can get Yesus in
your heart. He is my Saviour and He can be your Saviour. He is the

Light of the World. When I have Him I am not afraid. I cannot be afraid, for He has told me to lean on Him when it is dark and things go wrong. You should learn to pray to Him, boys. You should learn to kneel at His blessèd feet and ask forgiveness and ask Him to take you in His arms."

He had his own style of speaking straight from the heart, once saying, "Om Yesus says it anta possible den it anta" (If Jesus says it ain't possible then it ain't).

These words would come from John Swedenborg with his eyes having a fire in them and his lips shaking as he shaped the words, as his tongue gave the words, "We are not long for this world. My Yesus is waiting for me in the next world and it will be blessèd to see Him."

He lived sober, went to Wednesday-evening prayer meetings and special services, took his family to church Sunday morning and night. We saw him several times in coughing spells. There were days his shop was closed. His end, like Nig Bohnenberger's next door, came from consumption. Neither of them was afraid to go but John was more sure than Nig that he was going where he would have more shining happiness than he ever had on earth. I can see now the blaze in John's eyes, his mouth shaping his words, as he tried to teach us and lead us. I have no trouble imagining him at the Gate of Heaven and St. Peter saying, "Welcome, John Swedenborg. On earth you made bad shoes better. You wronged no man and cheated no one and the earth would be a better place to live in if there were more like you."

EIGHT

Kid Talk – Folk Talk

★

Kid talk would run to why women wore bustles, why they wore tight-laced corsets, why a woman with a pretty face would hide it with a black veil. When a young woman crossed a muddy street we watched whether she lifted her skirt high enough for us to see what her legs were like. We watched to see if Friday the thirteenth was unlucky and couldn't see it. We heard it was bad luck to step over a broom or to walk under a ladder, so some kids went stepping over brooms and walking under ladders to see what would happen and nothing did. When night came and the moon was up the same kids would look at the moon over the left shoulder to see if it would bring bad luck. None of us ever broke a looking glass, so we couldn't tell if that would bring bad luck for seven years. Some of us did try to make the warts on our hands go away. I took a string and tied four knots in it, one knot for each of my four warts. I buried the string under a maple tree in the light of a full moon. It was many weeks before my warts went away and I didn't believe the string and the moon had helped. One kid said that when an uncle of his had a bad cold he would kiss a mule on the nose and the cold went away. I heard that when new shoes squeak it is a sign they are not paid for. I had more than one pair of new shoes that squeaked and I was sure they had been paid for, so I knew that one was a fake.

Us kids did our talking with the rest of the town about the "Water Works" and the dirty yellow water with the bad smell that came out where they had faucets. The tower stood on the north side next to the Q. tracks, privately owned. The city got disgusted with it, dug its own artesian well, and has kept its own water system ever since.

We talked too of the rubber-factory fire. On a pasture east of Farnham Street near the path where we walked to the swimming hole we saw the three-story factory go up. A fire broke out a year or two later, and several girls had bad burns from their clothes catching fire as they ran downstairs. One young woman died from her third-floor leap to the ground. Whenever we passed the gutted building and its black walls we talked about why they hadn't put fire escapes on the second and third floors. Some of us got jobs knocking plaster off the black burnt bricks, and a boy might bust out any time, "They ought to have had fire escapes."

The saying was, "If you see a white horse spit quick over a little finger and if none of the spit falls on your finger you will meet a redheaded girl." There were kids who claimed it worked. I spit clean and dry more than once and the redheaded girl didn't show up. Another saying was, "If you see a redheaded girl look for a white horse." We tried that and the white horse didn't show up, one kid busting out, "Oh, the hell with white horses!"

In 1884 when a kid called me a mugwump I called it back at him. From the grownups we learned of high-up Republicans who didn't like Blaine's record, couldn't trust him, and were going to vote for Cleveland. The regular Republican Blaine men called these others "mugwumps." I heard a Blaine Republican say, "A mugwump is a man who sits with his mug on one side of the fence and his wump on the other."

When you didn't believe a fellow you might tell him, "Don't hand me that guff," or "I've heard that guff before." It was slang and "guff" was chatter and you were "spreading it on too thick." Politicians, salesmen, book agents, auctioneers, spielers, had "a line of guff." Later a farm machine came along that sent manure flying and spread it even over the soil, and a man talking too big was called a "manure-spreader." Of a man hoping for money to put through a scheme he had in mind they would say, "He's trying to raise the wind." All he needed to blow him and his scheme into motion was a good wind.

Us kids talked about how silly was the rhyme and who was so silly as to start it:

> It is a sin
> To steal a pin.

We believed that anybody who had one pin had a dozen or fifty or a hundred more and it was no sin to steal "a pin," "one single little pin."

Early we heard, "You can trust him as far as you can fling a bull by the tail" and "You're all right but your feet stink," which might get the answer, "I'll give you a brick house—one brick at a time." "You don't know whether you're comin or goin" was easier to take than "If I was as ugly as you, I'd sue my father and mother." A newly married couple "got hitched" and if they separated they "split the blanket."

Going home from Grammar School one boy said, "You're not such a muchness" and the other, "You're not much of a suchness." I forget where they went from there. Whatever it was they were too smart to fight about it.

In the late 1880's, on parting of an evening, we would say, "Good night, sleep tight, and don't let the bedbugs bite." Later this was considered babyish, which wasn't the case with what we learned from the old soldiers and marched to:

> Left, left, I had a good home and I left,
> Right, right, right back home to my wife and children.

Early us kids learned there was no use being sent for "a left-handed monkey wrench." The carrier boys at the *Republican-Register* learned from the printers about "type lice." You were told the lice were small and you put your head down close to see them. Then something squeezed and water spurted up into your face—and you tried to be on hand when a new boy put his head down to see "type lice."

Like grown men, on a payday we said, "This is the day the ghost walks." We said of a stingy boy, "All you get from him you can put in your eye." Or if a fellow promised to do something for you and you didn't expect he would, you said, "Yes, he'll do it—in a pig's eye." We tried to picture the man we heard of, "busy as a paper-hanger with the hives," and the fellow who was "quiet as two skele-tons wriggling on a tin roof." Hustling on a job we liked to say, "Get out of my way, I'm busy as a cranberry merchant," a smart saying and you said it even though you had never seen a cranberry merchant nor heard why a cranberry merchant is busier than other merchants.

I knew the fellow, and from what happened to him afterward John Kerrigan was strictly correct in saying, "He's so slick one of these days his feet are goin to slide out from under him."

He wasn't one of us but he could have been, the boy hitting the top of his head with a rock. A man asked why he was doing such a fool thing and the boy said, " 'Cause it feels so good when I stop."

They told it about Brown's Hotel and a traveling man who ate corn on the cob, one ear after another, till the waitress had brought him a dozen and more and then: "Don't you think you would save money if you went over and boarded at Andy Dow's livery stable?"

A man on Main Street was saying the mayor refused to renew the license of a certain saloonkeeper: "He tells us he can't give any more favors to the saloon crowd. Think of it, and him in his life has drunk enough whisky to float a battleship!"

When it wasn't clear how a man was making his living you might hear, "He's living on the interest of his debts." One year we often saw turning the corner of Berrien and Chambers a tall heavy-set man in a gray suit, double-breasted coat, and he walked easy and cool. He was gorilla-built and iron-jawed. The talk was that he was a gambler and you could find him any afternoon or night down on the Public

Square over a saloon dealing the cards till midnight or daybreak. We knew where he lived, with relatives who worked for the Q., but we never heard of his having a job except dealing at card games. Once a kid said, "Here comes the gambler," and another, "Wouldn't it be fun to hear him talk about his work!" and another, "He could tell about the suckers all right!"

In below-zero weather Mart and I were hurrying along Main Street about eight o'clock one morning. At the northeast corner of Kellogg and Main we saw a load of wood piled high on a wagon. The horses had no blankets and were champing. The driver sat high on his wood. Ahead of us we saw the butcher, Sam Swanson, stop and call to the man, "What do you think you're doing up there?" The man stopped beating his chest with his mittens and laughed as though it was the funniest thing in the world that morning: "I'm a tough sonofabitch from Old Henderson—do you want any wood?" Year after year Mart would keep asking me if I remembered it as though I might have forgotten.

The boy John Siebert had picked it up somewhere and when you said "Hello, John" to him he snapped back, "Hello yourself, and see how you like it."

John also liked to plump it straight at you, "That's what you *say* but how do I *know?*"

Charlie Hall taught a Sunday-school class and belonged to the Y.M.C.A. Driving a milk wagon for a small Jersey dairy, he wouldn't say "darn" or "doggone" to his old slow horse, those words too close to "damn." We heard him bark at the bonerack, "Get up there, Sinnania, what in all getout do you think you're doing? You diggle-depiggledy slowpoke, you're slower than molasses in January."

If he had a fall John Kerrigan might say, "The sidewalk flew up and hit me in the face." If you owed him a nickel or a dime he would say, "We'll write it in the dust and let the rain settle it." Then he might add, "You don't owe me nothin, paregorically speaking." You can never tell what a plumber's apprentice will bring away from working with master plumbers.

We heard of Horace Greeley making a correction: "I did not say that every Democrat is a saloonkeeper. I said that every saloonkeeper is a Democrat."

We said "Cheap at half the price" before we heard what the price was. We might say, "My ears are burning, someone is talking about me," when our ears weren't burning. A boy called another a liar and heard, "You're a double liar" and snapped back, "You're a double-double liar." They were learning the multiplication table.

We brought home to the folks the one about the Irish hod-carrier who said his work wasn't hard. "All I do is carry the bricks in me hod up the ladder to the man at the top and he does all the work."

A Norwegian told me his mother sent him to a store to get something and he came home saying he forgot what she sent him for. She sent him again with the words, "What you don't keep in your head your feet must make up for, my little man." When he ate with his fingers and his grandmother told him to eat with his fork, he said, "Fingers were made before forks," and she cornered him, "But not *your* fingers."

The best ball team the Seventh Ward had for several years didn't want a fancy name and called themselves the "Seventh Ward Red Mugs."

John MacNally met a hobo near the Q. switchyards, a New York Bowery boy who said, "Kuh-hay Cull, wot's duh chance fer duh next cab over duh rails—huh?" We practiced on that.

I went into Danny Flynn's saloon selling the *Sporting News*. They were crowding around a man knocked to the floor by a big husky. They asked the husky why he hit the man. He said, "I don't like his haircut." I saw it was a new and fancy haircut the man had. I saw friends of the big husky leading him out of the saloon and trying to explain to him that he oughtn't to knock a man down on account of his haircut.

In the two-bit gallery of the Auditorium I stood up to stuff into my pants my shirt that had wriggled up. A man in the seat behind

poked me, saying: "Is your father a glass blower?" It then came
over me that I was between him and the stage and he couldn't see
the show going on. I sat down feeling he had the best of it.

A young Swedish grocery clerk who was a fancy dresser kept
steady company for a while with a girl who was a good-looker.
When they quit going together, one kid said, "She gave it to him
where the chicken got the axe."

I read stories where men in New York said, "Pull down your
vest" or "Wipe that egg off your chin," but I never heard the like
in Galesburg. But in both New York and Galesburg people said,
"That joke is as old as the hills," or "Come off your perch." And in
New York and Galesburg they were beginning to say, "Most any-
thing can happen in Chicago and usually does."

Often in the Seventh Ward schoolyard I heard: "What's your
name?" "Puttin Tain, ask me again and I'll tell you the same," or
"What's your name?" "John Brown, ask me again and I'll knock you
down."

If I was clumsy on a job, Mart would say, "You're as handy as that
bird they call the elephant." And when he said, "I worked harder
than you did," I answered, "Yes, but I got more work done." When
someone in the house was slow getting started on a chore you might
hear, "Can't you make yourself useful as well as ornamental?"

A man who sang baritone in a church choir on Sundays kept a
store and was doing a good business. I heard another storekeeper
say, "He's making money hand over fist. He's got one ear for music
and another ear for money. He wasn't born last week."

I couldn't quite figure it out, a fellow saying, "I'd have a good job
if only I could use myself."

They told of a young fellow saying to his girl, "Let's go to the
picnic and after sundown we'll have a grass sandwich."

I was knee-high to a grasshopper maybe when I heard a neighbor
woman talking about a man who moved slow and took it easy. When
she said, "He's slow as molasses in January," I said to myself, "I've

heard that before. I heard fellows say it about me when I didn't run fast enough to first base." But then she went on and laughed about this man who took it easy, "He'll never set a river on fire!" I saw by the way she laughed it that she knew nobody could set a river on fire, but the man she had in mind would be the last anybody could think of that might set a river on fire. I had not yet seen a river but I knew that a river was just like the Cedar Fork Creek only bigger. For days I fooled around in my mind with the picture of a man trying to set a river on fire.

The first time I heard about a man "going to hell in a hanging basket" I did a lot of wondering what a hanging basket is like and why you couldn't fall headfirst down into hell instead of making the trip in a hanging basket.

It wasn't an insult among us kids to say, "You're off your nut" or "You're dippy" or "Say, your head wasn't screwed on wrong, was it?" or "You've got bats in your belfry."

From farmers we learned, "He don't know the difference between a furrow and a farrow."

A man without enough clothes to need a trunk married a woman with a farm and money in the bank. One boy said, "He got himself tied to a hunk of tin, all right." "Yes," said another boy, "before the wedding he was thinner than an old dime." They turned out to be a pretty good couple. Us kids were like many of the grownups, talking just to be talking.

Forty ways it was drilled into us, over and over, at home and in school and on the streets, "If you don't look out for yourself nobody else will." A thousand times in a year we heard it, "Save your pennies. They will grow into dollars. Great oaks from little acorns grow. Don't waste your money. Lay by what you can for a rainy day. A little money can be a big comfort. Money talks. Even when it stinks, money talks."

There were few divorced women in the town. When a woman was mentioned as a widow, the question might come, "Grass or sod?"

Of a boy no good at singing we said, "He can't carry a tune in a basket."

We tried to tease a rubber-factory girl about a fellow she had been seen with. She said, "Aw, shut up about him. He's the least of my troubles." Of a foreman at the factory she said, "He chews the rag. Listen to him and you get lint on your lungs."

Selling my papers I heard two men on a street corner. "How are they comin fer yuh, Bud?" "I'm all to the sandpaper, Bo. Got a snootful last night but now I'm all in the clear." "Could yuh slip me a couple uh sawbucks?" "Well, I could slide yuh out one little William the Fifth. If I could finger you more I would." "Ain't the gettin been good with you?" "Next you'll be tellin me givin is better than gettin." "Well, you know I never been a Wanderin Willie." "Well, you're a hard case, the way I look at it. My guff to you is you beat it in the hay tonight. You been lickin it up an throwin it in too fast." And handing over a William the Fifth (a five-dollar bill) he said, "Do a fade now, do a fade, Bo."

We heard of the boy on a job who was told, "Now come along tomorrow morning bright and early," and he answered, "Anyhow bright."

Mart had his word for a big-shot politician in Galesburg, "That man never loved anyone but himself." Many years later I heard of a woman who had "the heart of a cucumber fried in snow."

It was long ago I heard, "Every man has his price and every woman has her figure."

They meant in Galesburg that the woman was worn and cheap when they said, "She's just an old rip." They meant they were going to drink and have fun when they said, "Stick around, we're going to open a keg of nails."

The last word in many an argument was, "It's none of my funeral," or "It's no skin off my back."

We heard a grown man say, "I don't know nothin and what I do know ain't so." We heard him say of the man in a coffin on the funeral day, "Once in a while he wasn't as mean as he nearly always was." And we studied about his saying, "He might give you the shirt off his back but he wouldn't care who he gave the shirt off my back to."

The streetcar motorman was a little tired after his ten-hour day when I heard him say to another motorman, "There ain't no work to it—it's just goddam monotony."

It was fun to say to another kid, "Follow me and you'll wear diamonds," and hear him snicker, "Yes, paste diamonds."

We did hear of a loser in business whose story was short: "I started on a shoestring and all I've got now is the shoestring."

It wasn't an insult to tell another kid, "You've got a Henry Clay head—made of mud."

Along Main Street I passed two men, one well-dressed, the other shabby. I heard Well-dressed saying to Shabby in a rough voice, "Aw, don't try any sympathy racket on me." It stayed with me and I tried to think about it. Maybe one was right and the other wrong. And maybe each was half right and half wrong.

"Sympathy" was quite a word among the young and the grown-ups. You could hear, "He's had hard luck, I got a lot of sympathy for him" or "What's the matter with you? Haven't you got the least bit of sympathy for me?" It was later Bert Williams' song came, "All I Get Is Sympathy."

The Seven Sutherland Sisters—we saw pictures of them—and did they have hair! Every one of them had hair hanging thick and grand from her head to her heels. We heard of women buying their hair tonic but we didn't hear whether it made hair grow. When us kids saw a girl with extra long hair, it came natural to say, "Just like a Sutherland Sister."

The one sign on Main Street that hit people in the eye so they remembered it was in front of the Churchill & Weatherbee hardware store—at night an owl with its two electric eyes blinking and under it "We Never Sleep." Whenever we saw Mr. Churchill or Mr. Weatherbee, one of us would be saying, "Aw, I bet he sleeps."

For several years you could hear, "Chicago girls all have big feet." Then time passed and you didn't hear about the big feet of Chicago girls. But Mrs. O'Leary's cow who kicked over the lantern that started the Chicago Fire, you were dumb if you hadn't heard that. And once some kid pointed toward a man on Main Street and said to me, "See him? He was in Chicago when they had the fire." So I took a close look at the man and hoped sometime to hear him tell about the fire that only fifteen years before had nearly swept Chicago off the map. "There never was a fire like it"—we heard that for years. The nickname for Chicago was from the first syllable and pronounced "Shy." You could hear it often at the Q. depot: "Where yuh goin?" "Shy." "Well, look out for those slickers near the Union Depot. They'll ask yuh, 'Got a match?' and then they'll try to trim yuh."

Slickers in Chicago, we talked about them. They would sell you the Masonic Temple skyscraper, get a down payment from you, and then fade and the police couldn't help you. Or they would ask you if it wasn't worth ten dollars to see that skyscraper turn around on itself when you were on the top floor. If you paid you waited for the slicker, who had excused himself and never came back. Us kids had our doubts but it was fun to talk about.

A little creepy was the talk about that tank in the Joliet State Penitentiary. One of the boys said that when a convict refused to work he was put in the empty tank. In the middle of the tank was a pump. Water began coming in till it covered the floor. Little by little the water came to the man's ankles, then his knees. Little by little it came to his hips. If he started working the pump the water went down. If he refused to pump, the water came higher and higher. "He had to work or drown," said the boy. "My father says it's true."

We knew Joliet was a terrible place. We had heard that a convict refusing to work was "put in solitary," locked in a dark cell alone, and twice a day they shoved through the cell door his bread and water—in the dark—no one to talk to but himself except once a day they asked him if he was willing to work. Not till he said he would go to work did they open the door and let him into daylight again to see people and eat regular. We believed that. And we believed that maybe they had a tank where they let the water get nearly up to his mouth and nose but they wouldn't dare drown him unless a judge sentenced him to be drowned.

I could have got straight on how they did things in Joliet if I had gone to August W. Berggren and asked him. He was learning to be a tailor when he was fourteen years old in Sweden and his father brought him to Knox County, where he worked as a tailor. He played the violin, organized string bands, and wrote music arrangements. All the time he had an eye on business and politics and got to be a director and vice-president of the Galesburg National Bank, taking a hand in nominating candidates and electing them. I first saw him when my father took me into the clothing store of Berggren & Lundeen on Main between Seminary and Kellogg and I was maybe eight or nine years old. Mr. Berggren held a coat for me to put my arms into, held three or four more coats for me to get into, and my father picked the suit he wanted for me. It wasn't all wool, but Mr. Berggren was kind, showed respect for my father and me even though he was Sheriff of Knox County for eight years, a state senator for eight years, and president of the Covenant Mutual Life Association of Illinois. He was a born tailor and liked fitting men and boys into clothes. From May 1889 to March 1891 he was warden of the Joliet penitentiary and ran the prison. I could have hunted him out and asked him about that tank and about convicts "put in solitary." I didn't have the wit to do it and I didn't think about it later when I met penitentiary wardens in Joliet. So I'm still in the dark about that tank, though I would bet it was guff.

Walking to work one morning on South Street near Chambers I heard a Negro on the other side of the street call to a Negro a few feet ahead of me, "Waffo you sigashiatin this mawnin?" And the Negro ahead of me answered, "Who you 'ludin to?" Neither of them laughed nor smiled. They were saying good morning. "Waffo" meant "What for?" "Sigashiatin" seemed to mean showing up, ambulating and being around so as to be seen. As good an answer as any perhaps, from our side of the street, was, "Who are you alluding to?" made more brief and peremptory into "Who you 'ludin to?"

One evening on the Public Square Mart and I heard two "green" Swedes, the first one saying, "Haw yu got some snus, Olaf?" (Have you got some snuff?) and the second, "I hanta got none, Yon, if I got none I gif you any."

When the horsecars went out of business and the trolley cars came, we were tickled about the Chinaman in San Francisco seeing the first trolley car and busting out, "No pushee, no pullee, but go like hellee."

We liked Robert Fulton and how before he got his steamboat started there were people hollering, "You'll never be able to start it" and after he got it going the same people hollered, "You'll never be able to stop it!"

We liked too the story a young evangelist at the Methodist Church told us of the king who gave it out that anybody who could tell him a story running so long that he would cry, "Stop! Stop!" could marry his princess daughter. They came with long stories that ended before the king cried, "Stop! Stop!" and they had their heads cut off. Then came a young farm hand who began: "There was a king over people who had gone through a year of famine. And the next year when crops were good the king had them build a big store-house for grain to be kept. And a million grasshoppers arrived. And the grasshoppers hunted everywhere around the storehouse but they found only one little hole that one grasshopper could crawl through to get at the grain. And one grasshopper went in and came out with a grain of corn. And another grasshopper went in and came out with a grain of corn. And another grasshopper went in and came out with a grain of corn. And another grasshopper went in and came out with a grain of corn." And the king saw that he was in for a million grasshoppers going in one by one and coming out one by one with a grain of corn. And the king cried, "Stop! Stop!" and gave his princess daughter to the young farm hand to marry. Which shows that you never can tell what a young farm hand might be up to.

These sayings and stories on the streets and in the schoolyard stick in the memory like cockleburrs on a pants leg.

NINE

The Dirty Dozen

★

On the wooden sidewalks of Berrien Street we played one kind of mumble-peg and in the grass of the front yard or the grass between sidewalk and gutter ditch we played the more complicated and interesting one with jump-the-fence, thread-the-needle, plow-forty-acres, and plow-eighty-acres. The loser saw us trim a peg the length of the knife blade we played with. Then each of us took a whack at the top of the peg with the knife top, holding the blade, aiming to drive the peg as deep as we could. It was up to the loser to *mumble* his mouth and teeth around that peg and bring it out of the ground. On the wooden sidewalks we spun tops, flipped jackstones, chalked tit-tat-toe.

On the street, however, we played baseball, two-old-cat, choose-up, knocking-up-flies. Shinny was worth the time. For knocking a tin can or a block of wood toward a goal any kind of club would do, though the fellow with a plow handle had the best of it. Duck-on-a-rock has its points. The duck is a small rock that sits on a large rock. When you knock the duck off the rock, you have to run and pick up your own rock and get back to taw without being tagged. Or you can refuse to touch your rock and stand by it till another player knocks the duck off the rock and take a chance on picking up your rock and running for taw. If you get caught you're "it" and your rock becomes the duck. It sounds simple but it can be as scientific and complicated as some of the more famous games.

After we had been to see the commencement Field Day on the

Knox or Lombard campus, we put on our own little field day, bare-foot in the summer dust of Berrien Street. Some boy usually had a two-dollar-and-a-half Waterbury watch and timed us as we ran fifty yards, one hundred yards, a few seconds slower than the college runners, and five or six seconds under the world's record. We knew how near we came to the college records in the standing broad jump, the running broad jump, the hop-skip-and-a-step, the standing high jump and the running high jump. Whoever could throw a crowbar the farthest was counted put-and-shot "champeen." We did about everything the college athletes did except the pole vault. How can you have a pole vault setup on a public street where it would scare the living daylights out of all but the gentlest and weariest horses? The mile run we did of afternoons, breaking no records except some of our own, yet satisfying ourselves that there is such a thing as "second wind" and if you can get it you can finish your mile.

I haven't seen a field day since those days in the late '80's and early '90's. Yet because of the way we went in for those sports events in our own crude way on a dusty street, I can follow news reports and photographs of the Olympic games a little as though I had trained for some of the events. If as a boy you have put all you've got into a few hundred-yard dashes or running broad jumps you know better what is going on in the hearts, lungs, and minds of those who train, struggle, and hope for Olympic championships. Once in the cubicle of a magazine office I met in a near-by cubicle a fellow who had broken a world's mile-run record. He was a worn man, older than his years. He had trained too hard and run more miles than was good for him.

Of those days of play and sport in the street in front of our house one tender and curious memory stands out. The house next east to ours straight across the street was an average two-story frame affair, with a porch perhaps fifteen feet long. In the street in front of this house was our home base when playing ball. Often we saw on that porch in a rocking chair a little old woman, her hair snow-white with the years. She had a past, a rather bright though not dazzling past, you might say. She could lay claim to fame, if she chose. Millions of children reading the McGuffey and other school readers

had met her name and memorized lines she had written. For there
was in the course of her years no short poem in the English language
more widely published, known, and recited than her lines about
"Little Things":

Little drops of water,	Little deeds of kindness,
Little grains of sand,	Little words of love,
Make the mighty ocean	Help to make earth happy
And the pleasant land. . . .	Like the heaven above.

She was Julia Carney, her sons Fletcher and James being Univer-
salists and Lombard graduates, Fletcher serving three or four terms
as mayor of Galesburg. There she sat in the quiet of her backward-
gazing thoughts, sometimes gently rocking, while we hooted and
yelled over hits, runs, putouts. There she sat, an image of silence
and rest, while the air rang with boy screams, "Hit it bang on the
nose now!" "Aw, he couldn't hit a balloon!" "Down went McGinty
to the bottom of the sea!" Rarely she turned her head to see what
we were doing. She made no request "for the benefit of those who
have retired." To us at that time she was just one more nice old
woman who wouldn't bother boys at play. We didn't know that her
writings were in books and newspaper reprints that reached millions
of readers. The Carneys were good neighbors and she was one of
them—that was all we knew.

We should have heard about her in school. We should have read
little pieces about her in the papers. She has a tiny quaint niche in
the history of American literature under which one line could be
written: "She loved children and wrote poems she hoped children
would love." As late as the year 1952 Mrs. Dwight D. Eisenhower
in a magazine article quoted the poem "Little Things" as one of her
childhood delights.

It wasn't long before the fathers and mothers along Berrien Street
had new troubles with their boys. Under that electric light at Day
and Berrien the boys had a new playground. They could turn night
into day. There was night baseball, night shinny, night duck-on-a-
rock, night tug-of-war. There were winners yelling because they
had won. There were losers yelling that next time they would make
the winners eat dirt. Both winners and losers might be hooting each

other at the same time. "Yah, yah, yuh hayseeds you, you couldn't tell your hind end from a hole in the ground!" Vehement remarks like that floated in through windows into rooms where honest Q. shopmen and worthy railroad firemen and brakemen were trying for a little sleep because they had worked today and hoped to work tomorrow.

One of the sleepers who couldn't sleep had a voice like a big-league umpire and it was like shooting had started when one night he clamored from his bedroom window, "You boys shut up with your goddam noise and go home with you. If you don't I'll get the police on you." The noise stopped—no more hoots and yells. We sat cross-legged on a patch of grass next to a sidewalk and talked in whispers: "Do you s'pose he means it?" "Aw, what the hell, we got a right to holler, this is a free country." "Yeah, but what if he means it? We'll get run in." "Yeah, I don't want no patrol-wagon ride." About then came a woman who wanted her sonny-boy and she took him by one ear and led him away and his face had a sheepish look. Then came two men. They were fathers. They spotted their boys, collared them, and led them away like two sheep for slaughter. Mart and I went home. If we didn't get into the house by nine o'clock after our street play we would get scoldings or worse. We knew too what we would get if we didn't wash our dirty dusty feet. Into a wash basin they went—or we put them under the pump spout before coming into the house.

On a later night the boys forgot themselves and the hullabaloo they made could be heard a block away. Then as promised, the patrol wagon came. Before it could stop, five or six boys skedaddled to their homes. That left five or six of us who weren't going to run. If we ran it would show we were scared. We stood in a huddle waiting. Out of the patrol wagon under the electric light came two policemen in blue uniforms with a row of brass buttons shining, their nickel-plated stars shining too on their coats. One of them, Frank Peterson, weighed about two hundred and twenty pounds, and looked like a battleship coming toward us. We expected some hard words from Policeman Peterson. He spoke in a soft voice like what he was saying was confidential. "Don't you boys know you're makin a hell of a noise here and it disturbs people who are tryin to sleep?" What could we say to a nice quiet intelligent question like that? One boy said, "Yes," another, "Well, you know we was just tryin to have some fun." "Yes," said Peterson, again quiet and confidential like, "but ain't there some way you can have your fun without keepin people awake that's tryin to sleep?" We had come to like Policeman Peterson. We saw he wasn't mad at us and it didn't look like we were going to be put in the wagon and hauled to the calaboose. We said yes, we would try to have our fun without making so much noise. Before walking away to the wagon Peterson said, "Now that's a promise, boys, and I expect you to keep it. If you don't stop your noise, we'll have to run you in." And his voice got a little hard as he said, "Remember that. We don't like to arrest young fellows like you but sometimes we have to do it." That word "arrest" stuck in our ears. They could have arrested us. When you're arrested that means you're a criminal. And if you're a criminal, where are you?

The patrol wagon drove away. When the rumble of its wheels had died away we sat on the grass and talked in low tones near a whisper. All of us agreed that from now on we had better try to have our fun without hollering and yelling all the time like there was bloody murder or a house on fire. All agreed except the boy who had on another night said, "Aw, what the hell, we got a right to holler, this is a free country." This boy was saying, "Aw, that stinkin cop Peterson, I'd like to tie a bunch of firecrackers to his tail." He guessed he'd rather stay away and have some other kind of fun than come around and be a nice good boy like the police told him. And he did stay away and later he took to the poolrooms and the saloons and still later put in a year in the Pontiac reformatory for petty larceny.

We went on playing under the electric light and trying to keep quiet but it was a strain on us. What is duck-on-a-rock if you can't holler? I had got a job where I had to report at six-thirty in the morning and had gone home early one night, leaving the boys in a hot game of shinny, back in their old hooting and yelling. They told me the next day that a railroad fireman had come out in his nightshirt with a club and a revolver. He shot in the air twice to show the gun was loaded. He sent a bullet into a sidewalk plank and had them look at the bullet. He was wild-eyed, cursed them, slapped one of them in the face, kicked another, then took out a watch and said if every last one of them wasn't gone in two minutes he would shoot to kill. Half the boys ran and the rest went away on a fast walk. From then on there were not as many boys came to that corner for night ball, night shinny, night duck-on-a-rock. The corner became reasonably quiet, and decent people could sleep. There was hate for the shooting-iron fireman and when boys passed him on the street and he was out of hearing they called him the dirtiest names they could think of. And Policeman Frank Peterson they would point out with, "He ain't a bad fellow, do you know?"

One Halloween night we paid a debt to a man who had lectured and gabbed us for smoking cornsilk cigarettes we had made. He said we would go from cornsilk to tobacco and tobacco was bad. We strung a dozen tin cans on a rope, made another like it. We passed his house when it was lighted, came back later when it was dark. We threw our two strings of tin cans one after the other against his front door. Then we ran and hid behind a fence across the street. We saw the door open. We saw him come out and stand there looking suspiciously at the crazy tin cans on the porch floor. They might be bombs and they might explode, we guessed he was thinking. They might be a kind of dynamite can made by the Chicago anarchists we were reading about then. He kicked the cans around a little as though ready to run if any can exploded. He went to the front gate, looked up and down the street, muttering words we couldn't hear. He went back to the cans, picked up one string of them, and took it into the house, came out again and took the other string of cans in. Then we saw the door close. We waited a while, came out from behind the fence and ran lickety-split up the street. We had had our revenge and it was sweet. We talked about what smart devilish things we could think up when we hated somebody. Our next trick wasn't so good.

A quiet elderly couple had their home on the south side of Berrien west of Pearl. They had been there a year or two and we hadn't heard their name or what they lived on. When they sat on their front porch they might look at each other once in a while but they didn't speak to each other. When us kids passed by they didn't look at us. They just went on looking straight ahead at nothing in particular.

They seemed to be living in a quiet world of their own. They looked quiet and acted quiet. They were so still and peaceable that we got to talking about how still and peaceable they were and we ought to do something about it. One boy said, "Let's give 'em the tin cans." It wasn't a case of hate. We didn't hate them. We were just curious about them and we thought maybe something funny would happen. Again we strung together a dozen cans on each of two ropes. We saw their light on, waited and saw their kerosene lamp go out, waited a while longer and then sent the two strings of cans slam-bang against the front door. We skipped across the street, three of us and each behind his own tree. We waited. Nothing happened. The door didn't open. Nobody came out. We waited a while wondering whether the man had gone out the back door and was circling around to surprise us. We picked up our feet and ran.

It was several months later that one of the boys went into a Main Street grocery and saw this couple. For how many bars of soap they wanted or how many pounds of butter, they held up their fingers, two fingers for two bars of soap and so on. They didn't say a word. They were deaf and dumb. When the three of us heard this we were honest with each other. We asked why we had done such a fool thing. "What the hell," said one boy as he turned his back to me and stooped, "kick me." I gave him a swift kick in the hind end, then stooped for him to kick me. Each of the three of us gave the other two a swift kick. Once later when I passed the house and saw the couple sitting quiet and peaceable on their front porch I looked straight at them and touched my hat. They didn't nod nor smile. They just went on looking ahead at nothing in particular.

Andrew Munson over on South Street became part of our lives, a grown man with a crooked right leg, a crooked left arm, a crooked mouth, and a scraggly reddish-brown beard. The arm would have sudden twitching motions, the left shoulder joining. It came hard to get words out of his twisting mouth and they came with a spray of spittle. I saw kids like myself, at first near to laughing at him and then sobering, one kid saying, "You're lucky when you ain't born a cripple." Part of it was that the man had a sweetness to him, spoke as though life was pleasant and he had no complaints about what hard luck had handed him.

I have played baseball on a summer day starting at eight o'clock in the morning, running home at noon for a quick meal, playing again till six o'clock in the evening, and then a run home for a quick meal and again with fielding and batting till it was too dark to see the leather spheroid. On many a Saturday I had sold the *Sporting News* at five cents a copy, and I had read about the "leather spheroid."

Four lots to the east of our house was a vacant double lot where we laid out a small diamond. At the time a good-natured Jersey cow was pastured there for a few weeks. We never knocked a ball that hit the cow but when the ball landed near her and the fielder ran toward her it disturbed her. Also it disturbed the owner of the cow, who said he would have the police on us. So we played in the street till the day the cow was gone and we heard it had been sold. Then we went back to our pasture.

On the narrow lot next to the pasture lived Mrs. Moore, widow of a Civil War veteran, living alone on a Federal pension. She was a tall woman with dark hair streaked with gray and a face we liked well enough. She was a peaceable, quiet woman, smoking her tobacco in a clay pipe, keeping to herself and raising vegetables and flowers. She had the nicest all-round flower garden in our block, the front of her lot filled with hollyhocks, begonias, salvia, asters, and morning-glories climbing the fences. We had no ill will toward Mrs. Moore. But first base was only ten feet or so from her fence and every so often a fly or a foul ball would go over the fence into her potatoes, carrots, and hollyhocks. A boy would climb the fence and go stomping around hunting the lost ball. At such times as Mrs. Moore stood between the boy and the place where he believed the ball fell it was not pleasant for either party concerned. "Why must you boys do this to my place?" she would ask. When the boy answered, "We'll try never to do it again," her reply would come, "See that you don't do it again. I don't want to make trouble for you boys."

Again and again we sent the ball over into her well-kept yard. She tried scolding us but she just naturally wasn't a scold. She quietly hinted she might have to go to the police. She tried to look at us mean but couldn't manage it. It hurt her to see us scrounging among her garden plants. We were a nuisance and she could have gone to the police and had us abolished. And she didn't go to the police or to our parents living near by. She had property rights and we were trespassing on her property, and she forgave us our trespasses even though we went on trespassing. I would say now that she was a woman of rare inner grace who had gathered wisdom from potatoes and hollyhocks.

What is this fascination about making a hickory stick connect with a thrown ball and sending the ball as a high fly or a hot grounder for a safe hit? What is this fascination about picking up a hot grounder and throwing it to first for a putout—or running for a fly and leaping in the air for a one-handed catch and a putout? What is this peculiar shame of standing under a high fly and it falls smack in your hands and you muff it? What is this nameless embarrassment of being at bat with three men on bases and you fan the air three times with your bat and it's "side out" and you hear someone say, "You're all right only there was a hole in the bat"? These questions have gone round and round in the heads of millions of American boys for generations. I have many a night gone to bed and before falling asleep I imagined myself sliding to second, sliding to third, and stealing home. And I have had dreams of playing deep outfield and muffing a high fly with three men on bases and two of them scoring. Before falling asleep I would make plays that astonished players and people on the side lines. But in my dreams I always muffed the ball or when I tried to steal a base I was tagged out.

Our early games among the Berrien Street kids were played in the street, barefooted, keeping an eye out for broken glass or rusty cans with sharp edges sticking up. The bat was a broom handle, the ball was handmade—a five-cent rubber ball wrapped round with grocery string. The home plate was a brick, first base a brick, second base a tin can, third another tin can. We played barehanded till we learned how to get a large man-sized glove and stuff it with cotton, wool, or hair to take the sting out of a fast ball hitting the palm or fingers.

The days came when we played in the cow pasture with a Spalding big-league regulation ball. We gathered round the boy who first brought it to us and said we could play with it. "Well, what do you know!" we said, "A dollar and a half." And we told it around as a kind of wonder, "We been playin today with a dollar and a half." We would hear "Fatty" Beckman ask, "Is Skinny Seeley comin today with that dollar and a half?" Sure he was. He was bringing the same ball that Amos Rusie was throwing in the big league, the same ball Big Bill Lange was hitting so hard with the Chicago team. We had played many a game with a dollar-and-a-half ball that had the leather cover off and we could hit it and catch it but there wasn't the feel of that same leather spheroid that Big Bill Lange was hitting. When I carried Chicago newspapers and read sports news I learned about the "elusive pill" thrown by Amos Rusie. I was among those who grieved later to hear of Amos Rusie taking to drink, being dropped from major and minor clubs, and being found one day digging gas mains at a dollar-fifty a day. He was doing ten cents a day better than my father at the Q. shop but still I was more sorry for him than for my father.

Across a few years I could from day to day name the leading teams and the tailenders in the National League and the American Association. I could name the players who led in batting and fielding and the pitchers who had won the most games. I filled my head with this knowledge and carried it around. There were times my head seemed empty of everything but baseball names and figures. I could hear them rattling around in my head. I had my opinions about who was better than anybody else in the national game. Therefore I now understand the Great American Ball Fan and all his follies. I was an addict and I know why pop bottles have been thrown at umpires, though I have never at a season end thrown a good straw hat on the grandstand floor and jumped on it to crush the life out of it.

When Galesburg played Chillicothe or Peoria or Rock Island on the Knox campus grounds, there were always two fans to perform. Jim O'Brien, chief of the fire department, was on hand and took his stand near first base with an umbrella to keep the sun off him. And when the home team had a streak of luck, his umbrella would go into the air and he would catch it coming down and go into a fancy umbrella dance. Also there was the dentist Doc Olson. He could yell, whistle, and juggle a straw hat and make faces at the visiting team and cut up didoes. No matter how poor the home team played, these two fans performed and entertained those who paid their two bits to get in.

The Berrien Street kids lacking the two bits' admission watched
the games on the Knox campus through knotholes in the fence. Or
we climbed a tree fifty yards from the home plate, found a crotch to
sit in, and had as much fun as though we were in the two-bit bleach-
ers.

The most exciting baseball year the town had in that time was
when a City League was organized and played one or two games a
week. The Main Street clerks had one team, the railroad shopmen
another, and there were two other teams. I remember the pitching
styles of Bob Switzer, "Kill" Bruner, and Nelson Willard, the work
at shortstop and second base of Bay Sanderson and Grant Beadle.
One notable player was "Hump" Ostrander in right field for the
railway shopmen. In his younger days he had hopped a railroad train
and slipped and lost his left arm. The stump of it hung from his left
shoulder. All catches he made were one-handed. When he stepped
to bat at the plate he swung with one arm and hand. Hump's record
was fair and when he caught a fly or slammed out a base hit he got
extra cheers as a phenomenon. I had come to like him when we sat
across the aisle from each other in Swedish summer school and
studied "*Biblisk historia*" (Bible history) together.

Out of the tall grass around Victoria came a team that had sur-
prises. Galesburg had picked the best nine in the town to meet them
and the word was that maybe Galesburg would "goose-egg" them.
But the country boys played fast ball, among them the Spratt broth-
ers, Bob and Jack, who later went into minor-league clubs. Their
center fielder was a tall gawk wearing a derby hat. He may have
had a cap at home and couldn't find it. It was the first time the town
had seen in a regular ball game a player crowned with a derby. As
the game got going Victoria took the lead by one or two runs and
kept the lead till near the closing inning, when Galesburg with one
out got two men on bases and one of its heaviest sluggers came to
bat. He hit the ball high and handsome and sent it sailing away out
to deep center field. The tall gawk in the derby made a fast run,
made a leap for it, caught it with one hand and threw it straight to
second to catch a man off base—so Victoria was victorious in one of
the craziest, sweetest pieces of baseball drama I have ever seen.

One year Galesburg had a semi-pro team, its second baseman a professional named Bud Fowler, a left-handed Negro, fast and pretty in his work. A traveling salesman named Dushane, a stubby French-man with a brown mustache and every hair curled to the right moment, played third base one year. When the home team made a double play he would leap in the air, turn a somersault, and light on his feet. The crowd watched for it. It came in handy when the home team was losing, which it usually was when playing minor-league clubs.

An idea began growing in me that if I played and practiced a lot I might become good enough to get on a team where my talent was appreciated. Once on a minor-league team I would have my chance to show what I could do and I might end up in the majors—who knows about a thing like that? I didn't mention it. It was a secret ambition. I nursed it along and in what spare time I could find I played where the boys were playing, did fairly well in left field on a scrub team.

Then came an afternoon in early October. I was sixteen. Skinny Seeley and I went to a pasture in the second block north of the Lombard campus. Skinny and I knocked up flies. He was hitting some long and high ones to me. I had managed to buy secondhand a fielder's glove, a regular big-league affair I was proud of. I was running for a high one. I believed I would make a brilliant catch of it, the kind of catch I would make when maybe one of the minor-league clubs had taken me on. I was running at top speed. Suddenly my right foot stashed into a hole and I fell on my knees and face. When I looked at what had happened to my right foot I saw a gash in the shoe leather and blood oozing from the tangled yarn of the sock. I saw too that in the eight-inch hole there was a beer bottle, broken in half, standing on its bottom end, and into the top of this my foot had crashed.

I limped across the pasture, about a block, to the house of Dr. Taggart. He was at home. Out on his front porch he had me take off the shoe, then slowly the sock. He cleaned out the bleeding cut, picked out yarn and glass, applied antiseptic. Then he brought out a curved needle and sewed four stitches at about the middle of the foot just below the instep. I didn't let out a moan or a whimper through the whole operation. After my fall, when I saw the gashed shoe and the broken bottle, I did cry out, "Jesus wept! Jesus wept!" I moaned and groaned going toward the doctor's house, but when I found him in and when I watched the cool, sure, easy way he handled me, I gritted my teeth and smiled to him and told him I was lucky. He bandaged my foot and I limped home. My mother spoke sorrow and pity. My father asked when would I ever learn any sense and quit wasting my time with baseball.

From that day on I was completely through with any and all hopes and dreams of becoming a big-time ballplayer. I went on playing occasional games and have never lost a certain odd tingle of the hands at holding a bat or catching a baseball. Those four stitches in the right foot marked the end of my first real secret ambition. I began a hunt for new secret ambitions, but they were slow in coming.

We were between nine and twelve when we took in the Knox County Fair one year after another for three years. We walked the four and a half miles from Galesburg to the fair grounds just outside of Knoxville, Husky Larson, his brother Al, and one or two other boys. The dust lay one and two inches thick on the road. We walked barefoot, carrying our shoes and putting them on when we came to the fair grounds so we wouldn't get our bare toes stepped on in the crowds. We walked to save the round-trip railroad fare and after paying twenty-five cents admission, we watched our few nickels. Always one nickel went to the man who had the new and amazing Edison Talking Phonograph. Around the machine stood people watching what it did to the faces of those who clapped on the earphones and were listening. Some faces sober and doubting stayed sober and came away saying, "It works, doggone it, you can hear that brass band playing like it was right here on the fair grounds." Most faces, however, wore smiles, and came away saying, "It's pretty cute, I tell you. The machine talks like it's human." We stepped up with our nickels. We plugged our ears with the phone ends. We watched the cylinder on the machine turning. We knew the cylinder was the "record" of what came to our ears. We heard a voice saying this was the Edison Talking Phonograph and that next we would hear a famous brass band playing, which we did. We looked at each other's faces and nodded and smiled, "It works! I can hear it! Ain't it the doggonedest thingamajig? I wouldn't believe it if I wasn't hearing it."

We didn't know that the fair was part of our sex education, as it so definitely was, to watch the stallions and mares, bulls and cows, boars and sows, cocks and hens—and the judges awarding prizes and blue ribbons. We saw farmers proud of what they had bred and raised. And we saw gawdy young women, "dressed fit to kill," flirting with farm hands who had spending money. We felt something in the air very different from a circus coming to town. Many a farmer and his boy had come to learn. Their work the year round was in trying to make the land and the animals bring bigger crops and more food. In a way you could see and feel the farms they had come from. They had on their best clothes but their muscles stood out in little humps and bunches so that their coats hung on them rather than fitted them. Their women carried the signs of hard work and long hours, some of them taking pride in the jellies and preserves they had entered for showing. The biggest Knox County potato of the year was worth seeing, as also the largest rutabaga.

We didn't have the two bits for grandstand seats to see the horse races. We stood at the board fence next to the grandstand and watched the fastest horses in Knox County—saddle horses, thoroughbreds, pacers and trotters, with drivers in sulkies with high wheels, spokes of wood, and the rims iron. Several of the drivers, like Fred Seacord, we had seen on the streets of Galesburg exercising their horses and getting them used to the sulkies. The only time I ever talked with Fred Seacord was fifty years later after I had given a recital in the Central High School of San Antonio, Texas, and he wanted me to talk about my books and I wanted him to talk about his horses.

There came a "special feature." Occasionally we had seen Mr. Redfield with his Irish setter on Main Street. And we knew it was no common dog. Now we were to see what had earned its fame as "The Only Pacing Dog in the World." The world is large and there may at that time have been another pacing dog somewhere over the wide world, but if so its owner hadn't put in any claim and if he had Mr. Redfield would have challenged him to bring on his pacing dog for a race. So at last we saw Mr. Redfield come out on the track with his horse and sulky. Alongside the right wheel so the grandstand could see him was the Irish setter, handsome with his coat of brown hair gleaming, and his gait was that of a pacer, the legs in that peculiar continuous sidewise throw. Twice around the half-mile track went the pacing dog. His record for a mile I have forgotten. He wasn't as fast as pacing horses but the crowd believed he was the fastest pacing dog in the world and they cheered him and Mr. Redfield. We heard men saying that Mr. Redfield claimed no particular credit. He had noticed the dog just naturally pacing and encouraged him to go on pacing and never in an exhibition performance had the dog "broke" from pacing into a run.

That year we caught a ride in a hayrack from the fair grounds to Galesburg. Arriving home we talked most about having heard with our ears plugged the first Edison Talking Phonograph in Knox County and having seen the only pacing dog in the world go through his paces. About the dog the Old Man merely remarked in Swedish that it was interesting but not important. The Edison Talking Phonograph, however, giving you a band concert without bringing you the band, that was curious and he said, "Wat will dey tink up next?" When the talking machine later came to a vacant store on Main Street he spent several nickels listening to the newfangled contraption and did some independent thinking about how it ran and what it did.

When the circus came to town we managed to shake out of sleep at four o'clock in the morning, grab a slice of bread and butter, and make a fast walk to the Q. yards to watch the unloading in early daylight. A grand clear voice the man had who rode his horse a half-block ahead of the elephants in the parade and cried out as though there might be hell to pay, "The elephants are coming, watch your horses!" First to one side of the street and then the other he cried it and those who had skittish horses watched them.

After the unloading we went home for a quick breakfast and a run to the circus grounds, a big pasture at Main and Farnham near the city limits. If we were lucky we got jobs at carrying water for the elephants or lugging to the big tent the boards for the audience to sit on. After three or four hours of this useful and necessary work we were presented with slips of paper that let us in to see the big show in the afternoon. If we hadn't been lucky and if we didn't have the fifty cents for a ticket we tried to slide under the canvas and crawl to where we could peek through boards and between legs to see the grand march, the acrobats, the trapezists, the clowns, the hippodrome chariot race given before our eyes as it was in the time of Nero in Rome. Once as I was nearly through the canvas a pair of strong hands caught me by the ankles, yanked me out and threw me for a fall, and a voice told me I could get the hell out of there.

I walked around to the Side Show. There out front as a free show I saw the man with the elastic skin. He would pull it out from his face and neck and it would snap back into place. There I saw the tattooed man with fish, birds, brunette girls, ships, and many other shapes inked deep into his skin—and there too the Oriental Dancing Girl wearing few clothes and smiling about it to some giggling farm hands. The spieler, a man with a thick upcurled mustache, leaned toward the farm hands and said in a voice as if for them only to hear, "Go inside, boys. You can't lose. She takes off everything, every last stitch, and her muscles shake like a bowl of jelly. She makes a sick man feel like a wild monkey. What did you come here for, boys? She's got it. You can't lose."

Then the spieler dropped his confidential way and turned to the main crowd and let go in a smooth, loud voice. You could tell he was used to what he was saying and had spoken the same words in the same way a thousand times. "La-deez and gen-tul-men, beneath yon canvas we have the curi-aw-si-ties and the mon-straw-si-ties—the Wild Man of Borneo, the smallest dwarf ever seen of mankind and the tallest giant that ever came into existence, the most marvelous snake ever brought to your fair city, a man-eating python captured in the darkest jungles of Africa ever penetrated by man. And I would call your particular attention to Jo Jo the dog-faced boy, born forty miles from land and forty miles from sea." At this last you couldn't be sure but he was taking a laugh inside of himself, for his eyes twinkled. Us kids did imitations of him and when trying to rattle a pitcher or a batter, we would bawl, "Beneath yon canvas we have the curi-aw-si-ties and the mon-straw-si-ties," or "Look who's to bat. It's Jo Jo the dog-faced boy, born forty miles from land and forty miles from sea." And we learned too from the spieler, the barker, about the dime. "The price of admission, la-deez and gen-tul-men, is a dime, ten cents only, the tenth part of a dollar. Buy your tickets now before the big rush comes."

I had a dime and a nickel in my pocket. With the dime, the tenth part of a dollar, I bought a ticket. I went in and heard the ventriloquist and his dummy: "Will you spell a word for me, Danny?" "I'll try, what's the word?" "Constantinople." "Why do you tell me you can't stand on an apple?" I saw the Wild Man of Borneo and I could see he was a sad little shrimp and his whiskers messy. The Fat Woman, the Dwarf, the Giant, they seemed to me to be mistakes God had made, that God was absent-minded when he shaped them. I hung around the midget and his wife, watched them sign their names to photographs they sold at ten cents—and they were that pleasant and witty that I saw I had guessed wrong about them and they were having more fun out of life than some of the men in the Q. shops.

I stood a long while watching the Giant and noticed that he was quiet and satisfied about things and he didn't care one way or another whether people looked at him. He was so easy and calm about the way things were going that he reminded me of a big horse that didn't have to work and eats regular and never buys patent medicines. If a smarty asked, "How's the weather up there?" he might lift one eyebrow and let it pass, for he had heard it often enough. Nor did I feel sorry for the python. He may have been a man-eater but he was sleeping as if he had forgotten whoever it was he had swallowed and digested. After a third or fourth time around, the only one I felt sorry for was the Wild Man of Borneo. He could have been the only lonely creature among all the freaks. The Oriental Dancing Girl certainly was no freak, an average good-looking showgirl, somewhat dark of skin and probably a gypsy. She twirled, she high-kicked, did a few mild wiggles, and when it was over I heard a farm hand saying, "It's a sell. I thought from the way he talked outside that we was goin to see a belly dance." "Yeah," said another, "and she didn't take off a stitch. It's a sell."

Years later it came over me that at first sight of the freaks I was sad because I was bashful. Except at home and among playmates, it didn't come easy for me to be looked at. I didn't like the feel of eyes being laid on me. I would pass people on the street and when they had gone by, I would wonder if they had turned their heads for another look at me. Walking down a church aisle between hundreds of people, I had a feeling of eyes on me. If three or four men stood in front of a store when I came along and one of them made some remark like "Better hurry, kid, you're late," or "Does your mother know you're out, son?" I didn't have the answers and walked on with a feeling that their eyes were on me. This was silly, but when you're bashful you have that feeling of eyes following you and boring through you. And there at the side show were these people, the freaks—and the business, the work, of each one of them was to be looked at. Every week, day by day they sat or stood up to be looked at by thousands of people and they were paid to be looked at. If some one of them was more looked at than any others there was danger of jealousy on the part of those who didn't get looked at as much as they wished. Only the Wild Man of Borneo and the python seemed to be careless about whether anyone looked at them or not.

I walked out of the side show with my nickel still in my pocket. I passed the cane stand where a man held out rings and spoke like his tongue was oiled, "Only ten cents for a ring and the cane you ring is the cane you get." I watched fellows throw one ring and quit. One stubborn farm hand spent thirty cents for rings and didn't get a cane and laughed he didn't want a cane anyhow. I walked on and later came back and the man with the oily tongue was still calling out, "Only ten cents for a ring and the cane you ring is the cane you get." Now I saw a man ring a cane and look at it from end to end and laugh, "I spose maybe it's worth ten cents."

I stopped where a man was cheerfully calling with no letup, "Lem-o-nade, ice-cold lem-o-nade, a nice cool refreshing drink for a nickel, five cents, the twentieth part of a dollar." Then in a lower tone as if talking to himself, "Lem-o-nade, made in the shade and stirred with a rusty spade." I passed by him to hear a laughing voice, "Here's where you get your hot roasted peanuts, those big double-jointed humpbacked peanuts, five a sack." I passed him by and still had my nickel.

Then I came to a man sitting on the ground, a deep-chested man with a face that had quiet on it and wouldn't bawl at you. I noticed he was barefoot. I looked up from his bare feet to see his arms gone, only stumps of arms at his shoulders. Between the first two toes of his right foot he held a card and lifted it toward me and said, "Take it and read it." I read a perfect handwriting, every letter shaped smooth and nice. It said, "I can write your name for you on a card for you to keep. The charge is only ten cents." I looked into his face. I said, "I would if I had the ten cents. All I've got is a nickel." I took out the nickel and turned my pockets inside out and showed him that besides the nickel there was only a knife, a piece of string, and a buckeye. He took the nickel in his left foot. He put a pen between the first two toes of his right foot and on the card wrote "Charles A. Sandburg," lifted the foot up toward me, and I took the card. I looked at it. It was the prettiest my name had ever been written. His face didn't change. All the time it kept that quiet look that didn't strictly belong with a circus. I was near crying. I said some kind of thanks and picked up my feet and ran.

The great P. T. Barnum himself never met my eyes but I did see Mr. Bailey of the firm of Barnum & Bailey on a bright summer morning in a black swallowtail coat giving orders and running the circus in the big green pasture that soon was subdivided into city lots. I told the kids who hadn't seen Bailey that I had seen him real as life. And with the kids who had seen him I joined in saying, "Wasn't he something to look at? And think of it, he's nearly as great a man as Barnum himself."

We heard him three years straight. He came in October, harvesttime when the farmers brought money to town. He was a spieler with a wagon who stood at the end of his wagon with a gasoline flare lighting his face. He introduced a burnt-cork banjoist who sang, among other songs:

> Oh money is the milk in the cocoanut.
> Oh money is the milk in the jug.
>   When you got lots of money
>   You feel very funny,
>   And snug as a bug in a rug.

Then he stood up with a mischievous smile on his face and held before his eyes a box about three inches long, an inch high, and an inch wide. He squinted through it and then explained that by looking through this mystery box you could see what was going on around a corner from you. If the curtain wasn't down at the window where a woman was undressing you could stand under the window and see what was going on. "This for the unheard-of and preposterous price of only twenty-five cents." Having sold this to a few farm hands who only half believed him but were willing to give it a try, he came to his next spiel and this one I remember every word of: "We come now to the little Jerusalem Undertaker." He was holding up a fine-tooth comb. "Yes, what we have here is the little Jerusalem Undertaker, catches them one and all, both great and small. It is made of gen-you-wine buffalo horn. I was there myself when the buffalo was killed. Think of it, the little Jerusalem Undertaker, gen-you-wine buffalo horn—and only a dime, ten cents. Now don't crowd there. You boys down there, you get out of the way and give these people the chance of a lifetime."

Over the town on many a summer night went the Moonlight Quartette. Us kids would follow them for blocks. They could harmonize. They were in the going three summers and then vanished. They had voices, love of music, a love of life, and love of girls and women. Where they got their songs I never heard. "I Found a Horseshoe," "Standing on the Walls of Zion," "Mother, You Are Kind, I Know," "Sweet Chiming Bells," "We Are Four Bums, Four Jolly Good Bums," I heard from them for the first time and made them my own.

One Sunday afternoon a bunch of us had come together in front of the Olson store, most of us about sixteen or seventeen years of age. We were going to have a photograph made of the bunch. We counted and there were twelve of us. Someone said, "Then we can show people what the Dirty Dozen looks like." And the name Dirty Dozen stuck. It sounded like we were a gang and went in for gang fights. But the Dirty Dozen never fought another gang nor did we have any fights among ourselves. Seven of the twelve were sons of Americans from Sweden. Four were "native American." One was the son of a Frenchman. Only one of the dozen was ever convicted and sent to prison. That was years later and the offense was petty larceny and none of us held it against him. He had just been kind of forgetful and had come to like "nice things" and the women he went with liked "nice things."

Ed Rosenberg should have been counted with the Dirty Dozen. It was they worked out his nickname. He was pale and slim, a little undersized, always cheery and with his own sense of humor. He muffed an easy fly once and from then on we called him "Muff," or more often "Muffa." When running a race on a cinder path one day he stumbled and fell and got up to say, "I hit de grit." And from then on it was "Muffa de Grit." He knocked in a winning run in a ball game and was lit up about it and strutted around with his head high crying, "Who won the game? Eddie Ampa! Eddie Ampa!" Where he picked up the "Ampa" we didn't know but it sounded right, and now his name was "Muffa de Grit Eddie Ampa." Out of some sidewalk scuffling with a bigger fellow Eddie came saying, "He gave me de grunt." So for quite a while whenever Ed Rosenberg was seen coming to join the bunch he heard them calling all together and with laughing faces, "Here comes Muffa de Grit Eddie Ampa de Grunt." We missed him when he went over to Moline to work in the Deere plow factory, where they called him by his right name.

Charles ("Frenchy") Juneau is past any forgetting, one of the best chums I had. His father was a short, sturdy man with a head and beard for all the world like you see in portraits of Victor Hugo. And Frenchy himself had something of the Napoleon face and head. He could pull a lock of his black hair down the forehead, stick his right hand into his coat below the lapels, and ask, "If I'm not Napoleon, who am I?" He had worked as a metal-polisher in a stove factory in Aurora and when the works shut down he came to his father's home in Galesburg, held down several jobs he didn't like, and after a time went back to Aurora as a metal-polisher when the stove factory opened again. He didn't care for books nor singing as I did but we were "good company." We would go downtown, walk Main Street, buy a half-dozen cream puffs for a dime, walk Main Street eating our cream puffs till they were gone, walk around the Public Square, and go back to Berrien Street calling it a merry evening.

We went together to see William Jennings Bryan get off a train and get on a platform on Mulberry Street next to the Q. tracks and make a speech. Again later when Bryan was speaking in Monmouth, sixteen miles on the Q., we rode the cowcatcher of an engine from Galesburg to Monmouth on a cold October night. We were chilled through and Frenchy bought a pint of blackberry brandy. We drank it and it warmed us. This was the only time we went in for a little booze. After we heard Bryan speak and after we rode an engine cowcatcher back to Galesburg, we went back to our old ways of walking Main Street eating cream puffs.

We went that same fall to a big tent on the Knox campus and heard Bob Ingersoll give a speech lambasting the Democrats and Free Silver. But Frenchy and I went out of our way to get a sack of cream puffs and standing on the edge of the crowd we listened to the famous Republican orator from Peoria and munched our cream puffs. One night when the bakery was out of cream puffs we tried chocolate éclairs and decided, "Never again if we can get cream puffs." I remember nothing in particular of what Frenchy said or did that made him such good company except he had brightness and drollery and when we had nothing to talk about it was good just being together.

A half-block south of the Olson store lived the Swanson family. Billy Swanson sometimes joined the bunch and his nickname out of the Seventh Ward schoolyard stuck. When he was seen coming toward the Schulz store, the cry went, "Billy Billy Wanton, Bum Bum Bum." How that got started and why it went on for years I could only guess and guess again.

Billy's older brother "Monk" hardly ever dropped in on the bunch. His face was good-looking enough but by a little imagining you could say it had a monkey look. The nickname "Monk" stayed with him and he didn't mind it. We talked a lot about a mistake Monk made and a hard lesson he learned. He saw a watermelon car in the Q. yards over near Mike O'Connor's livery stable. He knew about cars and melons. The notion took him one afternoon that he would have to have a watermelon, cut it in two with a knife and eat the pink hearts of it. The taste of watermelon was there in a thirst on his tongue. So what does he do? He breaks the seal of the freight car. He pries and wrenches at the seal till it breaks. He pulls the door open, climbs up, and picks him one melon. He hides somewhere in the yards and has begun eating his melon. Then the yard police find him and he gets something like two years in the state prison. I remember how in later years Mart couldn't get over it. He would say of a sudden, with no connection with what we had been talking about, "Wasn't that a hell of a deal they gave Monk Swanson when all he wanted was one watermelon to eat on a hot summer day?" And once I said to Mart, "In a railroad town on a division point what is more holy than the seal on a loaded freight car? They have made it a law that breaking the seal is a penitentiary offense. Monk stole one melon to eat by himself. For that he might have got thirty days in the county jail. But in order to get the melon he broke a freight-car seal, which the law holds a crime worse than stealing. Monk didn't know that till they had him in court. They asked him why he didn't know it and all he could say was that nobody ever told him." Then Mart pressed me, "What I asked you, wasn't it a hell of a deal?" And I caved in, "Sure it was a hell of a deal, as rotten as what the law one time handed our Old Man."

There was a summer Sunday afternoon that eight of the Dirty Dozen could never forget. We had met in front of Schulz's, the sun pouring down hot and sweltering. Someone said, "Let's go out to that pond on the Booth farm and have a swim." So the eight of us started. On the way, on the edge of town, just inside the city limits, we came to the "Old Brick," as we called it, a pond about thirty yards long by twenty yards wide. Once there had been a small brickyard there and it was all gone except the pond and a big wheel we used to dive from. The bottom was slushy mud with broken bricks and pieces of tile and glass here and there. The water at its deepest was up to our shoulders. We had grown tired of it as a swimming hole and we had heard too that in the new homes built near it the people didn't like to have the boys swimming so close. But it was nearly three miles to the Booth farm pond and we decided we wouldn't walk those three miles on this hot day. We would have our swim in the Old Brick, dirty and mud slushy as it was. We began peeling off our clothes. All of us had stepped into the water except slow Ed Rosenberg, Muffa de Grit. Then came the surprise. "What the hell," yelled one of the boys. "Look! by God, that's Chief Wiley!"

And there on Day Street we saw the police patrol wagon and coming toward us big Policeman Frank Peterson and big Chief Wiley. The chief had his right hand raised away in the air and he was hollering, "Stay where you are, you're under arrest!" As he came closer we heard, "You boys ought to know you're not allowed to swim here. It's against the law and every one of you will get into the wagon and come along with me." We got into part of our clothes, some of us finishing dressing in the patrol wagon—all of us except Ed Rosenberg, Muffa de Grit. He had grabbed his pants and shirt and made a run for the Narrow Gauge Railway near by and the last seen of him he was nearly out of sight hot-footing it along the Narrow Gauge.

The patrol wagon had no top. The seats ran lengthwise. Four of us sat on one side, three on the other, looking at each other and wondering, taking side glances at Wiley and Peterson at the wagon end. We were going to be hauled along streets where people knew us. We would probably ride up Main Street for anybody and everybody to see us—arrested and on the way to the calaboose! And after a night in the calaboose we would be taken to court and there would be a trial and we wondered what would be the worst they could do to us—how did we know? The law is the law and anything can happen in the law. There was my nice brother Mart opposite me, the first time that any Sandburg in Galesburg had been arrested! There was Bohunk Calkins and "Jiddy" Ericson and Charlie Bloomgreen from their nice homes and decent people on Berrien Street and now in a wagon watched by two policemen, on their way in broad daylight on a Sunday to be hauled to the Cherry Street calaboose and thrown into stinking cells with the Saturday-night drunks and disorderlies.

The wagon moved north on Day Street seven blocks, reached South Street, and we had seen nobody we knew who had seen us. At South Street the wagon turned east. After two and a half blocks east the wagon was turned around in front of what was known as "Isa Magee's house." Chief Wiley stood up and yelled in his best slide-trombone voice, "Isa [Eye-sah], come out! Isa, come out!" No Isa

came out and again Chief Wiley yelled, "Isa, come out or I'll have to
go in and drag you out!" Soon a door opened and a blowsy heavy
woman in a thin gown stood looking toward us. We were wondering
if we were going to have a woman for company on our way up Main
Street, "a bad woman with a bad name." Then Wiley was yelling,
across the sidewalk and the fence, about twenty yards to the porch
where Isa Magee stood, "Isa, you've got a man in there, haven't
you?" Isa said something in a low voice that didn't reach us. Then
Wiley again, "Isa, I'm telling you to speak up and tell me if you've
got a man in there." Isa mumbled a feeble "Yes." Then Wiley, "Tell
that man to come out. If he don't come out there'll be trouble." The
man came out, all his clothes on, coat, pants, and all. He looked a
little scared, like he thought he would have to join us in the wagon
along with Isa. Then Wiley, "Now I've had a good look at both of
you, I'm telling you you better behave yourselves or there'll be
trouble. You better remember I gave you warning." That was all.
Then Wiley told the driver, "Drive on," and he drove on and we
were glad we were not going to have Isa Magee, a bad woman with
a bad name, for company up Main Street.

The afternoon was still hot and along Main Street we still didn't
see anybody we knew who knew us. At the calaboose on Cherry
Street we were locked up, three of us in one cell where there were
four drunks sobering up and the other four in a cell where there
were three drunks sobering up—no chairs, no cots, you sat on the
stone floor or kept standing. The air was thick with heat and with
stinks of whisky and the smells of sweating and puking drunks. We
had talked a little on the wagon. Now we talked more. Some of the
boys said, "They won't do anything to us. They'll let us out tomor-
row if we'll promise not to go swimmin in the Old Brick again."
Others said, "You can't tell what they'll do. The law is the law. It's
a hell of a note they should arrest us and throw us in the wagon and
then here in this dirty hole. If they've gone this far you can't tell
what they'll do."

It was about three o'clock that Sunday afternoon when they
locked us up. It was seven o'clock, when they were getting ready to
feed the drunks, that they unlocked our cells and said we could go
home. And they said more, "You're under orders to appear in court

tomorrow morning before Justice of the Peace Holcomb at ten o'clock."

We walked to our Berrien Street homes, talking all the way about what Justice Holcomb would hand us in the morning. After a lot of talking most of us believed the justice wouldn't give us jail sentences but maybe he would give us light fines, maybe "two dollars and costs." When Tom Beckum or Peg Hoey got their names many times in the papers for being drunk and disorderly Justice Holcomb fined them "two dollars and costs." The costs were five dollars and some of us wondered where we would dig up such money. I could pay the fine but not the costs. And I couldn't tell beforehand what my father would say if Mart or I told him, "You've got to let me have five dollars for costs or a son of August Sandburg goes to jail."

We stood before Justice Holcomb the next morning. We pleaded guilty to the charge that we had stripped naked and gone swimming in an old brickyard pond inside the city limits on yesterday's Sunday afternoon. Justice Holcomb gave us a little talk like he was a good uncle of ours and we should understand it was against the law to do what we did. He had us each promise we would never again go swimming in that pond inside the city limits. It crossed my mind but I didn't say it to the justice, "The nearest house to that pond is over four hundred yards away. The people there would have to use strong field glasses to see whether we were naked or not. They telephoned the police because they wanted to make trouble and to have fun watching the patrol wagon come."

We walked away, glad to be free and footloose again. What we agreed on was, "The damned police didn't have to arrest us and throw us in that wagon and take us to the lockup. Not one of us had heard there was any law about not swimming in that pond. Why didn't they put up a sign 'Against the law to swim here'? We have been swimming in that pond for years. If they had just got out of their damned wagon and told us we were breaking the law every one of us would have promised never to swim there again and we would have kept the promise. What's the matter with the police? We don't understand them and they don't even try to understand us. We went naked into the pond because we wanted to cool off on a hot afternoon and we didn't want to get our clothes wet by wearing them swimming. And if you're naked in water up to your shoulders who can see how naked you are? And if you're naked and not trying to show off you're naked, ain't it the same as the cats, dogs, cows, and horses that all the time go naked and nobody telephones the police about it? All right, the law is the law and the hell with it."

We had our feeling too about Chief Wiley having a wagonload of boys not yet fifteen driven around in front of the town's most notorious "bad woman," yelling for her to come out, yelling for a man to come out, then telling them they better behave themselves and driving on. What could it mean? We were sure there was something more back of it. It seemed to us that both Chief Wiley and the law were somehow silly and maybe crooked. We didn't know for sure. What we didn't know and what we wanted to know we couldn't learn from the police.

At home the father and mother were quiet and decent about the whole affair. They had seen their sons born naked, had seen them in washtubs naked, and though they didn't say so they seemed to agree with us that the law and the police had been somewhat silly.

It happened too that the policeman, Frank Peterson, who was with Chief Wiley, rented the second-story rooms of our house. I think Peterson went along under orders from Wiley and if he had been acting on his own he would have talked to us and given us warnings and let it go at that instead of hollering like Wiley, "Stay where you are, you're under arrest!" If you're a grown man and you hear a police chief say, "You're under arrest," it gives you at least a little shiver. And if you're not yet fifteen and you hear it there is something terrorizing about it—unless you're what they call an Old Offender who has been to reform schools.

I still refuse to feel the slightest guilt about the first time I was arrested and locked up by the police. I am sure Muffa de Grit would agree with me. He ran out the Narrow Gauge Railway till the police wagon was out of sight, put on his pants and shirt, sneaked back toward the Old Brick, saw no one was around, and picked up his stockings, shoes, and hat and went home. He half expected the police would come for him at his home but they didn't. The case wasn't that important. We all handed it to Muffa de Grit. He had quick wits and was fast on his feet.

Mart always claimed he put on his clothes before going to the wagon but that I took my clothes to the wagon and dressed there, which I insisted wasn't so. He claimed that in the wagon I had the blues and he was gay and cheerful. Year after year we enjoyed these disputes about what each one did when we were "thrown in the jug."

Jesse James became real to us. For years the paper-covered books came out about Jesse. I read five of them before I was fourteen, and us kids talked a lot about him. I talked with men who had read and heard about Jesse. He and his brother Frank had robbed banks and held up trains in states next to Illinois, just across the Mississippi River in Missouri, Iowa, Minnesota. I was four years old when Jesse was killed in his home in St. Joe, Missouri, where he was living under the name of Mr. Howard. He had trusted young Robert Ford but Ford was "the dirty little coward, who shot Mr. Howard," as the song has it. We could see Jesse standing on a chair to hang a picture on the wall and young Ford shooting him in the back to get the reward money paid to anyone who would "get" Jesse James "dead or alive."

We believed Jesse and Frank had good horses and could ride fast many miles after a train holdup or a bank robbery. And they could find friends who would hide them, or they could live two or three days in a cornfield or in caves or in thick tree clumps. Jesse could ride a horse past a telegraph pole and while riding put every bullet of his two six-shooters into that pole. He was a dead shot and those hunting him were sensible to be scared of his revolvers. And often he carried not only two but six shooting irons. Mostly it was the rich he robbed, and often he gave to the poor or he wouldn't have had so many friends willing to hide him. Jesse and Frank when they did a job on a railroad train or a bank, they did it more neat and handy and rode away faster and hid out quicker than any other robbers the country had ever seen. They were good to their one-armed mother, who had had her arm shot off by Northern Unionist guerillas. And Jesse read his Bible and never smoked nor drank whisky nor gambled nor spit "goddam" out of his mouth like real bad men. All this we had heard and read and more than half believed. These things caught our minds and hearts and made us believe Jesse James a hero worth looking at and remembering.

Later I came to believe that Jesse was a killer, a murderer who when the feeling came on him could put a bullet into a man and like it. The song helped Jesse's memory among folks. The song runs along as though Jesse was a good and brave man who had been wronged.

It was years later in Kansas City that I got on the phone the office of a lawyer, Jesse James, Jr. He had written a book, *Jesse James, My Father*, a well-written book that I had read. He may have been more than half right in his preface: "I defy the world to show that my father ever slew a human being except in the protection of his own life, or as a soldier in honorable warfare. His only brother, whose name was linked with his all the years of his life, is a free man today, acquitted of all crime." But the son of the famous robber wasn't in and I had to be taking a train. Then a few years after that I rode in a motorcar from Manhattan, Kansas, to Kansas City with a granddaughter of Jesse James. She was an intelligent and charming woman and I'm sure her grandfather would have been proud of her. She agreed with me that Robin Hood in England was probably much the same kind of fellow as her grandfather and if England can have her Robin Hood ballads we have a right to our Jesse James song.

Sometimes the names and faces of certain boys come back clear as daylight and the talk, the pranks, the games, we shared. Or again I look back to pieces of mischief or fun and I can't place the boys who were in on it. At baseball in a street or a pasture Fatty Beckman and Skinny Seeley and I were the craziest. We began playing earlier in the spring and kept on later in the fall than the other boys. We began playing earlier in the morning and we played later in the evening than the others. We played in late October and early November till the first frosts came and the last russet apple had fallen from a tree at the back fence of the pasture. Fatty wasn't fat—he was extra-stout and his cheeks puffed out a little. And Skinny wasn't skinny—he was merely lean and hard, with a quick smile showing a fine set of even teeth. I was "Cully," I suppose because it was considered a funny improvement on "Charlie." Fatty Beckman was the son of a widow and in September took days off from ballplaying to haul a wagon from house to house selling cabbages at five cents a head, earning fifty to sixty cents a day and jingling a pocket full of nickels when he came to the pasture for a last hour of two-old-cat before supper. Skinny began hanging around the Auditorium, the new theater, helping the stage carpenter "Husky" Johnson, and the property man "Cully" Rose. They trained him so when he went to Chicago he caught on as a stagehand and spent his life till old age as a stagehand there. Skinny had an elder sister Minnie, good-looking, prim, straight-laced, who for years clerked in the big O. T. Johnson dry-goods store on Main Street. She was always on time to and from the store. For years you could safely set your clock by when she came along Berrien Street.

The time came when I found other chums with different interests. There was Willis Calkins, a half-block away at Pearl and Berrien, his father a trolley-car motorman, clean and kindly, with a laughter for all weathers, his mother a beautiful woman whom we saw in one short year fade away from consumption. Willis was their only child. They were a singing family with Kentucky ancestors. Willis played the banjo, showed me the chords and how to accompany songs.

My first musical instrument had been a willow whistle I cut for myself. The pencil between the teeth and the tune rapped out by the right thumb followed. Then came the comb with paper over the comb's teeth and a mouth vocalizing—not so good. The ten-cent kazoo was better—you could imitate, in crude fashion, either a brass band or a rooster. A tin fife, a wooden flageolet, were interesting, and the ocarina surpassed all the wind instruments I fooled with. My first string instrument was a cigar-box banjo where I cut and turned pegs and strung the wires myself—not so good, neither tunes nor chords could be coaxed from it. A slightly disabled concertina, at fifty cents from Mr. Gumbiner's New York Pawn Shop on Main Street between Kellogg and Seminary, came next, developed wheezes, and was discarded. I tried the Old Man's accordion and it wheezed too often. Then came a two-dollar banjo from Mr. Gumbiner. This was a honey and from Willis I learned the chords. From the gracious Mrs. Schwartz on Ferris Street I had three banjo lessons at twenty-five cents a lesson. I should have gone on but it was Hard Times.

Willis could give the national popular songs, minstrel ditties, old ballads, a favorite of his about "Sweet Polly Perkins on Arlington Green." He had a smooth baritone voice, loved girls and women, and put an easy charm into his singing. He had a long nose on a horse face, his good humor was irresistible, and he was welcome at all parties. He had a lumbering torso, a rolling gait, and a rupture for which he wore a truss. Someone nicknamed him "Bohunk" and it stuck. One summer Bohunk and I walked a dozen times the three miles south and east to the pond on the Booth farm for the swimming there, "water up to your chin."

It was in these fields out near town we saw timothy hay growing and oats and wheat. Ever since when I meet a field of them I speak to them as old friends. It was Indian corn, though, that hit me deepest. There was sweet corn for corn on the cob at the dinner table and there were acres of broomcorn and sorghum. But the Indian corn stood tallest and ran for miles on miles, food for men and horses, and a wonder about the little white soft ears of June becoming the tough, yellow, hard, and husky ears of late September that could lie bare on the frozen ground and wait to be used. We saw old zigzag rail fences go down and the Osage-orange hedge take its place. I picked hedge branches with the right crook to them and cut with a jack-knife the club I wanted for playing shinny.

Walking back from the Booth farm pond Bohunk and I would make a decision where Farnham Street crossed the Peoria tracks. We could bear to the left, make a short cut across the Lombard campus, and on a hot day take a big cool drink of water from a cast-iron dipper chained to the Lombard pump. Or we could take a long walk on Farnham to Brooks Street and steal some luscious eating apples from Jon W. Grubb's orchard, tucking our pockets full and then circling our shirts over the waistband of the pants with a line of apples. The question we discussed at Farnham and the Peoria tracks was simple: "What'll it be? A short cut and a drink or a long walk and apples?" Forty years after that summer I met Bohunk in a hotel lobby in St. Paul, Minnesota, and with a wide grin of warm fellowship, he busted out, "What'll it be, Cully, a short cut and a drink or a long walk and apples?"

When the Calkins family moved out the Sjodins moved in—Swedes who had lived in Chicago fifteen years and lost their Swedish accent.

Mr. Sjodin was a journeyman tailor, could measure, cut, and sew a suit of clothes. Mr. Sjodin walked with his head high and his shoulders erect and thrown back as if to say, "I am a free man and I bow to no masters or overlords." He was the first real radical I knew as a boy. In his carriage of head and shoulders as I saw him many a time he seemed to be saying, "I cringe before no man." Then on talking with him you would find he wanted a new society, a new world where no man had to cringe before another. He was an anarchist, a Populist, and a Socialist, at home with anyone who was against the government and the plutocrats who rob the poor. I have not yet found out who were the "three tailors of Tooley Street," then famous, who met and drew up a declaration that began "We, the people." I am sure, however, that Mr. Sjodin would have been perfectly at home with them. He was a skilled tailor who took good care of his wife, one daughter, and two sons and liked nothing better than a few glasses of beer with plenty of talk about politics and the coming revolution.

There are companionships in early life having color and mystery. We cannot measure or analyze exactly what they did to us. And we like to look back on them. John Sjodin is one of these. He was two or three years older than I and had worked two years in a Milwaukee Avenue department store in Chicago. He had taken three lessons in clog dancing and from him I learned three steps to clog and never forgot them. He had absorbed much of Chicago's vivid and reckless flair and could give the feel of it in his talk. He had read widely. We lay on the grass next to the ditch on Pearl Street in front of his home on summer nights. He could talk on and on about the exploits of a detective named Macon Moore. We both rated Macon Moore higher than Old Cap Collier and Nick Carter. John was the first to acquaint me with the verb "snuck." Macon Moore could sneak and when he sneaked John had it that he "snuck." John appreciated having a listener who hung on through every bloody clew and every fight and escape till the arrest and punishment of the dastards.

John at that time could be jolly, liked jokes and funny stories and had plenty of them. I remember him saying more than once, "Keep the head, hands, and feet warm and the rest of the body will be fine." He was, like his father, a hard-and-fast political-action radical. "The

big corporations" were running the country, as John saw it, and the
time would come when the working people, farmers and laborers,
would organize and get political power and take over the big cor-
porations, beginning with the government ownership of railroads.
Always John was sensitive about the extremes of the rich and the
poor, the poor never knowing what tomorrow would bring them
and the rich having more than they knew what to do with. I never
saw John in a fight and I know he wouldn't have made any kind of
a leader of a mob or a riot. He would argue his points with anybody
but he wouldn't let an argument or a debate run into a quarrel. He
had his own reverence for life and said many a time that he couldn't
hate a millionaire and most of the rich were sorry fools who didn't
know what to do with their money except to put it to work making
more money. "He makes his first million and then wants to make his
second million," said John. "It's a fever that gets a hold on them and
they can't shake it off. They get into fights with other millionaires
about franchises and special privileges for robbing the people. Look
at Yerkes in Chicago. After serving a term in a Philadelphia peni-
tentiary as an embezzler he comes to Chicago and buys enough
aldermen to get the franchises he wants and soon he is running the
streetcar systems of Chicago and making millions. He won't go in
cahoots with other millionaires so they make war on him and say he
is no better than Jesse James, and the only difference is that Jesse
rode a horse."

I didn't argue with John. I asked him many questions and he
nearly always had answers. He believed deeply in a tide of feeling
among the masses of the people. This tide would grow and become
stronger and in generations to come the American people would
challenge and break the power of the corporations, the interests of
special privilege. There was no real difference between the Repub-
lican and the Democratic parties. Both took money from the cor-
porations and did what the corporations wanted done. John could
recite how many millions of acres the Union Pacific Railway got as
a free gift from the Federal Government, "every other quarter sec-
tion of land along the right of way besides billions of dollars to help
build the railway." Then John would chuckle, "And they say the
government should just govern and not meddle in private business."

John was not yet a voter but he favored the People's Party, the Populists. Later he became a Socialist. He learned the trade of a painter and decorator, joined their union, and over many years was active, and sometimes an officer, in the Galesburg Trades and Labor Assembly. He organized the Galesburg local of the Socialist Party. I had heard him often say he would like to be a merchant. "I have a head for business." He started a small neighborhood grocery and for years made his living out of it while year after year he ran for mayor on the Socialist ticket and introduced out-of-town speakers at Socialist Party meetings and rallies. His main influence on me was to start me thinking. He made me know I ought to know more about what was going on in politics, industry, business, and crime over the widespread American scene.

I was eleven when I had the first regular job that paid me cash. There had been odd jobs for earning money and there were Saturdays and after school hours when we took gunny sacks and went around streets, alleys, barns, and houses hunting in ditches and rubbish piles for rags, bones, scrap iron, and bottles, for which cash was paid us, my gunny sack one week bringing me eighteen cents. Now I was wearing long pants and every Friday was payday.

My employer was the real estate firm of Callender & Rodine, their office on the second floor of a building on Main midway between Kellogg and Prairie. Mr. Callender was a heavy man with a large blond mustache. His head was wide between the ears and in front of him, at his middle, he had a smooth, round "bay window," easy to carry. Mr. Rodine was the lean member and had a pink face with blue eyes. If a customer spoke Swedish and was a temperance man, it seemed Mr. Rodine handled him. If he was Irish and liked his whisky or a German who liked beer, it seemed Mr. Callender took care of him. They had their signals and worked together something like that when a man wanted to buy or sell a house, a lot, or a farm.

Their office was large and I would guess it was ten paces from the west wall where Mr. Callender had his desk to the east wall where Mr. Rodine had his big roll-top desk with pigeonholes to stick papers in and try afterward to remember into which pigeonhole this or that paper had been stuck. It was Mr. Callender who told me about pigeonholes in a desk and what they are for. It came into my head, but I didn't mention it to Mr. Callender, that some of the pigeon-holes were so thin you couldn't find a pigeon so thin that it could fly into one of those holes. Nor did I mention to Mr. Callender that it would be fun to bring in five or six pigeons and put them in the pigeonholes of the two desks so that when Mr. Callender and Mr. Rodine rolled back the tops of their desks the first thing in the morning, the office would be full of pigeons and wings flapping and fluttering. This idea, this scheme, I liked to roll around in my head and I told other boys about it, but no grownups. One of the boys said, "If you did that, they would prosecute you." So we made the boy tell us what it is to be prosecuted and for several weeks we saluted him, "Hello, Prosecutor" and "Here's Little Prosecutor again."

Mr. Callender and Mr. Rodine treated me nice and fair. The longest talk I had with either of them was when Mr. Callender told me what was expected of me, what my work was to be and how I should do it. After that, for month after month, about the only talk between us was on Friday morning when Mr. Callender handed me my pay, saying, "Here you are," and I said, "Thanks," and skipped.

They gave me a key to the office and I unlocked the door about a quarter to eight each morning, Monday through Friday. I took a broom made of broomcorn grown near Galesburg and manufactured at Mr. Boyer's broom factory at the northwest corner of Kellogg and Berrien. I swept out the office. I came to know every floorboard of that office, the cracks and corners where I had to dig in and push to bring out the dust. I swept the office dust out into the hall. I swept it along the hall six or eight feet to the top of the wide stairway leading down to the street. Reaching the bottom of the stairs I swept the accumulations of my earnest and busy broom out onto the sidewalk of Main Street and across the sidewalk. With two or three grand final strokes of my broom I threw a half-bushel of dust and paper and string and cigar butts and chewing-tobacco cuds out on the cobblestones to join other sweepings and layers of horse droppings. If a strong east wind was blowing, it would be no time until my sweepings had been scattered all along Main Street.

I would go up the stairs to the office, stand the broom in a corner, and then pick up the wide, round, flat brass spittoon that stood at

Mr. Callender's roll-top desk. If the day before had been a busy day with plenty of callers, the spittoon might be filled to capacity with fluid content in which floated cigar butts and tobacco cuds. I carried this container out in the hall to a cubbyhole with a faucet and running cold water. I dumped, washed, rinsed, and rinsed again and took the honorable and serviceable spittoon back to its place at Mr. Callender's desk. Then I did the same cleaning on Mr. Rodine's spittoon. About once in six or eight weeks I polished the spittoons till they were bright and shining.

This morning service of mine for Callender & Rodine took less than a half-hour. Sometimes I could whisk through all the motions in fifteen or twenty minutes. If at the time a man had come to me and said he was organizing a Spittoon Cleaners' Union, I would probably have joined, if only to meet with other spittoon cleaners to see what they looked like and to talk with them about our work and our wages, fellow craftsmen enjoying fellowship. At no time did I make a complaint to Mr. Callender or Mr. Rodine. I was pleased and thankful when on Friday morning Mr. Callender would bring his right hand out of a pocket and with a look on his face as though he had almost forgotten it, he would hand me a coin with those three words, "Here you are." And I would take the coin in my hand, say, "Thanks," skip down the stairway holding the money, and on the Main Street sidewalk open my hand to see what it held and there it was, twenty-five cents of United States money, a silver quarter of a dollar.

On the second floor a few doors west of the Callender & Rodine office was the printing press and office of the *Galesburg Republican-Register*. To this place we carrier boys went as soon as school let out at half-past three in the afternoon. As the papers came off the flat bed press, we took them to a table and folded them with three motions. When I had folded the fifty or sixty papers for my route, I counted them and took them to a man who counted them again to make sure my count was correct, with one "extra" for myself. If a single paper seemed a little thick, the man would look to see whether one paper had been stuck inside of another, a trick some boys worked too often. Then with a bundle of papers under my left arm, I went down the stairs to Main Street, turned north at the next corner, and went up Prairie Street. I learned how to cross-fold a paper so it could be thrown spang against a front door. If a house was near enough, I didn't have to leave the sidewalk to make my throw. On Prairie Street, however, lived the rich and the well-to-do, most of their houses set back so far from the sidewalk that I walked in halfway or near to the house before making my throw. These steps of my feet and motions of my hands and arms I went through six days a week through summer to winter and winter to summer for more than two years.

At one house set well back a man would often be at home and expecting me and more yet, expecting the latest telegraphed news over America and the wide world. This man expecting me would step out of the door to take the paper from my hand. He was the most roly-poly fat man in town. There were other fat men who stood bigger and weighed more, but no other so roly-poly. He was round everywhere you looked at him, no straight lines, even his back curved. He was a waddly barrel of a man, with a double chin, a round face, a gray silver mustache and goatee. This was the Honorable Clark E. Carr, mentioned often as the Republican Party boss of Knox County and having a hand in national politics. He had been appointed postmaster by Republican Presidents. He was to serve as United States Minister to Denmark.

He liked to be called "Colonel" Carr, encouraged people to call him "Colonel" and editors to print "Colonel" in front of his name. I believed "Colonel" Carr had sometime and somewhere marched his men on dusty roads in sweltering sun and had seen men fall wounded and dying. But later I learned that the Civil War Governor, Richard Yates, had appointed him a staff colonel, so he was a commander without a regiment, an officer who never reached the marching and fighting fronts.

At a later time I heard Colonel Carr in a campaign speech poke fun at himself for being so fat and roly-poly. At Copenhagen he had worked out some schedule that let American pork into Denmark at a lower tariff. He mentioned this and the collops of fat and flesh on him shook with his laughter as he added, "When I was the Minister to Denmark the American hog obtained recognition!"

As a young man he was the Illinois member of the Board of Commissioners who made up the program for the exercises dedicating the cemetery on the Gettysburg Battlefield. He rode in the parade to the battlefield and had written that he noticed President Lincoln on a horse just ahead of him and how Lincoln sat straight in the saddle at first and later leaned forward with arms limp and head bent far down. This roly-poly man taking the *Republican-Register* from my hand had met Lincoln in party powwows, had heard Lincoln tell stories, and Clark E. Carr said of Lincoln, "He could make a cat laugh." In 1864 he made speeches up and down Illinois for Lincoln and at Quincy had spoken before a wild crowd of ten thousand people from the same platform as Bob Ingersoll, the Peoria lawyer

Of course the twelve-year-old boy handing him his evening paper didn't know what made Clark E. Carr so important. I knew that he had for more than thirty years met and shaken hands with all the big men of the Republican Party. I knew he could make speeches and statements that got printed. I didn't know that even though he swung a lot of power in the Republican Party he couldn't get it to give him what he wanted most of all. I learned later that he wanted to be elected to Congress and go to Washington and be a statesman. Several times he came near getting what he wanted most of all and those against him stopped him. He would have stood a better chance of getting what he wanted most of all if he had belonged to the Grand Army of the Republic, the G.A.R. During the war, when Lincoln called for fighting men, Clark E. Carr made good speeches for his party but didn't manage to get into a Union blue uniform.

Having left Mr. Carr with the latest news about how President Cleveland and the Democrats were ruining the country, I went along Prairie Street and threw a paper on the front porch of the biggest house in town. People said, "It cost more than any house ever put up in Galesburg, eighty thousand dollars." It was gray stone, three stories, with towers and fancy curves. Here lived the Honorable George A. Lawrence. He married a good woman who had a big fortune. He was a lawyer with brown sideburns that stood out and waved and shook in a strong wind.

Also not far from the Carr house was the home of Howard K. Knowles. He was in the city directory as a "capitalist." He was the first man I ever met—the few times that I handed him his newspaper

—who used that word to name his occupation. Having put it into the
city directory in that style, I thought at a later time possibly he
would have wanted a brief and simple epitaph on his gravestone:
"Howard K. Knowles, Capitalist," and then the dates of his birth and
death.

I went on with my papers to the end of Prairie Street, went a block
west to Cherry, turned south to Main, and had one copy of the *Re-
publican-Register* left to take home. I had walked about two miles.
When there was mud or snow or stormy weather it took about an
hour and a half to carry my route and in good weather about an hour
and a quarter. The *Republican-Register* paid me one dollar a week.
I was more than satisfied with that weekly silver dollar.

Walking between rows of houses, many of them set widely apart
—wider lots than at a later time—I came to know yards and trees that
had personality. I spoke greetings to certain trees that I had seen in
sun and rain in summer, and cloud and snow in winter, branches
bending down with ice on them. Here and there in a back yard
would be a tomato patch, carrots asking to be pulled out of the
ground. Some yards had apple trees, and I helped myself to the wind-
falls.

For the little building in every back yard some said "backhouse,"
some said "privy." Carrying newspapers and later slinging milk I
saw all the different styles of backhouses—the clean, roomy, elegant
ones with latticework in front, those with leaky roofs and loose
boards where the cold rain and wind came through, a few with soft
paper that had no printing but mostly it was newspapers neatly cut
or catalogues. When you had to go to the backhouse you stepped
out into the weather—in rain or sleet. If the thermometer said zero
you left your warm spot near the stove and the minute you were out
the back door the cold put a crimp and a shiver in you.

About once a year a Negro we called Mister Elsey would come in
the night with his wagon and clean the vault of our privy. He lived
on Pine Street in a house he owned. We had respect for him and
called him Mister. His work was always done at night. He came and
went like a shadow in the moon.

I looked up the word "privy," finding it means "private or secret."
For hundreds of years every king of England had a "privy coun-

cilor" and when he wanted advice in private or secret he called in his privy councilor. When there was a secret deal on they would say of any man in on it, "He is privy to the affair." One of the oldest and most respectable words in the English language, I found out later, is the word "privy." When indoor plumbing came in the word "privy" went out, and it was "the water closet," which changed to the "toilet," the "bathroom," the "can," the "john," and worst of all, the "rest room."

I came to know the houses and yards of Prominent People. Their names were often in the paper. When they left for Kewanee, Peoria, or Chicago, I would read a "personal" about it in the paper. And I would notice the green blinds pulled over the front windows and three or four days of my papers waiting for them on the front porch when they came back from Kewanee, Peoria, or Chicago. If snow or rain was blowing in on the porch floor I would pull the doormat over the papers and have a feeling that I was not completely useless though it would be many years yet before I could vote for a President of the United States. Once I said, "When they come home they can read in the bottom paper that they left town, and the first paper I hand them when they come back will tell them they have come back and from where they have come back."

I had seen at his work one morning the man who went up and down Main Street and got the "personals," a short man with sandy hair, thin sandy sideburns, and a freckled face. He was writing in a notebook, standing and writing. I went closer and heard him asking a man how names were spelled. He was particular about the spelling of the names. Having written the names he shut his book, thanked the man, put the book in his left coat pocket and went into Kellogg & Drake's dry-goods store. There I saw him speaking to Ed Drake with the notebook again in his left hand as he wrote more names. Mr. Callender happening along, I asked him who was the freckle-faced man writing names in a book. "That's Fred Jeliff, reporter for the *Republican-Register*," said Mr. Callender.

I was fascinated. I could see Fred Jeliff walking back to the *Republican-Register* office and sitting at a table to write with a lead pencil on the same kind of paper the *Republican-Register* was printed on. I had seen him carry the sheets he wrote to a man standing at a case where each letter of the alphabet had its own little room. They called the man a "typesetter." He would read the names on the sheets of paper Fred Jeliff handed him, pick the letters with his right hand and put them in a "stick" in his left hand, the stick being exactly as wide as a newspaper column. After many other motions there would be ink on the type, and it would "press" on paper, and the *Republican-Register* for that day was printed and the names would be spelled like Fred Jeliff wrote them in his notebook up and down Main Street. I believed you could be a newspaper reporter if you could spell names and write them with a pencil on paper.

There came a year when I was deep in the newspaper business. I carried a morning route of Chicago papers at seventy-five cents a week and the afternoon route of the *Republican-Register* at a dollar a week. Every morning, weekday and Sunday, I was on a Q. depot platform when the Fast Mail train from Chicago came in at seventen. Out of a mail car as the train slowed to a stop rolled the bundles we picked up and carried across Seminary Street to the front of the Crocker & Robbins grocery where a covered platform kept rain or snow off us.

We were working for Mr. Edwards, who had a store on Main Street where he sold books and stationery and kept a newsstand. He had long red whiskers and a Santa Claus look if he wasn't excited. He told us what to do and he wasn't bossy or fussed up. I used to wonder whether he had been a boy one time and what a quiet boy he must have been. When two or three boys started scuffling he would step in like a mother hen who was going to have peace and no blood spilled.

We cut the ropes from the bundles, and there fresh as summer-morning dew or winter-daybreak frost were the *Chicago Tribune*, the *Chicago Record*, the *Chicago Inter-Ocean*, the *Chicago Times*, the *Chicago Herald*, the *Chicago Chronicle*. Each boy got his papers, giving each paper one fold, put them under his left arm, and started on his route, knowing well what he would catch if he threw a Democratic *Chicago Times* on the porch of a house where they were paying for the Republican *Chicago Tribune*. "When I pay for the *Times* I don't want the goddam *Chronicle*," a man blasted me when for once I gave him the wrong paper. I learned how wild and crazy a man can be if he doesn't get the favorite newspaper he has been reading for years. I noticed that the *Chicago Tribune* readers were usually regular Republican Party workers and those taking the *Chicago Times* were mostly red-hot Democrats. Where the other papers were two cents a copy, the *Chicago Record*, started by Victor Lawson, was one cent. You couldn't tell whether a man was taking the *Record* because it was cheapest or because it was the only Chicago paper independent in politics and giving what both sides had to say. When a house was taking two papers, one of them was the *Record*.

On the morning route I covered South and Mulberry streets and ended on Main Street. On Sunday mornings from seven-thirty till around noon, I pulled a little wagon of the Chicago papers, selling them at five cents a copy and getting one cent for myself out of each copy sold. I had about fifty regular customers and when there was extra-special big news, such as the assassination of Mayor Carter Harrison in Chicago, I sold ten to twenty more papers. Along with the other boys I would end up about one o'clock at Mr. Edwards' store on Main Street. After we turned in our money to Mr. Edwards, five or six of us would cross the street to a lunch counter. Always what we did was the same as the Sunday before. We climbed up on the stools and each of us said with a grin, "One and a bun," meaning one fried egg laid between a split bun—an egg sandwich. We were hungry and we smacked and talked between bites of our five-cent snack. Each of us paid his nickel and felt chesty about it. It was like we were grown men and we had money we'd earned and could eat away from home. We were paying cash on the line for what we ate. We ordered what we wanted and got waited on. Some of us had pants that needed patching but we were little independent merchants spending a nickel of our profits.

Often on my route in winter I stopped at the stove in the back of the Carlin grocery in the triangle at Main, Pine, and the Knoxville Road and looked through the Chicago papers. I tried to get my head around The Tariff. If I could really understand The Tariff I would know for sure whether it was too high or too low or whether we should forget The Tariff and have Free Trade. I tried to picture the Pauper Labor of Europe, people working for near nothing and living on near nothing and how if we didn't make them pay and pay to bring what they made into this country, the American factories would shut down, throw their workers out of work, and then what? Then "grass would grow in the streets." How do streets look when grass grows in them? There would be no iron horseshoes, no wagon wheels, so instead of dust in July there would be green grass. From there I couldn't go on. I did some guessing about what the men out of work would be doing but my guessing didn't get anywhere.

The day came when I was tired of reading in Chicago papers about "grass growing in the streets." Those who were saying it had picked it up from others and it was a kind of jabber they hoped to scare people with. I quit trying to imagine grass growing in the streets. And I quit trying to imagine the Pauper Labor of Europe. It was hard enough to understand the ten-hour workday in the Q. shops right under my eyes. Sitting by the Carlin hot stove drying and warming my feet, I read about the Tariff on tin and the Tariff on wool. They were a blessing to the American workingman, said one paper, and another said they were a curse. I began to doubt whether there were tariffs on tin and wool. It was some kind of a game they had made up so they could have the excitement of arguing to see if anyone would run out of arguments.

Once on a rainy Sunday I stopped under cover to read in the *Chicago Inter-Ocean* magazine section about a boy who had a visit with the poet Oliver Wendell Holmes. Holmes talked with the boy about how, why, and when he wrote his poems. I read the article twice and came away from it feeling I myself had had a visit with the famous poet and I would have to read his writings because I liked him as a man.

At the Carlin store I saw a young man carrying boxes and bags out of the store to a delivery wagon. He was a six-footer with big shoulders, a round head and face, a strong jaw and chin, a pleasant smile. How could I know, since he didn't know it himself, that he would go on and on and up and up? When later he began driving a handy wagon with a shanty on it out among the farmers and small towns he did well at getting new subscribers to the *Republican-Register*, yet also about the same time making friends with many key men of the Republican Party workers. He quietly smashed an old party machine, was elected county treasurer, took over two or three banks and joined them into one bank where he was at the head, took over the *Republican-Register* and joined it with the *Evening Mail* so he was the publisher of the new Galesburg *Register-Mail*. In politics it became a saying, "We won't know what the ticket will be till we see Omer Custer."

When I sat by the Carlin grocery stove, looking up from reading the Chicago papers, to see Omer Custer with a sack of flour on one shoulder and a sack of sugar on the other, he couldn't figure for sure that the day would come when he would be the top man in Knox County banking, politics, newspapers, owning the first modern hotel in Galesburg, carrying the name of Hotel Custer. Nor as Omer clucked to the horse and said "Giddap" did he have the faintest glimmering that some thirty years later he would be managing the campaign of Governor Frank O. Lowden of Illinois, a rather able and honest governor, for the nomination for President of the United States by the Republican National Convention. And when Lowden's chances looked bright and rosy, with the nomination almost in reach, and people were saying Omer Custer would be the next Postmaster General, there came out of St. Louis a scandal that wrecked the Lowden band wagon and the country got Harding instead of Lowden for President. Neither Omer on his delivery wagon nor Charlie with his newspapers at the stove drying his mittens, neither had a crystal ball for reading the moist, mystical future that lay ahead.

What with spading two or three gardens, picking a pail or two of potato bugs, selling Pennsylvania Grit along Main Street, and other odd jobs, I made about twelve dollars a month. One odd job was "cleaning brick." A brick house or store torn down, we took trowels, knocked off the dried mortar and tried to make an old brick look new. Our pay ran so much a hundred of brick cleaned. I worked at it between my paper routes and averaged about fifteen cents an hour. But it was more sport than work when we answered the cry, "The English sparrow must go!" The state was paying one cent for each dead English sparrow and I brought down more than thirty. I had tried killing them with a "rubber gun" of my own make, a crotched stick with rubber bands holding a leather sling where you put your stone in, pulled back your rubber, aimed at your sparrow, and let 'er go. Out of hundreds of rubber-gun shots I brought down one sparrow. Then I got an air rifle. There was a Swedish neighbor boy Axel Johnson who was an interesting liar and I half believed him when he said that an air rifle or a rubber gun was better for killing birds than a shotgun or a rifle using powder. "The birds can smell powder a mile off," said Axel, and he had me thinking hard about the smelling power of birds.

I was fourteen and coming near fifteen in October of 1892. My mother would wake me at half-past five in the morning. She had ready for me when I came down from the garret a breakfast of buckwheat cakes, fried side pork, maybe apple sauce or prunes, and coffee. I walked Berrien Street to Chambers to South Street to Seminary, where I always walked through the Q. depot, to pass the newsstand and the lunch counter where waitresses Mamie Sullivan and her sister would be joking with the railroad men and passengers. Up Seminary to Main and on across the Public Square to Academy Street, then north to near Losey and the house and barn of George Burton, who had two milk wagons. It was a walk of about two miles to get to where I was ready for work. I could have saved myself half of the walk by taking a trolley car but I saved instead the nickel carfare.

In this October were days I had a sore throat. I went to bed two days and sent word to Burton that I wasn't able to work. Reporting for work, I explained to Burton and he looked at me with suspicion and not a word, not a "Huh" nor a "Hum," nor "Well, it's too bad you had to go down sick but it's nice you're up and around again." I still had throat pains and was weak, for two days eating little on account of it hurt the throat to swallow. I didn't explain this to Mr. Burton—he already looked suspicious enough.

That same week Mart went down with a sore throat and it was four days before he was up and around. Then the two youngest boys of the family stayed in bed with throats so sore they couldn't eat. Freddy was a baby two years old and Emil was seven years old this October. Emil had a broad freckled face, blue eyes, a quick beaming smile from a large mouth. He was strong for his age. He and I wrestled, scuffled, knocked off hats, played tricks on each other, and

I read to him my favorites from the Grimm stories. We liked the same stories and he called often for "The Knapsack, the Hat, and the Horn."

We moved a narrow bed from upstairs down into the kitchen, our one room with a stove in it. Next to the west window, with afternoon sun sometimes pouring in, we put Emil and Freddie side by side in the one bed, each with a throat looking queer, what had been pink and red having turned to a grayish white. They seemed to be getting weaker. And though we knew it would be a dollar and a half for a call from Doctor Wilson, I walked to his Main Street office and told him the folks wanted him to come as soon as he could.

Doctor Wilson came in about an hour, stepping into our kitchen in his elegant long black coat, white shirt and collar, a silk necktie, thin reddish hair, and gold rimmed eyeglasses. He had a good name as a doctor. He took a flat steel blade from his case. It wasn't a knife, for we could see the edges weren't sharp. He put this on the tongue of Emil and pressed it down and looked keen and long at Emil's throat. He did the same for Freddie. Then Doctor Wilson stood up, turned to the faces of my father and mother and said three words. His face was sober and sorry as he spoke those three words: "It is diphtheria."

Late that afternoon the city health commissioner nailed a big red card on the front door of our house: DIPHTHERIA, warning people not to come to our house because it had a catching disease. When I went to work the next morning I did it with a feeling that Mr. Burton wouldn't like it if I stayed home, that he would be put to extra trouble if I didn't go and besides would be suspicious like he was when I came back after two days off. I told him we had diphtheria at our house and a red card on the front door. He didn't say anything one way or the other. So I went with my milk cans from one house to another across the town from seven in the morning till about one in the afternoon. The next two mornings again I worked peddling milk for Mr. Burton and there were houses where women were anxious, saying, "Do you think it right you should be handling our milk if you have diphtheria at your house?" I said I had told Mr. Burton about it, how we had a red card on our front door, but he didn't say anything one way or the other and I thought he wouldn't

like it if I stayed home—it would make extra trouble for him. And
the women had worried faces and said, "It doesn't look right."

On the third day when Doctor Wilson made his third call, he took
the pulse and the temperature of the two boys, looked long and
careful into their throats, and said they were not making any im-
provement. He shook his head and said something like, "All we can
do now is to hope. They might get better. They might get worse.
I can't tell." Late that afternoon we were all there, with a west sun
shining in on Emil and Freddie where they lay with their eyes
closed and still breathing. It was Freddie who first stopped breath-
ing. Mother, touching his forehead and hands, her voice shaking
and tears coming down her face, said, "He is cold. Our Freddie is
gone." We watched Emil. He had had a rugged body and we hoped
he might pull through. But his breathing came slower and in less
than a half-hour he seemed to have stopped breathing. Mother put
her hands on him and said with her body shaking, "Oh God, Emil
is gone too."

The grief hit us all hard. In the Front Room the marble-topped
center table with the big Family Bible was moved to a corner. In its
place in the center of the room were two small white caskets. Neigh-
bors and friends came, some with flowers. The Kranses and the
Holmeses came to look at the faces of their two little relations. The
Reverend Carl A. Nyblad spoke the Swedish Lutheran service. A
quartet sang "Jesus, Lover of My Soul." The undertaker moved here
and there as though it was like what he did any day, and you couldn't
read anything in his face. Mother cried, but it was a quiet crying
and she didn't shake her shoulders like when she said "Oh God, Emil
is gone too." Mart and I didn't cry. We kept our eyes dry and our
faces hard. For two nights we had cried before going to sleep, and
waking in the night we had cried more and it was our secret why
we weren't crying at a public funeral.

We saw the two little white caskets carried out the front door and
put in the black hearse with glass windows at the sides and the end,
four black tassels on the top corners. We followed in a closed car-
riage. At the grave we heard the words, "Ashes to ashes, dust to
dust," saw the two little coffins lowered and a handful of earth

dropped on them, the sober faces of the Kranses and the Holmeses being with us and having grains of comfort.

We were driven home in the closed carriage, the father and mother, the sisters Mary and Esther, the brothers Mart and I. We went into the house. It was all over. The clock had struck for two lives and would never strike again for them. Freddie hadn't lived long enough to get any tangles in my heart. But Emil I missed then, and for years I missed him and had my wonderings about what a chum and younger brother he would have made. I can see now the lights in his blue eyes and over his wide freckled face and his quick beaming smile from a large mouth. There have been times I imagined him saying to me, "Life is good and why not death?"

There were two days I didn't report to George Burton for work in that diphtheria and burial week. When I did report to him he was like before, not a word, not even "Hard luck," or "Too bad." Mr. Burton had a lean face with a brown mustache he liked to twirl in his fingers—and a "retreating" chin. Where the sloping chin ended the neck soon began sliding toward his Adam's apple. He had two or three fast horses he liked to drive with a sulky. One was a yearling bred from a glossy black mare Burton owned. The mare had a small head and her thin scrawny neck didn't match her heavy body. Burton said she was pedigreed and had class yet about half the time he had her hitched to his milk wagon. He enjoyed clucking at her to get a burst of speed and then pulling her in. He had a beautiful wife and his face lighted up at the sight of her. I think she meant more to him than all his horses.

Did I get to hating Mr. Burton? I might answer, "How can you hate a man you pity not because of his retreating chin but because you see him acting mean to himself? I felt so sorry over George Burton being what he was that I couldn't have hated him." Mr. Burton never sang for himself or me, never joked to me, never told a funny story, never talked like one time he had been a boy, never talked about what was in the newspapers or town gossip, never played any kind of music or talked about listening to it, never talked about men or women he liked or funny or mean customers.

I wondered sometimes whether George Burton had ever been a boy. What few times I tried to talk with him like I thought a boy could talk with a man and get along, he either cut me off short or he said nothing to me as though I had said nothing to him. He could stop the horse and wagon for a ten- or fifteen-minute talk with a man in a sulky driving a racehorse. On and on they talked horse talk, dams and sires and trotting records, each telling the other the good points of his own horse, each blabbering to the other about what mare or stallion would come along and break the records of Maud S. or Nancy Hanks. As time went on I came to see that Mr. Burton wasn't ashamed of being a milkman and neither was he proud of it. What he was proud of were two or three horses he had that he hoped to build into a string of horses that would make a name for him. He hoped the milk business might make him enough money to get more horses to breed some world record-breakers. I caught myself saying one day, "He don't know boys and if you don't know boys you can't know colts and if you don't know colts you'll never be a big-time horse man."

While with Mr. Burton, like all other milk-wagon helpers, I worked seven days a week, no vacations, no holidays, pouring the pints and quarts on the Fourth of July, Thanksgiving, Christmas, and New Year's Day, and we called each other "milk slingers."

In the Hard Times my father worked four hours a day, his month's payday check less than sixteen dollars. After Emil and Freddie died we were a family of seven and it took money to get bread, clothes, coal, schoolbooks. Papa had to make his payments or lose the house. Mary in her third and last year of high school had to have better clothes than in the grade schools. The twelve dollars a month George Burton paid me came in handy for the family. Doctor and undertaker bills, the cemetery lot, took regular cuts out of the month's wages of Papa. It was a hard winter and somehow I couldn't see my way to take out of my pay enough for a pair of two-dollar felt boots, or even a pair of dollar overshoes. On my milk route I had wet feet, numb feet, and feet with shooting pains. If it hadn't been for the five-minute stop at a grocery hot stove, or a housewife saying, "Poor boy, wouldn't you like to come in and warm yourself?" I would have had a case of bad feet for a long time. I learned a word for what my feet kept singing, "chilblains."

Once I was ten minutes late meeting Mr. Burton where he sat in his wagon and his felt boots. He said, and he wasn't laughing, "You're a slowpoke today." I said, "My feet were near frozen and I had to stop to warm them." He said, "Why don't you get yourself a pair of these felt boots like I have?" I said, "We're hard up at our house and we can't spare the two dollars." Mr. Burton sniffed a "humph" through his nose as though he couldn't understand what I was saying—which he couldn't.

I got tired of seeing him every day grumpy and frozen-faced, and somewhere early in 1893 when he had paid me twelve dollars for a month's work I told him I guessed I didn't want to work for him any more. He said, "Well, I guess that'll be no loss to me." And I thought of two or three answers I could make but let it go with, "Good-by, Mr. Burton." I was going to say, "You know where you can stick this stinkin job I've had with you," but I played a hunch and walked away after saying only "Good-by, Mr. Burton."

They knew at home that I was a helper through the Hard Times, that the little I earned counted. They knew I would rather have gone to school. When Mary graduated from high school it was the few dollars I threw in that gave her a nice white dress so she looked as good as any of them on Graduation Day when she stepped out and bowed and took her diploma. We knew that diploma would count. Now she could teach school and be a help and no longer be an expense to the family. The next fall she had a country school at thirty dollars a month. We hadn't planned it at all but her high-school books were a help to me. I didn't study her algebra and Latin textbooks, but I thumbed back and forth in them and got glimmerings. I read Irving's *Sketch Book*, *Ivanhoe*, and *The Scarlet Letter* and talked with Mary about what the teachers said those novels meant. I was doubtful of them then and I still look at them with a fishy eye.

The great book Mary brought home—great for what it did to me at that particular time, opening my eyes about law, government, history, and people—was *Civil Government in the United States* by John Fiske. Here for the first time I read answers to many questions: What are taxes? Who has the taxing power? What is the difference between taxation and robbery? Under what conditions may taxation become robbery? Why does a policeman wear a uniform? What is government? Here I first read the Constitution of the United States and tried to get my head around the English Magna Carta. Here I read many times the wonderful speech of Ben Franklin favoring the Constitution, quoting the French lady in a dispute with her sister, "I don't know how it happens, sister, but I meet with nobody but myself who is always in the right." Franklin explained there were parts of the Constitution he didn't like but he wasn't sure but that as time passed he might like them and, "Having lived long, I have experienced many instances of being obliged by better information, or fuller consideration, to change opinions even on important subjects which I once thought right but found to be otherwise. It is therefore that, the older I grow, the more apt I am to doubt my own judgment, and to pay more respect to the judgment of others." It was a honey of a book and I was glad we had all helped send Mary through high school if only that she brought that one book into our house.

I was glad John Fiske wrote the book. Once for several months I read every day in the *Galesburg Evening Mail* the column written in Washington, the national capital, by Walter Wellman. I did a lot of wondering about how one man could know so much about what the Government was doing. He seemed to make things so plain. I wondered what it would be like to live in Washington and have a job where you went out every day and looked in here and there at the Government and then wrote about it, making plain to millions of people what was going on. From John Fiske's book I learned there are three branches of the Government, the Executive, the Legislative, and the Judicial. Walter Wellman made me think I knew what all three branches were doing.

I had never seen John Fiske nor a picture of him. I imagined maybe he had a straight-out homely face like President John Finley of Knox College. Years later I met a Chicago woman who said when she was a girl of eight her father took her for a visit in John Fiske's study room in Cambridge, Massachusetts, on a hot summer afternoon. Mr. Fiske had his shirt off, and his undershirt was sweat-soaked, and he had finished several bottles of beer that stood next to a bucket of ice holding more bottles. Mr. Fiske had wide whiskers that dripped sweat. He was a heavy man with a big potbelly and when he asked the little Chicago girl to sit in his lap, she gave him a long look and said, "You haven't got any lap." And after hearing that I was still thankful to John Fiske. My hat was off to him and his ghost.

A book we owned each year till it got lost two or three years later was *Hostetter's Illustrated United States Almanac* meant "for merchants, mechanics, miners, farmers, planters and general family use." Where we came in was "general family." It had green covers and a string on one corner to hang it to a nail on the wall where it would be handy if you wanted to know when the sun would rise or the moon go down. Half the almanac was filled with good words for Hostetter's Stomach Bitters. The language was polite and you could read, "It refreshes the fatigue, imparts appetite, and affords tranquillity to overworked brains and oversensitive nerves. The facts relating to it we do not wish to embellish by hyperbole, or lessen the force by exaggeration." You went to the dictionary to get what they were trying to tell you.

There was advice in Hostetter's, how to get rid of warts, corns, boils, ingrowing toenails, hiccoughs, earache, how to get a ring off a swollen finger, what to do about a rusty nail in the foot or chicken lice. Five pages had funny drawings with jokes under them. A tramp comes into a business office and asks a bookkeeper sitting on a high chair at a high desk for a little money so he can eat. A man in a chair reading a newspaper cuts in, "Don't give him anything; he's been here before today." The tramp turns "loftily" to the man who has cut in and says, "Will you have the kindness not to meddle in my business affairs?" We read Hostetter's out loud in the kitchen and talked over the points of the jokes and what the "wise sayings" meant. Most of the jokes I have heard in one shape or other hundreds of times since I first read them in the 1880's in Hostetter's:

Railway Porter—"Well, sir, you've tipped me very handsomely, and I don't mind giving you a tip. Never get into the last carriage; it always suffers worse in collisions."

Mr. O'Bull—"Faith, why don't they leave it off then!"

"Are you in favor of enlarging the curriculum?" asked a rural school director of a farmer in his district. "Enlarge nothing," replied the old gentleman. "The building's big enough; what we want is to teach more things to the children."

A lady once went to Dublin Castle in such very full dress that more bust than barege was visible. "Did you ever see anything so unblushing?" said someone to Archbishop Whately. "Never, since I was weaned," replied the wit.

An Irish priest addressing his flock on the dangers of intemperance concluded with these words: "Drink, my children, makes you beat your wives, starve your families, and shoot your landlords—aye, and miss them, too."

They had their usual evening quarrel as they sat by the hearth. On one side lay quietly a blinking dog, and on the other, a purring cat; and the old woman pleaded with her growling husband: "Yust look at dat gat unt tog; dey never gwarrels unt fights like us." "Yah," said the old growler. "I know dot; but yust tie dem togedder one dime, und den you see blazes!"

A widow weeping over the new-made grave of her husband finally dried her eyes and said, "There is one comfort in it anyhow; I shall know where he is at night."

Sprinkled among the jokes you could meet some fellow like H. C. Yetter of Burnside, Illinois, April 25, 1887, writing: "When it comes to a question of genuine merit, Hostetter's Stomach Bitters leads them all. It is a strictly medicinal preparation, and for a tonic has no superior." Us kids heard that you could get drunk on one bottle of Hostetter's. We said we didn't care as long as Hostetter's gave us an almanac every New Year's Day. We read sayings:

A snob is a being on a ladder, who is quite as ready to kiss the feet of him who is above him as to kick the hand of him who is below.

When the girl who has encouraged a young man for several years suddenly tells him she can never be more than a sister to him, he can for the first time see the freckles on her nose.

You require in marriage precisely the same quality that you would in eating sausage—absolute confidence.

No man ever looked on the dark side of life without finding it.

The art of conversation is the art of hearing as well as being heard.

Silence alone is a powerful weapon. An Arabic proverb says, "Silence is often an answer."

The politician of the insect world is the flea. He is ever itching for place, creates no end of disturbance, and you never know where to find him.

Lincoln once said that some people not only believed that the earth moved on its own axis, but that they are the axis.

We didn't know we were getting education while having fun, Mary and Mart and I, in that little crowded kitchen when we read *Hostetter's Almanac* to each other. Besides pictures, jokes and sayings, it was crammed with all sorts of facts new to us and interesting —the morning and evening stars for any month in the year, the ocean tides, the velocity of the earth, eclipses, and so on. We were hungry to learn. We didn't write a letter to Hostetter's thanking them for letting us have a free almanac every year but we could have and maybe we should have. We left it to the fellows who said they could get drunk on one bottle of Hostetter's.

I remember reading Fowler and Wells' big book on "phrenology." To begin with, as I recall, they explained about physiognomy with pictures of different kinds of noses, the Aquiline, the Straight, the Executive, the Retroussé. I would go along Main Street and pick out noses like those in the book. Farther along in the book they got into heads and bumps on heads. This was phrenology. Look at a man's head and you could tell what kind of man he was. Thick between the ears he was Combative, good in a fight. If your head had the bump of Amativeness it meant you were good at love, handy with the women. If you liked children and raised a big family you had somewhere the bump of Philoprogenitiveness. Why did those big words stick in my mind? They were as useless to me as the curl in a pig's tail is to a pig. Why should I lug around in a corner of my mind that word Philoprogenitiveness? Yet I did. I have seen a man pushing a baby carriage on a walk with his wife and six children tagging along and I would say, "There it goes, that's philoprogenitiveness." Of course phrenology wasn't all nonsense. Nor, on the other hand, was it the science that lecturers and writers of books claimed. Audiences paid good money to hear a lecture with charts showing heads and bumps. It was a fad, caught on for a while and then faded.

In those years as a boy in that prairie town I got education in scraps and pieces of many kinds, not knowing that they were part of my education. I met people in Galesburg who were puzzling to me, and later when I read Shakespeare I found those same people were puzzling him. I met little wonders of many kinds among animals and plants that never lost their wonder for me, and I found later that these same wonders had a deep interest for Emerson, Thoreau, and Walt Whitman. I met superstitions, folk tales, and folklore while I was a young spalpeen, "a broth of a boy," long before I read books about them. All had their part, small or large, in the education I got outside of books and schools.

There was the late fall and winter I worked in the drugstore of Harvey M. Craig. I had a key and opened the front door at seven o'clock in the morning. I swept the floors of the store and the prescription room and about half-past seven I would see Mr. Hinman, the pharmacist, come in. I would take a chamois skin and go over the showcases. I took bottles from the prescription room that needed filling and went down in the cellar and turned the spigots of wine barrels and casks of rum and whisky and filled the bottles. There I had my first taste of port wine and claret and found they tasted better than I expected, though I was still leery of what they might do to me. I tasted whisky and decided it was not for me. There was a twenty-year-old rum that was so grand and insinuating and soft and ticklish that I decided it had danger and I never took more than a half-mouthful of it in one day. There were carboys in the cellar. A carboy is the champion of all bottles, standing three or four feet high, and the glass two or three inches thick. From the carboys I poured sulphuric acid and muriatic acid, wood alcohol, turpentine, and other stuff needed upstairs.

Before eight o'clock every day a regular, Jack Dee, would come in the front door. He was a lean, red-faced, hard-bitten Irishman from a livery stable across the street. He was a good man with horses and knew the way to all the graveyards, driving a hearse several times a week. He would hand Mr. Hinman a half-pint bottle, not saying a word. Mr. Hinman, not saying a word, would go back to the prescription room and fill the bottle with pure grain alcohol. I didn't hear whether Jack Dee had a prescription for the alcohol but I guessed he was a special case because time after time men would come in asking for liquor and Mr. Hinman wouldn't let them have it unless they had a prescription.

Several times across one week a man came in and begged Mr. Hinman to sell him morphine. He showed his money but Mr. Hinman wouldn't let him have it unless he could show a prescription. He had a chin beard and his face was pale, soft, and pudgy. He didn't walk easy—his legs were sort of wobbly. His begging was pitiful to hear. He lifted his pants leg and pulled down the sock to show the needle marks, the many scars where the needle had shot in the morphine. He claimed he was the father of Lottie Collins, the actress singer who was famous for the way she had started the song "Ta-ra-ra-boom-dee-ay" till millions were singing it. He said, "My daughter Lottie Collins would say it was wrong the way you refuse to let me have what I need." And Mr. Hinman would shake his head and say, "I'd like to help you but no matter who you are or where you come from the law says I can't sell it to you without a prescription." And tears ran down the man's face as he turned and wobbled toward the door, stopping halfway and moaning to Mr. Hinman, "Have a little pity. Think it over." And he did come back, two and three times in a day that week. Mr. Hinman said if it kept up he would report the man to the police. The man stopped coming.

At nine o'clock in the morning Harvey Craig would come through the front door and nearly always his wife with him. They seemed to be a fine couple. You could tell they got along well. Mr. Craig was a fairly heavy man, though not big-bodied like his father, Justice A. M. Craig of the Illinois State Supreme Court. He had something of his father's face, the mouth stern and the lip ends pulled down a little. He was kindly with Mr. Hinman and me, though there was no fun or frolics when he was around. His wife was a small package alongside of him. She had quiet and charm. She let Mr. Craig run the store and ask questions and see to this and that, usually leaving before noon.

I liked working with Mr. Hinman. He was slim, somewhat dark-skinned, with a neat small dark mustache like Edgar Allan Poe. His eyes smiled when his mouth did. He took an interest in being a pharmacist, had pride about handling drugs and medicines, kept studying the latest finds in medicine. His sense of humor was always there. He liked to tell about a boy coming into a drugstore on a hot summer Sunday and asking for "ten cents' worth of asafoetida." The clerk climbed up to a shelf and brought down a bottle, weighed out ten cents' worth of asafoetida, climbed up and put the bottle back, then climbed down and wrapped the asafoetida and handed it to the boy. The boy said, "Charge it." The clerk asked, "What's the name?" "August Schimmelderfer." At which the clerk busted out, "You little devil, run home with you. I wouldn't spell asafoetida and Schimmelderfer for ten cents."

In the prescription room was the biggest and thickest book I ever handled except *Webster's Unabridged Dictionary*. On the back and the front cover was the name: *The Pharmacapoeia*. In it were the names of all the drugs there are and what they will do to you. I rambled here and there in it. I asked Mr. Hinman questions about what I read in the book and he was patient and kindly. He liked to share his learning with a younger fellow who had more hopes than he knew what to do with.

For a month or two one winter I took a whirl at the mail-order business. John Sjodin sold me on the idea. He had taken several weekly and monthly papers that were filled with mail-order advertising. He pointed to *Comofort* in Augusta, Maine, with a million subscribers, the biggest circulation of any paper in the country, its columns filled with ads for selling medicines, chickens, kazoos, eye-wash, tool kits, medicines, knives, music boxes, toys, cheap watches, penny pencils, and more medicines. John said there had been fortunes made in the mail-order business. Men now millionaires had started with just a little printing press. John had bought somewhere for five or ten dollars a set of type and a tricky little press that would print a sheet five inches by four. I threw into the scheme two or three dollars I had saved. I was the junior partner and would share in the profits the same percentage as I had put in—that was fair.

We were going to print a "mail-order journal." John said, "We will have room in it for advertising only, so we can't expect to sell it. The subscription price will be not a cent. So we will name our mail-order journal *Not a Cent*." We ran off fifty or sixty copies, and at the top of the first page was the name of this new publication in the advertising and selling field: *Not a Cent*. We followed the first issue with a second. I forget what all we advertised. But I do remember we offered for sale one Waterbury watch "slightly used," a couple of knives "slightly used," and we gave the names of several books "slightly used." We couldn't afford the postage stamps to mail out our "mail-order journal." We gave out here and there among friends and strangers over half the copies and kept the rest to look at and say, "We're publishers and this shows what we publish."

The Sjodin family had moved to the north side in a working-class neighborhood east of the Q. tracks. We did our printing in the hay-loft of the barn, on cold days wearing our overcoats and running to the house once in a while to get warm. It was a mile walk across town for me and I ate with John in the Sjodin kitchen. John laughed from the beginning to the end of this plunge of ours in the mail-order business. We had a stock of goods and when you have a stock of goods you're in business. We got out a paper advertising our stock of goods and how can you do that unless you're in business? Away back in our minds, of course, was a slim glimmering hope. We would have bet one dollar against a thousand that something would turn up, that a twist of chance might come along and all of a sudden, like it happens every once in a while in a business starting small, we would be on Easy Street. When we quit the business, when *Not a Cent* stopped publication, we laughed the same way as when we first got set for the plunge.

*

ELEVEN

*

Learning a Trade

*

It came over me often that I wasn't getting anywhere in particular. I asked here and there about a job where I could learn a trade. I asked plumbers, carpenters, house painters, and they said there was no opening or I might come around later. When I asked Q. machinists and boilermakers what were the chances they said the Hard Times were still on, old hands waiting to go back. I heard that the Union Hotel barbershop wanted a porter. I said, "Barbering is a trade. A barber can travel, can work in other towns from coast to coast. At barbering you might be shaving a man who'll offer you a job with better money than you can ever make barbering."

I hired to Mr. Humphrey at three dollars a week, shoeshine money, and tips. The shop was under the Farmers' and Mechanics' Bank, in a half-basement with big windows that let you see the shoes of walkers on the sidewalk. By going up eight steps you could see the Public Square, down Broad Street to the courthouse park, and beyond that the Knox College campus. The floor of the shop was black and white square tiles. A white square dirty meant the black square next to it maybe was dirty too. I came to know every square of tile in that floor and said they could just as well have made the floor all black tiles. I mopped the floor every morning, with extra pushes of the mop on the white tiles. In rainy weather or snow, with mud tracked in, I gave the floor a once-over in the afternoon. The big windows to the street I went over once a week with soap and

water, sponge and chamois. And the four flat brass cuspidors had a
brisk cleanout of cigar butts and ashes every day.

Four barber chairs faced a long wall mirror and three times a
week my hands ran over every inch of that long mirror. First I
would put on a white cleaning fluid so you couldn't see anything in
the glass. Then with a chamois skin I wiped off the white stuff from
the glass so that any customer getting a haircut could see what the
barber was doing to him.

Mr. Humphrey, Head Barber and Proprietor, had the first chair.
At the second chair was a tall fellow with a mustache, his first name
John, and he was that nice with me that I'm ashamed his last name
slips me. At the third chair was Frank Wykoff, smooth-faced, with
silky golden hair. He had manners, had a reputation as a dancer.
When a customer wanted to talk Wykoff could go along, and it was
the same with the other barbers. Mostly the customers talked more
than the barbers. The fourth chair was worked by Mr. Humphrey's
eighteen-year-old son on Saturdays and before holidays when a rush
was on.

Mr. Humphrey was a barber and a gentleman. He could smile
and say to a regular customer with a nod of the head and a bend of
the back and shoulders that was nearly a bow, "Mister Higby, what
is the good word with you?" or "Mister Applegreen, how does the
world go round for you today?" or "Mister Hagenjos, it's about
time we were seeing your good face again." He had a round face
with a thin, straight-lined mouth and a pleasant voice. He was the
Boss of the shop and ran it smooth and all had respect for Mr. Hum-
phrey. The money drawer, with different holes for dollars, quarters,
and dimes, pulled out from a table near him. The two barbers wrote
with a lead pencil on a slip of paper twenty-five cents for a haircut,
ten cents for a shave, twenty-five cents for a shampoo, twenty-five
cents for a hair tonic, ten cents for a hot towel. The customer took
the slip of paper to Mr. Humphrey, who added it up and made
change.

Frank Wykoff could talk about the ballplayers up around New
Windsor where he learned his trade. He knew the Spratt brothers,
Bob and Jack, fast players I liked who had figured in beating the
Galesburg team and who later went into a minor-league team. Wy-

koff told about a Swede farmer near New Windsor who after a few drinks would say, "Come up to my haus. I got yankeehaw [alcohol]. I gif you yankeehaw you come to my haus." His favorite imitation was of a Swede who lost out in a horse deal: "Dat was deh bygyodest horse I naver did see. He wass no more fit to be horse dan spiting [in spite of] hal [hell]. He made me one time so mad I pick up a brickstick [brickstone] an hat him on deh behind lag so hard he could nearly walk. Dan I take him over to Olson wot trade him to me an I say, 'You take your bygyod horse and come long to hal wid you.'"

At half-past ten or eleven o'clock in the morning, when I saw there would be no customer out of a chair in ten or fifteen minutes, I would go up a back stairs, cross the big main office of the Union Hotel, and go into the most elegant saloon in that part of Illinois. There was a polished mahogany bar, a shining brass rail, tall brass spittoons inviting you to take a spit, a long mirror for those standing and drinking to see how they looked or to see the other faces at the bar without turning their heads, and wood carving like lace or embroidery on the top and sides of the mirror. I heard a farmer seeing it for the first time, "She's a bang-up affair, ain't she?" Near the end of the bar they set out the free lunch at half-past ten—ham, cheese, pickles, rye and white bread, and sometimes deer or bear meat. I helped myself, didn't care to buy a glass of beer, went down to the barbershop thankful to the bartenders for not asking what a minor was doing in the place, and thankful to Solomon Frolich and Henry Gardt, the two German Jews who owned the saloon. I tried to do an extra-special job when I ran my whisk broom over them or gave them a shoeshine. I had been in a grammar-school class with Henry Gardt's daughter and didn't feel exactly like a stranger to him, though of course I never mentioned to him that she was bright in her lessons, for he might have taken it as out of the way.

In the hotel office watching people come in and register I would try to figure out whether they were traveling men or show people dated for one night in the Auditorium across Broad Street from the hotel. I had heard and read a lot about swindlers, how they stopped at hotels, and maybe that very man signing his name in the register was one. We had the pink-sheet *Police Gazette* in the barbershop and I read it every week and I was on the lookout for the high-class confidence men and gamblers who always stopped at high-class hotels.

At the desk was James or "Jimmy" Otway, an Englishman who made me feel that the more I could know about him the better I would know England. Jimmy Otway reminded me of people and talk I had met in Dickens' novels. He was short with a blond face, blond hair combed back fancy and wavy, and a thick blond mustache that would have run out far only he kept it well curled, the curliest mustache in town, unless it was our grocer Will Olson. He wore light tweed suits, stiff stand-up collars and stiff starched cuffs, colored neckties, was spick-and-span. He talked brisk, said "suh" for "sir" and could say "What is yoh pleashaw?" in a way some people took as classy and elegant while others laughed. He bred blooded beagles and any day there might be two or three of his brown-and-white-haired dogs running around the office. The newspapers reported his sending his purebred dogs here and there over the country. Jimmy Otway belonged to the town and you were not quite a Galesburger unless you knew about him. I waited around sometimes to see whether he would drop his "aitches" when he talked and I learned there are Englishmen who don't drop their "aitches." Among the boys there used to be a question, "How does an Englishman spell *saloon?*" and the answer, "A hess, a hay, a hell, two hoes, and a hen."

Jimmy Otway was proud and had a temper. If a bellboy didn't come running when the bell rang, Mr. Otway cut loose. When a guest complained that a bellboy handled luggage wrong or was slow bringing ice water, Mr. Otway seemed to enjoy his tongue. The night clerk was different. I saw him a few times on days when Otway was off duty. I wouldn't try to tell what he looked like. I heard him classed as "the handsomest man in town." He was strictly what was meant by "tall, dark, and handsome" in the Laura Jean Libbey novels. The bellboys liked him. One of them said to me, "He's a lady-killer, if there ever was one, but we've never seen him take to a woman. He could take his pick of 'em but he don't do it. If I had his looks, Jesus wept, would I go down the line!" Time passed and I never did hear what happened as between him and women. When later I read in a book about Apollo Belvedere and saw pictures of Apollo, I said, "The nearest I can figure it, Apollo was the night clerk of the Union Hotel in Galesburg, Illinois."

In the barbershop on Saturday I was here, there, and everywhere. Next to the shop was a bathroom with eight tubs and partitions between, twenty-five cents for a bath. For those who asked it I would turn the faucets and get a tub of hot water ready for them. There were two or three regulars who would call me in to scrub their backs with a brush. One of these was a shoe clerk with a club-foot, who always said that the way I scrubbed him was good for his health. He would say "Thank you" when he handed me a quarter for myself. Nearly always those I gave special help to paid me a quarter. We had trouble with the tubs. They began looking dirty with a dirt you couldn't scrub away. We tried muriatic acid on them and they still looked dirty. So I would explain to each customer that what looked like dirt was the iron where the muriatic acid had eaten off the porcelain coat.

The worst mistake I made was one they guyed me about for a long time. The gentleman had had a shave, a haircut, and a shampoo. He looked good for a dime tip, at least a nickel. I gave him a shoe-shine. I swung my whisk broom over his Prinz Albert coat and his pants down to the shoes. Then I took his high silk hat off the hatrack. I began swinging my whisk broom up, down, and around his silk hat, the first hat of the kind I had ever handled. He had finished paying his bill to Mr. Humphrey when he looked over to where I was and saw what I was doing. He let out a howl and rushed over yelling, "You can't do that!" I saw at once what he meant. I had learned in a split second that I had been an ignoramus about silk hats. I tried to mumble something about being sorry. I saw the two bar-bers trying to keep from laughing. I saw Mr. Humphrey come up and heard him say the only sharp words he ever said to me, ending up with talking natural, "Charlie, you ought to have a soft brush for silk hats or a satin cloth." The customer had snatched his silk hat out of my hands and held it as though I might of a sudden jump at him and tear the hat away from him. I looked dangerous to him. He handed me a nickel for the shine and walked out as though he cer-tainly would never come back to this place. The next day I had a soft satin cloth on hand and a brush with hairs so soft you could hardly feel it running over the palm of your hand. And after that when once in a while a silk hat came into the shop I was ready for it. I had what they call "confidence" because I had been through what they call "experience."

The Union Hotel got most of the big-time people who came to town, show people, lecturers, minstrels, star actors who had been playing on Broadway and were taking their play from Galesburg to Omaha, to Denver, to Salt Lake City, to San Francisco. Galesburg made a nice one-night stand for them. I saw Eddie Foy get his face lathered and scraped one day and after I gave him a brush-off he handed me two nickels. It was later I saw him walk out on the Auditorium stage, and before he began singing, he said in a blurry hoarse voice, "It's a little dusty on the river tonight."

Of what us kids called "the big bugs on the North Side," many came to the Union Hotel barbershop. "You will meet the bon ton of Galesburg while you work here, Charlie," Mr. Humphrey had said to me. "It's a bluestocking trade comes to our shop and we want to keep the place shipshape, everything clean as a whistle."

The barbers, among themselves as barbers, talked about razors. Most of them swore by the Wade & Butcher razor. It interested me there was a razormaker whose name was Butcher. They talked about a customer whose face shaved smooth and easy. A fellow with a tough and tangled beard on his face they called a "squirrel." One of them had just gone out the door when Frank Wykoff, who had shaved him, was saying, "He was a squirrel, all right. After I started on him I knew I had to lather him again and rub it in deep. I stropped my razor six times. You can't cut his whiskers. You have to whittle 'em." There would be talk about what to say and how to say it nice to make a man want a shampoo, hair tonic, or a hot towel. It would end up with one of them saying, "It's a gift. Some barbers can just naturally talk a man into it without getting him sore. You can't go too far or they won't come back to you."

Outside barbers dropped in. There would be talk about what fool notions some people had about a face disease called the "barber's itch," how you could get it only in a barbershop, and you ought never go to a barbershop where anyone had got the disease. "What

poppycock!" barbers would snort to each other. Some of them said
they had never seen a case of it and it was gossip. Then there might
be talk about what barber had the "clap" and who he might have
got it from. This and that loose woman on the town might be named.
I remember one barber going on and on about fools he had heard
saying, "A case of the clap is no worse than a bad cold," and what
had happened to them and how they learned better. There was long
talk one day about a blacksmith-horseshoer. He was a strong, good-
looking, square-built fellow. I had seen him play catcher on a base-
ball team and he was a good backstop. Now, the talk ran, he had a
case of the "syph," one barber saying, "He's got a hole in his face
you can put your finger in." When later this blacksmith-horseshoer
died and I heard of it I did my wondering about whether it could
be true, whether a disease could eat a hole in your face.

Two or three times a week I would meet two other boys who
were portering in barbershops. We talked about what blacking was
best for a shoe, the rougher shoes that need two coats of blacking
before you put on the brushes, and how to look at a customer or
what to say that would make him think it would be a good idea to
pay you a dime instead of a nickel. One of these boys, Harry Wade,
thought he had a sidewise look up into the customer's face, along
with a smile, that sometimes brought him an extra nickel. The other
homely porter and I said to Harry, "You're a good-looker and wear
smart clothes and that's more than half of why you get more tips
than we do." Harry might not like the looks of a customer and after
he gave him a brush-off that had everything, if he got no tip, not a
nickel, he could say "Thank you" with a sarcastic sneer. The Head
Barber caught on to this and said, "You're a good porter, Harry, but
if you keep that up, we'll have to let you go."

Harry and the other porter used to dress in their fanciest clothes
and Sunday noon walk into the Brown's Hotel dining room and
order and eat a fifty-cent dinner. They called it "classy." They
liked doing it. Their home folks set a good table, but after being
barbershop porters all week they wanted to "sit with the bon ton."
Harry Wade had the only real and classy snare drum in our neigh-
borhood. He brought it to the Berrien Street pasture, where at night
the boys sat on the grass while he stood and gave us all the drum taps

he knew. Harry's arms and wrists were fast with the sticks. We knew he had practiced hard many hours and hoped to get on with a band and travel. Every one of us wished he had a classy snare drum and was good with the sticks like Harry. He had class enough without eating fifty-cent dinners at Brown's Hotel on Sundays.

Harry came along one night in 1893 to where we were sitting on the grass in the pasture. He had just got off a train from Chicago, where he had had three days at the World's Fair, the great Columbian Exposition. He sat down with us and talked for an hour about the fair. When he quit talking we put questions and he went on talking. We were sure there was a World's Fair up in Chicago and he gave us the feel of it. We couldn't afford to go and Harry brought parts of it to us.

Spring came after fall and winter months in the barbershop and doubts had been growing in me that I wasn't cut out for a barber. Spring moved in with smells on the air and Sam Barlow came into my life. He had sold his farm up near Galva and gone into the milk business. He was a jolly, laughing man, short, tough-muscled, a little stoop-shouldered, with a ruddy, well-weathered face, brown eyes, a thick sandy mustache, and a voice I liked. He had been a barn-dance fiddler, still liked to play "Money Musk," "Mrs. Macleod's Reel," "Pop Goes the Weasel," and other tunes.

Barlow stopped his milk wagon one day, called me from a sidewalk, and asked if I wanted to go to work for him at twelve dollars a month and dinner with him and his wife every day. I took him up on it. It would be outdoor work. I would see plenty of sky every day. The barbershop had been getting stuffy. I parted from Mr. Humphrey and it wasn't easy to tell him, "You've been fine to me, Mr. Humphrey, but I've got to be leaving. I don't think I'm cut out for a barber."

So every morning for sixteen months or more I walked from home at half-past six, west on Berrien Street, crossing the Q. switchyard tracks, on past Mike O'Connor's cheap livery stable, past the Boyer broom factory, then across the Knox College campus and past the front of the Old Main building. Every morning I saw the east front of Old Main where they had put up the platform for Lincoln

and Douglas to debate in October of 1858. At the north front of Old
Main many times I read on a bronze plate words spoken by Lincoln
and by Douglas some thirty-four years before I stood there reading
those words. They stayed with me, and sometimes I would stop to
read those words only, what Lincoln said to twenty thousand people
on a cold windy October day: "He is blowing out the moral lights
around us, when he contends that whoever wants slaves has a right
to hold them." I read them in winter sunrise, in broad summer day-
light, in falling snow or rain, in all the weathers of a year.

Then I continued along South Street to Monmouth Boulevard to
the house and barn of Samuel Kossuth Barlow. There I shook out
straw and shoveled clean the stalls of three horses, sometimes packed
mud into the sore foot of a horse, hitched a horse to a wagon. By
that time Bill Walters, a good-looking husky with a brown mus-
tache, would have come in from two farms west of town, bringing
in the day's milk to be delivered, and Mr. Barlow would be out of
the house. And Harry ("Fatty") Hart would show up. He wasn't
big nor fat but the boys had hung the nickname of "Fatty" on him
and it stuck. He was black-haired, straight and square-shouldered,
round cheeks maybe puffed out a little, black hair and black eyes
and a bright quick smile. He had ways with women. While Bill
Walters went with his wagon and worked to the north, Mr. Barlow
and Fatty and I covered the south side of town.

Sam Barlow was different from George Burton. He would take
a two-gallon can of milk and walk a route of a few blocks while
Fatty or I drove the wagon. He would keep telling us to pay re-
spect to any complaints of customers, never to "sass" them about
anything, whereas Burton used to act as though it was something
nice and special for people to get their milk from him. Mr. Barlow
had us keep an eye out for any house people were moving out of.
When new people came in we would be on the spot asking them did
they have a milkman and wouldn't they like to have milk from us.
Usually we got a new customer. From October on, when the cows
didn't have pasture, we sold eighteen quart tickets for a dollar, and
then in summer twenty for a dollar. Starting in early June till
about the middle of September we made two deliveries a day. Most
customers didn't have iceboxes and didn't like their milk to sour

over night. That meant Mr. Barlow and I would wash all the cans twice a day in the warm-weather months. The big eight-gallon cans that stayed on the wagon, the two- and three-gallon cans that we carried and poured out the pints and quarts from, all the cans got the same once-over from Mr. Barlow and me. We rinsed them with cold water and then sprinkled the bottom of the cans with yellow gold dust from the Gold Dust Twins, who had a big name then. We poured in hot water, reached down with a brush and scrubbed the inside of the cans, and then put them upside down in a rack outdoors. In the house we washed up and always had a good dinner set out by Mrs. Barlow and her daughter. Toward the end of a dinner of prime roast beef, baked potato, salad, apple pie, and coffee, Sam Barlow would ask, "Well, young man, do you think you have had sufficient to suffonsify?" At first I let it pass and then worked out an answer, "Having had a sufficiency I sure am suffonsified and I'm ready to sigashiate." Around the Barlow wagon any of us not feeling so good was "under the weather" or "below par" or "a little out of kilter."

Working for Barlow I got overshoes and no chilblains. One December week a cold rain or sleet came down every day for six straight days and none of us took cold, everybody on the job cheerful.

Three times a week I went to a house where two sisters, one about fifty-five and the other sixty, lived by themselves, unmarried. They seemed shy and their neighbors said they never "visited." They bought three pints a week, "only for our coffee," they said. They kept their pint of milk in a pail of cold water in the cellar. They watched their pennies close and they were my only customers who never let up telling me I didn't pour the milk up to the pint line.

To one house I always carried a small can holding the milk of one cow, the same one cow's milk every day. A doctor had ordered the baby in that house to have milk from one cow and every day the same cow. We were proud to be doing this for the family in that house because the man of the house, the father of the baby, was Frank Bullard. His name had been flashed to newspapers all over the country as the engineer on a fast mail train that set a new world's record for locomotive and train speed. I remember him a square-shouldered, upstanding man with a head of black hair, black mustache, walking out of his house and up the street carrying a wicker lunchbox, walking cool and taking it easy, and I would say, "I hope he breaks another world's record." We did the best we could to see that the baby never changed cows. But there were two or three times we couldn't help it, milk and cans got mixed up and the baby got the milk of several cows, and we never heard but the baby was doing well. There was a college professor who wanted skim milk when we could get it for him, two or three quarts a day. They had five children in his family and he said, "It's been worked out that cheap skim milk gives more nourishment for the price than the regular milk." So we got what we could for the professor.

The people who liked to ask about our watering the milk, we heard from them. One railroad man came out with his wife and as I poured the milk he would ask, "What is a milkman without a pump?" or "What kind of a pump does Barlow use?" or "Do you use that quart measure when you water the milk?" I think he lay awake nights trying to work up new ways of asking me about pumps, water, and milk. One morning I told him, "We're not using the pump any more. We're getting big bottles of pure spring water from Waukesha, Wisconsin, and we pour from the bottles into the milk cans." He was quick, "I noticed the milk had a new flavor."

Mr. Barlow toward noon might say, "I had a headache this morning, didn't feel so good—but I worked it off." His favorite song was about an Irishman in America named Patterson and he wanted his girl in Ireland, Bridget Donohue, to come over and marry him:

> Oh, Bridget Donohue, I dearly do love you,
> And if you'll take the name of Patterson,
> Then I'll take Donohue.

He liked to tell about an Irish couple on a farm near Galva who built a new house and invited the neighbors to a "housewarming." The woman of the house stood at the door welcoming friends and saying to the men, "Walk right in, gintlemin. We have ivery convaniance in the wurruld—lay your hats right on the bid." For Mr. Barlow this was a sidesplitter and you joined your laugh with his. When Sam Barlow said of a fellow, "He ain't got the sense Christ gave an oyster," I asked three or four questions about whether oysters have any sense at all and if it stood anywhere in the Bible that Christ had anything to do with oysters. Barlow said, "You can forget it, Charlie, we got our work to think about." I had respect for Sam Barlow when one day he spoke of a young fellow he had been watching for years. "He never gets started," said Sam. "He's always getting ready to begin to start to commence."

Most of the time I combed and curried two of the horses in the barn. But there were mornings when Bill Walters was supposed to tend to those two horses. A couple of times I told him the horses didn't look so slick as they might, and he said, "I let 'em go today with a lick and a promise." He could say this with a slant and a flicker of his eyes and I couldn't hold it against him. I studied about how to let chores go with "a lick and a promise."

Walters lived a few blocks away, with no children and a wife who sometimes came over to our barn to see how things were going. She was a quiet woman, well built with curves, easy in her motions like she might have made a good dancer. She had deep-black glossy hair, a sweet, well-made face with a sad mouth, full lips. When sometimes she flashed her black eyes toward Sam Barlow and held them on him, I thought she seemed to be sweet on him. He would hold his brown eyes on her a little dreamy and then suddenly break it off with a joke or going about fixing something. I was sure there was something away deep between them they couldn't talk about before other people.

The year of 1896 I followed politics in Victor Lawson's *Chicago Record* every weekday. I read the paper on the wagon and waiting for the wagon. That year too I read from cover to cover *The People's Party Campaign Book* by Thomas E. Watson of Georgia. I was leaning to the Populists. They had elected Senators and Congressmen in Kansas and Nebraska. They looked better to me that year than the Republicans or the Democrats. One day with our milk delivered and driving back to the barn, I talked a long streak to Sam Barlow about the rich being too rich and the poor being too poor, farmers losing their farms on account of mortgages and low prices for their wheat, corn, and cattle, millions of workers in the cities who couldn't get jobs, hell to pay all down the line, and how was it going to end and what was to come? Sam Barlow sat quiet for a spell and then said, "Well, Charlie, I'll tell you what's the matter. There's just getting to be too many people in the world, just too many goddam people. We've got to have a war and kill off a lot of 'em before times will get real better." I didn't let out a cheep. I was stumped. This was a point I hadn't read about in the *Chicago Record* or *The People's Party Campaign Book*. I knew I would have to read more and do more thinking of some kind for myself before I would know more that I was sure of.

At home, on the milk wagon, or waiting for it, I read several times William Jennings Bryan's "Cross of Gold" speech that swept the Democratic National Convention and swung to Bryan the nomination for President. I followed his speeches across the country and I heard him speak in Galesburg and in Monmouth. He was my hero, the Man of the People who spoke for the right, and against him were the Enemies of the People. He opened his mouth and the words pouring out were, for me in that year, truth and gospel. Later I would find out he was a voice, an orator, an actor, a singer, and not much of a thinker.

I enjoyed the fury of the campaign, so much to laugh at or to cry over if you liked crying. One Chicago newspaper kept after Bryan day on day calling him a "Popocrat," half Populist and half Democrat, and I liked the fun of it. When they called him the Boy Orator of the Platte I said that was all right. He was only thirty-five and if he had been a year younger he couldn't have run for President—and he sure was an orator—and he came from Nebraska where the Platte River winds over the prairie. Even when they said his mind was like the Platte River, "a mile wide and only an inch deep," I liked it as being smart and funny. It would be some time before I found it was half true.

I opened every day's newspaper to see what next the Honorable William McKinley was saying in Canton, Ohio. Republicans from Galesburg went to that Ohio town to stand on the lawn and see their candidate for President come out and give a front-porch speech. While Bryan traveled thousands of miles McKinley stuck to his front porch. I read of Mr. McKinley saying that the right Protective Tariff would soon have the smoke coming out of the chimneys of the idle factories and again the American workingman would have a Full Dinner Pail. Everywhere you could hear the Republicans talking about how nice it would be to see the smoke pouring out of those chimneys again and how the Empty Dinner Pail would be full. They gave words from Andrew Carnegie, "Soot on the window sill means prosperity." The big word was Prosperity, and you got it with soot on the window sill.

I read a ten-cent paper-covered book, *Coin's Financial School* by William H. Harvey, a smooth and tricky book. I read parts of it and believed the Money Question was simple as ABC or two plus four. Millions of people read it and, like me, believed the country would be saved if we could have—what? How we rolled it over on our tongues, how we rang it out of our mouths because the other side didn't like the sound of it—the Free and Unlimited Coinage of Silver! The other side we called "Gold Bugs." I learned to say, "In 1873 silver was struck down, silver was demonetized." And if I was asked, "How do you mean struck down and what is demonetized?" I could come up with forty different answers. My father stayed Republican. Not for a split second would he think about voting for Bryan and Free Silver. We had it hot and heavy over the supper table that summer. It was the first time in my life I enjoyed argument just to be arguing. I studied how to put the other side in a hole. Mary said I was so good at arguing that maybe I ought to be a lawyer. I sent for the prospectus of the Sprague Correspondence School of Law and considered if I could be a lawyer. Then I sent for the prospectus of the Sprague Correspondence School of Journalism and half decided I would make a better journalist than lawyer and time would tell.

Sam Barlow stayed Republican. One day I did some quiet arguing with him, not trying to put him in a hole, but just trying to change his mind into voting for Bryan and Free Silver. He heard me all the way through. Then the words came cool and kind from under his thick sandy mustache, "You make out a pretty good case, Charlie, but I can't see it. I've voted the Republican ticket all my life and it's too late for me to change. I wouldn't feel at home with the Democrats." From then on we talked about business, the customers, the weather—and women. Once he said, "There's more good women

than bad. I've found that out, Charlie. I don't know what my life
would have been without women." On a hot summer day when I
came out of a house after pouring a quart of milk for a woman, she
stood in the doorway and watched us drive away. She was rosy-
cheeked and her fine figure could be made out under her thin sum-
mer dress. She gave a nod of her head and a smile to us as we drove
away, and Sam Barlow said, "Wouldn't she be something to crawl
into bed with on a cold winter night!"

Barlow had dropped going to church. He had been a Methodist
or Baptist and said, "I've heard preachers who were good for me but
most of them just palaver, a lot of blowhards. I'm still in favor of
God and Jesus but I want to work it out my own way. I guess I
belong to the Big Church." I asked, "What's that?" And Barlow,
"That's the one that takes in all of 'em. I guess any religion is good
if you live up to what it says it stands for. They're all good but
they've all got too many hypocrites. I know when I do right with-
out any preacher telling me. And I know when I do wrong and I'm
ashamed of myself without any preacher telling me." Many a time
Sam Barlow put it like this: "It's a world we never made. We can't
have things as we want 'em. We have to take things as they come."

After sixteen or eighteen months with Barlow, at twelve dollars a
month and a good dinner every day, I asked him for a raise in pay.
He said the business couldn't stand it. I had to say, "My bones tell
me I'm not getting anywhere. I hate to leave you. You're the best
man I ever worked for but I can't see I'm getting anywhere." He
said, "If you have to go, then all right, Charlie. What has to be has
to be. You've been a good boy and we've had some good times to-
gether. I hope you'll come around and see us once in a while." I
dropped in a few times. They put in a new Edison phonograph with
a lot of cylinder records and I never got tired of hearing "Poet and
Peasant." Sam Barlow and I stayed good friends as long as he lived.

The tinner had his shop on Seminary Street a half-block south of
Main in a wooden building no bigger than a freight-train caboose
and the paint peeling off the boards. A sign in the window read, Tin
Work of All Kinds. I had often passed the place and seen the tinner
going in and coming out. He seemed to be worried and always

hustling, a medium-small man in clothes that hung loose on him and a slouch hat. crumpled on his head. He needed a haircut and hair would stick out from a hole in the hat. His face could look absent-minded as though he had thoughts far away and over the hills. I knew he had been in this shop a year or more and that people came to him for tinwork.

I opened the door and walked in one October day to ask him if he had a job where I could learn the tinner's trade. He said, without asking my name or where I came from or why did I want to be a tinner, "You can start in tomorrow morning at seven o'clock." He studied a knothole in the floor half a minute. "I can pay you three dollars a week. Come seven in the morning." He didn't ask whether I had any experience or recommendations or where I last worked or whether I ever had worked anywhere. He didn't ask my name and I didn't know his.

Next morning I was there at the shop door at seven o'clock. I tried the door, found it locked, and stood around and waited. Near eight o'clock he came along in a one-horse wagon. We loaded an outfit on the wagon and drove out to Broad Street and the house of the well-known Galesburg photographer Osgood. A cold October wind was blowing hard. We set up ladders, went up to the low slop-ing tin roof of the kitchen. I helped him pull loose old and worn tin sheets. Then the wind pulled at the tin sheets as we carried them to the ladder and on down to the ground. Sometimes the wind shook the sheets, twisted and crackled them. The tin sheets were rough, with cutting edges, and our hands couldn't get a full hold on them while we wrestled against the high wind. At twelve o'clock the boss said we could knock off. I ate a lunch I had brought in a paper bag. It was near two o'clock when the boss came back. I hadn't been sure in the morning nor the day before, but this time I did get the whiff of his whisky breath. He was fumbly going up the ladder. His feet slipped once but his hands kept their hold on a rung and he made it to the roof. I followed him and brought up a soldering out-fit, making two trips bringing up new sheets of tin. He soldered two or three of these sheets and near four o'clock said we would knock off for the day.

I remember the one and only time he smiled and then it was a

queer half-smile. A crazy wind had twists in it blowing over the roof
as he tried to solder two tin sheets. And as he pulled his hat tighter
down on his head so it wouldn't blow off, he looked toward me.
"You know, there never was but one tinsmith ever went to hell.
And you know why? He tried to solder with a cold iron."

The next morning I was on hand at seven o'clock, and now it was
nine o'clock when my boss came in the wagon, the whisky breath
still on him. We drove out to the Osgood house again and he soldered
maybe three or four sheets on the roof. At twelve o'clock he said we
would quit for the day. I was glad of it because he had slipped
again on the ladder, had nearly slid down the roof once, and his
hands were fumbly on the job. The next morning I was at the shop
at eight o'clock, waited till ten, walked around up and down Main
Street a while, and came back at eleven and at twelve to find the door
locked.

Then and there at twelve o'clock noon I decided I didn't want
to learn the tinner's trade. I felt sorry for the tinner. He had been
a good man once and then had gone too far with the booze. I said,
"I won't go back and ask him for my pay—he's too near his finish."
A few weeks later I saw the place closed and the sign Tin Work of
All Kinds gone.

When I took a job washing bottles in a pop bottling works one sum-
mer I didn't expect to learn a trade. I knew the future in the job
was the same as the past. You washed the same kind of bottles in the
morning and afternoon today as you would be washing in the morn-
ing and afternoon tomorrow, and yesterday had been the same. You
could see the used bottles coming in and the washed bottles going
out and it was "Here they come" and "There they go" from seven
in the morning till six at night. There was one point about the job
they told you when they hired you. You could drink all the pop
you wanted. Morning, noon, and afternoon, you could pour down
your goozle all the pop you wanted. It could have been that was
what made me want to try the job. I began drinking pop, bottle after
bottle. On the fourth day the diarrhea set in and went on for three or
four days. On those days I didn't drink pop. In the days after I didn't
drink pop. I had had enough pop to last me a lifetime. At the end of

two weeks I quit the job. I didn't like the sight of pop or pop bottles coming in and going out and today the same as yesterday and to-morrow.

There was the summer I was going to learn the potter's trade. East of Day Street, next to the Peoria tracks, stood a pottery that had been going a year or two. On the ground floor were the turners. You had to be a real potter, who had learned his trade, to be a turner. You had a "ball pounder" working for you, next to you at the bench. The ball pounder—that was me—put on a wooden scale and weighed enough clay to make a jug. I would throw this clay on the bench. I wouldn't touch it with my fingers—they wouldn't give it the lift needed to carry it in the air and bring it down and cut it in two across a wire. It was quite a trick to learn how to brace your wrists and throw the lower half of the palms of the hands into the clay and raise it and then cut it in two across the wire. I was warned that my wrists would be sore for a week or two, and they were. They ached and burned at times so I couldn't sleep at night. But after ten days the soreness was over and I could talk to the other ball pounders like I was one of them.

The "ball" you pounded out to a finish was cake-shaped, its size depending on the size of the jug to come. The turner threw it on a turning iron disk, sprinkled water on it, guided it with a hand scraper, and built it up into a jug. Then he stopped the turning disk and slicked out a handle that he smoothed onto the jug. Next, with my hands careful, I moved the jug off the disk and put it on a near-by rack to dry a little and then go for baking to a dome-shaped kiln outside the main building.

The turners were a gay lot who had worked in Eastern potteries and in Posey County, Indiana. They roared their private jokes about the kind of potters who learned their trade in Posey County. On the second floor were the molders, who didn't class up with the turners. They threw the clay into plaster-of-Paris molds on a turning wheel, scraped the inside of the crock or jar, and the mold and the wheel did the rest.

One morning I went down to breakfast to hear that the pottery had burned down in the night. I went out and walked around the smoking walls to see the fire had made a clean sweep of it. It was easy to decide I wouldn't be a potter.

On the main road running past the end of Lake George was a steep hill where the trolley-car motormen put on the brakes and watched close going down the hill. On the uphill trip it was slow and hard going. So they graded the hill. Men drove mule teams with scrapers, one man driving the mules, another man walking between the handles of the scraper, and when the big shovel of the scraper filled up they turned around and dumped it lower down the hill. They went on with this till the hill was a long nice slope and not a hill at all. I was interested because I was a water boy on this job for three weeks in hot summer weather. I carried two buckets of water from a pump a hundred yards away, two tin cups for each bucket. Some of the men called me "sonny," and it was, "This way, sonny," and "I can stand some of that, sonny," and "You come to the right man, sonny." Then between-times the mules had to have water. I would rather have been just water boy to the men and not to the mules. A mule would often drink nearly a whole pail of water. It was a hundred yards to where I could get another and the mules had no way of calling me "sonny." I remembered about camels going days without water and I wished I could change the mules into camels.

One summer I worked for Mr. Winfield Scott Cowan, who ran the boathouse and refreshment stand at Lake George near where the trolley cars stopped. Mr. Cowan had married a daughter of George W. Brown and lived in a big house across the street from the Brown Cornplanter Works. He was a medium-sized man with a dark-brown mustache and he knew how the business should be run, down to such fine points that nearly always he was worrying about this or that not going to come out right. If anything went wrong he acted as though something else was going to go wrong pretty soon.

My job was to let rowboats to people who would pay twenty-five cents an hour to sit in a boat and handle the oars or watch the scenery or talk to the women or girls in the boat. I would give them the oars, help them pick a boat, and help them shove off. I had charge of the refreshments and sold ice cream and cake or cookies, pop ginger ale, and a line of candies.

Mr. Bobbit had charge of the little steamboat that held ten or twelve people, twenty-five cents for a ride to the end of the lake and back. People said she was the prettiest steamboat in Knox County, and as there was no other steamboat anywhere in Knox County it was the solemn truth. Her name was *Lady Washington*. Mr. Bobbit kept up steam all day, and on some days had all the passengers he could handle and other days nobody riding. A man-sized man, Mr. Bobbit, he was tall, broad-shouldered, thick through the body, quick in his motions, always seemed to know what was going on and what to do. He had a blond mustache, keen eyes that could twinkle. He was English and had been a policeman somewhere, I heard, and I am sure he was a first-class policeman. He was good company and said, "I worry when it's time to worry and what you don't know sometimes is a help." Bobbit told about his boarding-house. After supper at night all the boarders lighted cigars and they smoked slow and careful. The first one whose ashes dropped off his cigar had to pony up for cigars for the bunch.

I saw the *Lady Washington* pull away from the wharf one day and she had one passenger worth a long look, a young woman with a fine face, a pale white face with a tight anxious look on it, and her hair very black against the white of her face. When the *Lady Washington* came back from her trip Bobbit and two men carried the young woman off—her clothes, shoes, face, and hair dripping wet. She had jumped off the boat and Bobbit had jumped in after her and brought her back to the *Lady Washington*. She lived, and they said it was a love affair that had made her want to die rather than live. Bobbit said, "When they told me she had jumped overboard and I saw her in the water I couldn't think of anything to do but to jump in after her. She tried to fight me off but I brought her in. She won't thank me now, I guess, but I'll bet the time will come when she'll say I did the right thing."

It didn't come hard to leave Mr. Winfield Scott Cowan at the end of the season, him and his worrying. He had no end of questions he would keep asking about this and that which wasn't going wrong. I wouldn't have been surprised to hear him say, "I'm not healthy unless I worry." Leaving the company of Bobbit wasn't so good. He was a hero to me. He was good for whatever ailed me. He said he ex-

pected a night-watchman job in the fall and winter. I said I hoped
I'd see him again, though I never did.

Two weeks of ice harvest on Lake George came one January, the
thermometer from zero to fifteen above. I walked from home six
blocks to catch a streetcar that ran the mile and a half out to the
lake. The night gang worked from seven at night till six in the
morning with an hour off at midnight.

The ice was twelve to eighteen inches thick. Men had been over
it with horse teams pulling ice cutters. In the first week on the job I
was a "floater." Rafts of ice about fifteen feet long and ten feet wide
had been cut loose. The floater stood on a raft and pushing a pronged
pole he propelled the raft and himself to the chutes at the big ice-
house. There the ice was broken into blocks or cakes, and a belt
carried them up where they were stood in rows with sawdust
sprinkled between to hold them cold till summer and warm weather.

I had overshoes and warm clothes and enjoyed the work, though
I was tired along about daybreak. The air was crisp. You could see
a fine sky of stars any time you looked up, sometimes a shooting star
and films of frost sparkles. The other floaters were good fellows and
we hollered to each other over the dark water our warnings that if
you fell in the water you'd find it cold.

At midnight we went up a slope to the Soangetaha Clubhouse of
the bon ton. On the porch, away from the windy side and out of any
cold wind blowing, we ate what we had carried out in paper bags.
My mother fixed me pork-chop and bacon sandwiches or roast beef
with pickles, doughnuts, and a small bottle of coffee. It was a cold
meal but I wolfed every mouthful and tasted it to the limit. I had
never had a night job that kept me till the sun came up. That week
I got acquainted with a little of what goes on over the night sky,
how the Big Dipper moves, how the spread of the stars early in the
night keeps on with slow changes into something else all night long. I
did my wondering about how that spread of changing stars was
made, how long it took to make, how long it could last, and how
little any one of us is standing and looking up at it.

The second week I was taken off as a floater and put in the ice-
house, where a dozen or so of us worked on a footing of blocks or

cakes of ice, the chute feeding us more cakes of ice. Each cake was about three feet long, two feet wide, and a foot thick. We threw our iron tongs into the end of a cake and then rassled and wrangled it to where it stood even with a row of other cakes. Heavy work, it had your back and shoulder muscles pulling and hauling like a mule. I had never before felt so sure that what I was doing could be done better somehow by mules or machines. I went home the first morning with muscles from ankles to neck sore and aching. I ate breakfast, went to bed right away, and lay abed trying to coax myself to sleep. But muscles would twitch and give signals and it was past noon before I went to sleep. Then three or four times I suddenly came awake and the muscles kept singing. When my mother woke me and said, "It's time to go to work," I was just beginning to sleep, it seemed. To get out of bed and into my clothes I had to slowly unwind myself, leg, back, and shoulder muscles stiff and sore.

The second night of clamping the tongs into those ice oblongs, dragging them twenty or thirty feet, setting them on end, getting back to the chute bottom where they kept sliding down and piling up—the second night was worse. Sometimes the tongs slipped and you hooked a new hold. Or your feet slipped on the ice underfoot. Or the ice slipped and slid because the ice cake you set it on had a slant and you had to call for sawdust on it. I would try for a rest by walking slow back to the chute. If I tried for a rest standing still two or three minutes, the foreman would come along, a quiet man saying in a voice that just carried over the noise of the rattling chute and the hustling men, "Better slide into it, Sandburg." If he had bawled it at me or snarled it, I would have quit the job on the spot. He remembered my name and I wasn't just a number, I was a person. And he said "Better slide into it" nearly like my mother waking me out of sleep to go to work. I had respect for him and hoped sometime I could be a foreman and act and talk quiet like him.

I didn't weigh much more than a hundred and fifteen pounds and each cake of ice weighed nearly as much as I did. I dragged and slipped and kept hauling away at my own weight all night long. Near daybreak I thought to myself, "Come seven o'clock and I'll tell 'em I'm quitting." I stood still thinking about it and getting a rest when the foreman came along. "Better slide into it, Sandburg. You know there's only a few more days on this job. I think we'll be through this week." And that gave me a different feeling. I went home, slept better, ate better, and the muscles all round weren't as stiff. I lasted the week through, and at a dollar and twenty-five cents pay a night I had earned higher wages than in any work before. One thing I noticed. I hustled a little too much. Most of the other men on the job had been railroad section hands, ditch-diggers, pick-and-shovel men, and they knew what my father sometimes reminded me of on a piece of work, "Take your time, Sholly." They worked with a slow and easy swing I hadn't learned.

Most of that week my sleep was restless. Those back and shoulder muscles would begin singing, "Wake up now and talk to us a little and think about us." I'm sure, too, that the rush and excitement of the work—ten hours straight with only that midnight hour to stop and rest, always expected to keep up your end—did something to my nerves and mind. One afternoon I was sleeping good and I had a dream. The house was on fire. I could smell the smoke. I woke out of my sleep. But in my waking I was still under the spell of that dream. I jumped out of bed, didn't stop to put on my clothes. I rushed down to the kitchen and cried to my mother, "The house is on fire! We've got to do something!" She turned from kneading a roll of dough and smiled. "No, everything is all right, Charlie. You go back to sleep." Then I came really awake. I couldn't smell the smoke I had smelled in bed upstairs. I saw there wasn't any fire. I said, "Mama, that dream fooled me." She said, "I know about it. I've had dreams fool me." She could say a blessing with her smile. I went back to bed and slept good again. Before going to sleep I said, "If that dream comes again I'll turn over and go to sleep and let the house burn down."

I thought of my ice-harvest days one year in May when the Glenwood Ice Company, the one I worked for, had big ads in the newspapers. There had been warm weather in May, and suddenly came a cold spell and you needed your overcoat again. The ads were asking how it had come to happen that such cold was sweeping over the town. And they would like to tell the public that it just happened because somebody had opened the doors of the big icehouse of the Glenwood Ice Company and let out the cold of their wonderful ice.

These clever ads were the first work of the Knox College student Earnest Elmo Calkins. He was practicing. He went to New York later and made a big name and money in advertising. More than that, he wrote a book, *They Broke the Prairie*, one of the most interesting histories ever written about a small American town, telling how they settled Galesburg in 1837 and what happened to the town over the next hundred years. When I met him we talked about our old days with the Glenwood Ice Company, the main ice company in Galesburg for many years. It folded and faded when the Weinberg brothers, across the tracks from the Q. depot, started the Galesburg Artificial Ice Company and made and sold ice cheaper and better. Then came the electric refrigerators, and they drove the artificial ice out of business. And when winter comes now there are no icehouses where men and boys hook tongs into ice cakes and set them up in rows and sprinkle sawdust between.

TWELVE

Cigarette Biographies

The first biography I owned was of a size I could put in any one of my four vest pockets. I didn't buy it. I found it and said, "Finders keepers!" I was going along to the Seventh Ward school when I saw it on a sidewalk on Seminary Street near Second, about two blocks from the house where I was born. I picked it up from the wooden board where it had been rained on. I brushed the dirt off and smoothed it where the top corner had been scorched. When I measured it later it was two and three-fourths inches long and one and one-half inches wide. The front cover had gloss paper and a color picture of the head and shoulders of a two-star general in a Confederate gray uniform. The title read *A Short History of General P. T. Beauregard.* I turned to the back cover and saw two soldiers, one sitting on a stretcher, the other standing and aiming a rifle at someone off somewhere. The color of their uniforms was halfway and I couldn't be sure whether they were Confederate or Union. Down below I made out the Stars and Bars, the Confederate flag. Inside the front cover I saw "Facsimile Signature" and the exact way he wrote his name "G.T. Beauregard" and under it his rank, "Gen. Comd." (the General Commanding). I could see he was a fancy writer. He made scrolls and windings like you see on wallpaper or like a skater cutting the figure eight. You could tell he wasn't in a hurry when he signed his name and he wanted it to stand out that he was the general commanding.

On the title page opposite I got his full name and how to spell it:

General Pierre Gustave Toutant Beauregard. After a blank page came thirteen pages of reading in fine print. Inside the back cover was a list of a "Series of Small Books," histories of Civil War generals, fifty of them, starting with Banks, Beauregard, and Bragg and running through to the last three, Sigel, Smith, and Stuart, with a notice of "other series in preparation." And here you learned how to get these books. It said "Packed in Duke's Cigarettes." The more packages of Duke's Cigarettes you bought the more histories you would have. If you bought enough packages and read all the histories, you would know a lot about the Civil War generals.

I couldn't think about buying first one ten-cent package of Duke's Cameo or Duke's Cross-Cut cigarettes, and then more and more of those ten-cent packages, for the sake of filling my vest pockets with histories, nice as they were. For one thing cigarettes had a bad name among us kids. We believed only "dudes" and "softies" smoked them. We had a name for cigarettes—"pimp sticks." We had never seen any pimps that we knew of but we had heard they were pale and slim and hung around bad women and died early. We had another name for cigarettes—"coffin nails." Every one you smoked was another nail in your coffin.

Our physiology books in school had warned us that tobacco has nicotine in it and nicotine is a poison. We half believed this and when we bought Virginia Cheroots at five for a nickel or the ten little "cigaroos" for a nickel and smoked them, we were like strong men not afraid of nicotine and ready to take a chance on what real tobacco could do to us. Then too with cigarettes you were supposed to inhale and take the poison straight into your lungs. This could lead you into consumption, or anyhow it would weaken your wind and slow you down as a runner or a ballplayer.

I scouted around and found three men who bought and smoked Duke's Cigarettes "once in a while for a change." One of them was saving the little books for himself. The other two saved them for me. One of them said, "What the hell do you want of those little fool books? I been throwin 'em away. But if you want 'em I'll keep 'em for you. There won't be many. I buy only one pack a month." The months went by and after a while I had the histories of Beauregard, Cornelius Vanderbilt, and Sarah Bernhardt, *The Life of T. De Witt*

Talmage, and the lives of George Peabody, James B. Eads, Horace B. Claflin, and Robert Ingersoll. They changed from *History of* to *Life of.* In their lives of "poor boys who have become rich" the list had fifty, starting with Russell A. Alger, Mary Anderson, John Jacob Astor, Jake Kilrain, and ending with Vanderbilt, Wanamaker, Whittier. I couldn't see where Mary Anderson was a poor boy who had become rich nor how Jake Kilrain after John L. Sullivan's knockout of him was on the way to being rich.

In the list I noticed John Ericsson, the inventor of the *Monitor,* the Swede who helped the North win the war. I tried but couldn't scare up a copy of the John Ericsson. A Swede boy pulled one out of his vest pocket one day and grinned at me. He knew I wanted it. I offered him a penny for it and went as high as a nickel and he shook his head. Then he let me borrow it to read and I let him borrow my Sarah Bernhardt. He had heard she kept a coffin in her bedroom and liked to stretch out in it to rest. I showed him where the book told about that and what kind of a woman she was. "They say she is the world's greatest actress," I told him, and then read to him from the book, how "she recites her lines as the nightingale sings, as the wind sighs, as the waters murmur." "Gee, I'd like to hear her," said the Swede boy, and I went on reading so as to get to the coffin:

She has been said to be dying of consumption for years, so she drinks brandy to heal her lungs, leads a life of feverish excitement, made up of keen, artistic labor as an actress, a modeler and a painter. In her salon she has a cerceuil, or coffin, placed on a stand. It is covered with white satin and white velvet, draped with expensive white thread lace. In this she lies during the day, as on a lounge, and it can be seen by her and her guests during their gayest, maddest hours of feasting.

"Gee!" said the Swede boy. "Do you believe that? She has the coffin she's going to be buried in right there before all those other people who will go to her funeral and she gets into that coffin and lays there where they can all see her only she isn't dead?"

"The book says so and I think she's that kind of a woman," I told him. "Now listen about her bedroom":

Her bedroom is hung with white satin, and rich white lace falls from the ceiling to the floor; but the bed alcove and bed are covered with black satin, and the curtains are black funeral velvet and black lace.

"Jesus, what a bedroom!" said the Swede boy. "I sure want to read that book." I offered to trade him the Sarah Bernhardt for his John Ericsson. He said maybe and the next day said he talked it over with his Swede father and mother and they said, "No, you keep the John Ericsson. He was a great man and this French actress is a bad woman."

The Beauregard book began with a little poem that made me expect he must be one of the greatest generals that ever lived:

> There is a page in the book of fame,
> On it is written a single name
> In letters of gold, on spotless white,
> Encircled with stars of quenchless light;
> Never a blot that page hath marred,
> And the star-wreathed name is BEAUREGARD.

After reading the book I felt the poem went too far. The book made him out a just fair-to-middling general and a good deal of an actor and said the Confederate President Jefferson Davis took it on himself one time "to encourage the report in Richmond that he [Beauregard] had become insane, and was no longer fit for a command." So I was left in the air and could only think either that Jeff Davis was a liar or Beauregard had gone crazy, and if so then the poem was wrong about no blot "hath marred" his "star-wreathed name."

I read each of my vest-pocket books at least once and went back to favorite spots in them. I believed more than half of what I read, mostly I suppose because they hardly ever said one thing on one page and the opposite on another page. I was sure that Cornelius Vanderbilt was the second-born of nine children and his birthday was in May 1794, though they didn't put in which day in May 1794 and that was a sign they didn't have a Family Bible where you could tell when each of the nine children came into the world and first saw the light of day. The first sentences in the book said it is good to be born poor and to be born on a farm:

America, the land of self-made men—the one country in the world where it is possible for a man to rise by his own effort from obscurity and poverty not only to the highest place in society, but to the more courted rank of millionaire as well—has witnessed no more remarkable career than that of Commodore Vanderbilt. Some one has aptly said: "Scratch a New York millionaire and you will find a farm-boy underneath."

I read how the boy's father "speculated," lost his money and was going to lose his farm. Then the mother, "a woman of rare qualities," climbed up to an old Dutch clock and brought out three thousand dollars in cold cash, "the careful hoardings of years," and saved the farm. From his mother he learned how to be careful and how to hoard, when it paid. He married at nineteen "his fair cousin, Sophia Johnson," began buying steamboats, went in for shipping, and was making plenty of money. I was interested where the book said:

While he was laying such sure foundations for the enormous wealth that afterward came to him, it is said he had certain radical socialistic ideas, among others that "no man ought ever to be worth more than twenty-thousand dollars." He then regarded John Jacob Astor as a "dangerous monopolist"; yet after leaving the command of his little steamboat Captain Vanderbilt made thirty-thousand dollars a year for the first five years, then doubled it in 1836. Before he had reached his prime the Commodore was worth half a million. When the gold fever broke out in California in 1849, he opened his famous Nicaraguan route to the Pacific. From the latter venture alone he confessed to having made a million dollars a year for a time.

He went into railroad buying and building and speculating in railroad stock. The country read how in one deal alone he cornered "Harlem stock" and cleaned up two millions. I was getting more clear on why men and boys, when asked to lend a dollar or a nickel, would sometimes say, "Who do you think I am? Vanderbilt?"

On the back of another book was a bare-shouldered woman worth looking at, one breast bare, and she held a shining green wreath and a banner that read above her "Charity" and below, "George Peabody, Philanthropist." It was what we called a "jawbreaker," the word "philanthropist," but the book made it clear. "During his long life he not only gave away millions of dollars but he placed his great wealth where it would do the most good." After making one fortune in America in the grocery and dry-goods business he went to London as a banker and made a bigger fortune. For all of his money he didn't marry and the book said: "The story is told that a young American girl who had refused him in the day when money was scarce married one of his friends, whereupon Peabody resolved to remain single —a resolve which he faithfully kept." I wanted to know more about that girl and how her husband did by her and what they talked about when George Peabody threw a million dollars to Baltimore for a free library, lecture hall, academy of music, and an art gallery—and later when he put three millions into tearing away tumbledown shanties in the London slums and building brick houses with a little grass around for children to play on—and later when he put another three million dollars into better schools for the Negro children of the South. The Queen of England wanted to give Peabody a title. He thanked her, said he could get along without it, and went home to Baltimore, where twenty thousand children met him and waved their hands and their handkerchiefs and he said, "Never have I seen a more beautiful sight." I wondered if the girl who had refused him was anywhere among the thousands of grownups looking on. On the front cover Mr. Peabody's white hair fell over his ears, and with his white side whiskers he reminded me of one of our Lutheran deacons.

Horace B. Claflin was the only one on a front cover who had his hat on. The back cover showed men tussling with big boxes marked "Dry Goods" and a horse team with a dray waiting to be loaded. I learned that Mr. Claflin was the greatest man in America in the dry-goods field in his time, and during the Civil War in one year his sales ran to seventy-six million dollars. He was born in a poor family in Milford, Massachusetts, and when his father said he ought to go to college and learn Latin and Greek he said he was going to be a merchant and the Latin and Greek would be wasted. There wasn't much more than that except what a good boy Horace was when he was a boy and what a good man Mr. Claflin was after he had made his millions.

The *Life of James B. Eads* was a little better, though not much. On page five it said, "He acquired a large amount of information on civil engineering and other subjects of the kind." Anybody would know that without being told. He invented and built ironclad gunboats to fight the Confederates on the Mississippi River, and he built the famous Eads bridge across the Mississippi River at St. Louis and did other fine things where he needed more than "a large amount of information." The best of the book was a picture on the back cover of the St. Louis bridge and three steamboats, one of them with smokestacks pouring smoke.

The *Life of Robert Green Ingersoll* showed on the back cover two little red devils with books, one of the books marked "Voltaire." I hadn't heard the name of Voltaire and said I would read extra-careful about him when I got to him in the *Cyclopaedia of Persons and Places* because the little devils seemed to be having such fun with Voltaire's books. I read this vest-pocket book up, down, and across five times and more. I had heard that Ingersoll was a "free thinker" and was against the churches and didn't believe in God. His home was in Peoria, only fifty miles from Galesburg, where he was a lawyer and would go out and give lectures. He had come to Galesburg and lectured but I didn't have the fifty cents to get in. He had a wonderful voice and they said he was "a wizard with words." When my mother said with a sad face, "He is a bad man and is doing the work of Satan," I didn't care so much to go and hear him even if I had the fifty cents.

Reading this little book about Ingersoll, I came to see why although he was a free thinker and made fun of the Bible, he had many friends even among the church people. He had been a Democrat before the Civil War, turned Republican when Lincoln called for soldiers, helped raise a regiment of cavalry, and after a year of hard fighting in Tennessee he was taken prisoner along with hundreds of his men. He became famous as a campaign speaker for the Republicans, and the speech he made nominating James G. Blaine for President at the national convention in 1876 "held all hearers breathless." I said to my mother, "You hear it on all sides that he is one of the greatest men in the Republican Party. I have heard Republicans say he is one of the best men living and there is nothing wrong about him except his religion." And she said, "I don't know about that. I know he is against the church and takes away the faith of people in God." From what I had heard and from what I now read of his life, I made my guess that Ingersoll wouldn't have been so well liked if it wasn't that he was such a grand fighter for the Republicans though people were saying that the Republicans would never try to elect him governor of Illinois. There had been talk about that but there were too many voters who looked at him like my mother did. Father said, "We won't talk about him." I am sure Papa was puzzled that so great a Republican, who made the grand speech nominating Blaine for President, could not be a good churchman like nearly all Republicans.

Half of the book about Ingersoll was taken from his speeches. Now I could see what they meant about how he could use language. "Newspapers all over the land," said the book, printed his speech in 1879 at the reunion of the Army of the Tennessee in the Palmer House in Chicago. Ingersoll had been a volunteer and had a right to speak on "The Volunteer Soldiers of the Union Army." He said at the end, "And now let us drink to the volunteers: to those who sleep in unknown, sunken graves, whose names are only in the hearts of those they loved and left, of those who often hear in happy dreams the footsteps of return. Let us drink to those who died while lipless famine mocked. One to all the maimed whose scars give modesty a tongue, and all who dared and gave to chance the care, the keeping of their lives; to all the dead; to Sherman, to Sheridan, and to Grant—the foremost soldier of the world; and last to Lincoln, whose loving life, like a bow of peace, spans and arches all the clouds of war."

I tried to picture him going to Washington to see his brother Eben C. Ingersoll, a Congressman, dying, how at the funeral while reading his speech he broke down and couldn't go on and with his eyes full of tears bowed his head on the coffin. Then he came to and went on. I read his strange words, part of the speech: "Every life, no matter if its every hour is rich with love, and every moment jewelled with a joy, will at its close become a tragedy as sad and deep and dark as can be woven of the warp and woof of mystery and death. This brave and tender man in every storm of life was oak and rock, but in the sunshine he was love and flower. He believed that happiness was the only good, reason the only torch, justice the only worshipper, humanity the only religion, and love the only priest." I was beginning to understand why Chauncey M. Depew, the famous after-dinner speaker, had said that Ingersoll was "the greatest living orator and one of the great controversialists of the age." I looked up "controversialist" and found that if you are a good one you are hard to beat in an argument.

I tried to get my head around some of Ingersoll's sayings. "Every schoolhouse is a cathedral in my religion." "Dignity is a mask some people wear to keep you from finding out how little they know." "I want to satisfy every mother rocking her baby that she is not raising kindling wood for hell." "When your child commits a wrong, take it in your arms, let it feel your heart beat against its heart; let the child know that you really and sincerely love it. . . . I have seen people who acted as though they thought, when the Saviour said, 'Suffer little children to come unto me, for of such is the kingdom of heaven,' that he had a rawhide under his mantle, and made that remark to get the children within striking distance." I could see that somehow I would go on and read more of Ingersoll. I wondered whether he would come again to Galesburg and I would get to hear him. He did come and I did see and hear him in a tent on the Knox campus in 1896 on a cold October night. He spent an hour saying the Gold Standard was correct and right and Free Silver was all wrong. I thought it wasn't much of a speech, even if he did have a rich warm voice with music in it. I had by then read several of his lectures and I would have walked miles to hear his rolling, swinging words about Shakespeare or Burns.

The last of the vest-pocket books I got hold of was the *Life of T. De Witt Talmage*. The way it was spread on right at the start made you curious: "When the future historian shall engrave on the Tablet of Fame the men and events which made the nineteenth century famous, a figure of unique personality will loom up before him in Brooklyn's far-famed preacher, Thomas De Witt Talmage. Scarcely a man occupies today a more conspicuous position before the American public than does this famous pulpiteer." I read this twice and said to myself, Where have I been? How have I missed reading or hearing about this man whose name future historians will engrave on the Tablet of Fame? I will read on. I will learn what a pulpiteer is. I have read what a charioteer is. Now I'll get a line on a pulpiteer. And maybe there will be more about the Tablet of Fame, how it looks and where the historians keep it and whether the names on it are polished every day or once a year. Something like that ran through my little noggin. And next I read:

The utterances of no American reach a wider or greater audience than do his. With his sermons published weekly in over three hundred American newspapers, and in over thirteen different languages of the world, covering the nations of Germany, France, Great Britain, Holland, Russia, and reaching to far-distant Poland, it may be truly said that the man has the world for his audience.

I didn't believe I was especially bright to notice that he wasn't reaching Asia and Africa and the yellow and black peoples weren't reading his sermons. But he was reaching the countries with white people, though here and there he was missing a few of them and I was one until now this book about Mr. Talmage was in my hands. I was sure, as I read on, that I would like to go to Brooklyn and hear him preach. The book made him out a powerful speaker. He filled his church. Six thousand came every Sunday and got seats to hear him, and hundreds who came late couldn't get in. If I went I would go early and slide into a front seat where I could see his face, clean-shaved except for brown side whiskers that hid his ears. I would look for when he lifted his two hands away up over his head like it showed on the back cover. I could see there were people who traveled to New York on business and then crossed over to Brooklyn on a Sunday to hear him so they could say when they got home, "We went and heard Talmage preach." It was a point with me that his sermons were printed after he spoke them. I believed if a sermon gets printed it's more of a sermon than if it is just left in the ears of those who hear it.

Talmage was born on a farm near Bound Brook, New Jersey, studied law, and turned to preaching. He had a church in Belleville, New Jersey, then in Syracuse and Philadelphia, then in Brooklyn, where he had to build big and bigger churches to hold the crowds that came. When at last he had seats for six thousand people to hear him, there were Sundays when one thousand people who came late had to be turned away and go somewhere else without hearing the great Talmage. I could see some of them getting home and saying, "We just couldn't get in. The place was jam-packed." He went to

England for a rest, but they made him preach and the London police
had to shush the crowds away that couldn't get in. He came home in
September 1885 and his ship was met by two big excursion steamers
filled with people cheering him. And at his church after six thousand
people had seats, there were over fifteen thousand outside crying to
get in. The police had to be called to keep order. The big pipe organ
played "Hail to the Chief." The book said "the scene beggared
description."

His church salary was twelve thousand dollars a year, lectures
brought him double that, his printed sermons five thousand dollars
a year, his salary as editor of a monthly magazine five thousand
dollars more. And, said the book, "his income today is easily seventy-
five thousand dollars a year." On this he and his wife, one son, and
five daughters managed to get along. He wasn't stingy. "He is gen-
erous to a fault, and gives thousands of dollars every year to chari-
table purposes." He was yet to go farther. "The zenith of his fame is
not yet reached." I said I must read some of his sermons after read-
ing "No man today is more caricatured or criticised." I looked up
the words and found that when you caricature you poke fun and
when you criticize you find fault. But the book didn't tell what there
was in him to poke fun at nor what faults they said he had.

Away on the last page was a clincher. "Dr. Talmage never
smokes, and to this fact, and to his abstinence from tea and coffee,
he attributes his good health." In a book that came in a package of
Duke's Cigarettes you could read that maybe your health would be
better by staying away from cigarettes. I thought it was pretty
honest for Duke's Cigarettes to let that stay in a book they gave
away. When I finished the book and put it in my vest pocket I said,
"The zenith of his fame is not yet reached." In geography we had
learned the zenith is the top of the sky and you can't go higher. And
the meaning was that Dr. Talmage's fame had gone high and would
go higher. That I could understand though I wished there had been
more about the Tablet of Fame where historians engrave names.

So there was my vest-pocket library of biography and history.
There were days I carried the eight books, four in the upper right-
hand vest pocket and four in the upper left. They had brought me
closer to eight famous persons who were still strangers to me. I

looked at them from a long ways off. I wouldn't know what to say if
one of them patted me on the head and said, "How are you, bub?"
If it was George Peabody I might say, "You sure gave away a lot
of money where it did good, didn't you?" though I doubt it. If it
was Robert Ingersoll I could say, "My father always votes the Re-
publican ticket," though I might find my tongue stuck against the
upper teeth and run away in a hurry. Sarah Bernhardt was too far
off over in Paris for me to think about meeting her. She was the
flashiest woman I ever read about and I would rather read about her
than meet her. But many years later I did see her in the Auditorium
in Chicago in a play called *Camille*, who was a woman with con-
sumption and lay in a bed and moaned "Armand, Armand," in a low
pitiful voice. She was dying and Armand was the man she wanted to
say good-by to. I heard a man say she had lost a leg and was acting
with a wooden leg and another man say it wasn't a wooden leg but
"the best artificial limb that money could buy."

I was proud in a sneaking foolish way about my vest-pocket
library. It was so handy and could be hid so easy. I didn't tell any-
one I was proud. That was my secret. I had books I didn't have to
take back to the Seventh Ward school or the Public Library. I was a
book-owner but it wouldn't do to talk about it.

THIRTEEN

The Auditorium

One night at home we heard the Opera House was burning and I ran down to the corner of Main and Prairie to watch it. I stood there across the street from the fire till midnight. I saw the second story go, heard the floor crash, and saw the firemen keep the fire from spreading. I didn't like to see the place go, I could remember so much about it.

On the stage there I had seen the Kickapoo Indians. They stayed six weeks and I went once or twice a week, admission free. We saw them in buckskins and feather headdress, in dances stomping and howling their lonesome war songs which we went away and tried to imitate. Then the white man they worked for would put in his spiels. If you had rheumatism or aches in muscles or bones you eased it away with Kickapoo Indian Snake Oil. If you had trouble with stomach or liver you took a few spoons of Kickapoo Indian Sagwa and your insides felt better and a bottle or two cured you. He was a slicker. We listened and did imitations of him.

On the stage boards now burning Doctor O'Leary lectured, admission free. Vegetarianism was his line. What he was selling I forget. He stayed three or four weeks telling what meat does to you and how when you eat it you have a tired feeling most of the time and you don't have strength for your work. If you quit eating meat and stick to vegetables your troubles melt away. Every night we heard Doctor O'Leary come straight out against meat in favor of vegetables. After he left town I didn't eat meat for two weeks. I found I had the same tired feeling not eating meat as when I did. I began eating meat again and I couldn't feel the poisons so I forgot about Doctor O'Leary.

There on five or six nights one month I had paid my ten cents to sit in the gallery and watch the first mesmerists I had seen. They looked in the eyes of fellows I knew, made passes in front of their faces, and had them fighting bumblebees, had them swimming across a carpet. There I saw the body of a living man, his head on one table, his feet on another table, his torso and legs stiff as a hard oak log. A rock was laid on his body and it stayed stiff. The powerful blacksmith Ben Holcomb swung a sledge on the rock and split it. And the body didn't give an inch. It stayed stiff and straight through the whole act. Then the mesmerist snapped his fingers in the face of the fellow who had a rock split on his body and nothing but air under his body. The mesmerist said something like "Right! right!" helped the fellow get to his feet, and the two of them held hands and bowed to the applauding audience. "It wasn't a miracle but it was a wonder," we said.

The curving and sizzling tongues of fire had licked away the stage curtain and boards where I had seen a diorama of the Battle of Gettysburg. A di-o-ram-a was what they called it when they told us at Grammar School admission was five cents. One diorama curtain after another came down showing different parts of the battle. The curtains were dirty and worn. The man with a long pointer explaining the battle had short oily whiskers you couldn't tell the color of. His clothes looked like he had slept in them and never brushed them. His voice squeaked. What he was saying ran along so you could tell he had said it so many times that it didn't interest him and his mind was away somewhere else. I got to wondering if he had children to support and what kind of children they were, and how many, and if there were five or six that was plenty to buy shoes for. I was so curious about how creepy and sad the man with the pointer looked that half the time I didn't see what he was pointing at. The main idea I got was that General Reynolds won the battle for the Union Army and General Pickett lost it for the Confederates.

Before my eyes the boards were burning across the street where I had first seen Shakespeare's *Hamlet* and was interested only in the killings at the end. I had heard people tell about seeing Edwin Booth play Hamlet on that stage. On those boards Congressman Philip Sidney Post had made a long Republican campaign speech, and I liked his looks and his voice and hoped I would grow up to where I could understand the kind of talk he was giving. I had seen a man walk out on that stage that I was terribly curious about. I had seen cartoons of him in the Chicago papers. I had expected from what I had read that he would tear the air and beat his chest and stamp his enemies under his feet. But he didn't. His name was John Peter Altgeld and he was running for governor of Illinois. He just stood in the same foot tracks through his whole speech, about an hour and a half, never sawed the air once with his hands. He just stood and talked in a quiet way as though if we should be quiet too we could make up our minds about what he was saying. The few times he did lift his hands to make a point the motions were as if he could be running a hand along the forehead of a sick friend. I went away saying I wasn't sure of all that he had said but from now on I would be more suspicious of his enemies than of him.

Where that stage was burning I had seen a young man with a soft tenor voice come out in a blue-velvet jacket and sing a dreamy song that we liked. I remembered and for years sang the ending lines:

> I never shall forget
> That pretty little pet,
> The maid with the dark blue eyes.

The next day I had a look at what was left. The balcony where I used to sit was empty air. Where the curtain went up, where the boards held together for the actors and speakers to walk and stand, the footlights, and the orchestra pit, they were all empty air except for a thin smoke and a thick smell coming up and spreading around.

On odd days I hung around the new Auditorium at Broad Street and Ferris. Often when out of work and puzzled where to go, I would end up at the Auditorium. It was an up-to-date theater with a main floor, a balcony, and a gallery that nearly everybody called "Nigger Heaven." The seats nearest to the stage, ten or fifteen rows, were the "parkay." On the tickets it said "parquet." It was supposed to be filled with "gay old birds" when a burlesque or leg show came, and people called it the "bald-headed row." Sometimes when I looked at that row I could see a few bald heads—and other times all the heads had plenty of hair. It seemed there were many people who just naturally liked to think there ought to be a row of bald heads come to see a leg show. The stage was big enough to handle any show from Broadway. Nearly every Broadway hit heading straight west made a stop at Galesburg on the Q. main line to Omaha and Denver.

Some of my work at the Auditorium I got paid for. Mostly I got to see the show for a little work I liked to do. The stage carpenter was American-born of Swedish parents, Oscar Johnson, and everybody called him "Husky." He could drive us and swear at us when there was a rush to be on time with all the scenes and props for the next act. We did our best and took it he was blowing off steam and had a right to. Husky Johnson could be withering, as I heard him one day. He came to where stagehands were talking about an actor who was a good deal of a show-off and they didn't quite know what to make of him. One of them asked Husky, "What do you think of him?" And Husky dragged it out slow as if he had been thinking about it: "Well—I'll tell you—I think he's got a pretty good mind— *for an actor.*" We could see that he meant "a pretty good mind" is scarce among actors.

The property man, Charles Rose, everybody called "Cully." He knew he knew everything a property man ought to know and if you wanted an argument any time he would give it to you. Usually he told you where to get off before you could start an argument. He was a corporal in the Galesburg State Militia, Company C, and could give orders in style. He believed in having props in order and on time. He could do quick headwork and we liked the way he ordered us around. Cully Rose hired the "supes." A "supe" was a supernumerary. He didn't travel with the show but they had to have their supes. I suped in *McFadden's Flats.* On the stage was an office scene on the eighth floor of a Chicago skyscraper. Off stage four of us supes watched the man in charge of us. When he went "Ahh-ahh-ahh" real loud and "Ohh-ohh-ohh" louder yet and "Ummhh-umhh-umhh" softer, we did the same. We made the sounds loud or soft following him as his hands went up and down like an orchestra leader. What were we doing? We were making the clatter and the rumbling of the Chicago street eight floors below the office on the stage. The audience out front heard us and some of them must have said, "Chicago sure does have noisy streets and that's the way it sounds from eight floors up." Later in the play the stage was showing the big Chicago fire of 1871 and us supes ran across the stage with boxes, packages, and bundles, moaning and hollering. Then we ran back around the stage, got different boxes, packages, and bundles, and ran across the stage again trying to give out new moans and yells.

It was told that a supe one time was to step out on the stage, open a door, and call out, "The Duke of Buckingham, my lord." That was all, just those six words. But he got flustered when he saw those rows on rows of faces out front and what came out of his mouth was "The Buck of Dukingham, my lord."

We worked as sceneshifters, pulling away a balcony and putting in green pastures with cows grazing, shifting away an old Roman temple and shifting in an old-time New York street end. As we finished there might be at our elbows a few steps away a famous star of the time waiting to make her entrance onto the stage. We would see a comedian in his comic make-up, his face solemn as the Ten Commandments, his eyes on the stage, waiting his cue to go on, his mouth sad. A minute later he would be out there before the footlights wriggling and twisting with his face and eyes all lit up and the audience roaring. Sometimes an actor would be saying in a whisper or a low voice the first line he would say when he stepped out on the stage. They brushed by us after their exits, breathing hard after a heavy scene, sometimes limp and sweating.

Once an actor was almost late. He had got into his costume and make-up and was in the wings ready to go on about ten seconds before he was due on the stage. He said to another actor, "Lordy, lordy, that was a close shave." The other actor: "Did you get bay rum with it?" And Willis Calkins, old Bohunk, said to me afterward, "He thought that was funny, about bay rum with a close shave. Do you think it was funny?" And I said, "I don't know. I'm going to think about it." Bohunk said, "Me too."

When we worked in the "flies" we got ten cents a night. We were up thirty or forty feet. On signals we would send up one curtain and let down another, pulling on ropes. If we got the wrong curtain we certainly heard from down below. Cully Rose could holler and he could be sarcastic. From where we were we could see parts of the play and if there was music or singing we caught it all.

We saw and heard John L. Sullivan close-up playing in *Honest Hearts and Willing Hands*. We could see he liked stepping out on the stage and he wasn't afraid of any audience. In one spot he sat at a table playing he was in trouble and had to use his wits. He put his elbows on the table, lifted his hands, dropped his chin into his cupped hands, and then in a whisper he was sure the audience could hear, "Now I must tink." He was the Strong Boy from Boston and if he wanted to say "tink" instead of "think" nobody was going to challenge him. When he took a curtain call he made a fine low bow to the audience, gave a little speech, ended it "I remain yours truly John L. Sullivan," and walked off the stage.

There was a melodrama where snow is falling and a father stands with his daughter and points to the lighted windows of a tavern. Then comes a line from him, a mouth-filling line, "Even now he is in yon tavern carousing with his boon companions." For months afterward us kids liked the way that line could fill your mouth. You can't say it without using every part of your mouth and tongue.

Some of us went the first year and then the second when the comedy *Eight Bells* came to town. Our favorite scene was where a prissy schoolmaster asks the class questions and they give answers. "What is the shape of the world?" "Square." "No, no, what is the shape of my snuffbox?" "Square." "No, no, the snuffbox I have on Sundays." "Round." "Correct. Now what is the shape of the world?" "Square on weekdays, round on Sundays."

The Star Gazer came once and then played return engagements. The star was Joe Ott. I went twice, and I can't remember the plot nor any lines of the play. What made the play a go was the face of Joe Ott. He could say nothing with it. And the way he said nothing with his face was so interesting that you either had to pity him or take a laugh—and you took the laugh.

After we saw Joe Jefferson play Rip Van Winkle, we liked to give the toast Rip gave: "May you lif long und brosper."

Fridtjof Nansen came. I had read his magazine articles that went into his book *Farthest North*, but I couldn't scrape up the fifty cents to hear him lecture. I was on hand when his train pulled in at the Q. depot. It was snowing and I thought he looked like a Scandinavian hero, tall in a long fur coat, as he walked the platform and through the station to where I watched him get into a Union Hotel hack.

When Henry M. Stanley, the African explorer, came to lecture, I was there again at the Q. depot to see him get off the train and to tag at his heels through the depot. He wasn't as much to look at as Nansen because to me he was mostly a Famous Writer while Nansen was a Great Norseman and a Viking with a heart for all human strugglers.

If I was on a milk wagon or some other job when minstrels came to town I would manage to have two bits for a ticket to the top gallery. I would try to be on Main Street when the minstrels paraded in tan top hats matching their tan cutaway coats and tan spats, with horns and music in the lead. The curtain went up and always there would be that Middleman, Mister In-ter-loc-u-tor, on one side six burnt-cork faces over white boiled shirts clicking the rattlebones, on the other side six more with tambourines, opening with a song. More than once we heard an End Man ask the Middleman, "Why do the policemen in Monmouth wear rubber boots?" the Middleman saying he couldn't think why in the world the policemen in Monmouth wear rubber boots, and the End Man: "Why, everybody in Monmouth knows the policemen wear rubber boots so as not to wake up the other policemen." We laughed because Galesburg and Monmouth, sixteen miles apart, were jealous of each other and we liked any joke that made Monmouth look silly. We learned later that over in Monmouth the minstrels asked why the policemen in Galesburg wore rubber boots and the answer was so they wouldn't wake the other policemen in Galesburg.

The question "How can you tell whether the man or the woman runs the farm?" had the answer, "If the wind is from east to west and the smoke from the chimney blows from west to east, then the man runs the farm." We giggled at that minstrel joke and passed it on as we did another: "I have pants from Pantsylvania, a vest from Vest Virginia, a coat from Dacoata, and a hat from Manhattan—am I not an American?"

At least two minstrel shows had an actor who was asked if he would bet ten dollars that he could answer "Yes" to three questions. The first came, "Was your father hanged in Texas for stealing sheep?" "Yes." The second, "Did you buy a big sack of candy and it was a bitter-cold winter night and you met a little girl on the street and she was ragged and walking barefoot in the snow and she begged you to let her lick just one stick of candy and did you say to her, 'No, you little brat, I wouldn't even let you look at this candy I've got,' did you do that to that poor little girl?" "Yes." The third question: "If I lose this bet will you pay me ten dollars?" "Yes." And the house roared. And for a few days it was told along Berrien Street and I've never heard it since then, back about 1890.

I missed none of Al Field's minstrel shows. I believed that Al Field was "the undisputed King of the Banjo." When I went to a minstrel show I was satisfied I got my two bits' worth in "Nigger Heaven." You could hear the peanut-eaters cracking the shells, working their jaws, and dropping the shells on the floor. That was expected in the top gallery. On the main floor and in the parquet nobody would dare be seen eating a peanut. And down there they couldn't yell and holler for a good act nor "mee-ouw" at a bad one.

James J. Corbett, world's champion boxer, came in *Gentleman Jim* and his bag-punching opened our eyes. I was following big-league baseball and when I heard that Arlie Latham, the dandy second baseman of the Cincinnati Reds, would do a song and dance in a show, I went to see it. The show wasn't much and Arlie Latham was no star at singing and dancing but I had seen a hero and got my two bits' worth. I didn't see Bob Fitzsimmons, another world's champion, in his show. But I did see him on the Q. depot platform, tall and lanky, with salmon hair and pink skin. He was leading a pet lion back and forth. I couldn't figure which was most worth seeing, Fitzsimmons or the lion. Either was worth laying your eyes on.

I helped on the stage when *Monte Cristo* came to town with James O'Neill the star. The sea that he swam when he made his escape, the rolling of that canvas sea, was made by some other boys and myself. We were told how to make the sea angry and we did. The high spot of the show for us kids was where O'Neill playing Edmond Dantes swims the rough sea to an island where he is to find treasure gold.

Reaching dry land, he stands on a rock with his hands stretched out to high heaven and the cry comes from him, "The world is mine!" For weeks we tried imitating O'Neill in that grand, wild cry, "The world is mine!" We couldn't hit it off but it was fun trying. It was many years later I saw and read plays by a son of James O'Neill and met a granddaughter of James O'Neill soon after she married Charlie Chaplin. She and Chaplin laughed when I looked her in the face and said, "Oona, I worked on the same stage one time with your grandfather."

There was the *Uncle Tom's Cabin* show I peddled bills for and got paid ten cents and a ticket to the show. The bills said there would be two Uncle Toms, two Evas, two Simon Legrees, two Elizas crossing the Ohio River, and two packs of bloodhounds. We were puzzled how there could be two of everything. We went expecting something new and different. What we saw was just one more Uncle Tom show, with one of everything instead of two. The trick brought out a good crowd that would be suspicious about again paying cash to see two of everything.

Ole Olson, full of Swedish accent, came one year and two years later the same show under the name of *Yon Yonson*. We saw *Shore Acres*, and after *East Lynne* bragged, "It didn't make me cry." We got used to melodramas where the mortgage hangs over the house and you can hear the mortgage gnawing in the night under every floorboard and in the end the villain with the mortgage gets what is coming to him. Or it might be the will of a dead man and they poked here and there hunting for it, saying "The old will, the old will." Regular on the calendar came a Civil War play with a Union spy in love with a Rebel girl or the other way around, but always wedding bells and apple blossoms in the end. I suped in one of these, *Shenandoah*. Quite a stir was raised when *The Black Crook* came. It had the name of being the classiest burlesque ever, a leg show with costumes running to black. It was said, "Every woman-chaser in town will be there," and they had a packed house. At one Eddie Foy show there were those who heard him say, "A hair on the head is worth two in the brush."

Two famous theater names were Anna Held and John Drew. In cigar stores and saloons hung a picture on the wall. In a woman's hand were five cards from a deck and the words "This is the hand that Anna Held." And under five cards in a man's hand were the words "This is the hand that John Drew." I heard a Swede boy, after looking at this picture, mimic an English actor he had hung around at the Auditorium, "Clevah—eh wot?"

Mary, with her chum Bessie Wardale, went to a few plays at the Auditorium. After a time Bessie moved to Chicago, having married a traveling man, Hugh McMullen. On a visit to Galesburg, Bessie was nursing a baby, and I tickled the baby under the chin and in the ribs. She was one of many babies that I as a boy tickled under the chin and in the ribs, sometimes kissing a big toe if the baby was barefoot. But this particular girl-baby of Bessie Wardale had fate in her chin and ribs. She went on to be a grown woman and an actress who played on Broadway two thousand nights the part of Ellie May in *Tobacco Road*. I missed seeing her as a player because I had read the book on which the play was based and I don't care for plays made out of a book I have read. But had I known Bessie Wardale's baby was the star, I would have gone one night and then back-stage I would have tickled the star under the chin again. Ruth Hunter, her name was on a book she wrote and sent to me, *Come Back Tuesday*, an interesting book about theater life where the players "at liberty" are so often told to come back Tuesday. I wrote her that when I see her sometime in New York I won't recognize her because it's so long since I saw her and she was so little and has changed so.

I have heard of alumni societies where graduates get together and talk over the old days. I wish there was an alumni society of the old Auditorium in Galesburg and we could get together. I'm one of the graduates. I give the old place my blessing. When I last saw it the building was closed, dark. It faded and folded with the coming of the silver screen, the photoplay, the "moom pitchers," the flicks.

★

FOURTEEN

★

Prairie Town

★

This small town of Galesburg, as I look back at it, was a piece of the American Republic. Breeds and blood strains that figure in history were there for me, as a boy, to see and hear in their faces and their ways of talking and acting. People from New England and their children owned much of the town and set the main tone in politics, churches, schools and colleges. I heard Yankee old-timers and how they talked "through the nose." Up from Kentucky and Tennessee had come English and Scotch-Irish breeds who were mostly Democrats in favor of the saloons and farther back in favor of Stephen A. Douglas as against Lincoln.

Many Swedes had become voters and a power in politics and business. Their Republican leader for years was a banker, Moses O. Williamson, known as "Mose." He was on the Illinois State Committee of the Republican Party, and if you wanted a state or Federal office the word was "See Mose."

And the Irish? I had Irish schoolteachers and playmates. I would stand still in the Q. yards to watch the switchman, Tom Carmody, walk. He was a prize-winning dancer and his way of walking had a music to it. Tom Beckum, the happiest drinking man in town, I can never forget, nor Mark Connelly, a Q. shopman. At parties, sociables, picnics, political rallies, among the shopmen, or in a cigar store, Mark, the young Irishman, would give his Swedish dialect stories. He was as good as any Swede at imitating a green Swede. One of his stories that us kids learned ran:

"Goliatt vas a grate beeg fallow, femteen [fifteen] feet high. Dawveed vas a leetle fallow, he hawrdly come up to de knees of Goliatt. Goliatt, he say, 'Dawveed, I goin' to keel you an' eat you.' An' Dawveed, he anta been scared. Dawveed he go to de crick an' he peek heem five stones. An' he put a stone in hees sleeng an' he trow it at Goliatt. An' vat you tink? De stone he trow hit Goliatt right in de stomach an' knock all his brains out!"

The Irish liked it. The Swedes liked it. The "pure Americans" laughed till their ribs shook. Frank Pollock, of one of the native-born American families, at parties and concerts gave imitations of green Swedes. Like Connelly he was a born comedian, though he ended later as a grand-opera tenor. I didn't notice Swedes being sore about these imitations of green Swedes. Along with other young Swedes I did some imitating myself. I had been among the Irish enough so that I picked up their brogue. At times in later years I would drop into the Irish brogue not knowing I was talking it, and I have been taken for one of the Irish. Their brogue and the Swedish accent are the only ones I can put on and be taken for the real thing.

There were names us kids liked to use. We liked them mostly because they sounded funny. A Jew was a "sheeny." The Irish were "micks." A Swede was a "snorky." A Yankee was a "skinflint." The Germans were "Dutch." The Italians were "dagoes." A Negro was a "nigger" or a "smoke." I heard Irish boys say of themselves, "Us micks" and Negroes speak of themselves as "Us niggers," and one Swede boy to another, "Hello, snork." When you hated and wanted to be mean you said, "goddam mick" or "goddam nigger." We believed that the "sheenies" on the quiet might be calling us "snorkies" and calling the Irish "micks" and that would be all right with us because that's what we were. But if they called us "goddam snorkies" or "goddam micks" then we would look for bricks to heave.

Two German Jews, Sol Frolich and Henry Gardt, owned the Union Hotel and bar, and the biggest saloon in that part of Illinois, the White Elephant on Boone's Avenue, next door south of Main Street. Gardt was the quiet one of the two, a smallish man with a black mustache. People said he did the thinking and his partner the talking. Sol Frolich was tall and bald, one of the breeziest laughing men in town. He could mix in any bunch of men with his thick and comical

German accent and his sense of fun and fellowship, and they would listen to him. Being in the liquor business, Frolich and Gardt were up to their ears in politics but their foot tracks were not easy to find. Somehow I can't remember any scandal that was raised about them unless it would be that the Reverend W. H. Geistweit mentioned from his pulpit that the White Elephant had been open after midnight. They were strict about not selling liquor to minors and no women allowed at the bars and no gambling in their places. Many people had a way of laughing when they mentioned "Frolich and Gardt," maybe with a wink of the eye, as though they might more than once have stepped up to the most elegant bar in town at the Union Hotel or into the big barroom of the White Elephant that sold more drinks to more men than any other saloon in town. Frolich and Gardt gave Galesburg color and fun.

The Gumbiner pawnshop, the only one in town, what else was there like it? Where else were there so many different watches to look at—gold, silver, and nickel watches, big old-fashioned "turnips" too big for a vest pocket, a Waltham or two pawned by railroad engineers? But we heard an engineer say the Walthams came "from pickpockets a thousand miles away" and "No engineer would hock his Waltham unless he was drunk and wanted to get drunker." Here at Gumbiner's we saw gold, silver, and brass watch chains, silk and satin watch fobs, big hunting knives and small penknives, pocketknives we wished we had the money to buy, brass knucks and slung shots you could knock a man senseless with, shotguns and rifles and old squirrel guns, Colt's revolvers and the old-time one-shot pocket pistol. And when it came to fifes, flutes, flageolets, clarinets, ocarinas (here I bought my fifteen-cent ocarina, my "sweet potato"), fiddles, accordions, concertinas, banjoes, and guitars plain and fancy, there was no place like Gumbiner's. Nor was there any auctioneer like the slicker at Gumbiner's. His tongue and throat never went back on him. He seemed to wind himself up and then let go on his spiel and he didn't have to stop to oil himself. We were thankful the Gumbiner Jews had come to Galesburg.

Finest of the Jews, said everybody, was Max J. Mack of the men's clothing firm, Jacobi & Mack. Every year a few days after New Year's their front windows would blaze with red price tags and they would have page spreads in the newspapers about their "Annual Red Tag Sale." You couldn't get away from it. They made you want to buy a new suit of clothes.

Max J. Mack for many years was elected alderman from his ward. He was regular at city-council meetings, had his head in all the facts and figures of city business, watched every ordinance, and if a deal was crooked or wasteful he would vote against it and tell why without insulting anybody. The plainest people could go to him with a complaint or a question and he would give them his time as if they had a perfect right to it. He had a warm heart for all people, and when he said, "I'm for what's good for the city of Galesburg and its people," he wasn't just one more blabmouth politician. There came a time when Mart tried for several years to get Max J. Mack nominated for mayor, but the Boss couldn't see it. So a Swede failed at giving Galesburg a Jew for mayor.

Among the Negroes I had friends. Morning after morning at the Q. depot I would see "Tip" Murray with his shoeblacking kit hung by a strap from one shoulder. Passengers getting off trains would hear him, "Shine 'em up—a nickel a shine." Tip and I talked baseball, how the big leagues were doing, and what Galesburg might do in the Three-Eye League (Illinois, Indiana, and Iowa). Tip was lean and wiry and could pitch a good game. I could connect with his outcurve but he nearly always fooled me when he put a drop on it. He had his days, he told me, when nobody wanted a shine, other days when he made a couple of nickels, and circus days, holidays, and "big days," when the score ran up to fifteen or twenty nickels.

While I was in short pants I would meet the King brothers from Pine Street. They were shorter than I and lighter weight, but the older one would shine his eyes at me and say, "You want to fight?" I could see he would like to fight me if I was willing, a "snork" and a "smoke" bloodying each other's noses. He didn't holler it nor make a face at me. He said it kind of soft as if he was listening to hear himself say, "You want to fight?" I told him I wasn't looking for a fight and we went on our ways without another word. I figured that Willy King had been saying to himself, "Am I scared to fight a white boy?" And then to make sure he wasn't scared, he puts it to the first white boy he meets, "You want to fight?"

Often walking along South Street a Negro would come in sight and some boy would be sure to say, "There's Double-headed Bill." He was of medium size and build, had a good face, and an extra-big head. You couldn't say he was a freak of nature. He just happened to have a head that was bigger than most people had though you had to look twice to notice it. You didn't draw back from looking at him like when you saw the double-headed calf at the county fair. It was a well-shaped head he had, good to look at even if it was extra-big. But someone had hung on him the nickname "Double-headed Bill" and us kids thought it smart to be saying it.

"Nigger" Duke lived in the Q. yards and shops. He found warm corners for sleeping in the winter, and anywhere would do for him in summer. His meals came out of leftovers in the dinner buckets of shopmen and the wicker baskets of trainmen and enginemen. His legs were two short stubs. He had many years back gone to sleep in a boxcar in zero weather, and the doctors had to saw off his legs a little below the hips. On the bottoms of these stumps he had leather pads. He took short steps and walked himself where he pleased around the Q. yards. Going to the Seventh Ward school we saw him many times near the machine shop or at the Peoria tracks flag shanty. He was thick-chested, a heavy man with fine straight shoulders, a well-shaped head and face. His teeth were white and even, and when he smiled or broke into a laugh from his black-skin face, it was like promises and flowers. He had a greeting, a smile, or a laugh for everyone he met. I heard him say, "We've all got our jobs and my job is to chase away the blues." His voice was high and clear and words tumbled fast from him.

From the Swedes in the shops he had learned to talk Swedish and liked gabbing with the Swedes. There were Swedes hunted him out in the Q. yards to hear a crippled black man talking like any good Swede. We were told in our school days that Nigger Duke happened to be at the Q. depot once when a train loaded with green Swedes fresh from Sweden came in, headed for Nebraska. Nigger Duke lifted himself to a car platform and walked along the aisles of the cars talking Swedish and telling the newcomers, "After a while when you have been in this country as long as I have you'll turn black like I am." His Swedish was perfect and his white teeth glistened and his laugh rippled as he told this to Swedes who had never heard a black man speaking Swedish. Some laughed at him. Others looked sober and then gloomy, for they half believed him. And it was told there were women on the train who broke into tears and sobbed.

In later years Mart said that Susan Allen, a Negro woman who did cleaning at his house, claimed it was her husband John Allen who got on the train and had the Swedes worried about turning black. I think something like it must have happened though I believe most of the Swedes on the train took it as a good joke. I could see a certain kind of tough Swede saying, "So we're going to change to black, are we? All right, let it come. It'll be fun watching it happen."

I didn't hear what became of Nigger Duke. I can't forget him and wouldn't try to. He was made to laugh through life, to laugh at life, and to bring others to laughing with him. He was a strong man. There were railroad men who said that when he would be gone from the Q. yards a few days or a week he was away with Negro women who enjoyed him—and this could have been just talk. The railroad men were proud of him and said no other railroad had anything like him. And the Swedes were proud of him because he could talk to them in a language the Americans and the Irish hadn't learned. He could say, "Hur mår du i dag?" (How are you today?) like a blessing with promises and flowers.

The Negro voters expected and were given two city jobs. There was always one Negro policeman in uniform. And a Negro drove the police patrol wagon.

One Negro had a bad name in the hobo world. His name was Richardson and he was the night policeman for the Q. in the yards. His club had been bloody many a time from beating the head of a hobo. I talked with hoboes who showed scars on their heads where they said the scalp was broken by Richardson's club. The word for him among the hoboes was "that goddam nigger bull in the Galesburg yards." Why the head men of the Q. railroad kept him on duty year after year I didn't hear. Galesburg was a division point and it could have been there were gangs stealing from the cars. Or there may have been hoboes who had ganged up on Richardson and given him a beating and he was hitting back at any and all hoboes. Anyhow he made a name for himself as a terror to those who tried to ride railroad trains without buying tickets.

I first heard German spoken when I played with Mickey Artz in his front yard on Brooks Street. His mother didn't like the way we had run over her flower garden. What she told him was plenty. It was all in German but he heard it and we went to the street to play catch. She reminded me of Grimm's fairy stories and such sentences as, "Hans' wife became enraged and she threatened to cut his head off."

The Italians came late but they pushed their carts and cried their bananas and oranges over every street in town. Before they came by carloads there were two well-known Italians. Father Costa was the priest at the Corpus Christi Church at Kellogg and South streets near the center of town. He was a short, thin-lipped man, with deep small black eyes. I would come near speaking to him on the street but his little black eyes would fix me and I didn't let out a peep. Father Tonelli had the other Catholic church, St. Patrick's, a mile away, off in the Fifth Ward among the Irish. He was handsome, like picture-book Italians. To him I would say a good-morning and he would smile back a good-morning worth at least a dime on a rainy day.

Frenchy Juneau and his father were the only French I knew. I didn't get to know any Poles, Bohemians, Slovaks, Russians, Hungarians, Spanish, Portuguese, Mexicans, South Americans, or Filipinos. I did stop in to watch our two Chinamen ironing and wrapping laundry two doors south of the fire department on Prairie Street. They wore black blouses. Their heads were shaved, and running down from the crown of the head two or three feet was a braided pigtail of hair. They talked singsong up and down to each other, maybe saying, "He's a funny little brat come in to look at us." Through their window I saw them early mornings and late at night ironing, starching, wrapping bundles, and marking the bundles with Chinese letters in big black crayon. They made me think about the human race and how different some parts of it are from others.

Often in the 1890's I would get to thinking about what a young prairie town Galesburg was—nearly twenty thousand people, and they had all come in fifty years. Before that it was empty rolling prairie. And I would ask: Why did they come? Why couldn't they get along where they had started from? Was Galesburg any different from the many other towns, some bigger and some smaller? Did I know America, the United States, because of what I knew about Galesburg? In Sweden all the people in a town were Swedes, in England they were all English, and in Ireland all Irish. But here in Galesburg we had a few from everywhere and there had even been cases of Swedish Lutherans marrying Irish Catholic girls—and what was to come of it all? It didn't bother me nor keep me awake nights but I couldn't help thinking about it and asking: What is this America I am a part of, where I will soon be a full citizen and a voter? All of us are living under the American flag, the Stars and Stripes—what does it mean? Men have died for it—why? When they say it is a free country, they mean free for what and free for whom, and what is freedom?

I said I would listen and read and ask and maybe I would learn. By guessing and hoping and reaching out I might get a hold on some of the answers. Those questions in those words may not have run through my mind yet they ran in my blood. Dark and tangled they were to run in my blood for many years. To some of the questions I would across the years get only half-answers, mystery answers.

FIFTEEN

"College City"

Knox College, Lombard College, Brown's Business College, gave Galesburg the nickname of "College City." Living in a college town had its points for us kids. What is education? As a barefoot boy I asked that and talked about it with other boys. After our school terms were over Lombard College would hold its Commencement Exercises. We didn't know what "commencement" was, nor "exercises." The college was a few blocks away and we heard you could go in free. We ran our bare feet up to the third-floor chapel and on up the narrow stairs to the little gallery where nobody would mind our bare feet. We learned by listening to the speakers that "commencement" is when you finish your education and go out into the world and commence living and using your education. And the "exercises" were what we saw them doing on the platform. The president of the college spoke, members of the graduating class spoke or read papers, some man from far away who had a big name spoke. They used many long words we had never heard before and a good deal of the time we couldn't understand what they were saying. But they were all educated, and we knew that by listening we might learn a little about what it is to be educated.

I remember how I watched one graduate. Only a few years before he had been a farm hand and I had seen him plowing his father's cornfield. Now I saw him in a fine black suit of clothes and a stiff white stand-up collar and he was educated and getting a diploma that he could show to prove he was educated. When he spoke he used the word "theory" several times. I had never heard of a theory. He said, "This is all very well in theory, but how will it work out in practice?" I knew what practice is, how if you don't practice at stopping grounders and catching flies you're no good in the infield or the outfield. I saw that theory is what you have in your head about how to make a play, and practice is where you work out your theory. Spots like that gave us a beginning idea of what they meant by education. We liked best, of course, the musical numbers, piano solos and singing by graduates of the music department. But here and there among the speakers, even those we called "kinda dumb," I caught sight of a world of books and people it would take me a long time to know better. We spotted show-offs who didn't quite know how to handle their education and we laughed at them. But we knew we were a little ignorant ourselves or else we would be able to tell just why we knew they were show-offs. All we were sure of was that they didn't know how or why they were show-offs with their educations. When later we saw in a circus an educated dog and an educated horse showing off we liked them. If they didn't make a show of their education they wouldn't eat.

I worked at reading a book by Edward Eggleston, *How to Educate Yourself.* He set me going on the questions: What do I do when I think? What is thinking? What do I do when I see? Can I be too careful about what I think I see? Can my eyes fool me? Can my thinking about what I have seen fool me? What I meet in streets and rooms, what I see out of windows, what I look at in the great outdoor world—all these become part of me and I become part of them if I know how to really see them and then know how to think about them. Every outside has its inside worth thinking about how and why it is what it is. I read several times one sentence of Eggleston: "An unreasoning skepticism is as bad as the unreasoning credulity, but the habit of holding the mind open to conviction, and the habit of questioning everything for the sake of learning more about it, are certainly exceedingly valuable ones." I rassled and wrangled with that. He pointed to people who heard and believed that if you put a living fish into a pail of water it doesn't add to the weight of the water. What Ben Franklin did was to weigh a pail of water and then put in a living fish and weigh that. And Ben found that it weighed as much more as the fish weighed. Another sentence I read more than twice: "When I read in my chemistry that oxygen, hydrogen and carbon are elementary substances, the authority of the eminent chemist who tells me this is sufficient to convince me that this is a correct statement of the fact so far as the fact is understood by the chemists, but in holding myself ready to believe that all these substances may after all be compounds, and may ultimately be discovered to be such, I only do precisely what the chemists themselves do, and what they must of necessity do if they hope to make any new discoveries in their science." It was tough going and I had to hunt around in dictionaries and cyclopedias to get clear on it, but it was worth the time.

Peeking around here and there one summer morning, just looking to see what there might be to see in the Lombard building, we opened the door to the room at the east end of the second-floor hall. The three of us stepped into the room, took a quick look at a tall glass case at the east wall of the room, then stepped out into the hall in a hurry, closed the door, and talked in whispers asking if it was right and if it was safe to go into the room and look around. In the glass case at the east wall of the room we had seen a tall human skeleton. We had seen rat, cat, dog, and horse skeletons but this was our first look at the bones of a human being and it looked almost as though it might walk out of the glass case. The jawbones and teeth had a big white grin and we didn't know but it had put on the grin for us as if saying, "Why do you come in here where I am having a quiet time by myself?" One kid said, "I was scared at first but I'm not scared any more. Let's go in." He opened the door and we followed him. I walked tiptoe at first till it came over me that walking barefoot on a floor you don't clump. We spent a while getting acquainted with the skeleton. We had many questions—about the skull that holds the brain, the nose so flat with no meat on it, the grinning teeth that must have done a lot of chewing, the arm bones, hip bones, knee bones, toe bones. And then: "Who was he? Could he have been a murderer? Who took out his insides and scraped all the bones so white and clean? Was he ever buried, or did they dig him up from a grave? When you're grown-up and die would you like to have your skeleton in a place like this for people to look at? Ain't it

spooky how that big grin never comes off his face? Would you like
to have it in your room at home to talk to when you wake up in the
morning?" We went around to other cases, with rocks of many
kinds, a hundred stuffed birds. Before leaving we had another long
look at the skeleton, one kid saying, "He's the champeen in this room
all right." We went back on other days to see the rocks and the
birds, but mostly the skeleton.

John Van Ness Standish I saw many a time on the streets and at col-
lege exercises and public events. I studied his figure and walk, his
well-trimmed beard that covered the entire face, his bald head on
whose top we counted the hairs, his beaming eyes and smile. Why
shouldn't I look at him with curiosity, respect, or wonderment? I
couldn't give the names of even one of my two grandfathers or my
two grandmothers, except the single fact that my mother, Clara
Anderson, had a father and a mother named Anderson. And Profes-
sor John Van Ness Standish had a chart with trunks and branches.
He could show you where he traced six generations straight back to
Captain Miles Standish, the toughest Indian-killer and the hardest
fighting man of the Mayflower Pilgrims who founded Plymouth
Colony. More than that, he could show you where his line of blood
went back to Thurston de Standish living near the village of Chorely,
Lancashire, England, in the Year of our Lord 1222. That, of course,
is going away back. No one else in town I heard of could go that far
back and give names and dates as to ancestors. We knew we were
descendants, most of us, but few could go farther back than a hun-
dred years and specify what loins and wombs we came from. The
important point, with most of us, was that we had actually been born
and the question had been from the beginning for each of us, "What
are you going to do about it?"

Our Galesburg Standish was out of Vermont folks, at sixteen
taught winter schools, and in summer did farm work to pay his way
through Norwich University. At twenty-nine, in 1854 he was acting
president of the Illinois Liberal Institute, which became Lombard
College, and for thirty-eight years he was professor of mathematics
and astronomy, though at times he taught logic, Cicero, Virgil, and
Livy. He organized a horticultural society and directed the tree-

planting of the county courthouse park. I have a soft spot in my heart for him because of what he did with the Lombard campus. On its area of four city blocks that campus had the most lovable set of trees in or around the town. The great elm near the college pump had a wider spread than any other tree in the county. There were clumps of pine and single pine trees where I went many a time to lie on the brown carpet of dry needles, to look up through the dark-green branches, alone with a wonder and a reverence that was vague and beyond words, with mysteries that never failed me and never cheated me. I was thankful to Professor Standish for his tree-planting work. What he said and wrote about trees and how we should love them and care for them didn't interest me. What the trees did to me was something different from what they did to him. What they did to either of us is our personal secret. It is true that only God can make a tree. It is also true that only God could make either Professor Standish or me. It may be too that having made both Professor Standish and me, God then looked at the great elm by the college pump and spoke to Himself about which was the more worthy creation.

Professor Standish married Augusta Kendall, teacher of drawing, French, and Italian at Lombard. He had seen her in fair weather and foul. She wore rubber boots when heavy rains drenched campus and streets. They traveled round the world three times, seeing every country in Europe, Egypt, the Holy Land, the North Cape and the Midnight Sun, and every state in the Union except the Carolinas. They had come into money and brought home ransackings from ancient Rome and the more ancient Greece and the still more ancient Assyria, the daily papers telling where they had been and what they brought back. I read about them in the papers and looked at the Standish couple and wondered what they got out of what they had seen and heard where they had been. I would look out of a milk-wagon door passing by them on a street and have half a notion that my thirty Italians in the two houses on Berrien Street near Seminary had told me a few things about Italy and the sons of Tuscany that the Standishes never even suspected. The Standishes were what my friend Tom Ferril of Denver calls "Culture Vultures."

In 1892 Lombard trustees elected Standish president of the college. Three years later he resigned in some kind of a huff. Earnest Elmo Calkins wrote that Standish was "peppery." We may be sure he was peppery when he quit Lombard. Three years after leaving Lombard he made a gesture, he gave out with a sign and token. He made a free gift of one hundred thousand dollars, not to the college where he had served forty-one years and sunk his deepest life roots. He slam-banged the whole hundred thousand dollars into the hands of Knox College. He knew it was needed and would be useful there. His house and home next to the Knox campus, its grounds laid out with handsome arrangements of bushes, shrubs, and trees, all this on his deathbed he left to Knox College. His dying words could have been, "All that I have and am I give to Knox. I have forgotten the name Lombard if I ever knew it." He may have been wronged by Lombard. Somehow I never found the time to really look into what happened. I merely knew that he read a thousand important books in several languages, that he lectured to hundreds of teachers' institutes on how to educate the young, that he traveled three times round the planet Earth, that he loved trees and did a work with trees, for which I am infinitely thankful, that somehow all his travel and reading and love of trees couldn't help him when his heart nursed a hate, couldn't keep him from acting "peppery." Why travel three times round the world and then act peppery?

Standish's last important position had the title City Forester of Galesburg. That could go on his gravestone. I still love him as a forester. If the roots of trees tangle in his frame under the grass roots we can imagine an inaudible voice whispering, "These bones shall rise again." He might have said to St. Peter, "On earth it was men failed me. I was ever kindly to trees and no tree ever betrayed me." He could have had no memory that once after Lombard commencement exercises in the third-floor chapel he passed in a lower hall three barefoot Swede boys who had sat in the chapel gallery. He laid his hand on the head of one of them and smiled and went on. Maybe he meant to give me a blessing. He died thirty-three years ago, as this is written, and now I give him my blessing for the trees he gave me and so many others.

Lombard College graduated its first class in 1856, four men and two women. No one predicted that one of them would be the first Galesburg woman to be titled by the British Crown. Lucy Adaline Hurd, daughter of Erastus Hurd, a civil engineer working at railroad construction, was not hard to look at, being "tall, slender, and dignified, with softly waving black hair, hazel eyes, and apple-blossom complexion." When in 1858 Abraham Lincoln came to Galesburg for the debate with Douglas, it was Miss Hurd, having beauty and personal distinction, who was chosen to read the city's address of welcome to Lincoln, so legend has it. She was one of a group of Lombard girls who presented satin banners to both Lincoln and Douglas. On the banner for Lincoln the girls sewed the inscription: "To Abraham Lincoln, Champion of Liberty, by the Lombard students, October 7, 1858."

Six years later Miss Hurd was living with her widowed mother near Joliet, Illinois, once a week going to Ziegfield's College of Music in Chicago. Coming home on a late night train she found no one at the Joliet station to meet her and she had no umbrella against the falling rain. The young telegrapher in charge of the station stepped up to her with an umbrella and in a shy way asked if he could help her to her home two miles away. He looked nice enough to her, though at school he had been a fighter and had been thrown out for drawing a picture that made the principal look silly. His father, a lawyer, had met Lincoln and Douglas, was elected the first mayor of Joliet, died in a cholera epidemic, leaving the family an honorable name, five children, and a mortgaged roof. Since then the family had often gone along on three meals a day of hominy and molasses. As a telegraph messenger boy he learned to play poker, later calling it "not a game but an education." A book told him that a pocket piece he carried was a "crinoid" a million years old and he began collecting fossil forms, many a Sunday searching quarries and creek beds for specimens. He spent days and nights copying by candlelight a borrowed book—Hitchcock's *Elements of Geology*—copying every page, text, pictures, and index, hungering to know about the crust of the earth. He returned the borrowed book and then found it was no use to look in the one he copied, he had learned it so well. A telegrapher at fifteen, he had taken over the wire a full report of one of the Lincoln-Douglas debates.

Miss Hurd saw him as one more Corn Belt boy, raised in Will County, and he had an umbrella and it was late at night and to her it seemed he could take care of himself and her. She said, "Yes," and they started to walk, the umbrella in his right hand, in his left hand the pipe he had been smoking. He was struck with her black hair, hazel eyes, and apple-blossom face and he was stealing side glances at her as he crammed his pipe into his coat pocket. They had gone but a few steps when he smelled something burning, ran his hand into his left coat pocket and found that his lighted pipe had set his coat on fire. He said nothing to Miss Hurd and quietly smothered the fire.

Some three years later he was a train-dispatcher at Bloomington, Illinois, and they were married. She stayed at home while he went on and up in the railroad world, whirling away riding thousands of miles a month, general superintendent first of the Chicago & Alton, then general superintendent of the Chicago, Milwaukee & St. Paul system. He went on to make a name as one of the mightiest of railroad-builders. He was the brain center directing day and night gangs of over five thousand men and seventeen hundred teams clearing land and laying rails up at Winnipeg, ten thousand men east and west, building the Canadian Pacific Railway. This was the human dynamo the Galesburg girl had married, to see him go away for weeks and months, driving himself hard and driving his men as hard as himself.

This was William Cornelius Van Horne, of whom a Winnipeg reporter wrote, "Van Horne is calm and harmless-looking. So is a she-mule and so is a buzz-saw. You don't know their true inwardness until you go up and feel them. To see Van Horne get out of the car and go softly up the platform you would think he was an evangelist on his way to preach temperance to the Mounted Police. But soon you are undeceived. If you are within hearing distance, you will have more fun than you ever had in your life before."

The Canadian Pacific Railway got built, ran transcontinental freight and passenger trains, and the Van Hornes moved into multi-millions. In 1892 came appointment as Honorary Knight Commander of the Order of St. Michael and St. George, and the news came to

Galesburg that Adaline Hurd of the Lombard class of '56 was now
Lady Van Horne. She probably heard from him about an office at-
tendant making a lickspittle low bow and solemnly mumbling, "Good
morning, Sir William," and his brushing past saying, "Oh hell!" He
was slightly bald over the forehead, wore a close-trimmed full beard,
and once in Paris a head waiter mistook him for King Edward of
England and had the orchestra play him "God Save the King." He
bought most of an island in Passamaquoddy Bay, six hundred acres
where he was his own architect and landscape gardener, laying out
roads, gardens, hedges, orchards, and bathing pools, raising Dutch
belted cattle, importing plants and flowers and growing acres of
mushrooms on wooded slopes, giving the place the ancestral Dutch
family name of Covenhoven.

Here Adaline stayed while he roved thousands of railroad miles
a month. Here she could go with him from one canvas to another,
Rembrandt, Hals, Velásquez, Goya, El Greco, Renoir, Gainsbor-
ough, Hogarth, Millet, and the work of Japanese and Chinese paint-
ers. In their first days of courtship she saw his drawings and had
watched him become a fair painter in his own right, putting his
frescoes on the walls of Covenhoven, sometimes in his waggery sell-
ing one of his own paintings as an "Old Master." She heard him ad-
vise, "Never buy a picture that you do not fall in love with. The
purchase of a picture, like the selection of a wife, can hardly be done
by proxy." She saw him do card tricks, mind-reading, play practical
jokes, spend hours with his fossils. She heard of men speaking to him
their amazement at his working hard all the time, playing hard all the
time, dining at midnight and playing chess or billiards all night, ask-
ing, "How do you do it?" and her husband, laughing, "Oh, I eat all
I can, I drink all I can, I smoke all I can, and I don't care a damn for
anything."

She tried to know when he strictly meant what he said, as once
in a letter: "The greatest men of the past were all Masters of Hum-
bug, and so are the greatest men of today, including our friend J. J.
Hill, and I don't say this in any derogatory sense, for I feel a real
respect and admiration for him, because in the main he has applied
his mastery of Humbug to very useful purposes, which cannot be
said of most of the great masters in this line."

She could remember their early years in St. Louis when she went down with smallpox. He couldn't think of sending her to the city pesthouse. He swore the doctor and the family to secrecy and had his wife isolated in his attic study where he kept a fossil collection. There he spent his days with her and his rock specimens, a life-hobby with him. At night he changed his clothing, thoroughly disinfected himself, went down to his office when the staff was gone, attended to the day's work, then home near daybreak for a little sleep and the care of Adaline. She recovered, with scarcely a face disfigurement, and no one else came down with the dread smallpox.

When, years later, rheumatic fever had him in bed and was followed by a carbuncle on the knee, he was not a willing patient. He had been in the habit of smoking at all hours day and night, and now the doctor limited him to three cigars a day and three only. So Adaline saw him in bed with a cigar about one foot long and an inch and a half thick, and he was laughing. "I have had these specially made for me and I smoke three of them a day and each of them gives me a good smoke for two hours."

Few of the Corn Belt girls ever had a more elusive, versatile, and dynamic husband. If she had taken an earlier train from Chicago to Joliet, arriving before the rain began that night in Joliet in '64, she might never have become Lady Van Horne nor heard him snort about his being a "Sir" and she a "Lady." He died at seventy-two saying he'd like to have five hundred more years of living.

"All my religion is summed up in the Golden Rule and I practice it," he once said to a man, who asked if he were really serious. "Yes, I am serious," came his answer. "I practice the Golden Rule and I think I am the only man in business who does. What are you laughing at?" This was when Kaiser Wilhelm was in the news and the man who had laughed was saying, "Well, I have heard of *Me und Gott*— but Van Horne and Jesus Christ is rather a new——" Van Horne saw the point and gave a broad grin. "Well, I do the best I can."

In the fiftieth year after he had begun as a telegrapher in Joliet, he and his Adaline went back to that town for a Homecoming Festival and he joined with the folks as a home-town boy. A few years later Montreal put on mourning and thousands followed his coffin to the train that carried his body to the States and on to Joliet for burial.

His most famous exploits had been on Canadian soil but it was his wish he should be buried in Will County, Illinois, U.S.A.

I never saw Jonathan Blanchard, though I did hear the echoes that lingered in the air of his roaring and crying when he was president of Knox College from 1845 to 1857. I heard enough about him as a boy so that I could almost see the ghost of him flitting around Old Main on the Knox campus or the doors of the Old First Church. He ran Knox College for thirteen years, brought in more students, brought in much-needed money, built it up, and raised a harvest of hate that nearly wrecked the college. He hated slavery, preached and wrote against it, passed along runaway slaves. He needed more yet to hate. Secret societies he hated and the Masons worst of all, crying, "Freemasonry is an accursed religious imposition and cheat!" All forms of whisky, wine, and beer he hated. As a boy he broke a jug of cider brandy meant for his father's harvest hands and told them cold water was God's choice for them.

Any and all "Sabbathbreakers" he hated. In 1854 he heard that the new C.B.&Q. railroad had run a train through Galesburg on a Sunday. He was surprised, shocked, and the next Sunday he was there at the little old brick depot, a committee and a crowd watching him. He was a figure to look at, a tall man, big of frame, a heavy beard covering all his face except the shaved upper lip, and a mouth pulled down at the corners, wearing a long black clerical coat and a high silk hat. The dinky little engine, with its funny smokestack pouring out plumes of black soot from a wood-burning furnace, had pulled in. The passengers stepped off and the conductor was ready to call "All aboard!" Then Jonathan Blanchard moved out from the crowd, raised a commanding flat hand toward the engineer, and gave an order, "Take that engine to the roundhouse." The engineer looked down from his cab to ask who was giving the order and heard, "I am President Blanchard of Knox College and again I order you to take that engine to the roundhouse and not run this train on Sunday." Then from the cab came the reply, "Well, President Blanchard of Knox College, you can go to hell and mind your own business, and I'll take my train out as ordered."

The ghost of Jonathan Blanchard still goes stalking around Knox

County. He was a lion, a bear, a buffalo, and in the realm of human behavior rated himself half horse and half alligator. Cardplayers he hated and let them have it in his sermons that ran three hours and longer. Men and women who liked to step out in a quadrille or Virginia reel, these he blasted as children of the Devil headed straight for a hell of everlasting fire. He hated Universalists, Unitarians, Free Thinkers, Roman Catholics, actors, drunkards, and fiddlers who played "Comin' Through the Rye" on Sunday. He enjoyed controversy, seemed to create antagonisms for the secret fun he could have out of them. He saw himself as a crusader hurling spears at Hydra-headed monsters of sin. He invited, or rather instigated without knowing he was doing it, a storm of jealousies and rivalries that ran for years and came near being the ruin of Knox College. He fathered five sons and seven daughters, lived to be eighty-one, and died fighting Freemasonry as a blight and a curse.

The new Knox County courthouse had its cornerstone dedicated in 1885, and I was barefooted and seven years old when I joined the thousands who surged around the speakers' stand. It didn't mean anything to me when that day I saw solemn men wearing white aprons and heard that the Illinois Grand Lodge of Masons was going through the right motions with the help of delegate Masons from forty-three other Illinois counties. Nor did it mean anything special to me that the orator of the day was Alfred M. Craig, a justice of the Supreme Court of the State of Illinois, even though later it would turn out that I was to be the chore boy in a drugstore owned by Justice Craig's son Harvey. It was a big day and I went home wondering what a courthouse would be without a cornerstone.

And I didn't know till years later that Jonathan Blanchard, old and gray, had to write a letter and have it published in a Galesburg paper. In this letter he was still roaring and moaning about the Masons. His old Knox pupil, Alfred M. Craig, had presided over public Masonic ceremonies, surrounded by men from lodges whose members were sworn to commit perjury and shield "murder most foul and horrible." The judge should have known better than to lend a hand in such "monkey business." Blanchard raved at the Baptists for feeding the Masons, at a Galesburg church for going so far as to have a Mason for its pastor, at Knox College for having a Mason as its

president. He blamed secession and the Civil War on the treacherous
Masons. He wrote for Judge Craig and the public: "To hope that
Masons will do as they are sworn by cutthroat oaths not to do, is to
profess your belief that Masonry means nothing."

Jonathan Blanchard was born to wrangle and enjoy wrangling.
He is a show piece in the museum of American freedom. He spoke
his multiple hates and lived unharmed. I have seen his autograph.
Having written his name he underlined it with fancy scrolls. He
lived without coming to know that he was not one bigot but several.
He strode and roared and the echoes of him linger for me in certain
Galesburg corners and I almost catch the ghost of him. I am sure
there are plenty of living sinners he would like to haunt and haunt.

Several times when carrying a two-gallon can of milk I met on
streets near Knox College a little man who would nod his head to me
without speaking and I would nod my head to him without speaking.
He wore a tight-fitting, square-cornered, single-breasted black coat
to his knees and the buttons ran up to his chin. You couldn't see his
collar from in front because of his white beard that spread like a
fan. His face would light up and his eyes be half-smiling when he
met me and as he passed me. I had the notion once that maybe he
went to sleep at night with that half-smile and it was there when he
woke up in the morning. His beard covered jaws, chin, and upper lip
and you had to guess what his mouth was like. Once on Main Street
I saw a man point at him and say to another man, "That fellow used
to know Abe Lincoln." I knew he was the president of Knox Col-
lege for many years, but it was later I learned he had been elected
Superintendent of Public Instruction of the State of Illinois seven
times and served fourteen years. His room in the State House at
Springfield was next to one that Lincoln used when a candidate and
he and Lincoln had had friendly talks.

This was Newton Bateman, sometimes nicknamed "Little Newt,"
and he said that Lincoln would introduce him as "My little friend,
the big schoolmaster of Illinois." He said that Lincoln once brought
him a letter asking if there should be any corrections in grammar and
saying, "I never was very strong on grammar." He said he saw Lin-
coln walk back and forth, troubled about the storm that was to

sweep the country, saying, "I am nothing but truth is everything." He said he was the last man to shake hands and say good-by to President-elect Lincoln before the train pulled out from Springfield bound for Washington and Lincoln's inauguration.

Newton Bateman was born in New Jersey in 1822. His father, a weaver and a cripple, took wife and family of five children West to Illinois in a covered wagon in 1833. Near Jacksonville the Asiatic cholera struck the mother, and people in a panic fear of the plague saw to it that she was buried in fast time, so quick that the grave wasn't marked. Her youngest son Newton in after years made searches for it but couldn't locate the grave. In his struggle toward an education, he lived for a time on mush and milk at eleven cents a week, walked with a peddler's pack on his back and sold pins, needles, thread, "notions." He had aimed at being a minister, and then changed to teaching. He was principal of the Jacksonville schools and organized the State Teachers Association. As president of Knox from 1875 to 1892, the longest time any president of Knox had stayed, it was said that under him there were more graduates who went out into the world and made big names for themselves than under any president before him. "He had character," I heard one man say, "and it reached the students."

I am sure he had more character than I suspected when of a morning I met him and he would nod to me without speaking and I would nod to him without speaking. He made me feel that I could come to him with troubles and he would talk them over with me. Maybe that was his character reaching me.

Little Newt dropped out as president of Knox when he was seventy, went on teaching a few classes while a new president took the chair—John Huston Finley, twenty-nine years old and "the youngest college president in the United States." I met Finley several times, carrying my two-gallon can of milk, but he passed me by, his head down, thinking, his mind far away. Years later his wife said that her husband didn't wake up in the morning till our milk wagon came rattling and banging past their house.

Finley had a face you could say was both handsome and homely. He was an educator, an orator, a politician, a salesman, and could make a speech on anv subject on two minutes' notice. He made

Knox known over the country as a college where Lincoln and Douglas debated on the campus, the debaters standing on a platform next to the college Main Building, facing an audience of twenty thousand people on October 7, 1858. Finley was the first to connect the name of Lincoln with that of Knox College in a big way. The country heard about Lincoln and Knox on October 7, 1896, when Finley put on an Anniversary celebration. I got away from the milk wagon in time to wedge through the crowd for a good look at Chauncey M. Depew in a Prinz Albert coat, with side whiskers, and a fedora hat on his head as he spoke. The day was cold and men on the platform wore overcoats with the collars turned up. I don't remember a word Chauncey Depew said but I could say I had seen the president of the New York Central Railway and a man who in 1864 made stump speeches over all of New York State for Lincoln for President. Depew had the name too of being "the most popular after-dinner speaker in the United States." He was a humorist and could make people laugh but this day he tried to be solemn and didn't make the grade. He was neither funny nor solemn. We enjoyed hearing him because we had heard so much about him.

Robert Todd Lincoln, the son of Abraham Lincoln, made a short speech that afternoon. I puzzled about him and wondered what kind of talks he had had with his father in the White House, what kind of a Secretary of War he had been in the cabinets of Presidents Garfield and Arthur. I had read of how at one Republican National Convention after another some delegate always nominated him for President and he would get one vote. I had read too that he was the lawyer for the Pullman Company and he was all for the company and against the strikers in the bloody strike of 1894. In his short speech he didn't say anything I went away thinking about.

Senator John M. Palmer spoke. He had a better right than any of them on the platform. He had been a Democrat who refused to go along with Douglas, had helped found the Republican Party in 1856 and had gone to Chicago as a delegate to nominate Lincoln for President. He had commanded troops in battle and risen to be a major general, had been governor of Illinois, and had shifted back to the Democratic Party. And in the year of 1896 he had broken from the regular Democratic Party and organized an independent party that favored the gold standard as against free silver. I was for free silver but I liked the independence of this silver-haired old soldier who, when I saw him, had only a year to live.

While Finley brought national fame to Knox College he made a big name for himself. I knew people who said they would like to see his homely face in the White House.

Knox was lucky in having George Fitch as a student. I saw him at the ball games of the City League and read every line of his reports the next day in the *Evening Mail*. He was a king of slang, with a reckless humor about hits, putouts, errors, and slides to home. Later, while on the *Peoria Transcript*, he wrote a series of short stories for the *Saturday Evening Post* about Siwash, his name for Knox College. The name stuck and "Siwash" became an enduring and endearing nickname for Knox.

One June night in the year of 1895 the town of Galesburg was, as people said, "turned upside down." Church bells and the Knox College bell rang all night. You could hear gunshots. Cannon cracked and boomed. Fireworks sprayed the sky and firecrackers snapped. Railroad-engine whistles tooted. City and farm boys rampaged around bonfires on the campus and in the streets. Glee clubs sang and wild yells came on the air from before midnight till past daybreak. You could hear voices getting hoarse from crying "Hurrah for Knox!" followed by "Hurrah for Harbach!" We knew what Knox was, but what was this Harbach? For those who hadn't heard the news, it was there the next day in the *Republican-Register* and the *Daily Mail*.

A Knox student, Otto Harbach of Salt Lake City, Utah, after winning first place in an oratorical contest at Knox had gone on to win in a state contest and again to win in an Interstate Intercollegiate contest held in the Auditorium in Galesburg. Harbach of Knox won the high medal, the nice money, the sweepstakes. The Knox Silver Cornet Band, the Glee Club, and a wild mob followed the students who hauled Harbach to the campus on their shoulders. With songs, bells, yells, bonfires, they not only made the welkin ring but they swept the deck and threw the broom in the sea in so far as that could be done in a prairie town.

Not until forty-four years later did I meet Harbach. He had moved into Broadway with such plays as *The Firefly*, *Katinka*, *Madame Sherry*, *Roberta*, *The Cat and the Fiddle*. "Smoke Gets in Your Eyes," "Indian Love Call," "Rose Marie," "Who?" "The Night Was Made for Love," "One Alone," "Cuddle Up a Little Closer," are some of his lyrics sung by millions. He told me that in faraway Utah he had heard of Lincoln and Knox being linked, that something of the portentous Lincoln shadow lingered there, so he picked Knox as the college he would work his way through.

Harbach was a member of the Knox Club of New York, which was putting on a party at Delmonico's on this evening when I first met him. And it was in the heart of Harbach to throw in with a one-act play that went straight back to boys and girls, moonlight on the campus, dreams and the fathomless heart of youth. He placed the scene in that east doorway of Old Main. Knoxville, Lombard, old Newton Bateman, young John Finley, each name had its meaning to the Knox Club. In one scene Harbach had the ghosts of Bateman and Lincoln in a conversation about my Lincoln book. I had trouble with my eyes and looking over to my friend Catherine McCarthy of Harcourt, Brace, I saw that with her too smoke got in her eyes.

Harbach titled his little play *The Baffling Eyes of Youth*, a phrase from an ode I read in 1937 at a rededication of Old Main at Knox, the closing lines:

One thing I know deep out of my time: youth when lighted and alive and given a sporting chance is strong for struggle and not afraid of any toils or punishments or dangers or deaths.

What shall be the course of society and civilization across the next hundred years?

For the answers read if you can the strange and baffling eyes of youth.

Yes, for the answers, read, if you can, the strange and baffling eyes of youth.

SIXTEEN

"Where Shall We Go?"

★

"Where shall we go?" was often a question. At the Public Library, on Main near the Square, on the second floor, you heard no talk. At the librarian's desk they whispered like they had secrets. It was as still as in a church when the preacher reads the text. You could cough or sneeze if you had to. You were supposed to read and think. When two of us kids looking at a funny picture happened to snicker out loud, we would find eyes on us. You came to be quiet and learn something.

On reading tables were magazines and the Galesburg and Chicago newspapers. I went through the catalogue back and forth, reading titles of books and trying to guess what was good for me. The catalogue was an eye-opener on how many books and how many different books there are in the world. I wondered if anyone in Galesburg had read all the books in the catalogue and how you could make a catalogue without reading all the books in it.

As soon as I could I wanted to get a card to take out books and they told me I had to make an ap-pli-ca-tion. So I learned how to apply by filling out an ap-pli-ca-tion. I got my card and began taking out books, one by one, and the date I took the book out got stamped on my card. One by one I read all the books in the library by Horatio Alger, Oliver Optic, and C. A. Stephens. When all the books by those authors were out, I tried Hans Christian Andersen, and if he was out then some kind of *Strange Tales* of this and that.

One day in a library book I noticed that the population of the earth in the year I was born was 1,439,029,600. I puzzled over whether they had counted me and how if they hadn't counted me the number should be changed to 1,439,029,601. I was beginning arithmetic and it was fun to add one, which was me, and make a big number so odd you couldn't divide it by two and make it come out even. And when I read in the same book that fifteen million Chinese people had died in a famine that year I was born, I puzzled over whether they had been subtracted from 1,439,029,600.

Miss Phillips, the librarian, was perched on a high stool back of a high desk and I stood tiptoe to hand her my card. She had a prim face, a long straight nose, and eyeglasses. I believed she had read many of the books in the catalogue and was the best-posted woman in Galesburg on books. One afternoon the books I wanted were all out, and I went back to the catalogue and wrote more numbers of books. Only one I wanted was in. It was named *Queer Stories for Children*. As Miss Phillips handed the book toward me and I reached up for it, she said with a smile I didn't like, "Here you are, little Queer Stories." I could have thrown the book in her face, though I didn't. She called me little and I had got over being little. Worse yet, she as much as called me "queer" and if you're queer you act queer, think queer, and talk queer. I said to myself she deserved the long nose she had and I wished it would get longer. And if I was queer she was snippety and I would rather be queer than snippety.

We went to hear Methodists and Baptist evangelists. Mormon missionaries, and Seventh Day Adventists. We saw the Reverend W. H. Geistweit in his rubber boots and black costume take the new member of the First Baptist Church by the shoulders and dip the whole body in water. We heard both Lutherans and Catholics say "sprinkling" is as holy as "immersion." We heard Mr. Geistweit lead the fight against the saloons. Was the White Elephant or Danny Flynn's saloon open after midnight or selling whisky on Sunday? Mr. Geistweit in his pulpit named the time and place. The newspapers printed it and the police swung into action or forgot it.

Most of the saloonkeepers were careful about the word "saloon." Nearly every saloon had a sign in front: "Sample Room." They had tables where a traveling man could lay out his samples for buyers to

look at. Or they meant you could step in and sample their whisky
or beer.

Mr. Geistweit went on to Chicago to a big church and made a
national reputation, became a national anti-saloon leader. Mr. Geist-
weit had a spare frame and face, a thin brown beard over the face.
I felt he was not afraid to suffer and take punishment for what he
was saying and doing, the same as old-time speakers and preachers
who agitated against slavery and were run out of town by mobs.

We went to meetings of the A.P.A., the American Protective
Association, calling on Americans to protect themselves from the
growing power of the Roman Catholic Church. Reading a few copies
of their weekly paper, *Liberty*, I felt they were all one-sided. The
editor of *Liberty* spoke at one meeting. He had reddish chin whiskers
and we heard him go on and on saying the same things he put in his
paper. I said to John Sjodin, "He's a flannelmouth. He's against and
against and what he's for is only being against. I'd rather go with the
Populists. They are *for* some things that might work out." And
John, being a Populist, said I was on the right track and maybe yet
would come clean over into their party. The A.P.A., after excite-
ment for a year or two, fizzled out, though occasionally in saloons
and streets a fist fight broke out between an A.P.A. man and a
Catholic.

On one summer day the stores closed and Main Street was dead.
The Grocers and Butchers Annual Excursion took a thousand or
fifteen hundred people by train to Rock Island, by Mississippi steam-
boat to Burlington or Quincy, and by train back to Galesburg. It
meant a dollar I didn't have or couldn't spare, so I missed it from
year to year. Boys who went could talk for an hour about the trip
—the girls, the band music, what they saw and ate, the pop they
drank, who flirted with who, who got drunk and went to sleep and
didn't get a sight of the big Mississippi River, who lost their shirts
shooting craps. They could talk on and on, and all I hankered after
was to see that Mississippi River.

The Y.M.C.A. had two big rooms on the second floor near Main
and Prairie. Tables held the latest *Youth's Companion*, *Harper's
Weekly*, *Golden Days, St. Nicholas*. Even if I didn't agree with the

full-page color cartoons of Kepler and others in *Puck* and *Judge*, they were fun. I tried to imagine whether the cartoonists felt truly as mean toward Blaine or David B. Hill or Cleveland as they made out. One cartoon I couldn't forget showed Queen Liliuokalani of Hawaii, a big fat round woman, plopped in the lap of President Grover Cleveland, his face puzzled.

There were games there too. Crokinole and chess had their points, but I favored checkers and came near to a reputation as a checker player. I could win against Theodore Lindquist, a Swede boy with a pink squarish face and eyeglasses, who stood highest in mathematics in high school and later became a college professor teaching mathematics. Here I met Mr. Doyle, a retired furniture merchant, who played in local championship matches. Against Mr. Doyle I got several draws and a few times won over him. When I delivered the *Chicago Inter-Ocean* to him at his home on East Main Street near the Knoxville Road, he would ask me in for play or to work on the checker layouts in the *Inter-Ocean*, "black to win in three moves" or "white to win in four moves." His house was the last on my route and sometimes we played an hour or two. When I got three or four draws I was satisfied. And when a few times I won a game in Mr. Doyle's house I felt victorious and tickled.

The most interesting book in the Y.M.C.A. library was *The Life of Mason Long, Gambler*. The first half told about gamblers, their ways of cheating, how they trick their victims, what their fingers do with a deck of cards. This first half of the book the boy readers had worn dirty and ragged. The second half of the book, where Mason Long is a convert to religion, this was clean with no pages ragged or dirty.

The Y.M.C.A. secretary, Godfrey Haas, had a light reddish mustache and sideburns and we liked him. He ran the place to give boys clean fun. He would invite us to prayer and gospel meetings and you could go or not. He made the Y.M.C.A. a good hangout and in some connection or other I said to him one time, "God bless you, Mr. Haas."

I chummed with Vic Lundgren. He was shorter than me by a head and he had quiet ways and an innocent face anybody would trust. His habits were steady and had to be, as he was the support of his mother and an older sister. His job was on the "check row" of the Brown Cornplanter Works, a dollar and twenty-five cents a day. His father had quarreled with the mother. He had a hot temper that got where he was threatening to kill her. The family told him to go, and he went. Vic had had some kind of word that his father was out in Larned, Kansas, and doing well. Vic would do his guessing about whether his father would leave him anything or would have anything to leave to anybody. He liked to think maybe some relative of his would show up or would die and he would be notified of money or property left him—or it might be somebody that just accidentally took a liking to his face and named him to have money or property. He had seen consumption creep up on people and take them all of a sudden and he was anxious of his lungs and would say, "You never can tell who it is going to get next." Vic didn't hate anybody, not even his father. He didn't have any complaints about life. He was doing his job and always wanted to be in bed by ten o'clock at night so as to be in shape for his job and the ten-hour day tomorrow. We could talk or we could walk a block or two without any talk. We went to band concerts on the Public Square in summer on Friday nights and joined the crowd at Loescher's drugstore ordering ice-cream sodas.

Vic and I would stop and watch Tom Beckum on a payday night when Tom "had a jag on." He was a pick-and-shovel Irishman, keen-witted, and with a few drinks in him he loved everybody in the world, including Tom Beckum. He would step in front of a stranger, pull at the man's coat lapel, and say, "Tom Beckum, that's me, I'm Tom Beckum." Or he would throw his two arms wide apart and stop in front of three or four people coming abreast as if he was flagging them down. They would stop and listen to him and see his quizzical face as he said, "Who built the courthouse? I'm askin yuh. Who built the courthouse? Tom Beckum, that's me, Tom Beckum."

There would be complaints and the police would take Tom to the calaboose. The next day the papers said, "Tom Beckum was before Justice Holcomb again today, drunk and disorderly, two dollars and costs." I heard of people coming to Galesburg to visit and their relatives or friends took the visitors up Main Street hoping to show

them Tom Beckum, one of the sights of the town. I never heard
where he came from nor where he went after he was gone. The
few times I saw him performing on Main Street, he seemed to me a
fine comedian and the happiest man in the United States. Everybody
knew the Knox County courthouse had just been built a few years
and was the biggest and grandest building in five counties. And the
way Tom Beckum could hold up a pointing finger and ask, "Who
built the courthouse?" and then tap himself on his chest with the
finger and say, "Me, Tom Beckum," that was comedy as good as
they were playing over at the Auditorium.

On several cold winter nights Vic Lundgren and I ended up at
the Salvation Army, a second-floor hall on Prairie a block south of
Main. We had seen them march, eight or ten, to the beat of a bass
drum and the blasts of a cornet. Only bitter cold or nasty weather
kept them from marching out and holding a street-corner meeting,
with the drum laid in the center of their circle and the people stand-
ing by invited to throw nickels, dimes, and quarters on the drum.
Once we saw a drunk throw a silver dollar on the drum. Another
wanted to step inside their circle and do a dance. They let him in
for a few steps and then one of them walked him home. On Satur-
day and Q. payday nights they got their best crowds and more drum
nickels. They sang, "We'll roll the chariot along . . . And we won't
drag on behind." The second verse: "If the Devil's in the way we
will roll it over him . . . And we won't drag on behind." The last
verse was sure "the collection will help us to roll it along . . . And
we won't drag on behind."

A trim, sweet-faced brunette played a guitar to her singing and
went weaving in the crowd shaking the tambourine before men who
caught her smiling face close up and couldn't resist dipping into their
pockets for a stray nickel or dime. Her favorite song always had the
crowd very quiet. I have never heard it from any other singer nor
seen it in print. The tune I remember, and these lines:

> As we roll along we all are record-makers,
> Records black or white,
> In the wrong or right.
> As we roll along we all are record-makers.
> Oh be ready when the train comes in.

Working men and women who after a hard day's work were supposed to be tired, would come to the hall night after night and join in singing, "Oh, I'm Glad I'm in the Army," "Are You Coming Home Tonight?" "Are You Washed in the Blood of the Lamb?" and "There Is Sunshine in My Soul." They smiled at humor and slang in a gospel song:

> There are flies on you,
> There are flies on me,
> But there ain't no flies on Jesus.

Maud Bliss had joined the Army. We had seen her at the Seventh Ward school, shy and having few words. Now she had the words. Now she could drop to her knees and make a prayer as long and solemn as any of them. A little woman, with a full contralto voice, her body shook as the words of prayer and testimony poured from her. I had played ball with her brother Roger Bliss. We called him "Rusty" on account of his hair. He had a way of moving quick and smooth with his hands and feet, a rich grin showing many yellow teeth. He had been sent to the Pontiac State Reform School for stealing. We all liked him and we couldn't see him as a thief. We saw him holding different jobs and turning most of his wages over to his mother, a widow woman. What times we saw him across *a* few years he was "going straight."

Among the captains and majors of the Salvation Army were men and women out of England. They told about the slums of London, pits of sin and filth, where they had brought souls to the feet of Jesus. Their world-famous leader, William Booth, was to them the world's greatest voice leading men and women out of "the wilderness of sin." To them Booth had the stuff of Moses on the mountaintop or Daniel in the lion's den. They were sorry, they were sad, when Booth's son William Ballington Booth and his beautiful wife Maud rebelled and seceded and started the Volunteers of America. After that in many a town, as in Galesburg, the Army had its bass drum on one street corner and the Volunteers theirs on the other side of the street.

Fellows two to four years older than us were putting on a dance once a month, renting a hall and paying two fiddlers. They picked a name for themselves, the Golden Rod Club, and it sounded fancy. Husky Larson, Jiddy Erickson, and others of the Dirty Dozen said we could match the Golden Rod outfit. After thinking of different names, we decided to call ours the Monarch Club. We were not monarchs but it sounded like a fifty-cent Havana cigar. We rented a hall. paid a couple of fiddlers, and it came to twenty-five cents apiece each night we danced. We were two-bit monarchs. A fiddler called the quadrilles, and between we danced the waltz, two-step, polka, and schottische. I learned the polka redowa, soon forgot it, but never lost the waltz and the two-step. Young people worth remembering were on the dance floor from eight till eleven o'clock, when the fiddlers played the sad "Home Sweet Home." The Hanson sisters, Allie Harshbarger, Gertie Gent, others, they were lovely girls who could have gone anywhere and held their own for looks, manners, and smooth dancing.

There were the weeks I hung around the Knox County courthouse and heard trials. If the testimony wasn't interesting, the court stenographer always was. He was a pudgy fat man with a pink face and a thick bunch of pinkish whiskers on his chin. The way his right hand would travel along and get every word of the witness on paper, and any time the lawyers or the judge asked him what the witness said he could come up with it in a flash—I thought that was as wonderful as a pitcher striking out one batter after another.

I dropped into the courthouse one day to find the Knox County lawyers holding a memorial meeting for James MacKenzie, who had died a short time before. I had watched MacKenzie trying cases and I liked the way his mind worked. One lawyer after another got up and spoke words of praise for MacKenzie and they were saying just what I wanted said. He had iron-gray hair and mustache, a sharp wind-bitten face, and chewed tobacco except when addressing the jury. I could see that the lawyers meant what they were saying about his rare mind and fairness. It was no time for any of them to mention MacKenzie's one bad habit. Regularly he got drunk. He would know beforehand the day he would be getting drunk. When he was to be in court he was sober. A lawyer told me that a man came to MacKenzie's office late one afternoon as MacKenzie was closing the office. The man said, "I have a case I want you to take for me. Suppose I come in tomorrow." "No use for you to come tomorrow," said Jim MacKenzie. "The door will be locked and I'll be drunk."

I still remember the man with a wooden leg charged with stealing a gold watch from Mr. Stromberg of the Stromberg & Tenney bookstore. He wore a plain gray suit, looked neat and respectable, and told a story that seemed straight. I thought maybe there was some mistake, that he wasn't the kind of man who would steal a gold watch. He wasn't ruffled at all when he testified. And when the evidence against him was all in, it was plain that he was a liar and a thief. They sent him up for grand larceny. If it had been a two-dollar-and-fifty-cents Waterbury watch it would have been petty larceny. He got extra years in Joliet because the watch was gold, so the larceny was grand and not petty. I was learning law.

Where shall we go tonight? What will one night bring? I was loafing in the Q. depot one night. A man came in and I heard him saying, "There's a mob over at the county jail. It looks like they're going to lynch Ed Jackson." I had heard about Ed Jackson and seen him often. He was the handsomest mulatto in town, about medium height, nice rounded shoulders, well muscled, nose and chin well shaped, a neat dark mustache. He walked erect with an easy roll of body. He had been a prize fighter for a few years but drink had slowed him down. In a fight in Danny Flynn's saloon, he had knocked a man into a heavy pane of glass that broke. One piece of glass cut into a leg artery and the man bled to death. So Ed Jackson was in jail and the charge was murder. He had been in jail two or three days and I had heard of wild talk going round, but I didn't know what to make of it. The town had never had a lynching, I had never seen a mob. Galesburg wasn't much of a place for mobs. I had been reading in the papers about the "White Caps" in the South, masked riders in the night who lynched Negroes. Some of the telegraph stories in the papers hinted there was something not all wrong about the lynchings. Anyhow I picked up my feet and ran the three blocks over to the Knox County jail.

Here was a mob, sure enough. And a crowd was looking on at

the mob, with once in a while someone from the crowd stepping over and joining the mob. There would be a hum of many men talking loud and excited, and suddenly it would break into a roar and you could hear yells, "Kill the nigger!" and "We'll get the murderer, the black sonofabitch!" As I wedged in closer, I could see maybe forty or fifty men around a long telegraph pole. They had it pointed at the jail door. You could hear them yelling to the sheriff that they were going to batter down the jail doors and take out "the murderer" and give him what he had coming to him. Sometimes they flashed revolvers and dragged ahead with the telegraph pole.

The mob had broken down part of the fence next to the sidewalk and I wasn't sure what was going on till I ran into the yard next door. From there I could see Sheriff Bob Matthews and a row of deputies, each with a Winchester repeating rifle at his shoulder ready to shoot. The mob leaders at the front of the telegraph pole would move ahead about three feet, and when the sheriff ordered them back they would go back maybe two feet. They had been creeping closer to the jail doors. The sheriff had been calling out, "Get back there!" but the time came when he said he wasn't going to stand for any more fooling and if they came toward him with their pole another step, his men would shoot.

Mayor Fletcher Carney came and talked to the mob and to the crowd, saying the thing was wrong and they should let the law take its course. A doctor everybody liked, William O. Bradley, drove his buggy through the crowd and stood up in the buggy and made a speech to the mob that they ought not to disgrace the city and they ought to obey the law. Yet the howling and the yelling of the mob went on. Their leaders stood looking into raised rifle ends that looked ready to shoot, and there was something about the way Sheriff Matthews said if they came on another step with their pole they would get bullets, he would give the order to fire. It seemed like the sheriff meant it. The mob leaders had been figuring on more and more of the crowd joining them and there would be such a sweep and a rush on the sheriff and deputies that they wouldn't dare shoot—and the jail doors would be crashed and Ed Jackson hauled out and strung up or shot. It seemed to me the mob was more like forty men than fifty, and a few of them had drifted away.

I had been watching those wild-eyed yelling men around that telegraph pole maybe half an hour as they moved up a few yards and then moved back not as far as they had moved up. Then I saw Sheriff Bob Matthews tell his deputies to lower their rifles, and he called the mob leaders to come up to him for a talk. He told them that Ed Jackson wasn't in the jail, that he had been taken away where no mob could get at him. There was a humming and then a roaring from the mob when they heard this. They wouldn't believe it. The sheriff invited them to name a committee to go into the jail and see for themselves that Ed Jackson wasn't there. The committee went in and searched all cells, halls, and corners of the jail and couldn't find Ed Jackson. Then the air began to cool down. There wasn't going to be any hanging or shooting. The crazy show was over. We drifted away into the night, some of us glad it turned out as it did, others sad and disappointed that Ed Jackson was away somewhere and alive.

A few weeks later Ed Jackson, who had been in the Peoria County jail, was put on trial in Galesburg and sentenced to Joliet for life. Members of the mob went on trial, and their head man was sent to Joliet for a short term. Many years later I happened to be in Joliet and went with a friend to the Sunday-morning services in the prison chapel. We sat on a platform with the chaplain and the warden. There was singing and a sermon. My eyes ran from face to face of the convicts. And at one face my eyes suddenly stopped. I had forgotten about Ed Jackson, and there was his face. His eyes caught mine. His eyes saw that I knew him. How I knew his face and where we might have met he didn't know. At least a hundred times during an hour I found my eyes looking into his, and he was saying to himself, I am sure, "I wish I could place you and I wonder why my face is familiar to you." He was steady in the way he could keep his eyes on me and I was the one who turned my eyes away as though saying, "You win." He didn't know I was saying to myself, "What a pity it was that when your fist hit that man in the saloon he didn't slam into a wooden wall instead of a pane of glass that broke so it cut a leg artery and he died. It was an accident and you didn't mean it to end like it did." Maybe he read my eyes and had an inkling I always liked his looks and thought he would have made a great actor if the chance had come along.

Straight across the street from the Knox County jail was the Knox College campus. Straight west was the east front of the college where Lincoln and Douglas debated. The howls and yells of the mob, "Kill the nigger!" and "We want that nigger!" could be heard across the same air where the words of Lincoln came clear on an October day, "He is blowing out the moral lights around us, when he contends that whoever wants slaves has a right to hold them," those words in bronze at the north door of the college. Fred Jeliff, as editor of the *Republican-Register*, wrote years later: "The writer was an eye witness to the proceedings in front of the jail. We doubt if the mob would ever have taken the trouble to hang Jackson to a Lincoln elm. The probability is that they would have shot him. The outstanding fact is not what the mob proposed to do, but that they were prevented from doing it. As one thinks back to that sensational night, he becomes aware, first, that Jackson was given a fair trial and was sentenced to the penitentiary; second, that the mob leaders were punished; and third, that the scene of the Lincoln-Douglas debate was not desecrated. It can be further said that in the handling of this whole case, there was no stain on the reputation of Galesburg."

The key man and the hero, if any, was cool Bob Matthews standing with his deputies and their Winchesters ready to shoot—and his quick wit in sneaking Ed Jackson out the back way for a ride to the Peoria County jail. He had a little of his pay in the cheap looks on the faces of the mob leaders after they searched the jail and found their bird had flown away.

SEVENTEEN

Theme in Shadow and Gold

★

Earnest Elmo Calkins so loved Galesburg and Knox that his book *They Broke the Prairie* can stand as a classic portrait of a small town and college in the Midwest from 1837 to 1937. In a section on "Culture" he mentions physiology being taught in both school and college "as if the two sexes were identical and lacked reproductive functions." He quotes a disgusted senior: "You can go clear through Knox College and never learn that babies are not found under gooseberry bushes." He gives "an embarrassing incident" from high-school days:

The Shakespeare used was Hudson's edition, expurgated to protect the morals of high-school students from the facts of life. The worldly old Polonius was commissioning Hamlet to inquire discreetly into the possibly gay life of his son, Laertes, in Paris,

"I saw him enter such and such a house of sale."

What was a "house of sale"? The next line had been excised by Hudson, and no one could explain the phrase until a student who had an unexpurgated edition read the next line—"evidently a brothel." There was a painful silence; some of the boys snickered; others evidently did not know what the word meant. The teacher recovered first, and with heightened color said, "We will now go on."

As to the pure and the impure observed by Calkins in the 1880's and 1890's, he wrote: "An expectant mother was a disgraceful spectacle followed by whispered comment. Childbirth was never discussed, either in school or society. Children imbibed no beautiful associations with maternity. The obscene passages in the Bible were always skipped in the Sunday-school classes." Once a year the high-school boys were called into a session for males only—but not for a talk on sex hygiene. "No, the lecture was a stern admonition against fouling the public privy and writing on the fences with chalk words now found in current novels. The Puritans who warred against slavery, intemperance, Sabbath breaking, with beating of tom-toms, evaded the subject of sex completely. Whatever a child learned was from contemporaries, and it w~s years before most of them got the matter straight in their minds."

We would point out Cushman walking his slow suspicious walk along Main Street. The first boy seeing him would say, "There's Cushman." He had a face that would have been handsome if he could have wiped off what was sad, evil, and secret on it. He was the Galesburg reporter for the *Chicago Sun*, a scandal sheet that came from Chicago for the week end. Sometimes it gave names but mostly it was rotten gossip without names, like "The daughter of a Main Street livery stable keeper took a trip to Chicago last week with a Quincy traveling man." Or "Who was the man in the brown suit who took the wife of a leading dry goods merchant for a buggy ride to Knoxville last Sunday afternoon?" The *Chicago Sun* didn't last but a year or two, but while it was going we expected to hear most any time that Cushman was shot dead one night and nobody knew who did it and nobody cared.

A gentle human soul was Edward Higgins. His father and mother were out of old-line Pennsylvania Dutch and New England stock. The father had a good job at the Brown Cornplanter Works. They were Methodists, pious but not sanctimonious. They said grace at the table. They gave their five children what is termed "a good up-bringing," sending them to high school and keeping them fairly regular at church and Sunday-school attendance. They had books in the home, and besides the *Galesburg Republican-Register*, they took the *Chicago Tribune*, the *Youth's Companion*, *St. Nicholas*. The father voted the national Republican ticket and was a total abstainer.

voting in the local elections the No-License ticket which aimed to dry up the saloons. They were a clean American family, the atmosphere healthy and wholesome. I delivered milk to them, came to know them, and liked them. There were cold winter days when Mrs. Higgins asked me into the kitchen for coffee and fresh doughnuts.

Edward was the oldest of the five children. He finished high school, became a certified public accountant, and half the time was out of town on business.

Then a blow fell, one of those things beyond prediction before it happens, almost beyond belief after it is a fact staring you in the face and saying, "What's to be done about it?" In the realm of relations between man and woman is a platitude that anything can happen and usually does. Edward Higgins, a bright and good-looking fellow, with a reputation for being "honest and upright" and keeping company with decent and respectable people—Edward Higgins had suddenly married a woman. And they had set up housekeeping in a large house on a respectable North Side street, and the woman Edward married was known as one of the sorriest, blowsiest whores that had ever hit the town. There too to that house I went with my milk can and poured out the quarts for the loose-mouthed, slipshod, barelegged, loose-gowned slattern who ran the house and while Edward was away on business trips had men and drinking parties in the house. I saw this affair going on and Edward's mother sad-faced about it. I moved on into another job and didn't hear how it came out, though I am sure Edward couldn't have stood it for long. One night when I passed the Higgins house and saw their lighted windows I said to myself, "You can read happiness or anything else you want in the lighted windows of a house at night."

Once in a blue moon, possibly more often than the appearance of a white crow, a lyric love may arrive to a prostitute and a man's need of her. My good Swedish friend, Dr. Thor Rothstein, with a reputation beyond Chicago in his day in the medical profession, told me of a case. The man had syphilis. The woman who had given it to him he wanted to take out of the house where she was and marry her and have children, and he was asking if both of them could be cured of their disease. The doctor said, "Yes, you can both be cured, but it might be a terrible wrong to the children if you should have

cohabitation until a year after the cure. Can you promise me that?"
The couple hesitated and then promised. They were married. They
met the doctor's condition. "The children came, three of them," said
Dr. Rothstein. "I can say they were wellborn, and it has been for
twenty years a successful marriage and still is." Perhaps one moral in
the realm of the relations of men and women is: "You never can tell."

At the time it happened in Galesburg the papers were full of it,
everybody talking about it. I don't remember the name of the young
woman in the case. I am not sure her name was printed, nor do I
recall whether she came into court as a witness. My recollection is
that she did appear in court though I believe the newspapers spared
her the ordeal of her name being there in plain print.

Nor did the newspapers say, as is the custom now, that she had
been "raped." They said a criminal assault had been committed on
her. The name of the man, of course, was published. He went on
trial and day following day the testimony came, the details of the
crime, with care about not going too far in anatomical procedure.
The man was known as "Jungle" Riley. The place was among tall
weeds at a spot on the Knox College campus about two hundred
yards from the east side of the college Main Building where some
thirty years previous Lincoln and Douglas had stood before twenty
thousand people. There were bloody garments brought into the
courtroom. The woman had fought him but he overcame her
and had his way. I have forgotten how many years his sentence in
the Joliet penitentiary was to run. But I have not forgotten and
never can forget how this tale of violence swept the town, how us
kids read the papers, how we tried to get into the courtroom for a
look at Jungle Riley and the witnesses, how well we knew that "a
criminal assault" meant "rape," how we discussed the details of the
fierce and wild action and speech involved in an affair of rape. We
had sisters. We knew some fine girls. We would have joined up
with any mob. There was talk of a mob breaking into the county
jail and "stringing up" Jungle Riley but it simmered down. We had
come to the age of puberty. We were not clear about sex, about the
love life of either boys and girls or men and women. One boy said,
"When a man does what Riley did he doesn't know what he's doing.

He's gone clean crazy. He comes out when it's all over saying he wished to God it hadn't happened." We more than half agreed with this boy. We were sorry for Jungle Riley like that boy was. We asked the boy if he was on the jury, would he vote to send Riley to Joliet? And he said, "Yes, that's the hell of it. I'd send him to Joliet because he might do the same thing again to my sister or yours." What us kids were talking about then was human life being sacred and related to a question, "What is justice?"

I try to look back and fathom what good or harm came of the reporting in full with gory details. I am sure that rather than sending men and boys on the prowl for women and girls, the case threw fear into them, fear of the realm of sex, fear of danger, filth, and blood, much of the same dark fear that lurks in Hawthorne's *The Scarlet Letter*. There was, of course, a deepened respect for the police, the law, and the courts of justice. A creature of violence, a human being shaken out of all controls, had been caught and removed from where he could not again play at his ruthless game. There was, too, an aftermath of a bad taste about it all. We would as soon it hadn't happened. Yet the act recurs. In cities and in country neighborhoods it recurs. It may be found in the oldest folk tales and ballads. "He took his way with her." Or more vividly, "He knew it would mean death for him, but he took his way with her." In the big cities such a case stirs actual interest only in the local neighborhood where the crime occurs and the accused or the victim is personally known. In a small town it sets people agog. They go look where it happened and discuss the details. I know us kids for days were overexcited. I can't now figure what was the main thing it did to us unless it taught us that life can be brutal and that sex holds no easy and ordered pathways but is a mysterious labyrinth.

Walking around Chicago once with William Allen White, editor of the *Emporia Gazette*, I asked him how his paper would handle a Jungle Riley case. He said, "We never print the woman's name. We leave out the gory details as far as possible. In divorce cases, no matter what juicy morsels of gossip and testimony there may be, we print nothing but the names of the parties to the suit and on what grounds they get their divorce." Then he added, "It saves a lot of trouble—and white paper, what we call newsprint."

The case of Fred Burley and Jennie Bernberger was something else. It didn't get into the papers. Nothing occurred that might have brought it into the newspapers. The two of them had been going together in a rather easy way. They were teased more or less about how often they were seen wandering by themselves, keeping away from others. They were both fourteen, nothing special about either of them as to looks or cleverness, a very ordinary couple. The talk about them, however, was away out of the ordinary. One cool late-fall afternoon they were seen by three boys we knew who couldn't have twisted what they saw into something else than what they saw.

On the way we often took to the Seventh Ward schoolhouse we passed the roundhouse of the Fulton County Narrow Gauge Railway. It was a small affair, this railway, running some sixty miles from Galesburg to Lewiston, Illinois. The roundhouse was a small affair too, at times with no locomotive there and no one to attend a locomotive. The round table where the locomotive was turned around so it wouldn't run backward on the next run was seldom used and had a lonesome look. Under the rails and beams of the turntable, weeds and grass grew thick and there were many odd corners. We had played hide-and-seek and follow-the-leader there. The place said, "I will hide you" to any who might want to be hidden.

The three boys passing by took a notion to run out and chase each other along the beams. Suddenly in the grass and weeds of an odd corner two boys saw Fred Burley and Jennie Bernberger. They motioned the third boy to come look. They watched a minute or two and then ran away. They told it to the gang. One or two told it at home. It became one of those quiet scandals that don't spread far. Fred Burley's father was a railroad engineer of good record who liked his liquor. Jennie Bernberger's father was a Q. machinist and they were known as a quiet decent family. Fred was neither handsome, clever, nor reckless in any unusual way. He was a good ball-player and in a fight took pretty good care of himself, having an older brother who had been brutal in two schoolyard fights. It seemed hot blood ran in the family. What had happened, said some of those who talked about it, was one of those things that happen and you can never be sure why they happen. Someone got word to the Burley and Bernberger parents, and Jennie and Fred were never seen walking together again. In the course of time it passed away as nothing to talk about. No baby came.

Everybody passed it over as a little affair to forget—except one Swede boy. Of the five or six other boys I knew who talked about it while it was still a live and warm scandal, none of them mentioned it to me in the years that came after. This one Swede boy, however, was haunted by it. He had a mind and temperament for religion. He was a mystic and over his manhood years became a cultist in weird Christian sects and doctrines, writing tracts and speaking of himself, by inference, as a purist and a perfectionist. He carried himself as one who has attained holiness. I met him occasionally at intervals of ten and twenty years, and each time in our talk he brought up the sin of Fred Burley and Jennie Bernberger under the Narrow Gauge turntable long years ago. It was more than forty years after that boy and girl fell into their act of folly and passion that my religious friend wrote a letter to me and went out of his way to write his horror of those childhood sinners. He asked if I remembered the affair, with the implication that if I wasn't haunted by it as he still was, then I should properly be. I haven't yet figured out what it did to him and why, as with nobody else, it never changed for him in its color of blood scarlet. After forty years he shrank from the shame of their loathsome and evil act.

I am sure that if I had been struck as deep as he was by the infamy of this one event so memorable to him, I would go on a search. I would seek all items of information that would throw light on what happened afterward to Fred and Jennie. Did they marry, and how did their marriages turn out? Are there children, and how have they turned out? What does either of them, now in their seventies, have to say about one sudden event away and far back in the storms of their lives which they perhaps remember only dimly? Could one or both of them have gone on farther in sin so that if my friend should meet and hear them speak frankly they would paralyze him with what they know of the ways of evil? That could be. Or again they might tell of plain humdrum lives and perhaps one or two sons with Distinguished Service Medals or Purple Hearts. If we could know the facts we wouldn't do any imagining. We can make one inference to the effect that a zeal for holiness can be carried so far that it is both pathetic and comic. Unless this should meet the eye of my old Swede-boy playmate I expect next time I meet him he will again mention with pious aversion the piteous and unholy affair of a boy and girl under that Narrow Gauge turntable—sixty years ago!

Quite different was the atmosphere of another affair tinted with scarlet. Where I worked in the pottery at the southeast corner of town I often saw the young man Harry Wilson. He was a molder. He threw a lump of clay into a plaster-of-Paris mold of crock shape, put the mold on a turning wheel, kept the clay moist with the proper amount of water his hands kept throwing on it, and held a scraper taking the excess clay away. It was fun to watch him. I used to go when the chance came from the ground floor where I worked to the second-floor molding room. There I would see the crocks taking shape while I listened to the fascinating singing of Harry Wilson. Aye, the lad had tunes to him. Handsome he was, with a clean-cut face, straight nose and chin to match, liquid brown eyes, wavy brown hair, and a mouth for carving song words. Like his mother back in Ohio, he was an Irish Catholic. He had from her some old Irish jigtime ditties and come-all-yes. These he could sing, and shift to "Kathleen Mavourneen," "In the Gloaming," "The Last Rose of Summer," and other sad and poignant lyrics. My favorite was "Juanita." The fountain, the summer moon, the parting lovers in their last kisses, they came alive. He believed in love and its hungers and could give them in shadowed tones. I, a kid apprentice, had the nerve to say, "You ought to be with Al Field's minstrels." He smiled, "Just a molder. Once a molder always a molder."

The girls in the molding room carried the moist clay molds to a kiln for heat, drying, baking. One of the girls, Hilda Ellquist, of Swedish Lutheran peasant parents, was slow-minded, of robust build, with a comely face and a sweetness of clean strengths. You might see her in some of the paintings and sketches of Jean François Millet. I saw a rare dreaminess come over her face when listening to Harry Wilson sing "Juanita" or "In the Gloaming." The days arrived when Hilda wasn't coming to work. After a week or two, a girl who had seen Hilda reported with a sorry face, "She's in the family way." In this same week Harry Wilson didn't show up for work. The word was, "He's skipped town." And no report ever came back on where Harry Wilson had gone and what might have become of him and his voice and the further girls and women he met and sang for.

Hilda's baby came wellborn. She had an elder sister who was a perfect companion and comforter. Hilda carried herself with a quiet dignity, with neither pride nor shame. She worked as a housemaid, took a job in a laundry, kept on going to church, and brought along her boy with care and affection. Her father, a Q. day laborer, and her mother joined in care and affection for the little one.

A young farmer came along and began "keeping company" with Hilda. He played with the growing boy and had fun. He said to Hilda, "Why shouldn't we have a boy or girl of our own?" "You mean," asked Hilda, "we should get married?" "Sure—why not?" he said and he wasn't laughing. So they were married and Hilda bore him four bouncing babies, "thumping bantlings," worth looking at.

And her firstborn child? The years ran fast. He went to school, he went to war, he went into the selling game, a hardware line. A woman who saw him at a party reported to me, "He's made a success. You can see it the way people take him. He's a Presbyterian, an Elk, a Moose, a Mason, and is active in the Veterans of Foreign Wars. He saw combat duty in France in 1918. One of his three boys when last heard from was flying a helicopter in Korea." I had to say, "At this party did they ask him to sing?" "Not that I noticed." "Did any of them mention him as a singer?" "Not that I heard. Why do you ask?" And I passed it off with no word about a fellow she had never heard of, that sweet-singing bad-boy Harry Wilson, gone where the wind listeth, singing of love and its hungers.

There were a few folks who raised their hands as though to brush away evil, and they as much as called Hilda a slut and a strumpet. Still others laughed at the mention of Hilda's trouble but their laughter was as though someone had taken a fall on a slippery place—and no telling who's going to be next. I can't remember among the young people I knew that there was any of the spirit of Mr. Hawthorne's novel *The Scarlet Letter*, which was required reading in the high schools then. I missed going to high school but I read Mary's copy. I recall another boy who had got hold of *The Scarlet Letter* and how he told us, "It's about a preacher who knocked up a woman and a baby came and there was hell to pay. It got worse and worse, everybody fussed up. I quit reading it. I didn't care how it ended." He said more and I got the impression that the book not only told him that sex is a dangerous fire to fool with at any time, full of secrets and cruelties, but worse yet, sex is a sort of filth and flesh is nasty. Could it be that *The Scarlet Letter* reeks with Sex Education?

"Bud" Hogan was older than the fellows in our gang and went mostly with an older set. But he stopped in often at the Schulz cigar store, sometimes spent afternoons and evenings with us. He didn't get drunk, only "liked to get a little jingled." He knew by name most of the women "on the loose" in Galesburg and many of them in Monmouth and Peoria—and they knew him. I was getting a haircut one afternoon in the LeMatty barbershop on Seminary Street when a woman passed by in front, a flaunt to her walk, her hair cut short. Bob LeMatty said, "She's new here—who is she?" Bud Hogan sitting in a chair piped up, "That's a new chippy from Peoria" and gave her name and told her points.

We believed Galesburg was a decent well-behaved city compared to Peoria. In Peoria, we believed, were big distilleries and breweries making whisky and beer and the saloonkeepers ran the town. When a Galesburg man wanted a "bad woman" for the night it was safer to go to Peoria than to try it in Galesburg, where the police made raids. Gambling too was safer in Peoria. It was years later that the song came, "I Wisht I Was in Peoria Tonight." We usually said "Pe-or-y." Years back, it was told, the great Shakespearian actor, Junius Brutus Booth, father of John Wilkes Booth, rode a Q. train from Galesburg. And when the brakeman called out, "PE-OR-Y" Booth stood up and in his clear tragic voice gave the four syllables, "*Pe-or-i-a.*"

The Hogans lived near us. The mother was Swedish, short and sturdy, pleasant, hard-working, using none of her Swedish on the large calm Irishman she had married who had a good job with the Q. and a well-trimmed red beard on the lower half of his face. Bud had flaring red hair, heavy red eyebrows, fair clean skin, a scattering of freckles on his face, a nose with a slight upward angle at the middle, a mouth not small, with lips that parted to flash lines of even teeth when he laughed. The face muscles, eyebrows, shoulders, all joined in when he laughed. His body to his heels went into a sort of jigtime when he laughed in a long ripple. What he was saying might not have any particular wit or humor, but it was catching. Others felt gloom chased away when he merely said, "Ain't it fun to be alive and in circulation?" He was a swift-moving lightweight, had won prizes at waltzing, and his walk had the grace of a good dancer. We had seen him in his back yard, in pink circus tights, practicing on a trapeze hung from an apple tree. He was working as a switchman for the Q.—with an off eye on getting to be smooth enough on a trapeze to go with a circus, a hankering that didn't last long. We heard him wish once he could be a circus clown. The chance never came, though we were sure he could have cut original monkeyshines before audiences. The Q. switchmen knew him for one of the best of them. He could swing arms, body, and feet onto a moving boxcar as though it was a dance with music. He wore gay clothes, light checked suits, red neckties. Once I blossomed out in a new suit, not at all a loud one, but I must have looked a little fresh, for Bud Hogan stood before me, sized me up and down, and rippled, "Why, Charlie, you look like you had just jumped out of a rosebush." A trimly built girl passed by in a bright neat summer gown and a wide picture hat with flowers, and Bud laughed, "Ain't she sweet? She looks like she's just been unwrapped brand-new from a bandbox."

He brought up the talk going around about Fred Burley and Jennie Bernberger and took a quiet laugh for himself. "What a place that is, that old Narrow Gauge turntable! One summer night I went to a band concert on the Square with a pretty girl who was always good to me. After the concert we took a long walk. It was a cool evening after a hot day—and a full moon, a big wagon wheel of a moon, a fine moonlight you could sift through your fingers. We walked and talked. We walked and held hands and didn't say anything. We stopped, put our lips close, and walked on. We walked to the end of Pearl Street, came back to the Peoria tracks, and stood there for another kiss. It was near midnight. Our eyes lighted on the Narrow Gauge turntable maybe forty yards away. We went over there, slipped under the beams and found us a nice corner in the black shadow of one of the beams. After a while we heard little sounds and we looked where they came from. And there was another couple. They had seen us and were giggling. In the next hour we made out two more couples who had picked their places in the black shadow under a beam. We laughed and made our getaway. Nobody said a thing. Nobody saw nothin! Nobody knows who was there. I'm sure little Jennie Bernberger wasn't there. Her old man wouldn't let her out that late. She and Fred Burley had to have the daytime."

There came a winter when I saw Bud Hogan with a serious face and his laugh wasn't in jigtime. He dropped his old-time clowning. He wasn't skylarking any more. He said, "I'm in love, Charlie. First time I was ever really hit with it. Not on the booze any more. She's got me. I worship the ground she walks on. Diamonds in her eyes. We're going to get married next spring. I'm going straight."

This dancing joker, this clown, this gay bright blade Bud Hogan, was going in for Holy Matrimony. "She lives in Peoria, a fine old family, a strict father and mother, two brothers in college, clean every way. She didn't like my boozing, even a little. I told her I'd swear off and I have. No more redeye for me, Charlie. I'm lucky to get her. Jesus, I'm lucky!"

This was early December. I saw Bud twice before Christmas and he was still serious, sweet and happy serious, with a dark streak about it. No more night prowling, no more booze, and, "I'm the luckiest man alive!" He went to Peoria, had Christmas Eve at the girl's house, and slept in the Spare Room. He joined in a big Christmas dinner and in the afternoon went with her two brothers to a skating party on the Illinois River. The day was zero-cold and the ice perfect. What happened I heard in early January when Bud was back in Galesburg. We sat in the back room of the Schulz cigar store. Bud had been down to the White Elephant and he was jingled, lightly so, the redeye on his breath. He told about Christmas Day:

"It was a grand skating party, a dozen couples and extra girls for my girl's two brothers. I cut figure eights and did some fancywork on the ice. One girl and I put on a waltz for the others. She was good. Then I noticed the two brothers and another fellow every once in a while would skate out of sight around a bend of the river. I could see they had something going on between them around there. And I skated around and caught them at it. They had three quart bottles of whisky and they were hitting it hard. The two brothers of my girl held out bottles to me. 'The finest Kentucky bourbon,' they said. 'Take a swig. It's the real goods.' I said, 'You know I've told the folks I've sworn off. I'm on the wagon.' They said, 'We don't tell the folks. And you won't tell the folks. They think we're good Y.M.C.A. boys. Hit the bottle. It's smooth stuff and'll keep you warm.' They kept at me, 'We won't tell and you won't tell.' They pushed a bottle into my mouth. I took a long drag of it. It tasted like no other liquor I ever had. It was like my system cried for it. After that when those fellows went around the bend I went with them, though once when I held back they took me by the arms, one of them saying, 'Now we're going to have one big drink to our sister and happy days!' We cleaned those three quart bottles. I got going like a damned fool and put away my share, I guess. You see, it was zero-cold, and when you're outdoors you can take a lot of it and not feel it except it warms you.

"The two brothers went to some college party for dinner. I went back to my girl's house. I'd forgot about cloves or peppermint. They were suspicious of my breath. Right off I could see something wrong there. 'We'll have dinner in about an hour,' said my girl. 'Sit by the stove here and warm your feet.'

"I sat by the stove—sure—I snuggled up close to that red-hot hard-coal burner. And in about two flickers, I was dead asleep. I didn't know nothin from nothin. They tried to wake me for dinner but I was a bag of salt, dead to the world, and around me a rich bouquet-of-whisky stink.

"After a couple of hours my eyes came opening slow and I wasn't sure where I was, my brain thick and hazy and my head aching. Then I could hear them speaking to me. I got their voices. I came awake. I came awake and ashamed and scared like never in my life before. They brought me a plate of turkey and mashed potatoes they had kept in an oven. I tried to eat and had no taste. I drank two cups of black coffee. I tried to talk but it was a foozle. What was there to say? I could tell by their faces it was all up—no hope—not a chance.

"They had me stay in the Spare Room for the night. I went to sleep, had a crazy dream, and came out of it to stay awake and tossing around all night. When I saw daylight coming into the room, I put on my clothes, packed my valise, wrote a little note, 'I'm sorry and you don't know how sorry, good-by.' I rode home on the first caboose out of Peoria. You don't know what it is, Charlie. There she was in bed the next room to me. And all night long I knew when daylight came I was going away from her forever."

We saw Bud drinking harder, getting more than "jingled." Where he used to be particular about women, now we heard a man say, "Any old snaggletooth will do him." The next spring he was around the cigar store much of the time, ugly red sores on his face. With neither pride nor shame, and as though telling hard luck and asking no pity, he said he was taking mercury "for the syph."

The next year he was in the United States Army in the Philippines. He marched in rain, slept in mud, proved himself a good soldier. He got an honorable discharge, came back to his home town, went switching again, married a good woman, and the last news I had of them they were still living together and he was a sober provider. I could believe that he might be meditating, "I had my years of flame. So many a time red roses poured over me. There were days I was a ball of fire. Now I am near burned out but I like what I can read in the eyes of young people I meet."

On the credit side of Bud's record as a sinner were many points. He was peaceable, kept out of brawls, slid away from the fights, got no girl "in the family way," wasn't interested in gambling, never was arrested for disorderly conduct, had a straight record for work on the job, made good cheer and good will in the company he kept, a born funmaker. A letter I still have from him, written in the Philippines, has the shine of his laughter. His nickname for me was "Backup Charlie" and through the four-page letter he keeps calling me Backup. "Tell the girls," he wrote, "that they had better stay off the streets when I get back, for we look like Moros. Say Backup I have got the Moros dance down pat and it is the prettiest dance you ever saw in your life." In rain, mud, and bloody work, he had no complaint and put his laugh into his letter. Love and the ladies, fun and liquor, pride in his work, made his life till those jolts came and he settled down. I don't know why I write with such detail about Bud Hogan unless for a feeling that he was an artist and a genius and that if we overlook a few slips that were minor rather than major, he made the world brighter for many people in everyday life. I never knew a man more convincing and truly affirmative at saying, "Ain't it fun to be alive and in circulation?" That could go on his gravestone.

David Horn lived not far from our house. He was the only child. His father had given the best of his life to the Q. at common labor, had been sober, careful, and thrifty and had laid by enough to keep him the few years left to him when his old bones were no longer any good on the job. David Horn's mother too had seen her best years, had swollen legs, and walked with slow halting steps. They lived in a little three-room cottage they had paid for. They believed, as the saying went, they would "never have to go to the Knoxville poorhouse" five miles away. Old Man Horn was interesting, appealing, to look at. His fine head of hair had gone snow-white, as also his venerable side whiskers, and he seemed to be a piece of Old Sweden.
Different stories were told about why the son took to gambling, how and why he kept going to a hoard of some four hundred dollars in the house, how and why he lost at the gambling rooms on the Public Square till every dollar was gone. One story that Mart and I were inclined to credit had it that a buxom, good-looking widow of a railroad brakeman had got some kind of a hold on David Horn. He had been seen coming out of her house. We couldn't believe that David on his own had gone in for gambling every last dollar he secretly took from his father's savings of years. We knew him as a steady lad, no boozer, nothing rakish about him. We heard him talk about his winnings early in the game, with a light in his eyes as though he was going somewhere and what he was doing would pan out big. He may have been swept along by the well-known amateur gambler's passion, the fools' fever of hope that lures them on. We blamed the flip, buxom widow. To us she looked the part.

The money ran out, the last hoarded dollar gone. The cottage took on one mortgage after another. When the mortgage money was gone, there was only one road to take for Old Man Horn and his wife with her slow halting step. They ended in the Knoxville poorhouse and their son David left town with several personal secrets. I met him later and we didn't hit it off or I might have learned whether he was just naturally hit with a fever to "buck the tiger" or whether the widow really did have a hand in the tragic finish.

A Knox College student, Peter Holmquist, came from a small Illinois town, of pious Swedish parents, it was said, well-to-do folks. He taught a Sunday-school class in a Swedish church, and paid social calls on some of the Swedish girls in our block. He was tall, lean, well muscled, passed up athletics for scholarship and made brilliant records, won prizes. His face was a marvelous mask. He had a strongly carved nose with a slight curve, a mouth of fixed melancholy when in repose. After a joke his face would lapse into the fixed look that had perhaps grave meditation rather than sorrow. The girls in our block liked him. He didn't put on airs. He could have gone with girls at the college Ladies' Seminary but he held to his Swedish friends. He graduated with honors. I forget the important positions he went into where a great career was predicted for him. I have forgotten too the malady that suddenly laid him low. When he died there was sorrow, for "he had high promise."

Forty years went by and a thousand miles from Galesburg I went for a visit with an old Swedish woman who had known and loved my folks. We talked about many old and odd remembrances. I mentioned Peter Holmquist and the times my sister and I had seen him. The woman was in her eightieth year and I had noted her memory as unusually clear and exact in all matters familiar to me. Otherwise I wouldn't have accepted the curious meditation that came from her, brief though it was. She had lived in the community where Peter Holmquist was raised, and her words came slow as though the memory was distinct, as though a thing she recalled definitely had been forgotten a long time and now came afresh. She spoke her brief reminiscence as a queer and memorable fact. "Peter Holmquist, yes,

I remember. He was an illegitimate child, his mother a deaf-and-dumb woman."

I didn't know how to go from there except to ask whether it was known and accepted as fact and her answer came, "All the leading people in town knew it. After enough time passes you have to think back to what it was that made such talk away back. If I should think hard about it for two or three days it would come back to me, who was the father and the name of the deaf-and-dumb mother. His mother was one of three unmarried sisters. They left him their property and he was well off."

My memory went roving back to the face of Peter Holmquist. Besides my recollection of him in life I have a photograph he gave Mary. Aware that mind and memory can work tricks, I don't completely trust my impression about a mute look on the face of the man. There is a hint of the mute, the inexpressible and unfathomable, about any melancholy face. What I find myself meditating about is the unknown, what Peter's secret did to him. It was probably a spur to him. He so carried himself and managed his life that if at any unforeseen moment he should learn that at college, and in his Galesburg church circle and among his Swedish girls, his secret had become known, there would be good people saying, "Well, what of it? It's nobody's business but his. He doesn't smoke, drink, swear, nor go prowling and skylarking, and he makes high records in his studies and he isn't snooty. Don't be a gabmouth." I would not have entered this matter in these crude annals were any person concerned still alive. Peter is gone and all his next of kin vanished.

Tiskilwa, on the Rock Island line, was not far from us. A young woman who had moved from a farm near that town to Galesburg told me of her grandmother and a grand-aunt. Those ancestors of hers were among the First Settlers. One evening there came to their cabin a man not drunk, for he was steady on his feet, but the breath of liquor was on him and he was wild-eyed, full of wild talk. The two women saw a long white scar running from one ear and along half his throat, as though someone had tried to cut his throat and finish him. He was a big scrawny fellow and his clothes hung upon him like he had been sleeping in the timbers in the rain. He had found out that the farmer and his hired man were away for two or three days, driving hogs to market.

"My grandmother was thirty then," the young woman from Tiskilwa went on. "She was rosy-cheeked, strong and full of wit. When she saw the cabin door pushed open and this strange man come in and begin his wild talk she said to herself she'd keep cool and use all her wits. He took my grandmother by the two wrists and said he knew what he wanted and he was going to get it and nobody would stop him. His eyes blazed and his throat scar got whiter. My grandmother said there was nothing less than rape and murder for her and her sister, the way the man talked. They looked at each other knowing the man couldn't be in his right mind. They kept their wits, though, and began cooling him down. The grandmother said, 'We've got roast pork in the oven, can you smell it? We can give you potatoes with gravy and fresh apple pie. Wouldn't you like to sit down here at this table and eat first before you do anything else?' He sat up to the table. He ate his fill and a change began coming over him. It was late afternoon, near sunset. Then one of them said, 'Maybe what you need is a good night's sleep. We can give you a good bed with clean sheets and you'll get the rest you need.' They put him in a clean bed. He woke up in the morning after a twelve-hour sleep, asked if he had behaved foolish the evening before, ate three fried eggs for breakfast, and gave them sheepish smiles when they told him the half of his wild-eyed talk. He stepped out of the door saying to the two women, 'The blessing of the good Lord be on you all your days,' and was on his way." They were pioneer women who kept their heads in danger.

"My grandmother," said the young woman from Tiskilwa, "took a dinner basket to the men in a field quite a ways off. She told me she always carried raw meat to throw to the wolves when going through a piece of timber on the way. The morning came when two wolves followed her and kept coming closer. When they were about five yards from her she threw them the raw meat. While they stopped to eat it she ran and came safe to the men in the field. She was good at handling either a hungry man or a hungry wolf.

"I asked her if ever a child fell into a well on their place, as had been told, and she said, 'No, but one time when we saw Indians coming we hung a little girl in the well till the Indians passed.' "

One brave woman I saw almost incredibly loyal to her marriage vows and family was the wife of a Q. shop laborer. Six healthy children had come to them. The man was known to the grocers as "good pay." He could buy "on tick" and no questions asked. They were among the families classified as clean and decent. Then the husband and father came down with consumption. They were living in the little house on South Street where our family had moved from my birthplace. I was delivering milk to them. The time came when their bill for milk tickets had run so high that my boss ordered me to let them have no more tickets. The sick man lingered, grew pale and thin till he seemed a bag of bones. Over two years he lingered, holding to life with white skeleton fingers. During that long struggle to live and make a comeback his wife "took in washing." I saw her at the tub many a time. She was the support for a family of eight in a three-room house. Day after day her hands ran along the washboard, ran clothes through a wringer, hung out the clothes and ironed them, one of her boys hauling the finished work on a little wagon to the customers.

She was not a large rugged woman who could take such work in her stride. She was small and well muscled, but the endless monotony of one wash after another and the same nice lace every week from one family and the same red-flannel underwear from another—it wore her till she was pale and thin. Friends and neighbors wondered if she would go down like her husband. But she didn't. Something in the pith of her bones told her to stand up and go on. This invisible something might have been devotion to her husband and little ones. It might have been some code in her blood from her Swedish ancestral stream, telling her life is a battle and you fight to the last with whatever you've got. In what she did there was love of her man and of her brood of those born from her—and there was also pluck and valor as strictly as that for which genuine heroes are awarded medals of gold with rich inscriptions.

She saw her husband die in the house where she had endlessly attended him and where she and the children had for nearly two years borne their burden of pity at the spells of racking coughs and the toils of keeping floors and garments clean. The widow slowed down somewhat in her battling at the washtubs, brought her boys along to where their earnings helped and she could rest her bones and look back on harder days and worse nights. I heard of her boys and girls on different jobs, decent and honest. I heard her say once, "I did my best with what I had. Sometimes I nearly give out, but I went on. My husband was a good man. The children have come out pretty well. They were such handy little helpers. All we can say is we did the best was in us." A spare and a gaunt life she had. A citation could be written over her grave: "She was in her humble pathway a heroine who illustrated the meaning of true love."

There was a stanch little woman, strong-bodied with a rich full bosom, whose husband thought the world of her, whose neighbor women spoke admiration of how neat and handy she was with her housework. She could fix a pie for the oven or do a washing with the least number of motions needed, singing at her work. And her neighbors knew she often whispered a prayer about a deep wish she had. When her first child came it lived only two days. Her second child lived only a day, and I heard of two neighbor women who talked to each other about it and suddenly the two of them had their aprons to their eyes drying the tears. I heard a boy say that his mother had gone over to help in any way she could. She had seen the dead child and there came from the mother the half-choked words, "I think God ought to entitle me to one child, don't you think so?"

When Hattie Hoffenderfer left our block and her home and her folks we wondered a little about how she would do in Chicago. "She's got nice hips and a good bust, but her face ain't nothin extra," I remember one boy saying. In a year or two we had forgotten Hattie. Then news came dribbling back that in one of the big department stores she had moved up from clerking to an important office job. Another year or two and we had again completely forgotten Hattie. Then one summer she came back to the home town, on a two weeks' vacation, visiting with her folks and looking up old acquaintances. The word went around, "Have you seen Hattie

Hoffenderfer?" And some who had seen her said, "God, the clothes she's got on!" She was the flashiest-dressed woman who had ever walked around our end of town. She had the tightest-fitting corset and the highest-heeled shoes we had ever seen. Her walk was a continuous strut. When she talked with old neighbors and friends she didn't overdo it but she let it be known that she had come up in the world to an important position. What she held down was a "position" rather than a job.

The silk she wore looked genuine and the three gold rings on her fingers, set with jewels, and the diamond brooch at her throat. Had she talked more about her work and what she did to earn the money to buy such apparel and adornments, there wouldn't have been the kind of talk that went around. She liked Chicago. "Chicago's been good to me," we heard her say, and we answered, "It sure has." No one we knew of dared to ask her, "Hattie, where in all time did you get the fancy duds and stones you're wearing?" We doubted that when she took the train back to Chicago she had the least notion of what kind of gossip buzzed around her. The slang of the day had it, "She certainly could put on the agony." How her German peasant father and mother took her visit I didn't hear. The father kept on going regularly to his job in the Q. shops.

There were two Negro women who for two or three years walked Main Street and the Public Square on Saturday nights and Q. payday nights. They didn't stroll. They walked fast as though they had an errand, as though going somewhere to work, to a party, or to church. They caught the eyes of those on the watch for anything of interest and out of the ordinary. One of the women was over six feet in height, slender, light of color, a good-looking brown-skin. The other was short, her head below the shoulders of her partner, her skin black, her face somber. And this pair, these partners, had been given nicknames known to hundreds of men and boys, the tall one "Rattlesnake," the short one "Guinea." They were never seen on Main Street with either Negro or white companions. They swept along Main Street and around the Public Square, on some nights once or twice, and more than that on other nights. They didn't look at men or flash any signs. They were never arrested. They were not flagrant. They were two interesting, picturesque persons. With a little training they could have made a hit in vaudeville.

Talk ran that men followed them to their rooms, which may have been so—or again not. They could have been two housemaids or cooks or washerwomen. They were out to see Main Street on the nights when that street was crowded and spectacular with faces and store windows. They wouldn't have been noticed in particular except for the fact that they were a striking and charming spectacle, complete contrasts. And the nicknames helped give them a certain comic distinction. People who had heard of Rattlesnake and Guinea would go downtown and keep an eye out for a glimpse of them. It is an even bet they were on the loose. Anyhow they are in my album of faces and forms seen when I was a boy.

The next face is that of a white woman who walked alone. On Saturday nights always, and often of weekday nights, summer and winter, she walked Main Street alone. She was of medium height, somewhat slender, with dark hair, brown eyes, a pale face. She was open-mouthed and below her upper lip shone a row of gold-filled teeth. Someone had nicknamed her "Klondike." The Alaska gold rush was on and the nickname stuck. Her worn face and the droop of her shoulders gave me the impression she had been struck hard blows and heard harsh words and whatever might happen to her couldn't be worse than what she had had. I stood on street corners with other boys and heard them snicker, "Here comes Klondike," and I joined in the snickering. I don't know who followed her to the darker streets, nor what kind of men might have wanted her, nor how meager her earnings were. And I think maybe she wouldn't be in my album of memory except for her open-mouthed row of gold-filled teeth and the many men and boys who called her Klondike. Life had already whipped her, while Rattlesnake and Guinea still had miles of vital living to go.

There was Stella Garrity. Her name was in the papers several times when her house was raided and the men in the patrol wagon tried to hide their faces. She kept a house next west of the Narrow Gauge Railway on Berrien Street. She was a massively constructed woman, with the curves of a burlesque star. In her case I can use her right name. I believe she would prefer to be mentioned rather than have her name omitted. She was a show-off, no other woman of the town quite so flagrant about being seen publicly in dashing fine clothes. On many a summer Sunday afternoon she could be seen in a fringed-top surrey, with one of her girls and two men. They were out to be seen and to look proud and gay to those who gazed at them. They meant to be impressive and they were. Stella was in décolleté, showing her well-rounded shoulders and shapely bust, a picture hat wide-brimmed with laughing flowers. When she saw one of her customers who would welcome a greeting, she gave it with a wave of a blue-silk kerchief or the throwing of kisses.

After her place was raided and she was fined several times and her customers were fined and men were afraid of being caught in raids on her house, Stella left town. She and Isa Magee were the only two women in town sufficiently notorious, with their names often published, so that they had reputations in many little towns beyond Galesburg. One of us had a good word for Isa, though. Johnny Thompson had a route carrying the *Republican-Register*. When I told him that a Q. engineer on my route had handed me a dime on Christmas morning, he said that one of his customers had handed him a dime. "And guess who it was?" said Johnny. "The only house on my route where I got a Christmas dime was from Isa Magee. If anybody asks me about Isa I'll say a good word for her."

Next door east of our house, after the Bonhams, lived the Homers, Mr. Homer a Q. engineer. His son Bert and I chipped in and bought a punching bag, hung it to a basement ceiling, and made the walls ring with our fists drumming the leather. We had seen Jim Corbett in his lightning fists and arms at the bag, and all we wanted was to be half as good. Then I saw less of Bert for a time and noticed a change come over him. He had been shy, more bashful among people than I was. I forget what Bert's job was and what people he went with who might have helped to change his ways, but all of a sudden he was bold instead of bashful. He was well built, had a round pink face, blue eyes, rare even teeth, and a dangerous smile. The girls took to him and he took to the girls. Women older than he played for him and he took what he wanted. Spring and summer came and the punching bag was forgotten. I went my way wishing I could be as bold and handy with girls and women as Bert Homer. I knew too that as a "good-looker" he had it over me and, like Nicodemus, I would have to be born again.

The Spanish-American War came along and Bert enlisted for service in the Philippine Islands. He wrote to me from Bongao in November 1900:

Dear Friend Charles:

Your letter received and is quite a treat down in this part of the country. Well, Cullie, I had fever up to one hundred and five but I am all O.K. now. . . . I went in the kitchen the other day to try it and you ought to see us sling out the slum. We sure have some fun at it and of course we get a few extras to eat our-self. . . . Say Cullie you must excuse this poor writing for there are three of us writing on a table about the size of a cigar box and they keep talking and slapping me on the head so that I can not write hardly at all. You said that there was not any news back there I dont know what you would think if you was down here. We only get mail about once every two months and then it is old to you people back there. It is get up in the morning at first call and work all day building roads, or hike over the mountains hunting for negroes. I suppose you are having good cool weather now but it is mighty hot down here. We are all as black as Indians but the heat does not bother me like it did when I first came over here. Say Cha's it has been so long since I saw a white woman that I have almost forgot what they look like. They have got six Japanese girls here in camp for the benefit of the Co. and you can guess what it is like to one hundred and seventy eight men. It is the next thing to nothing. We would not know how to act around a white girl if we had a chance to get with one. How is my old Irish Swede getting along or has she went up the spout? And Old Joe tell him I will write to him soon and that I am going to send him some shells for Christmas. And my Mother if I have time before this boat goes out I will write to her but you tell her that I send her my love and that I am getting along fine and I hope they are all well. . . . I would like mighty well to get to come back to the States again but I dont know how soon we will get the chance so we take everything just as they come and say nothing. I have found out that is the best way to take things over in this country. Well Cha's I guess this is about all I can think of for this time so I will close hoping to hear from you as soon as possible, and tell my Mother that I am well and getting fat. Well good by for this time. Write soon.

So goes an American soldier portrait we may value for clean candor, affection, and fellowship. Bert came back in fine trim, the family moved West, and we lost track of each other. The Irish Swede he mentioned was a housemaid, taller and older than Bert, who made free with many men and Bert her favorite. She was long-legged, swift of body, with black hair, flashing black eyes, shaggy black eyebrows, and a daring face. She liked men and her eyes said, "I'm a man's woman." I saw her once with Bert and I thought her eyes played on him with a hunger for him. She couldn't keep her hands from smoothing him at arms and shoulders, with now and then a hand along his face. I heard she left town soon after he did. No news came of either of them but I would like to think they got married and had four children, two boys and two girls, the boys having his face and the girls hers.

Henry Cameron and Dorothy Elwell kept steady company at college two years, and the third year it was no surprise they were engaged, onlookers saying they were a perfectly matched couple. Henry was tall, with a sunny face, a winning smile, popular in college activities and elected to responsible offices. Dorothy was smaller, a smooth dancer, a bright student, with a touch of gravity near melancholy at her mouth. They were seen together so often and seemed so fond and constant that all bets and forecasts had it they would have smooth sailing. They graduated and Henry Cameron went to his father's farm in Wisconsin, Dorothy Elwell to her father's farm near Knoxville. They waited only to fix the date of their wedding.

One day a letter came to Dorothy. She opened it to find only a newspaper clipping. She read it and it stunned her. The short news item said that Henry Cameron and his brother David Cameron were in a rowboat that overturned and both of them were drowned. That was all. Only a few lines of print with no details given. She wrung her hands, she stood puzzled. Why no added lines from whoever mailed the clipping? She made a telephone call to a friend in Wisconsin who lived close to the Cameron brothers. His words burned in her ears: "Why, there's nothing to any story that Henry and David Cameron have been drowned. I saw Henry Cameron yesterday and talked with him." Dorothy Elwell broke into tears and

sobbed into the phone, "Tell Henry it's all over. I never want to
see him again." Henry took the first train for Galesburg and drove
out to see Dorothy. He explained to her that he had nothing to do
with the hoax, that it was David's idea to get the news item in a
country weekly and mail it to her. Dorothy couldn't hear him and
held to her first words to him, "It's all over. I never want to see you
again." He stayed and begged and pleaded and found her heart
fixed and stony. She refused to take his word that it was meant as a
practical joke and he had no hand in it. She told him there was no
glimmer of hope ahead and all their fond kisses in the past were
ashes of roses—she told him to go and he went. Each of them later
made a marriage more or less successful but that is another story
with many windings.

There was a wild and crazy wedding night that set the town by the
ears. Those who enjoyed scandal had the time of their lives. A col-
lege boy, the son of a professor, was marrying the daughter of a
livery-stable keeper. He was handsome and well liked and she was a
stunning beauty—so it was told by those who remembered that far
back, to a time when some of the best people considered it indecent
to serve and drink wine. At this wedding the corks popped, the wine
ran free, and the empty bottles piled high. It went to the heads of
young bucks in spiketail coats and boiled shirts. They went out and
fixed up a dray with flags, festoons, and flowers, with a throne for
the bride to sit on, the groom to stand at her side as they were to
ride to the Q. station for their honeymoon train.

Somehow the wedding guests split into two parties, wets and drys,
on whether the bride and groom should ride the dray. Fighting be-
gan, noses got bloodied, chairs were thrown, coats and pants got
ripped and torn, and as the fighters moved out of the house there
were drunks flung on their faces in the dust of the street. Those who
were trying to drag the bride to the dray found that the groom had
a mean pair of fists. He pulled her away from them, rushed her to
his buggy, and drove to the Q. station, his hat lost and his clothes
rumpled and dusty. It was one of those scrimmages where so many
were squabbling, tussling, and trading punches at one time that no
one could tell the whole story. One side held they had a right to a

little fun. The other side answered, "Wine is a mocker and leads young men to folly."

A farm hand from near Henderson Grove they called "Sliding Sam" because of tricky ways he had of sliding in a barn dance. His father had died, leaving him a big farm loaded with mortgages. He tried to work the farm and make it pay while he went with his girl to one barn dance after another where they opened one keg of beer after another. He lost the farm and was taken on by a neighbor farmer who had been an old friend of his father, so close a friend, it was said, that he gave the young man a promissory note his father had signed and told Sliding Sam to tear it up. He treated Sam like a nephew and let him have any horse and buggy on the place.

I first saw Sam one Fourth of July afternoon at Highland Park when he was the caller for quadrilles. He had laid his small-sized tan sombrero on a chair. He wore a light-green shirt with a red necktie pulled through slits cut in a white poker chip. He was an extra-fancy caller, singing some of the calls, stretching his arms and waving his hands. It was a hot day and the sweat rolled down his pink face that turned strawberry red. You could call his face handsome except it had a rough look around the big mouth and the crinkled forehead as though he had temper and could slide into a fight and like it. Up over his forehead his glossy black hair was combed back wavy and pretty. You could tell he had looked in a glass and put every wave of hair where he wanted it. Why some wave of it didn't fall down on his forehead as he sweated and called and swung his arms, I couldn't figure out. Every hair stayed stuck where he put it.

His girl was there and his eyes picked out hers. The other dancers saw him giving her special smiles and bows as she swung on the corners or went through the grand-right-and-left. They knew he was jealous of her. I was near a corner where I saw him walk up to a fellow saying, "You're huggin my girl too close. I didn't miss it when you was swingin on the corner." He wasn't mad yet. He didn't threaten. He was just giving a warning.

His girl was the prettiest of the lot. She was a standout—slim, with curves, hips, and quick easy feet. Her black hair hung in two thick

braids down her back. She had a picture mouth and chin and a man
in a grand-right-and-left laughed to her, "Howdy, angel-face."

I saw Sliding Sam late in the afternoon in a rowboat with his girl.
As he pulled the oars he was looking at her as if maybe he owned her
from feet to head and anyhow for the time he had her where no man
but him could touch her.

On a mild winter evening I next saw Sliding Sam. I was on Main
Street with Frenchy Juneau and a railroad man we knew came along
saying, "There's a hell of a fight down on the Square." We ran to
where a crowd was circling around, pushed our way in, and saw the
two men fighting. You couldn't call it much of a fight, it was so one-
sided. Sliding Sam was standing watching a young fellow face flat
on the sidewalk. The young fellow wriggled around onto his back,
sat up and rubbed his bleeding mouth and nose. One eye was shut.
His light hair had blood streaks where he had run his hand. He got
to his feet, wobbled around, and stood looking at Sliding Sam. Then
he lurched toward Sam and tried to swing his right fist at Sam's face.
He swung slow and weak as though his strength was about gone
but he was going to give Sam whatever he had left in him. Sam swung
a right-hander that landed on the fellow's jaw and he crumpled to
the sidewalk and lay there down and out, stone-still. We heard a man
say, "He was drunk when the fight started. He was easy to lick."

We had heard one man call out, "It ain't a fair fight" and another
rough voice, "No, it ain't a fair fight." This was while the fellow on
the sidewalk was twisting around and trying to get to his feet. We
saw Sam turn toward the men who were saying it wasn't a fair fight
and tell them, "I'm goin to stand here and keep knockin him down
long as he keeps askin for it." We heard a high trembling voice cry-
ing, "Come on home, Sam!" and looked where it came from. There
was Sam's girl half in shadows between two men. After the knockout
I looked past Sam and saw the girl with her hands lifted up near her
shoulders, the palms of her hands turned away from her and the
fingers wriggling and her lips white and twisting.

Two policemen stepped in and asked what was going on. Sam
said, "This is my girl here. The two of us was goin to get into my
buggy. Then I said I'd stop in for a cigar before we started to drive
home to Henderson Grove. She stands here waitin for me when this

bastard comes along drunk as a fiddler's bitch. An he makes one nasty crack after another to her. I heard him when I came out. He was actin like she was a cheap streetwalker. I let him have it. I knocked him down and he got up and came back for more and I let him have it." The fellow on the sidewalk was beginning to moan and one policeman went to phone for a doctor while the other policeman took the names of witnesses.

A few days later we read in the papers that Justice Holcomb gave the fellow who got beat up a lecture on not getting drunk and if he did, to watch where he went and what he said while drunk. Sam got off with a fine of ten dollars and costs and a lecture about not being so handy with his fists. I never heard who Sam married or whether he did get him a wife. The girl he was so jealous of ended up marrying a thick six-footer who had a big stock farm out in Iowa near the Nebraska line. He was steady and sober and went to church and there was one baby after another for six years.

Farnham Street where it meets Fifth was a country road when I walked barefoot in its dust, the land pasture or cornfield. On a piece of ground a house went up there and in that house Galesburg had the bloodiest crime of passion in its history. The man had been drinking but he couldn't have been clumsy drunk, for the fast and horrible work he did on the night he came home to find a man in bed with his wife. He sent a bullet into the man's body and a bullet into his wife's right arm. He put two razor cuts in the palm of his wife's right hand and slashed a deep cut in the left side of her neck from below the ear to the mid-line of her throat. Across the man's throat his razor swept from the left ear nearly to the right ear, severing the jugular vein. The bed was blood-soaked and the pools not yet settled when police officers arrived in the morning.

"The fight lasted two or three minutes," the killer testified when on trial. His movements around the unlighted upstairs room must have been fast, his feet quick and his hands working in a wild fury. He was found guilty of manslaughter and sentenced to fourteen years in the state penitentiary. Mart joined eighteen character witnesses—among them a college professor, a physician, and men the killer had worked for—who testified that "before his recent trouble his general reputation as a peaceable and law-abiding citizen was good." He served his time in Joliet, came back to Galesburg, lived a quiet life, and died, having had occasional news from his two married daughters and grandchildren in Chicago. Mart said to me, "He was that gentle and easy-going that he was about the last man in town I would have expected to hear was a killer and a double one. He told me that once before the last awful night he had caught the same man in bed with his wife. He warned them but they stayed in bed and jeered at him and said he didn't have the nerve to kill a flea." After he had served five years, Mart and others tried for a pardon or a parole but couldn't swing it. The affair was involved, complicated in motives, and not lacking in light on why hard liquor in excess is termed "tanglefoot."

As a boy I met unfinished stories, small scraps of everyday life not rounded out. On a streetcar to Highland Park, one of two men in the seat in front of me raised his voice at one point to say, "My wife doesn't like it and what she doesn't like I just naturally have to hate." I know sophisticates of this later age who would remark, "There seemed to be a maladjustment between them."

I heard a boy telling, as he heard it from his mother, of the woman next door to them. "She found a loaded revolver he had brought home and hid. She took out the cartridges, afraid he was going to kill himself or her. She didn't tell him about takin out the cartridges. A week later she found the revolver again and it was loaded and she took out the cartridges and didn't tell him about it. It's a kind of a game they play now. He don't tell her about loadin the revolver and she don't tell him about unloadin it and my mother wonders if somebody is goin to be shot. She wonders if she could give advice that would be any use. She's gettin nearly as nervous as the woman next door."

There was a house where a railroad engineer lived. He had moved into that house with two children and had seen six more children arrive there. He had made good money and most of his children finished high school. One child died early of diphtheria, another met an accident and would walk lame through life, two of the girls married men who drank hard and ran with other women. Only two of his children turned out somewhat as he would have liked. I happened to be selling the weekly *Sporting News* in the Q. depot and overheard the father saying to another engineer that he was waiting for a train to bring in one of his boys who had done fairly well. And I can't forget the offhand yet positive way that he remarked, "Eight children is too many."

Walking a few feet ahead of me on Main Street one day were two railroad men, young brakemen. An interesting brunette in a wide picture hat passed and one of the men turned his head for another look at her. Then as they walked along he said, "I don't think any man should stop lookin!" And after a pause he gave his second thought, "If my wife heard me say that she'd raise hell."

On a warm Saturday evening one summer on the Public Square near the Union Hotel I saw two young sports flashily dressed, a little flush with liquor, and I could tell by their voices they were in a quarrel or a hot argument. As I passed what I heard stayed with me, one of them holding the other by the coat lapel and snarling, "I know you better than you know yourself and I'm tellin you you're a damned queer duck and you're goin to have a hell of a time when you get tied up with any woman. You'll never get what you want and if you do it won't last."

I heard a high-school girl tell of her "strict" mother worrying about her. A boy with a name for being wild with both boys and girls had taken this girl for a long walk one night. She told her mother that they walked as far as the Lombard campus and she refused to go strolling among the pine clumps or the tall grass with him. Then came the questions: "Did he get fresh with you?" "How do you mean?" "Did he touch you, did he lay a hand on you?" "No, but I wouldn't care if he did." What came about later in that house between mother and daughter I didn't hear but I am sure there was a conflict of wills.

I was perhaps twelve years old when I got a job in haytime on a farm near town, twenty-five cents a day and a noon dinner. My job

was carrying to the men in the field a jug of cold water, wet gunny
sack wrapped around the jug to help keep the water cool. They
were rougher men than I had ever worked with. I couldn't follow all
their jokes and brags about women they had been with. At the
dinner table, after their first attacks on the food had broken their
hunger the three men talked and laughed. Suddenly Mr. M., the man
of the house, the tenant farmer who was our boss, went into a blaze
of anger and snarled a mean remark to his wife, who kept the house
and had cooked and served our dinner. I have forgotten what he said
and what he was blaming her for. At our house I hadn't seen or
heard the like. The woman stood still. The men were quiet and we
all looked at the woman. We saw she didn't shake nor choke. She
just stood still and cried without making a sound. The tears ran down
her face and she lifted her apron and wiped her eyes and cheeks.
Mr. M. mumbled and muttered, like storm thunder dying away. We
took up our eating again and there was no more talk and laughing.
The men went to the field and stuck their pitchforks into the hay-
cocks. The man on the hayrack pitched and shuffled it into a nice
oblong stack and I brought them the jug they lifted and tilted so the
cool water ran down their throats. And over and over I would
wonder about the woman at the house and her crying and how many
times he had snarled at her and slapped her face and done worse,
maybe hitting her with his fist. What I caught was that he got some
kind of enjoyment out of snarling at her and shaming her before
other people. I couldn't make out what was going on, only whatever
was wrong I was on her side and against him. After three days the
hay was in. I was paid off and never heard what became of Mr. M.
and his wife that he mistreated and before other people.

What was there so strange and sad when it first came to your ears
about a man and his wife, "There's no love lost between them"? You
worked on it and it came out that they had found a love between
them and then lost it.

There was printed without names the letter of a young fellow
who took out a marriage license and a week later wrote to the
county clerk, "I send you the licence that you gave me to get mar-
ried with and state that I was not married for this reason because the

girl whose name is on the paper went back on me because she could get another feller." He gave the name of the other "feller" he wanted the license sent to and signed himself "most hart broken."

A Henderson township pioneer yoked his oxen to his big two-wheeled wagon, mostly hand-hewn, and drove to a cabin where a young woman climbed into his wagon, and with her parents' consent they drove to Henderson village to get married. In the village road they stopped the oxen and the groom asked a man standing in the road, "Squire, are you the man what marries a couple fer a dollar?" "Yes," said the squire, "just climb down here." "Oh no, we'll stand right up here in this wagon. Go ahead." And so, standing in the ox wagon, they were married. The dollar was paid and they drove away for their honeymoon on the groom's farm.

Roland Worth was a college athlete, a fine quarterback, with black hair and black eyes, bright in his classes. His father held one of the most important and responsible positions in the city. They were well off as to money. Mrs. Worth many a time held out a crock for a quart of milk I poured. I would have believed that her son could have had any girl in Galesburg he wanted. It was years later that I talked with a trustee of Knox College, a beautiful woman whom I had adored at a distance in my milk-wagon days. She gave me a conversation she had with Mrs. Worth, who opened it, "You ought to marry my son." "Why, he's never told me that he loves me." "He does love you, he worships you." "If anyone loves me I expect him to tell me so again and again, then I'll believe him." So there in the house of one of my milk customers was the play of *Love's Labour's Lost*.

"Why don't you pick you a nice young woman and marry her and settle down?" was asked of a slick young passenger brakeman, who answered, "Why should a man stick with one woman when he can satisfy all of them?" He ran wild for a while. Then he did meet a girl he couldn't get away from, married her and settled down. Two children came. He was promoted to conductor. Two more children came. And what you heard about him was, "He's dependable every way you take him."

Later a Peoria lawyer told me about one of his cases, a suit for divorce, the husband charging adultery. The leading witness worked as a chore man at the house where it was alleged the offense was repeatedly committed. He testified that on a certain afternoon of a day he named he suddenly remembered a piece of repair work on the front porch of the house. He had put it off for weeks and decided to get the job done on this afternoon. At the end of the porch, before starting work he happened to take a look through the window of a bedroom. He was asked by the husband's attorney what he saw. He answered that he saw the accused woman in bed with a man. Then came the question, "What did you see them doing?" His answer came with no hesitation, "What did I see them doing? Well, there they was, toes to toes!"

A Galesburg man had a visit with a Chicago relative of his who was in Joliet for life for killing a woman and was saying, "There's lots of time to think here. The only thing I miss in the pen is women." He hesitated, and then, *"But if I was outside I might meet another woman like the one I killed."*

There was a period with my playmates, mostly Swedish boys, when going to and from the Seventh Ward school, we had ideas or little frames on which we tried to weave ideas while lacking the skeins of experience. We were along ten or twelve years of age. When we talked about our families and what class of society we were in, we said, "We ain't rich and we ain't poor." As a statement it would hold good. We were on that boundary line where so definitely we needed ten thousand times what we owned as property in order to be rich, wealthy or affluent, and a drop of thirty to fifty per cent in wages would have put us strictly into the classification of the poor, the genuinely poverty-sunken. Those who have lived on that delicate, shifting, and hazardous boundary line have had an experience that some use as help in understanding economic issues and the labor history underlying the swirling human currents of our times.

At this time we ten- to twelve-year-olds had positive views on marriage. We were against the institution and practice of holy matrimony. Most of us were sure we would never go in for marriage. We had seen enough of it. I recall how bluntly one boy put it, and the rest of us chimed in and agreed with him: "If you marry you have to sleep in the same bed with the woman. Then the babies come. And you have to raise children and they eat and get sick and wear out clothes and take up room and make a mess around the house and they cost more than they are worth." Each of us was sure he would somehow get along without getting tied to some woman and a house full of children that cost money and the man has to earn the money. In later days the question didn't seem to come up whether we were rich or poor and we seemed to move into a viewpoint that if a man found him the right kind of a woman it might be worth the time to marry though it was still a gamble.

A boy in our block I knew well, and I saw his love for a girl in the next block. They walked and held hands and life made rainbows for them. She had him do most of the talking. She was a slim figure, stunted in growth but shapely, and had an ivory-pale beautiful face. At fourteen they began "going together" and kept "steady company" for two years, saying they would marry at eighteen. Then came what was called "galloping consumption," lung hemorrhages, and for six weeks he went nearly every day to see her white-faced smile and to hold her thin little white hands. When Madeline Clark died he went to the funeral and came away and said to me, "Be a long time before I can look at another girl." He was years getting over it. Sometimes what the superior elders call "puppy love" runs deep and leaves scars.

I had my "puppy love." Day and night her face would be floating in my mind. I liked to practice at calling up her face as I had last seen it. Her folks lived in the Sixth Ward on Academy Street next to the Burlington tracks of the Q. They usually left a crock on the porch with a quart ticket in it. I took the ticket out of the crock, tilted my can and poured milk into my quart measure, and then poured it into the crock, well aware she was sometimes at the kitchen window watching my performance, ducking away if I looked toward the window. Two or three times a week, however, the crock wasn't there and I would call "Milk!" in my best boy-baritone and she would come out with the crock in her hands and a smile on her face. At first she would merely say "Quart" and I would pour the quart, take my can, and walk away. But I learned that if I spoke as smooth and pleasant a "Good morning" as I could, then she would speak me a "Good morning" that was like a blessing to be remembered. I learned too that if I could stumble out the words, "It's a nice day" or "It's a cold wind blowing" she would say a pert "Yes, it is" and I would go away wondering how I would ever get around to a one- or two-minute conversation with her.

I was more bashful than she. If she had been in the slightest as smitten as I was, she would have "talked an arm off me." But she didn't. It was a lost love from the start. I was smitten and she wasn't. And her face went on haunting me. Today I can call up her girl face and say it's as fine as any you'd like to rest your eyes on, classic as Mona Lisa and a better-rounded rosy mouth. I had no regrets she had smitten me and haunted me. I asked for nothing and she promised the same. I could say I had known my first love. It was a lost love but I had had it. It began to glimmer away after my first and only walk with her.

I dropped in with another boy one summer night to revival services at the Knox Street Congregational Church. There I saw her with another girl. After the services a chum of mine took the other girl and I found myself walking with the girl of my dreams. I had said, "See you home?" and she had said, "Certainly." And there we were walking in a moonlight summer night and it was fourteen blocks to her home. I knew it was my first or last chance with her. I said it was a mighty fine moonlight night. She said "Yes" and we walked a block saying nothing. I said it was quite a spell of hot weather we had been having. She said "Yes" and we walked another block. I said one of the solo singers at the church did pretty good. And again she agreed and we walked on without a word. I spoke of loose boards in the wooden sidewalk of the next block and how we would watch our step, which we did.

I had my right hand holding her left arm just above the elbow, which I had heard and seen was the proper way to take a girl home. And my arm got bashful. For blocks I believed maybe she didn't like my arm there and the way I was holding it. After a few blocks it was like I had a sore wooden arm that I ought to take off and have some peace about it. Yet I held on. If I let go I would have to explain and I couldn't think of an explanation. Not for a flickering split second did it dawn on me to say, "You know I'm crazy about you and crazy is the right word." I could have broken one of the two blocks we walked without a word by saying, "Would you believe it, your face keeps coming back to me when I'm away from you—all the time it keeps coming back as the most wonderful face my eyes ever met." Instead I asked her how her father, who was a freight-train conductor on the Q., liked being a conductor and did he find it nice work.

We made the grade at last. The fourteen blocks came to an end. I could no more have kissed her at the gate of her house than a man could spit against Niagara Falls and stop the water coming down. Instead of trying to kiss her I let go her arm and said "Good night" and walked away fast as if I had an errand somewhere. I didn't even stand still to see if she made it to the front door. I had made the decision I wasn't for her nor she for me. We were not good company for each other. If we were, at least one of us would have said something about what good company we were. I still adored her face and its genuine loveliness, but it had come clear to me that we were not "cut out for each other." I had one satisfaction as I walked home. My bashful right arm gradually became less wooden. The blood began circulating in it and my fingers were loose instead of tight and I could wiggle them.

I have an album of faces in my memory, faces that were a comfort. One I saw many times. She would be walking a street or driving a surrey. Her face was a blossom in night rain. She married a small storekeeper and children came. And her face was still to me a blossom in night rain. I never spoke a word to her. What I adored about her might have been mostly imagination. Yet I heard long after from those who knew her that she had an inside loveliness matching her face.

I remember several beautiful girls and women of my home town. Their personal loveliness compares nicely with that of notable stage stars and society women. I remember an Irish girl with a turned-up nose, flashing brown eyes, and a swift impudent mouth. She had her kind of beauty, as did a Swedish girl whose slow smile had a prayer

in it while her walk was the water willow moving to a morning
wind. There was the singer heard on many local occasions, her con-
tralto voice and personality lovable. She was the wife of a railroad
fireman and there were gossips malicious in their talk about her.
There was Mary's chum of many years, Anna Ersfeld, as stunning
a brunette as any in the Floradora Sextette. There was Anna Hoover,
the public librarian, with a rich bosom and an apple-blossom face
framed in dark hair. There was Janet Grieg, the young matron of
the Knox girls' dormitory, Whiting Hall, Miss Grieg a mezzotint by
Copley, a country girl from a farm near Oneida teaching manners
to the Knox country girls. There was fair-haired Ollie Linn and
bonnie Lois Smith, the robust and rosy Rilla Meeker, the gay singing
Nell Townsend, Alice Harshbarger, whose head would have been
welcomed by any painter seeking a model, Frankie Sheridan with a
face of Maytime bloom. And so many times Mary spoke words of
faith that counted with me.

Over in the Fifth Ward near St. Patrick's Church of a morning
on the milk route I would meet Theresa Anawalt starting to her job
in a Main Street store. My eyes would be on her walk and the ways
of her head and shoulders long before we met and passed by each
other. As she came closer, my eyes fed on the loveliness of her face.
I'm sure her face is there in certain Irish ballads of wild fighting over
such a face. A hundred times I met her about eight o'clock of a
morning coming along the same sidewalk in the same block. She
seemed to have thoughts that were far away and over the hills.
About the fiftieth time we met I figured it might be time for me to
say to her with a bright smile, "Well, here we are again." And then,
figuring some more, I believed I would leave it to her for such a re-
mark. It wasn't with me a case of love at first sight or the hundredth
sight. It just happened that I found her wonderful to look at, a mys-
teriously beautiful young woman with a sad and strange mouth. We
didn't speak to each other there and then on that sidewalk in that
block in the Fifth Ward—nor ever afterward. And I haven't heard
her name or any scrap of news about her since that year—Theresa
Anawalt. And if this stray item about her should meet her eye, she
can't say I've forgotten her. I have in this chronicle, for the sake of

convenience, given fictitious names to some persons, but not in the case of Theresa Anawalt.

I could go on. It would be quite a little gallery. I could say that I carried faces with me and could turn album pages looking at them when they were gone I didn't know where. I enjoyed their loveliness in my boy's mind in ways they could never have guessed. I once heard a man say, "The town I grew up in didn't have a woman worth a second look." Either his eyes were not so good or it was a hard town for him to grow up in. Of course, I could mention the drab and the tragic that came to some of my album women, but I knew them in their Springtime Years when a freshness of dawn was on them before time and fate put on the later marks.

EIGHTEEN

Pioneers and Old-Timers

There was no standard pioneer cut to a regular pattern. Most of them could stand hard work and streaks of bad luck. The winter blizzards cut through them as they rode their horses, drove their wagons. They sweated along the corn rows of summer. Many had vivid personalities, their lives striped with color. I saw some of them on Main Street, at the County Fair, at celebrations, at the Old Settlers' picnics held at Gumm's Grove near Knoxville. I came to know some of their children and grandchildren. Others I heard about from men and women who had seen and talked with them. Others I read about. They became real to me. They had broken the prairie, laid the first roads and streets, built the first schools and churches, colored the traditions of the town and country where I was born and raised.

They knew wagons, the pioneers and first settlers. They had eaten and slept in wagons and under wagons. They had studied every cubic inch of certain wagons, where to put their skillets and blankets, their plows, axes, hoes, seed corn, their six, eight, or ten children. When a wheel broke or a harness tug, they fixed it or got along somehow till they arrived where there was help. Some had made part of their trip on flatboats or paddle-wheel steamboats, the generation who arrived before the railroad came to Knox County in 1854. They had the color and the distinction of those who could say they had left Ohio, New York, Tennessee, or Kentucky in a wagon, driving their horses over wilderness trails where often the feet of horses, the rims and spokes of wheels, tangled in underbrush. They camped where night found them and took up their journey again at daylight.

As a boy I saw some of these old-timers, in their seventies or eighties, hard-bitten, grizzled and fading. I tried in my boy mind to picture them standing where there wasn't a wall or a roof on Main Street not yet a street—no streets anywhere and no houses. There they looked around and decided where to clear for the first row of houses, the Public Square, the church, the blacksmith shop, the general store—and the college to be the focus of light and hope for the youth and the coming generations. They saw their little town rise to be a place and a name where before had been silence broken only by wild-animal cries, by the recurring rains and winds.

Those old-timers became part of my mind and memory, working dimly but definitely. They were living segments of history, specimens and vestiges, breathing evidences in the building of America. What they wrought by their ventures and struggles was likewise wrought in many other places where pioneers had taken empty land and given it human life, made it a human community with a name spelled on the maps.

Some had blank, dumb, scrawny faces, and their wives' faces matched. Some had twinkling eyes and could give out with raucous, infectious laughter. There were heroes with dreams of making an America to light the worlds overseas. And there were misfits and wanderers who had drifted to where they were, who would go on drifting.

We saw at Old Settlers' picnics, in Gumm's Grove, men of failing sight and hearing who told of seeing virgin prairie grass that rose "standing six feet high," grass roots tough and tangled so deep they often broke the wooden plowshare that tried to break them. Some had cut a field of grain with a hand sickle and threshed it by horse feet trampling out the wheat. Their corn meal they ground by turning a hand mill. Before they could afford glass they used greased paper for windows. Some had shot wolves and sold the skins for bounties the state paid. Some had worn for years the big warm overcoats they made from skins of deer they hunted and shot down and skinned. "You had to be handy with what tools you had," was a saying. On the handles of knives, axes, plows, on horse reins and fence rails, their hands were at home and became tough yet flexible.

Some went by antique names as quaint as their weather-beaten faces. Benjamin Briley married Cassandra Smiser and called her "Cass" for short. Elder Ziba Brown, the preacher who later became professor of languages at Abingdon College, baptized one member with the name of Adoniram Judson Thomson. Philip Nelson Terwilliger was united in matrimony to Sosa Welch. An Abingdon banker had Kentucky parents who brought him up a Democrat, and his name was Strawther Givens. Saloonkeeper Charles Brechwald married Barbara Waltz, and they believed dancing was no sin. The parents of Gad Dudley Colton took sober thought before giving him that first name. More particular were the Kentucky parents of Lemuel Cibley Meadows. Postmaster Brainard at Oneida had raised Shorthorn cattle and Poland China hogs till his farmhouse burned down. Then, being sixty-three years old and a Democrat, he took appointment from President Cleveland to the post office and moved to Oneida, where cronies called him "Jep." His first name was Jephtha as likewise in Connecticut his father's first name was Jephtha.

At the Knox County Fair or an Old Settlers' picnic, I may have seen Gladdial Scott, his face probably there among hundreds of faces I saw. But if I did see him nobody pointed him out and said, "See that old fellow? That's Gladdial Scott, born in Tennessee in 1809, came to Sangamon County, Illinois, in 1833, married Susan Sexton there, drove his wagon here to Knox County in 1834, settled four miles north of Knoxville, and raised many crops, including six children. They say he's the first man ever broke sod with a plow in Galesburg Township." Or among the faces might have been Richard Mathews or Daniel and Alexander Robertson, who seemed to hold the record for being the first settlers in Knox County, looking over their seed corn in Henderson Township in late February 1828, figuring what their plows might do in April to the sod and tough wild grass of virgin prairie. To any one of those three pioneers, if I had met them at the pens of blue-ribbon hogs or prize stallions, I could have said, "You came to Knox County exactly fifty years before I did. Does the fifty years seem long to you?" And they would have chuckled, I'm sure, "It seems only yesterday."

Harmon Way could have been pointed out to me for what he was.

He came to Chestnut Township in 1841, and besides farming,
trapped and hunted. In 1862 he killed twenty-five deer, for several
years killed sixteen to eighteen deer each winter. Up to the year of
1878 when I was born he had killed somewhat over three hundred
deer. It is not strange that in all my born days in Knox County I
never saw a living wild deer.

I saw Charles W. Elliott, who graduated from Lombard College
in 1892, and I saw a photograph of his pioneer father Burgess Elliott,
who shaved his upper lip and most of the underlip and then wore
elaborate chin whiskers. One photograph I would have treasured, of
Burgess Elliott "breaking" prairie with his plow and him goading
four yoke of oxen. He raised flax that his mother wove into cloth for
his shirts and his axe cut ties for the roadbed of the C.B.&Q. railroad.

When us kids walked the four and a half dusty miles of the Knox-
ville Road to the County Fair, we passed the old home of Isaac
Guliher. Neither the house where he had lived nor the barn where
he had milked his cows interested us. We didn't know that Isaac
Guliher, born in Christian County, Kentucky, had moved to Sanga-
mon County, Illinois, in 1830, and at seventeen years of age in 1832
had enlisted for the Black Hawk War and served as a private under
Captain Abraham Lincoln, moving to Knox County in 1833. Nor did
we know that in 1858 when Lincoln was on his way from Knoxville
to Galesburg for the debate with Douglas, they told him this was the
house where Isaac Guliher lived and Lincoln got out of his buggy
and a mile of buggies and wagons stopped for ten minutes while
Lincoln walked in and drank a dipper of cold water with old Sanga-
mon County friends. Had we known this, some one of us would
have said, "Let's go in and have a drink of water from the same pump
Abe Lincoln drank from."

At the time I was born one pioneer stood out above all others in the
town and county—the name, George W. Brown. A farm boy in
Saratoga County, New York, he learned the carpenter's trade,
worked on the earliest railroads of the Mohawk Valley, heard from
relatives in Illinois of good land out there cheap. In 1836 he was
twenty-one and with his wife rode a covered wagon west and ever

west for weeks on weeks while the rains came nearly every day and
the wagon wheels stuck in mud and clay and had to be lifted or pried
loose. Some nine miles from Galesburg in July of 1836 he stopped
and looked around, not a house in sight. He traded his team of horses
for an eighty of land. His wife ran the farm while he built houses. In
Galesburg, Knoxville, Henderson Grove, in later years they pointed
to houses well built by George W. Brown. He laid by what he could
of his earnings while thinking, studying, and then studying some
more. In 1846 he was seen at his small log house near Tylerville,
barefooted and wearing only a straw hat, a hickory shirt, and jeans
pants. He was putting together and experimenting with a machine to
plant corn. He wrestled and wrangled with his crude materials, and
in 1851 assembled a machine with which two men and a team could
plant sixteen to twenty acres of corn in a day. Alone in the little log
house, he was his own designer, tooler, assembler, and demonstrator.

In the spring of 1852 he planted with his machine sixteen acres of
corn for himself and eight acres for a neighbor. He planned that
year, and hoped to finish, ten machines and he completed only one.
He sold livestock, sold his last horses, for means to clinch his patents.
In order to go on and produce and sell his cornplanters, he sold his
farm, borrowed money at ten per cent interest, sometimes one to
two per cent a month, one month paying three per cent. In 1856 he
got his shops in Galesburg going and made six hundred cornplanters
and the next year a thousand. His machines spread far over the Mid-
west during the war years, 1861–1865, and they were credited with
food-production increase that helped the North in winning the war.

Manufacturing costs ran high, however, and after the Brown
Cornplanter Works had been going for ten years, it was said in
Galesburg, "George W. Brown isn't worth a dollar." The ruthless
competition against him slowed down when the United States Su-
preme Court validated his patents and ordered one competitor to
pay him two hundred thousand dollars. The tide turned and his
plant produced and sold eight thousand machines a year. He had
two hundred men working for him, his shops covering all of a city
block except the corner lot he reserved for the new Methodist
Church of which he was a regularly attending member. The bare-
foot farmer and carpenter of 1846 enjoyed walking around from

the woodworking department to the machine and blacksmith shops, then to the pattern rooms, the construction department, the painting and finishing rooms, the storage sheds. Also he had a massive throne-like chair built, and it was placed on the platform near the pulpit of his church. There on a Sabbath morning Mr. Brown sat facing the congregation and they could see him while he saw them.

Mr. Brown was mayor of Galesburg when I was born. I saw him driving on the streets of Galesburg and I was perhaps eight years old at the one and only time that I am sure Mr. Brown saw me when I saw him. It was a summer morning and I was walking alone and barefoot on a dusty road nearly two miles east of Galesburg. I was heading for a swimming hole we called "The Root" where a blown-down tree and its large root made a creek dam and we used to brag that the water was "nearly up to your belly button." I had not quite reached the front gate of Mr. Brown's large farm when I looked back, slowed down in my walk, and kept on looking back. I saw a pair of glossy black horses, a spanking team, on a slow trot, pulling a well-kept, shining buggy. The man driving was stockily built, wore a black hat, a black coat, a white shirt with a lay-down collar, and a black bow tie tucked under the collar. His face was broad and pink, a straight nose, the upper lip and cheeks smooth-shaven, and a smoothly rounded, carefully trimmed white beard at his chin.

He pulled in on the reins and slowed the horses to a walk. He gave me a sidewise passing glance, looked me in the eye as he rode past. I couldn't have believed that he was going to stop the buggy and ask me in for a ride—I couldn't and didn't so believe. I was satisfied that he didn't come to a halt and ask me questions. He looked like he had the law with him and had authority to ask me questions that would bother me to answer. I was ten or fifteen feet behind him when the buggy stopped. I saw him reach up one arm and with one hand pull a rope that lifted a lever that moved up and opened the gate. Having never seen a gate open so smooth and easy for a man who didn't get out of the buggy or wagon, I enjoyed seeing it. And I especially enjoyed watching it performed by a nationally known inventor who was the founder of the Brown Cornplanter Works covering nearly one city block. I watched him close the gate by the same easy one-arm pull that had opened it. Then I walked on past the first brickyard, past Highland Park, and joined other kids in water "nearly up to the belly button."

I heard Alfred M. Craig spoken of as "the richest man in town." He owned several farms and Main Street buildings. He was president of the Bank of Galesburg, the Bank of Altoona, the Farmers' State Bank of Alpha, the Bank of North Henderson, the Bank of Prairie City, besides being a director with heavy interests in the Farmers' National Bank of Knoxville and the State Bank of Victoria. I saw him several times when I worked in the drugstore of his son Harvey Craig.

At such times as the elder Craig came in to see his son I would try to manage to be giving an extra polish to the showcases and have a look at him. For there was a rather strict sense in which the elder Craig was the most important and distinguished citizen of the town. I didn't eavesdrop. I had heard so much about him that it satisfied me as a fifteen-year-old boy just to have a look at him. He was tall, broad-shouldered, deep-chested, with sideburns that ran down the cheeks and under the jaws. His face was impressive with a look of quiet power, a large aquiline nose running to a pointed end and the nostrils wide. His baffling eyes looked from under bushy eyebrows. His chin was strong and his mouth as baffling as his eyes. He gave me sidewise glances several times as I looked up from my work with the chamois skin. I knew better than to expect him to say, "How are you getting along, bub?" He wasn't that kind. He didn't smile often and when he did it came slow as though it cost him.

I was suspicious of him because I had heard so often that he was the richest man in town. And I hadn't heard so it came clear what a remarkable life he had had. His Irish grandfather left Londonderry and arrived in America with a working capital mainly of two bare hands. His mother was of Kentucky folks who came from Virginia. His father was Scotch-Irish out of Pennsylvania, a Fulton County farmer and a millwright who built a string of flour and feed mills along the Spoon River in the 1830's and 1840's. The boy went to Knox College, got his degree in 1853, opened a law office in Knoxville, rode the circuit, saw both Lincoln and Douglas when they came on errands to Knox County. When the Whig Party passed out he became a Democrat. In 1873 he was elected a judge of the Supreme Court of the State of Illinois, elected again in 1882 and in 1891. He wrote opinions in several famous cases. A railroad had charged a shipper $65 for hauling a carload of grain from Gilman, Illinois, to New York while the same railroad for the same kind of a carload and the longer haul from Peoria, Illinois, to New York charged only $39. The railroad contended it was incorporated in another state and therefore Illinois had no say-so as to rate charges. Judge Craig laid it on the line as a rule and the Supreme Court of the United States upheld it that a state does have power over traffic inside its borders even though carried on by an outside corporation. It was Judge Craig too who wrote the opinion holding that the City of Chicago and not the Illinois Central Railroad had the right to fill in and use land on the Lake Michigan front—out of which came Grant Park, Soldiers Field, and the crowded lake-front beaches enjoyed by the people of Chicago.

Had I been told these things about Judge Craig, I would have had a different curiosity as I looked at him while polishing the glass cases with a chamois skin. The nicest thing about him was not that he was the richest man in town but that up on a high bench of authority the railroads couldn't make him do what they wanted done. The railroads couldn't say, "He is our man." There was talk at one time of his being nominated for Vice-President on the Democratic ticket. It was said too that in 1888 he came within an ace of being named Chief Justice of the Supreme Court of the United States, President Cleveland finally naming Melville W. Fuller.

All this I would have liked to know when I saw him come into the drugstore one winter morning shaking the snow off his heavy fur overcoat. I would have liked to hear him tell of how he was assistant prosecutor in 1872 of the murderer Osborn, the only man ever legally hanged by the neck till he was dead in the County of Knox, State of Illinois. Of course what I don't yet understand is why a man who owned several farms and Main Street buildings should in his late sixties want to bother with being president of five banks and director of two more banks. I don't understand it unless Alfred M. Craig as a Man of Affairs to the end of his days liked to know as much as could be known of all dealings in money and land in his county. He had keen instincts about money and land and played a

game with them that to him was fascinating. I am not sure he would
have agreed with Tom Edison's innocent question, "What does a
man need more than just board and clothes?"

Benjamin Ramp I saw at the Knox County Fair. Having seen him
once, you knew him when you saw him again. His left leg was gone.
So was his right arm below the elbow. When he came to Knoxville
in the winter of 1848 he had a wife, five children, and twelve hun-
dred dollars. He bought an eighty-seven-acre farm and, needing extra
money, began hauling or "teaming" from Knoxville to Peoria. The
first two trips went well. Leaving Knoxville on the third trip, he
came soon to the down road of the Spoon River Hill, afoot and hold-
ing the reins. When the staple of the neck yoke broke, he did his
best at holding the scared and tangled horses. He was thrown to the
ground. The wheels and the heavy wagonload ran over his leg. After
help came and the doctor was through with him, his left leg to the
upper thigh was gone.

In the spring when he moved to his farm with wife and five chil-
dren, he was thirty-three years old, near his last dollar, and he had
debts. Good people of Knoxville raised two hundred dollars for him
but he refused the free gift. He went at his farm chores with one
good leg and a crutch, his wife, nine-year-old Elizabeth, eight-year-
old William, five-year-old Mary Jane throwing in with their help.
He had good cheer, a round face shaved smooth all around the large,
full-lipped, laughing mouth. He managed well and had luck till fif-
teen years later. As he was driving a mower, a wheel went wrong and
he was thrown to the ground. The sickle bar cut off his right arm
below the elbow. As the years clocked away, he came to own, in Haw
Creek, Persifer, and Truro townships, one thousand seven hundred
acres of cultivated land and three hundred acres in pasture, eight
of his thirteen children living. And I have no doubt that at the Knox
County Fair I saw the faces of two or three, maybe five or six, of his
then living forty grandchildren and his six great-grandchildren. As
the boys grew older they, with his advice, ran the farm, and he served
four years as a justice of the peace, voted Republican, and went every
Sunday with his wife to the Knoxville Presbyterian Church. I heard

a preacher make brief mention of him once: "The doctors amputated on him but they couldn't amputate his strong will and his gift of laughter, his love of God and right living."

Out on the Seminary Street road were farms to which we drove our milk wagon for more milk when we had sold out and needed two or three gallons for our last customers. At no time did we drive the four miles out to the five-hundred-and-forty-seven-acre farm of Daniel Green Burner. We had heard and read about Mr. Burner. He came to Knox County from New Salem, Illinois, where he had lived four years and had seen the young Abraham Lincoln march off to the Black Hawk War. He had traded at the grocery where Lincoln served customers and he had noticed young Lincoln's ways with people. Mr. Burner told a reporter for a Galesburg paper that Lincoln sold whisky but never drank any himself, and "Lincoln would swear under strong provocations, but this was not often. I don't think he made any pretensions to special goodness. The community was raw and green and he was one of us. Lincoln was as full of fun as a dog is of fleas. . . . He would back up against a wall and stretch out his arms; I never saw a man with so great a stretch. He did little things like that to please people. . . . He did not go to others for his amusement, but if they wanted fun they came to him and found him full of it. . . . There was a singing school but Lincoln couldn't sing any more than a crow. So he did not go often." Mr. Burner had many memories of Lincoln and New Salem. I am sure that more than once he drove into town passing, as he had to from his farm, the Seventh Ward schoolhouse at noon or recess and that I saw Mr. Burner, though I didn't know who he was and his face meant nothing to me. It would have been nice if I could have worked on his farm in hay harvest and sat at table and heard him talk about New Salem days.

The best-remembered of the Swedish pioneers came in 1851, three years before the railroad. In the 1880's I saw him often, on the streets, and in the church where I heard him preach and pray. He was in his late sixties, a gray muffler beard at his throat, a rugged

body and face. This was the Reverend Tuve Nilsson Hasselquist. He
had need to be rugged. He earned his passage across the Atlantic by
serving as pastor for some sixty Swedish emigrants. He rode hun-
dreds of miles on stagecoaches over the rough roads of the Midwest
prairie. He had traveled on horseback and afoot, organizing congre-
gations and schools, sleeping in log cabins, in sod houses, in hay-
stacks. In 1852 at thirty-six years of age he became the pastor of the
new Lutheran church in Galesburg which had been founded the
year before by the Reverend Lars Paul Esbjörn. The same year of
1852 he was elected president of the Augustana Evangelical Lu-
theran Synod of Northern Illinois.

He could write and he believed in printing. He started in Gales-
burg the first Swedish-language newspaper of any kind in America,
Hemlandet (Homeland), its office later being moved to Chicago. He
could sing or tell a story. He was a natural persuader of men. He
carried good-fellowship with him, though never to the point of
touching alcoholic liquors. It was known that high church authori-
ties in Sweden couldn't take to him because he had outside of his
church lectured on temperance. He looked the pastor, the shepherd
of his flock. He had been an early president of Augustana College,
teaching theology and fifteen other subjects while he edited *Augus-
tana*, a weekly paper, and preached weekly sermons.

His face spoke of granite and had gargoylish carving. His mouth
stretched wide and solemn while hinting it was ready for a laugh.
Once on Seminary Street near the church he nodded his head and
smiled to me and two other boys, the only time I saw him up close.
His eyes crinkled and I was sure that he could let out a rollicking
laughter, which was a feeling I didn't have about most of the preach-
ers I had seen and heard. As far back as 1853, in January weather he
made a stagecoach ride across the State of Illinois, from Moline to
Chicago, to help organize the first Swedish Lutheran church in that
big wicked city. He was a strong man and he may have been domi-
neering, riding roughshod over others to win his points. I don't
know. I know I like the memory of him and his face and his rugged
shoulders. I like to remember that he loved music, put a piano in his
house, and the claim was made by people pointing to it, "There is
the first Swedish home in the United States to have a piano."

I remember one old-timer I saw only once as he passed by in a G.A.R. parade, and I didn't get a full look at his face though I could see his nose looked out of place. Joe Elser told Mart and me that this fellow had been in the fighting at Murfreesboro and had come out with face wounds. And Joe Elser heard this veteran laugh at his handicaps. "I can't see with my right eye and my nose gets in the way of my left eye."

In looking back I tried to locate the fall and winter I worked as a porter in the Union Hotel barbershop. I couldn't fix the year. I racked my memory, asking what was the job I had before and what was the next after the barbershop. I would have made a poor witness at answering a lawyer's question, "Now will you give us the dates when you began work and when you quit your job as porter in the Union Hotel tonsorial emporium?" I would have said, "I can't answer that question. It was sometime between 1893 and 1896." Then if the lawyer went on and asked, "Do you mean you cannot definitely recall a single date in some one year when you worked at that barbershop job?" I would have gone on and said, "Yes, I wouldn't swear to a single date."

Then in some odd corner I met the fact that General Philip Sidney Post died on my seventeenth birthday, January 6, 1895. Here was something. Now I could be absolutely sure of where I was on that date and several weeks after.

General Post, the Congressman from our district, had served five terms and was beginning his sixth when he died. He was a Knight Templar in Masonry, member at large of the Republican State Central Committee, and had been Commander of the Department of Illinois, Grand Army of the Republic. Senators and Congressmen, old soldiers of the Civil War, politicians from far and near, came to the funeral.

At the Q. depot I saw a noon train from Chicago pull in with a special car loaded with men wearing Prinz Albert coats and high silk hats. I watched them get off the special car. And—this is another fool trifle that sticks in the memory—I heard one of the silk hats say to another, "He was concerned over the loss of his umbrella." I didn't hear who had lost the umbrella, but I knew, whoever he was, he was "concerned." He wasn't bothered nor troubled nor anxious. I would remember that. If I ever got to wearing a silk hat and lost an umbrella I would say I was "concerned" about it.

I walked to the Union Hotel barbershop to find every barber chair filled and a line of customers in the waiting chairs wearing Prinz Albert coats, the hatrack filled with silk hats, and more of the same shiny hats in a row on two window ledges. It surely was silk-hat day in Mr. Humphrey's tonsorial emporium.

I took to my shoeshine stand, where already the first customer had taken the seat and was waiting for me. I shined his shoes, the next, and the next. I shined the shoes of four Senators, eight Congressmen, two or three mayors, and two pairs of knee-high boots of the kind Lincoln wore. Some had their feet in square-toed shoes, wide with heavy soles. A few wore what we called "gunboats"—thick leather spread east and west under a man's foot soles, anchoring him so no wind could blow him over and neither man nor mule push him down. My wrists got sore swinging the two brushes over the leather, flicking a cloth in jigtime for the finish, and then taking my whisk broom and swinging it in jigtime over the smooth broadcloth of the Prinz Alberts, back, shoulders and sleeves.

It was a big day, my banner day as a shoeshine boy. Most of them handed me the regular nickel pay. About a fourth of them gave me a dime and two whose breath told me they could have been at the Union Hotel bar dropped a quarter into the hand I held out. "You could have knocked me over with a feather." For the first time I earned $1.40 in one day, besides meeting close-up many important men. I could see they were the kind of men who were running the government—in Chicago, Springfield, Washington, they were running the government—and if they had had time and had cared to talk with me they could have told me plenty about how the government is run.

That was the day, about January eighth in 1895, just after General Philip Sidney Post died on January sixth. I knew exactly where I was working then and could swear to it in any court.

I had been going along thinking Philip Sidney Post was one more politician and I didn't see him as any special hero. I had heard him make speeches that didn't stick with me. I had seen him on the streets, a man of stocky build, thick through the body, a round head and face, straight nose, a little bald over the forehead, a longish dark mustache and a little goatee you had to look twice to see, a stand-up collar and an ascot tie. Below the left lapel of his double-breasted coat hung his badge of G.A.R. Commander.

Philip Sidney Post had come back to Galesburg in 1879 after serving thirteen years as consul and then consul-general at Vienna, Austria. John Hay, then Assistant Secretary of State, wrote Post a letter that was published, "praising him to the skies." You couldn't ask a nicer letter of praise than Hay wrote. Hay could be gingerly with words but for Philip Sidney Post he went the limit. Hay probably knew the letter would be used in Post's first campaign for a seat in Congress. Hay probably was well informed on Post's record as a soldier at the time Hay was a secretary to President Lincoln.

I didn't know when I heard Philip Sidney Post making a speech at a Republican rally or when I saw him walking on Main Street that I was looking at a great fighting man, one of the best soldiers that answered Lincoln's call for troops in '61. He was a young lawyer out in Wyandotte, Kansas, when the call came. He went east to Galesburg, enlisted, and became second lieutenant of Company A, 59th Illinois Volunteer Infantry, fought in some of the bloodiest battles of the war, taking wounds, getting honorable mentions, moving up to major, colonel, and brigadier general. Pea Ridge, Perryville, Murfreesboro, Chickamauga were bloody grounds, and Post was there.

After the war his corps commander, General George H. Thomas, asked the Secretary of War to make him a colonel in the regular army, writing that after the Pea Ridge battle Post "even before his wound was recovered . . . rejoined his regiment." General Thomas, a man careful with words, wrote on of what he knew: "In the great battle and decisive triumph of Nashville, General Philip Post's brigade did more hard fighting and rendered more important service than any like organization in the army. In the grandest and most vigorous assault that was made on the enemy's intrenchments, near the close of the fighting on the second day, General Post fell, and as it was at first supposed, mortally wounded, at the head of his brigade, leading it to the onslaught. A discharge of grape instantly killed his horse under him and tore away a portion of his left hip. I know of no officer of General Post's grade who had made a better or more brilliant record."

The War Department, after his wounds healed, sent him to San Antonio, Texas, in command of sixteen infantry regiments. It was nearly thirty years later that General Post with two other men came into the Union Hotel barbershop. All three had shaves. Two had shines. One of the two whose shoes I shined was Philip Sidney Post. If I had known where those feet had been in their time I would have tried to turn out the best and brightest shine I ever put on shoe leather.

I haven't looked up General Post's record in Congress. He lived a plain life, didn't come into big money and didn't seem to need it. When he came back to Galesburg after Vienna he went into the real estate business. He must have been a man away out of the ordinary to get such a comment as the scowling and grumpy *Chicago Times* gave him March 28, 1874: "The American Consul at Vienna is an impetuous son of Illinois, of more service to the country in a month than many in a year. Free from humbuggery and devoid of the nonsense of affectation, he has a cheery greeting alike for the traveling millionaire and the penniless sailor."

In his day and time I took him for just one more politician, his right hand not sure what his left hand might be doing. And now I have a sneaking fool pride in my heart that one time I shined his shoes without knowing where the feet in those shoes had been.

Robert W. Colville, born in Scotland in 1839, crossed the Atlantic when he was twelve years old, and came to Galesburg in 1856. He volunteered for the infantry and took a hand in the fighting at Fort Donelson and Shiloh. He worked up from a railroad fireman for the Q. to roundhouse foreman at Aurora, coming to Galesburg again in 1878, where he was nothing less than master mechanic of the Chicago, Burlington & Quincy division. We heard about him across the 1880's and later, how he was here, there, and everywhere in anything of the Q. that was mechanical. "Better have things in shape, Bob Colville might be coming around," was heard. And us kids had a saying we took from the grownups. When a kid talked big and gave orders like he was a boss, he would hear from others, "Who do you think you are, Bob Colville?" The years went by and Bob Colville was a pretty good man on his job. For thirty-one years after I was born he went on with his job as the Q. master mechanic, till his death came—under a C.B.&Q. locomotive.

Mr. Hultgren was tall, broad-shouldered, with large arms and hands, had a wide face and a harmonious wide mouth, a thin black muffler beard under his jaws. Mr. Hultgren's smile was an October harvest moonrise. He was born in Sweden with good will to all men, and crossing the Atlantic to Knox County, Illinois, hadn't changed it. He lived alone near the Lombard College campus, planted two or three acres, kept a cow or two in a pasture. He walked with long steps and a slow easy roll to his body. I remember passing him once on the street and stopping to look back at him and saying to myself, "He looks like one of the Twelve Apostles and I don't know which one only I'm sure it isn't Judas." He had been cut off from membership in one of the Swedish churches because of his refusal to accept belief in eternal punishment for all unbelievers. He was the only man in town to wear a broad-brimmed Quakerish black hat. When he met man, woman, or child, he touched his hat with right hand and gave out with his moonrise smile, every front tooth shining. He was the only man I have known who touched his hat in salute to men and boys he met.

Gersh Martin died in 1894 at sixty-six years of age, his life given to liberty, free speech, printer's ink, and hard liquor. In the six years that he owned, edited, and wrote his weekly, the *Press and People*, I saw him many a time on Main Street or Boone's Avenue walking around to get news items, gossip, and advertising, or "another little drink." In the summer he went on the streets with no coat, his vest pockets full of pencils, wearing a white shirt and no necktie, a wide battered felt hat of light gray, a muffler of snow-white hair around his throat. He had been a canal mule-driver, a tramp printer, and when he came to Galesburg he made a newspaper pay by dipping his pen in an ink bottle and writing "hot stuff." He would breeze straight into scandals that other papers wouldn't touch. The churches and colleges, politicians and "city fathers," the Woman's Christian

Temperance Union, they heard from him, some reading him on the sly while saying, "I wouldn't read that dirty sheet." A Baptist Sunday-school superintendent found short in his accounts the *Republican-Register* took as "another good man gone wrong," but the *Press and People* had it, "No, another bad man found out."

Gersh Martin as a writer had style and ideas and saw his editorials widely reprinted. Looking toward the Illinois tall grass, Charles A. Dana of the *New York Sun* saw a kindred spirit and reprinted several meditations from the Galesburg weekly. Gersh Martin read good books, told smutty stories, mocked at the smug and self-righteous, liked nothing better than to hook a hypocrite and "nail his hide to the barn door." He was the spokesman of the Wets as against the Drys. He was Frolich & Gardt's answer to the Reverend W. H. Geistweit.

I was sixteen or seventeen when I carried water, ran errands, a few times helped sponge and dry a sweating horse, over six weeks of racing at the Williams racetrack. What I earned in quarters and half-dollars ran maybe up to ten dollars. But I had a pass to come in at any time and I saw up close the most famous trotting and pacing horses in the world, how they ran, and what the men were like who handled and drove them.

C. W. Williams came to Galesburg from Independence, Iowa, where he had what they called a "kite-shaped" racetrack, though some said it was more like the figure eight. He had been a telegraph operator and had picked up, at prices that later looked silly, two mares. The world-famous stallions Axtell and Allerton were foaled from these two mares "bought for a song." In 1889 the three-year-old Axtell cut the world's trotting record for stallions down to two minutes and twelve seconds, and on the night of that day was sold to a syndicate for one hundred and fifty thousand dollars, said to be then the highest price ever paid for a horse of any breed. Two years later Mr. Williams could have sold his stallion Allerton for more than he got for Axtell. This was after Mr. Williams himself drove Allerton to cut down the world stallion record to two minutes and nine and three-quarters seconds.

So when Mr. Williams came to Galesburg in 1894 he had a reputation, organized the Galesburg District Association, and laid out a new racetrack on one hundred and twelve acres on the Knoxville Road east of Farnham Street, the same land where I had carried water for a hay-harvest crew, and across the road from the house where I had seen a man make a woman cry with words he snarled at her. The new racetrack, Mr. Williams gave it out, was "the only dead-level track in the world." Shaped like a railroad coupling pin, the long sides of it were dead level, with the ends graded for the sulkies to make the turn. In the great six-weeks racing meet that Mr. Williams put on there were rainy days when races had to be put off and other days when small crowds came, even though the trotters and pacers had national reputations. But there was one big week of good weather and one smashing big day in that week. That was the day we saw the black mare Alix come down the home stretch to break the world's record for trotters. Away later I wrote of it: "I see her heels flash down the dust of an Illinois race track on a summer afternoon. I see the timekeepers put their heads together over stop-watches, and call to the grandstand a split second is clipped off the old world's record and a new world's record fixed. I see the mare Alix led away by men in undershirts and streaked faces. Dripping Alix in foam of white on the harness and shafts. And the men in undershirts kiss her ears and rub her nose, and tie blankets on her, and take her away to have the sweat sponged. I see the grandstand jammed with prairie people yelling themselves hoarse. I see the driver of Alix and the owner smothered in a fury of handshakes, a mob of caresses. I see the wives of the driver and owner smothered in a crush of white summer dresses and parasols. Hours later, at sundown, I see Alix again—and I want to rub my nose against the nose of the mare Alix."

That day put Galesburg on the map for horsemen and horse-lovers over the whole country. At the center was Mr. Williams. I saw him several times on the track and on the Knoxville Road driving Allerton and other stallions he had "placed at stud." He was a medium-sized man with an interesting face. I thought his face looked like he had secrets about handling horses yet past that there was a solemn look that bordered on the blank—I couldn't make it out. He made a great name in the horse world and breeders came from the

country over to see him. The blood of his stallions ran for many
years in winning horses. A horse named Lee Axworthy, who ran a
mile in 1:58¼, was a grandson of Axtell.

Then harness racing began to run down in style and fashion. Mr.
Williams sold all his horses for good money and put it into Canada
land dealings. He hit "the sawdust trail" at a Billy Sunday revival.
The last time I saw him was on a Q. passenger train from Chicago to
Galesburg. He sat quiet in a seat by himself. And I could no more
read his face than I could twenty years earlier. I like to think about
him as I saw him once on an October morning, a little frost still on
the ground, in a sulky jogging around the only dead-level racetrack
in the world, driving at a slow trot the stallion Allerton, being kind
and easy with Allerton, whose speed was gone but whose seed were
proud to call him grandsire.

NINETEEN

⋆

Hobo

⋆

I had my bitter and lonely hours moving out of boy years into a grown young man. I can remember a winter when the thought came often that it might be best to step out of it all. The second thought came, "What would be the best way?"

I had read in detective stories how prussic acid gives death in an eyeblink but I didn't know a doctor who would give me a prescription for it. "Rough on Rats" and carbolic acid were the only poisons I could think of and they would mean you wriggled and moaned with the pains and twists of dying. A revolver bullet through the head, that was clumsy to think about. To hang myself I would have to get a strong rope, find a place to fasten it, fix a box to stand on, kick the box loose and then drop. And it might be that while strangling my tongue would slide over my underlip and when they found me I would be too ugly a sight to think about. You have to work at several chores to hang yourself. It is more bother than any other way of killing yourself. I could throw myself into Lake George but I couldn't be sure but that I would swim to the bank and live on. The handiest way of all, I decided, would be what as kids we had talked of when there had been that suicide on Pearl Street—to stand in front of the Q. Fast Mail train and the *Evening Mail* would have a headline "Sandburg Boy Killed by Train" and it would look like an accident and no disgrace to the family.

After thinking about these different ways of doing away with myself, I would come out actually feeling a little cheerful. The idea came to me like a dawning, "If death is what you want all you have to do is to live on and it will come to you like a nice surprise you never imagined."

After that winter the bitter and lonely hours still kept coming at times, but I had been moving in a slow way to see that to all the best men and women I had known in my life and especially all the great ones that I had read about, life wasn't easy, life had often its bitter and lonely hours, and when you grow with new strengths of body and mind it is by struggle. I was through with *Tom the Bootblack*, *From Rags to Riches*, and all the books by Horatio Alger. Every one of his heroes had a streak of luck. There was a runaway horse and the hero saved a rich man's daughter by risking *his* life to grab the reins and save *her* life. He married the daughter and from then on life was peaches and cream for him.

There was such a thing as luck in life but if the luck didn't come your way it was up to you to step into struggle and like it. I was beginning to see some light. I read Ouida's *Under Two Flags*. The hero lost everything he had except a horse, lived a dirty and bloody life as a fighting man, with never a whimper. I read Olive Schreiner's *The Story of an African Farm*, sad lives on nearly every page, and yet a low music of singing stars and love too deep to ever be lost. I believed there were lives far more bitter and lonely than mine and they had fixed stars, dreams and moonsheens, hopes and mysteries, worth looking at during their struggles. I was groping. I was to go on groping. I read a definition that had won a prize: "Pluck is fighting with the scabbard when the sword is gone." I couldn't see it as a prize-winner. I preferred the hero who cried, "We'll fight till hell freezes over and then we'll fight on the ice!" That, if it didn't make sense, at least gave you a laugh.

I was nineteen years old, weighed one hundred and forty-two pounds, nearly a grown man. And I was restless. The jobs I had worked at all seemed dead-end with no future that called to me. Other boys were handy with girls and I had never found a "steady." Among the boys I could hold my own. With the girls I was bashful and couldn't think of what to say till after I left them, and then wasn't sure.

I read about the Spanish General Weyler and his cruelties with the people of Cuba who wanted independence and a republic. I read about Gómez, García, the Maceos, with their scrabbling little armies fighting against Weyler. They became heroes to me. I tried to figure a way to get down there and join one of those armies. I would have signed up with any recruiting agent who could have got me down there. I believed I would have made a fair soldier in one of their armies. Nothing came of this hope.

What came over me in those years 1896 and 1897 wouldn't be easy to tell. I hated my home town and yet I loved it. And I hated and loved myself about the same as I did the town and the people. I knew then as I know now that it was a pretty good home town to grow up in. I came to see that my trouble was inside of myself more than it was in the town and the people.

I decided in June of 1897 to head west and work in the Kansas wheat harvest. I would beat my way on the railroads and see what happened. I would be a hobo and a "gaycat." I had talked with hoboes enough to know there is the professional tramp who never works and the gaycat who hunts work and hopes to go on and get a job that suits him. I would take my chances on breaking away from my home town where I knew every street and people in every block and farmers on every edge of the town.

There had been a little traveling for me. Once when eight years old and a member of the Junior Epworth League at the Mission I had been a delegate to a convention in Monmouth. I traveled that sixteen miles to Monmouth, and that was the farthest I had been away from Galesburg till I was fourteen. Then John Sjodin and his brother Albert, Mart, and some other boy, we all chipped in and bought one bonerack horse for two dollars and another for three dollars. We hitched these to light wagons we borrowed, drove some fifty miles to the Illinois River between Peoria and Chillicothe opposite Spring Green, where we camped, fished, and went swimming. The three-dollar horse died on us and we buried him with respect and many jokes. We had expected that if one of them died it would be the two-dollar horse. We scraped our pockets and raised the five dollars that bought us another horse for the trip home to Galesburg, where we sold it for three dollars to the man who sold us the three-dollar horse that died. The man who sold us the two-dollar horse wouldn't let us sell it back to him and I forget what we did with it, though we spoke highly of it as a willing horse that had staying power.

I was sixteen when for the first time I rode a railroad train for fifty miles. I opened a little bank of dimes and found I had eighty cents. My father got me a pass on the Q. to Peoria and I rode on the train alone to Peoria and felt important and independent. I saw the State Fair and sat a long time looking at the Illinois River and the steamboats. I drank the "sulphur water" at drinking stands here and there. I was a traveler seeing the world. I went home with my last dime gone, but I couldn't help telling other people how Peoria looked to me and how she was quite a town and bigger than I expected.

I was eighteen when I made my first trip to Chicago. I had laid away one dollar and fifty cents and my father, after years of my begging for it, got me a pass on the Q. I put my head out of the car window at one town after another. For years I had heard their names. Now I laid eyes on them and said, "So this is Galva," "Well, if here ain't Kewanee," "So this is Mendota," and at Aurora, "Here's Frenchy Juneau's town, but where's the stove factory where he was a metal-polisher?" I was traveling light, no valise or bag. In my pockets I had my money, a knife, a piece of string, a pipe and tobacco, and two handkerchiefs.

John Sjodin had coached me on how to live cheap in Chicago. The longer my dollar and a half lasted, the longer I could stay in Chicago. I ate mostly at Pittsburgh Joe's on Van Buren near Clark Street, breakfast a high stack of wheat pancakes with molasses and oleo and coffee with a dash of milk in it, all for five cents. Dinner was a large bowl of meat stew, all the bread you wanted, and coffee, at ten cents. Supper was the same.

A room on the third floor of a hotel on South State Street was twenty-five cents a night. The rickety iron bedstead with its used linen sheets took up most of the bare wooden floor space. In the corners were huddles of dust and burnt matches. You hung your clothes on nails and went down a dark narrow hallway to a water closet and washroom with a roller towel. It was a change from the Berrien Street house where I had had the same clean room year after

year. I didn't feel lonely but I did have a feeling that even though
I wasn't dirty I needed a scrubbing. And I did know that a few
blocks away was the Grand Pacific Hotel where I could get a big
clean room for three dollars a day. But the thought no sooner came
than it went.

I was seeing Chicago for three days on a dollar and a half. I went
two nights to the Variety Show, vaudeville, in a top gallery at ten
cents. I mustn't miss at ten cents the Eden Musée on South State,
John Sjodin had said, and there I saw in wax Jesse James, several
murderers, a line of faces showing what syphilis does to your face
at first and then later if you don't get cured. I walked through the
big State Street department stores that I had heard about for years
from Siegel Cooper's at Van Buren and north to Marshall Field's.
I walked and stood in front of the Daily News Building, the Tribune
and Inter-Ocean buildings. I had carried and sold so many of their
papers that I wanted to see where they were made. I had great re-
spect for Victor Lawson and his *Record* and *Daily News* and I
would have liked to go into his office and speak to him but I couldn't
think of what I would say to him if I did get in.

I walked miles and never got tired of the roar of the streets, the
trolley cars, the teamsters, the drays, buggies, surreys, and phaetons,
the delivery wagons high with boxes, the brewery wagons piled
with barrels, the one-horse and two-horse hacks, sometimes a buck-
board, sometimes a barouche with a coachman in livery, now and
again a man in a saddle on horseback weaving his way through the
traffic—horses, everywhere horses and here and there mules—and the
cobblestone streets with layers of dust and horse droppings. I walked
along Michigan Avenue and looked for hours to where for the first
time in my life I saw shimmering water meet the sky. Those born
to it don't know what it is for a boy to hear about it for years and
then comes a day when for the first time he sees water stretching
away before his eyes and running to meet the sky.

I walked around every block in the Loop, watched the frame-
works of the Elevated lines shake and tremble and half expected a
train to tumble down to the street. I dropped in at the Board of
Trade and watched the grain gamblers throwing fingers and yelling
prices. I walked out to the Desplaines Street police station and

walked the route from there to where eight policemen were killed by the "anarchist bomb" and stood wondering whether they would ever find out who threw the bomb.

The afternoon of my third day in Chicago I stopped in at a saloon with a free-lunch sign. I helped myself to slices of rye bread and hunks of cheese and baloney, paid a nickel for a glass of beer, and sat down at a table by myself. I didn't care much for beer then but I had heard so much about Chicago saloons and their free lunches and funny doings that I wasn't going to leave Chicago without seeing the inside of a saloon. I was "feeding my face" when a woman came and took a chair alongside me. Her face looked young, with hard lines at the mouth and eyes. She smiled a hard smile and said, "What are yuh doin? Lookin fer a good time?" I said, "I'm polishing nail heads for Street and Walker." It was a saying then. If you were out of work and looking for a job you walked the streets where the wooden sidewalks had nail heads sticking up and your shoes polished those nail heads. Her face lighted up and she blazed it at me: "I'm goin to polish your nail head fer yuh!" She was terribly alive and the words came hard through her teeth and her pretty mouth. I waited a few seconds fumbling around with what to say and then told her, "You're up the wrong alley, sister. I ain't got but two nickels and they wouldn't do you any good." She stood up, said "All right" cheerily and skipped along toward men at other tables.

What those last two nickels went for I don't remember. I had seen Chicago on a dollar and a half. I hadn't met anybody I knew who knew me and I couldn't think of anybody in Chicago I knew who knew me. I knew Victor Lawson, but he didn't know me and it would be twenty-one years before I would meet him and tell him I read a good paper that was his. I rode home to Galesburg and tried to tell the folks what Chicago was like. None of them had ever been there except Papa and Mama and they had stayed only long enough to change trains. The great World's Columbian Exposition had come and gone in Chicago in 1893 and our family saw it only in newspaper pictures. I was glad to be back in a room with a clean floor and a bed with clean sheets. It was good to have Mama's cooking after Pittsburgh Joe's. Yet there were times I wished I could be again in those street crowds and the roaring traffic. And I had thought about it in Chicago and it didn't yet come clear to me why the cartoonists drew Chicago as a tall robust woman with a big bosom and over her forehead a crown with the words, "I WILL." Chicago seemed to me many women saying, "I will," "I won't," "I can't," "I wouldn't," "I couldn't."

Now I would take to The Road, see rivers and mountains, every day meeting strangers to whom I was one more young stranger. The family didn't like the idea. Papa scowled. Mama kissed me and her eyes had tears after dinner one noon when I walked out of the house with my hands free, no bag or bundle, wearing a black-sateen shirt, coat, vest, and pants, a slouch hat, good shoes and socks, no underwear, in my pockets a small bar of soap, a razor, a comb, a pocket mirror, two handkerchiefs, a piece of string, needles and thread, a Waterbury watch, a knife, a pipe and a sack of tobacco, three dollars and twenty-five cents in cash.

It was the last week in June, an afternoon bright and cool. A little west of the Santa Fe station stood a freight train waiting for orders. The conductor came out of the station and waved a yellow flimsy in his hand. As the train started I ran along and jumped into a boxcar. From then on I stood at the open side door, watched the running miles of young corn, reading such station names as Cameron and Stronghurst, names of villages and towns I had heard a thousand times and had never had sight of. Crossing the long bridge over the Mississippi my eyes swept over it with a sharp hunger that the grand old river satisfied. Except for my father, when riding to Kansas to buy land, no one of our family had seen the Father of Waters. As the train slowed down in Fort Madison, I jumped out and walked along saying, "Now I am in Iowa, the Hawkeye State, my first time off the soil of Illinois, the Sucker State." Never having seen a penitentiary, inside or out, I walked for a look at it, saw the guards in their towers, saw the high stone walls blank and dumb except for saying, "Here we hold, where they can't get away, the thieves and murderers caught in Iowa."

I bought a nickel's worth of cheese and crackers and sat eating and looking across the Father of Waters. The captain of a small steamboat said I could work passage to Keokuk unloading kegs of nails.

I slept on the boat, had breakfast, sailed down the river watching fields and towns go by, at Burlington, Quincy, and Keokuk shouldering kegs of nails to the wharves. At Keokuk I spread newspapers on green grass near a canal, and with coat over shoulders, slept in the open with my left arm for a pillow. I washed face and hands at the canal, using soap from my pocket and drying with a handkerchief. Then I met a fellow who said, "On the road?" I said "Yes." He led me to where he had been eating bread and meat unwrapped from a newspaper. "I got three lumps last night," he said, and handed me a lump for myself. A lump was what they handed you if they wanted to give you something to eat at a house where you asked for it. My new friend said, "I got a sitdown before I got the lumps." At one house he had been asked to sit at the kitchen table and eat. That was a sitdown. Then because he wanted to spend this day free to look at the canal and the blue sky, he went from house to house for lumps, hiding them under wooden sidewalks so his hands were empty. "At the last house," he said, "they offered me a sitdown and I couldn't tell them my belly was full but would they please wrap it up."

The lump he gave me had four slices of buttered bread and two thick cuts of roast beef. "This is breakfast and dinner for me," I said. "You're a good sport." He said, "I'm hoppin a freight for St. Louis tonight. I always feed good there."

He was long-boned. His flesh seemed to hang on his bones, his cheeks loose and his wide mouth loose-lipped. His face and hands were pudgy as though your fingers would sink into them if you touched them. "I'm a Noo Yawkah," he said. He had come out of a Brooklyn orphan asylum, had taken to The Road, and said he had never done a day's work in his life. He was proud he had never worked and had found a way to live without working. "The real tramp can't even think about work," he said, "and it gives him a pain in the ass to talk about it." He named Cincinnati Slim and Chicago Red and other professional tramps he had traveled with, mentioning them as though they were big names known to all tramps and I must have heard of them. He named towns where the jail food was good and how in the winter he would get a two or three months' sentence for vagrancy in those jails. "Or I might go South for the cold weather," he said, "keepin away from the towns where they're horstyle." So now I had learned that where they are hostile they are "horstyle" in tramp talk and it has nothing to do with horses.

He had a slick tongue and a fast way of talking. It seemed to me he liked hearing himself talk about himself. At noon he ate his lump of two pork chops with buttered bread and I ate my bread and roast beef. After about an hour he happened to lay a hand on me in a way I didn't like. Soon after that I walked away, leaving him where he lay on the green grass looking at the blue sky, his face and hands pale and pudgy. I would have felt sorry for him if he wasn't so sure he could take care of himself. I could see he wanted to take care of me in a way I didn't care for.

Two policemen on Main Street looked me over from hat to shoes and I felt safe. During a heavy rainstorm that night I slept in the dry cellar of a house the carpenters hadn't finished and I was up and out before they came to work. I had a fifteen-cent breakfast, found an old tomato can, bought a cheap brush, had the can filled with asphaltum for a few nickels. Then I went from house to house in several blocks and got three jobs that day blacking stoves that were rusty, getting me seventy-five cents, and two jobs where my pay was dinner and supper. I slept again in the house the carpenters hadn't finished and the next day went from house to house and got no jobs with pay brushing asphaltum on rusty stoves, though I did get breakfast, dinner, and supper for three jobs. The next day I bought a refill of asphaltum, earned three meals and twenty-five cents. The next day was the same as the day before. I found that the housewives were much like those for whom I had poured milk in Galesburg. I found too that if I said I was hoping to earn money to go to college they were more ready to help me. The trouble was there were not enough rusty stoves.

The next day was the Fourth of July, with crowds pouring into Keokuk. I saw a sign "Waiter Wanted" in a small lunch counter near the end of Main Street. The owner was running the place by himself. He said I could make myself useful at fifty cents a day and meals. He showed me the eggs, lard, and frying pan, the buns and ham for sandwiches, the doughnuts and the coffeepot. Soon he went out, telling me I was in charge of the place and to be polite serving customers. This was ten o'clock in the morning. Three or four people drifted in before eleven-thirty, when he came back, feeling good, he said, and he would help through the noon rush. Five or six customers came in the next two hours and he sat in a quiet corner taking a sleep while I handled the trade. There were not more than two customers at any one time and I flourished around, got them what they called for on our plain and simple bill of fare. I felt important. Maybe after a while I might work up to be a partner in the business. I ate a ham sandwich with two fried eggs and coffee.

The owner woke up and went out saying he would be back soon. Three o'clock and he came in feeling better than the last time he came in. He had forgotten to eat at noon and there being no customers around, I offered to fix him two fried eggs, which I served him with a bun and coffee. He went out saying he would be back soon. I served two customers while he was gone. Five o'clock and he came back "stewed to the gills," slumped himself in a corner on the floor, and went to sleep. I fried myself three eggs and ate them with two buns and coffee. I fixed two sandwiches with thick cuts of ham, put them in my coat pockets along with two doughnuts, opened the money drawer and took out a half-dollar. With my coat on one arm, I closed the front door softly, and that night slept in a boxcar that took me halfway across the State of Missouri. For a poor boy seeking his fortune I hadn't done so bad for one day. And the next two weeks I wouldn't do so good in any one day.

Next was the railroad section gang at Bean Lake, Missouri. My Irish boss, Fay Connors, hired me at a dollar and twenty-five cents a day and I was to pay him three dollars a week for board and room in his four-room one-story house thirty feet from the railroad tracks. There were five of us in the gang and you would have known Connors was the boss. He liked his voice and his authority. At no time did he get mad and bawl out a man, but he had a frozen-faced way of letting men know he was once a section *hand* and was now a section *boss*. The one time I saw a tool in his hand was when he wasn't satisfied with the way another man showed me how to tamp a tie. He took the pick and swung it clean and straight, tamping the gravel or rock under the tie so the bottom under the tie would be tight and not loose I tamped ties several days from seven till noon, from one till six in the evening. I hadn't trained for it and my muscles ached at night like when I worked in the ice harvest at Galesburg. Then came weed-cutting. We swung our scythes along the right of way, the same motions hour after hour, ten hours a day. So I had to train a new set of muscles and *they* ached at night. On Sunday I washed my shirt and socks.

At morning, noon, and evening, the meals at the table in the Connors house were the same, fried side pork, fried potatoes, and coffee. Connors seemed to like it. So did his wife and the three small children. I hoped for some greens, for pork chops instead of side pork, for an egg or two, for one change to beef or lamb stew. At the end of two weeks, on a Sunday morning, I hopped a freight for Kansas City and left Boss Connors to collect for my board and room out of my paycheck. The rest of the pay was still owing and was never collected. If Connors did get it he couldn't have sent it to me, as he didn't know my address and I wasn't expecting to have any address for weeks or months.

In Kansas City Mrs. Mullin had a sign in the window of her restaurant on Armour Avenue, "Dishwasher Wanted." She took the sign out when the Swede boy from Illinois made himself at home in the kitchen with the mulatto chef and the one waiter, also a mulatto. I had good times in that kitchen. The chef was fat, jolly, always cheerful. The waiter was handsome, brown-faced, gay, and he could sing. Noontime was the rush hour of the workers from the meat-packing plants near by. It was a fight in that dish trough to get enough dirty dishes cleaned for serving the customers. I swept the eating room morning and afternoon and mopped it on Saturday.

My sleeping place was the end of a hallway with my cot curtained off, and I washed and shaved, using my pocket mirror, at a sink and faucet in the hall. I was tired one morning when I said to the chef, "I don't care whether school keeps or not." I remember the laugh of the chef as he told the waiter, "Gus says he don't care whether school keeps or not," and George the waiter laughed. I was going by the name of Gus Sandburg. Why I changed from Charlie to Gus I don't know. George could sing either old-time songs or late hits. One afternoon he sang a sad song that had me melting. I said, "That's pretty fine, George. It sure gets me." He said, "I'll sing that for a sweet girl tonight and she'll give me anything I ask her for." I believed him. Only a woman with a heart of stone wouldn't soften to the way George sang, I believed. He took a liking to me and would sing again special songs I called for.

I was up at six in the morning and had the eating room swept for customers who began coming in at six-thirty when we opened. I worked every weekday till eight o'clock at night except for an hour or two in the afternoon. I had three good meals a day. The chef would ask me what I wanted and fix it for me as though he was an uncle of mine and nothing was too good for me. I had Sunday off and walked miles around Kansas City comparing it to Galesburg, Peoria, Keokuk, and Chicago.

In a week or so the wheat harvest in western Kansas would be ready. Mrs. Mullin paid me my second week's pay of one dollar and fifty cents. I thanked her and said good-by and saw the sign "Dishwasher Wanted" whisked back into the street window. Shaking hands with George and the chef and saying good-by wasn't so easy. They were goodhearted men who had made everything easier and brighter for me.

I slept two nights in a fifteen-cent second-floor flophouse. Here were forty men all in one room, each with a cot about an arm's length apart from the cots on each side. At any time a near neighbor might be snoring, "sawing wood," and at two or three in the morning there might be a scream from a fellow waking out of a bad dream. I heard one man cursing, whether asleep or awake, cursing people and conditions. Worst of all were the flat brown creepers who could bite into your skin so you were awake on the instant. They had homes in our blankets. We had no sheets.

I was tempted to spend ten cents for a dish of ice cream. The temptation got the best of me. I ate it in a big place full of gold chairs and mirrors. A diarrhea began. An abcess in the palm of the right hand ached and pained. It had probably started from handling the pick and scythe on the section job. I went to George and the chef at Mrs. Mullin's and told them I couldn't stand a doctor's bill. They sent me to a Catholic hospital. There, with few questions, a doctor had me lay my right hand on the table. He cut in with a knife, took out what was inside the swelling, and I fell to the floor in the first faint of my life. I came to in a second and he washed the hand, bandaged it, and said it would soon be well. I told him the diarrhea had weakened me. A nurse in nun's dress took me to another room, gave me a large spoonful of brown liquid that tasted good and gave me a bottle of it to take away. I guessed she was Spanish from the way she said, "Theez eez varry gooood fawr the di-oh-ree-ah." With her good voice and good heart I could have said, "You are an angel," but I was bashful.

Hopping freight trains on my way west I had one bad afternoon. A shack (hobo for brakeman) had ordered me off an open coal car where I was crouched hiding. When the train started I got on the same car again. The train was running full speed when he climbed down from the car ahead and another shack followed him. He put his face close to mine. "I told you to stay off this train. Now you'll come through with two bits or you'll take what you get." It was my first time with a shack of that kind. I took it that I might owe the railroad money for fare but he wasn't a passenger-fare collector. So I didn't come through with two bits. He outweighed me by forty pounds and when his right fist landed on my left jaw and his left fist slammed into my mouth I went to the floor. I slowly sat up and looked up toward him. He was snarling, "Stay where you are or you'll get more." Then as he and his partner turned to go he gave me a last look and laughed, "You can ride, you've earned it." He was the kind of shack who was surprised at a later time when the I.W.W. Wobblies took over trains, ganged up on him, and gave him the kind of bleeding mouth he handed me. I met brakemen who were not small-time grafters. One who spotted me in a boxcar corner said, "If you're goin to ride, keep out of sight."

I stood up and watched the passing land. The trees were few, no such timbers as in Illinois and Missouri. I had come to the Great Plains. I was traveling, though my handkerchief was splotched red from putting it to my mouth. When the train slowed down I got off and found myself at a hobo jungle, two men leaving to catch the train I had quit, two more washing their shirts in a shallow creek shaded by three cottonwood trees. I washed my shirt, socks, and handkerchief. The two men were gaycats, said they had spent their last nickel for a loaf of bread and a half-pound of Java and could I scrape the nickels for a few weenies? I said fair enough and went for the weenies and we ate well. I caught a freight that night that had me in Emporia, where I walked past the office of the *Emporia Gazette* but didn't have the nerve to step in and ask the editor, William Allen White, how he came to write "What's the Matter with Kansas?" I didn't agree with it but I liked his style. After a big two-bit meal I went to the city park, where I lay on the grass for a sleep and then talked with two men who got me to singing for them. It turned out they were professional tramps. They wanted me to go along with them. They were sure I could make money singing in saloons. They had the idea we would all share in the money so made. It seemed a little queer to me.

That night a bright full moon was up in a clear sky and out past the Santa Fe water tank waiting their chances to catch a freight train west was a gay bunch of eight men. One of them, a big husky, had a black eye from a fight with a shack and he was sure he had blacked the shack's eye. We told stories. The best-dressed man in the bunch had a bundle under one arm and had a laugh that said he could take care of himself. He told about a hobo at a back door asking a hatchet-faced woman for something to eat because he hadn't had a bite of food for two days. The woman said she would get him something. He waited. The door opened and the woman's skinny hand went toward him with a thin dry crust of bread in it as she said, "I give you this not for your sake nor for my sake but for Christ's sake." As he took the crust of bread and looked at it he turned his face toward her face and said, "Lady, listen to me. I beg of you not for my sake nor for your sake but for Christ's sake, put some butter on it!" Another of the bunch told about a Missouri boy who hadn't had much bringing-up. A woman at a back door had a pan of fresh doughnuts. She said, "Would you like a couple of these?" as she handed him two, and he busted out, "Missus, I could eat a thousand of them goddam things!" They seemed to be a keen and clean lot of travelers in the moonlight there that night, most of them heading toward the wheat harvest.

In a windy rain I jumped out of a boxcar and found a sleeping place under a loading platform for stock cars About seven o'clock in the morning I read the station sign and learned I was in Hutchinson, Kansas. I had heard it was better not to hit the houses near the railroad. They had been hit too often by 'boes. I walked eight or ten blocks and hit two houses. "Have you got any work I can do for breakfast?" They took one look at me and shut the door. At the third house a woman sent her daughter to get me a saw, showed me a woodpile and a sawbuck. For an hour I kept the saw going, piled the wood, and went to the house. The smiling mother and daughter led me to the family table, set fried ham and potatoes, apple sauce, bread and coffee, before me. After I had eaten they handed me a large lump. I thanked them forty ways, walked Main Street to see what Hutchinson was like, and went on to my loading platform. Unwrapping the lump, I found fried chicken and bread that would make dinner and supper, along with two pocketfuls of apples that had come down in the wind and rain the night before.

I tried to get acquainted with a fellow I had seen at the other end of the platform in the early morning. What few words I could get out of him were German. He seemed about sixty years old, hump-shouldered, with a gray scraggly beard. He sat cross-legged for hours looking straight ahead of him. He had a neat bundle at his side and would put his hand on it once in a while to make sure it was there. His clothes were neat and clean. I asked him, "Which way you going?" and "How long you been here?" At each question he turned his head and gave me a slow look in the eye and turned his head back to go on looking at nothing straight ahead of him. At noon he slowly opened his bundle and took out a loaf of rye bread, cheese, and baloney. He slowly munched looking straight ahead at nothing in particular. I held toward him a small piece of fried chicken and the look he gave me was as though the chicken might be poisoned.

He took out a New Testament in German type and read for a time while I smoked a pipe and read the two newspapers I had picked up on Main Street. There was plenty to talk about but I couldn't get him started. It could have been that he had secret sorrows and he was nursing them as he sat looking straight ahead. He couldn't have been sick or he wouldn't have chewed, smacked, and enjoyed his rye bread, cheese, and baloney. When I brought him a can of water from the station pump and drank of it before his very

eyes, he did reach out and give himself a drink of it, but not a word
from him nor a look of the eye saying thanks, it was good water I
brought him. When I caught a late-afternoon freight he didn't re-
turn my wave to him from the train. He still sat on that loading
platform looking straight ahead of him, a human sphinx shrouded
in his personal secret sorrows. I did my imagining about what loves,
hates, or murders might have made him crawl into an impregnable
silence where he defied any shafts of laughter to break through his
armor.

Lindsborg, Kansas, was Swedish, and Pastor Swenson, the head of
Bethany College there, was a Lutheran Synod leader I had heard
preach in Galesburg. It was either hay or broomcorn harvest I
worked in with other Swedes on a farm near Lindsborg. I stayed
three days at a dollar a day and meals, sleeping in a barn hayloft.
On my third and last morning I had been awake a few minutes when
I heard voices down below. One voice came clear to me, a Swede
saying, "Is that *bum* up yet?" I said to myself, "Am I a bum?" And
I answered, "Yes, I am a bum." I had bummed my way to Lindsborg.
I had no baggage nor bundle and I expected to bum my way on a
train out of Lindsborg. The first time in my life that I heard myself
referred to as a bum was among Swedes I had made a detour to see.
I wouldn't have expected him to say, "Is that young stranger up
yet?" but he could have said, "Is that Swede from Illinois up yet?"
To him I was a bum and he was giving me no such hand of fellow-
ship as George or the chef in the Kansas City kitchen.

Newspapers said the country was pulling out of the Hard Times,
more factory chimneys smoking, the full dinner pail and the prom-
ised McKinley prosperity on the way. Yet there were still many men
out of work, many men who had left their homes hoping for jobs
somewhere. You could see these men riding the boxcars and sitting
around the jungle hangouts. Some had learned hobo slang. Some
didn't care for it. There was always a small fraternity who knew
each other at once by their slang. They were professional tramps,
who divided into panhandlers and petty thieves. I heard panhandlers
talk about "how to work Main Street," what kind of faces to ask
for a dime or a quarter. "Never mooch a goof wearing a red neck-
tie," I heard. Panhandlers would argue about the best story to melt

the heart of the citizen you walked along with on Main Street. "I'm lookin for work and haven't had anything to eat for two days, and I've just had a letter my wife and two children are sick at home," takes longer and makes the citizen more suspicious than if you say, "I have to eat, could you spare a dime for a cup of coffee?" The longer you make your story, the more is the danger of the citizen asking you questions and while you are answering maybe a cop comes along "and he sees you're a vag and jugs you."

The petty thieves did less talking. The only one who got confidential with me wore a good brown suit, a brown shirt with a brown necktie. His face and mustache were like the pictures of the hero in the *Family Story Paper*. His quiet words to me were, "I'm a second-story man. I could use you." He would have me stand on his shoulders and climb up on a porch, go through a window, and search for money and jewels we would split. He hadn't been doing so well lately but he had seen many good times and they would come again. He would find girls to travel with us, he had a way with women, he said. He had a soft voice. He was polite. I told him I would think about it. I managed to get away from him without telling him what I thought about it.

A panhandler, for no reason I could think of, got confidential with me and two other gaycats. He pointed to a spindly fellow somewhat well dressed who seemed shy about mixing with other fellows around. "See that squirt over there?" he said. "He's a pimp. They beat him up and threw him out of a Kansas City whorehouse last week." It could have been, and then maybe not. He was speaking his mind and made it clear that as a panhandler he had little respect for a pimp and there was a social chasm between them. I remembered him at a later time when a panhandler told me, "I always get a good feed at a whorehouse unless there's a pimp around. The pimps are too goddam jealous of us."

I was meeting fellow travelers and fellow Americans. What they were doing to my heart and mind, my personality, I couldn't say then nor later and be certain. I was getting a deeper self-respect than I had had in Galesburg, so much I knew. I was getting to be a better storyteller. You can be loose and easy when from day to day you meet strangers you will know only an hour or a day or two.

What girls I was meeting on a job or at a sitdown usually wanted to know where I was from, where I was going, what kind of a home and folks I had, and I was working out of my bashfulness. Sometimes I spread it on a little thick about what a good home and education I had. They liked it when I said I would yet be going to college, though in my own mind I hadn't the slightest idea of how, where, and when I would go to college. But if a young stranger mentioned that he wanted to go to college, it gave the girls and women a higher opinion of the young stranger in their midst.

On one boxcar ride there was a young farm hand from Indiana of my own age. He had a face and a way of talking I liked so much that I asked him how it would be for the two of us to travel together and share and share alike for a few weeks. He said he would shake hands on that if I would go with him to the Klondike. The gold rush was on and he was heading for Alaska. He had expected to stop for the Kansas wheat harvest and earn money he needed but now he figured that might make him a little late in getting to the Chilkoot Pass and the gold waiting for the early ones. We were sorry to part. He reminded me of my brother Emil. He is one of those misty figures in memory that have you saying, "I wonder what ever became of him."

In one jungle was a little fellow in his middle forties who said that every summer he would break away from Chicago and take to the road, working now and then. "What I like," he said, "is to sleep under the stars. Do yuh know the stars is a great study? I never read a book about the stars but I never get tired of lookin at 'em and watchin how they move and change. The stars make me feel that whatever is wrong with the world or with me sometime is goin to be made right. The stars is the only book I read." He had a question he said kept bothering his brain: "Why does God make it rain on the ocean where there is plenty of water and not on the desert where the rain is needed?" He wanted more light on that. "I like to watch the workins of my own mind," he said. "The longer I live my mind gets to be more of a mystery to me."

"Along next October you'll need a benny," I heard in one jungle and learned that a "benny" is an overcoat. "I think I'll try the goat in this town," said one and I learned the goat in a town is the Catholic priest. One fellow saying, "I had a good snooze in a knowledge box last night," meant he had slept in a country schoolhouse. "Have you scoffed?" or "Have you had your scoffins today?" meant "Have you eaten?" or "Have you had your eating today?"

I had bought for a nickel in an old bookshop in Kansas City a small *Cyclopaedia of Useful Information.* Many a time it came in handy to pass the time rambling through facts and figures. On one page there was a poem it said was a favorite of President Abraham Lincoln. As the days passed I learned by heart half the verses, finding that to say them made loneliness less lonely, such verses as:

> Oh, why should the spirit of mortal be proud?
> Like a swift fleeting meteor, a fast-flying cloud,
> A flash of the lightning, a break of the wave,
> He passes from life to his rest in the grave.
>
> The leaves of the oak and the willow shall fade,
> Be scattered around and together be laid;
> And the young and the old, the low and the high,
> Shall crumble to dust and together shall lie. . . .
>
> The maid on whose cheek, on whose brow, in whose eye,
> Shone beauty and pleasure—her triumphs are by;
> And the memory of those who loved her and praised,
> Are alike from the minds of the living erased. . . .
>
> The peasant, whose lot was to sow and to reap,
> The herdsman, who climbed with his goats up the steep,
> The beggar, who wandered in search of his bread,
> Have faded away like the grass that we tread. . . .
>
> 'Tis the wink of an eye; 'tis the draught of a breath
> From the blossom of health to the paleness of death,
> From the gilded saloon to the bier and the shroud.
> Oh, why should the spirit of mortal be proud?

At Larned, Pawnee County, Kansas, I refused to regard myself as a hobo. My father had owned one quarter section of land in that county which he sold and then bought another quarter section which he sold. My father had set foot in this town when he came to look at the land he bought. I had written for my father the letters sending tax payments to the county treasurer of Pawnee County. When I walked past the courthouse I felt like an important, respectable citizen, even though I was sleeping in empty boxcars that stood on the Sante Fe tracks waiting to be loaded with wheat. You could walk the few blocks of Main Street in about three minutes. You could see empty houses here and there. People had moved away because of conditions, Hard Times. On one corner scood a big ghost hotel empty of travelers, no business, and here and there on Main Street a place where they once were open for customers and now spiders and cobwebs had taken over. The weekly paper was worth reading if only for its name, the *Tillers and Toilers Journal.*

Having promised Vic Lundgren that I would look up his father, I did so, and wrote back to Vic that his father was suspicious of me and didn't care to send back any word to his wife, son, and daughter in Galesburg. I worked at seventy-five cents a day helping a carpenter for three days. I worked five days with a crew threshing wheat—three days on one farm and two days on another—pitchforking bundles of wheat onto the tables of the thresher. It was hard work but the crew was jolly, the meals and cooking good, the barns clean where four of us slept on hay, the pay a dollar and twenty-five cents a day and board. Then there was to be no more work till five days later. I decided to head west to Lakin, where I heard there was more doing.

In the days between work I had long talks and shared meals at the Santa Fe water tank with an odd bird from Kansas City. He said he had been a bookkeeper there for a coal firm several years. They had let him out because business was slow. He seemed to have money and he did have a six-shooter that he took out once in a while and fingered as if he could use it in a pinch. He said that a teamster at the coal firm had been out of work for months and came to him one day and offered his sixteen-year-old daughter, saying, "You can have her for ten dollars a week. I need the money. So does she and the family." The way he told it, with many details, I thought it was probably a true story. He said he turned the offer down on account of not having the money to spare, and, "The girl was a good-looker but I was laying by money because I expected any day to be let out. And I would rather go along with the women I had than to take on a good girl only sixteen." He had fairly nice clothes, an interesting face with a hawk nose, a good mouth, and a chin that pointed out. His blue eyes had some kind of danger about them that I couldn't make out. He was warm and friendly with me and seemed to hint that maybe we could travel together. I was to meet him some weeks later farther west and learn what was the game he had in mind and what was hidden in the sudden danger gleams of his blue eyes.

At Lakin, Kansas, I noticed on a timetable that I was six hundred and eighty-four miles from Galesburg on the Santa Fe. I figured what with detours I had traveled a thousand miles since I left home. I worked with a threshing crew some three weeks around Lakin. The job finished on one farm, we moved to another farm with a different farmer and family. The work came easier with getting used to it. The dust in your nose and eyes, the chaff sliding down your sweating back, you got used to. One evening at six o'clock the boss said there was only two hours of threshing left and a full moon would be up. We ate supper, at seven went on threshing by the light of a bright full moon, and finished at nine o'clock. At ten o'clock the crew and thresher moved to another farm where we started in at seven in the morning.

A shack put me off the bumpers of a fast freight I caught out of Lakin. When you ride the bumpers you stand on the couplers between two cars and keep a good hold on a brake rod. The shack had leaned down and called, "You get off at the next stop or there'll be trouble." A minute after I got off, who was there but my blue-eyed friend I had chummed with at Larned. It was near midnight. We went to a lunch counter and he insisted on paying. He had a roll of bills. He said, "I'm flush," and he was. I told him I was catching the next freight out if there was an empty boxcar I could sleep in. He walked with me to the water tank, where he pulled from his hip pocket the same revolver he had shown me at Larned. He said, "This gat comes in handy, boy. It saves you a lot of hard work." Then it came out. He was sticking up harvest hands for their money. Once at a water tank and once in a boxcar he had pulled his gat and, "I pushed the gat into his guts and told him to come through with every dollar on him or I'd pull the trigger, and he came through." I had thirty-odd dollars on me and was wondering why he didn't push

the gat into my guts. I think I would have come through with my
last dollar. I think he still hoped I might buy a gat and go along with
him as a partner, something like that. I forget the town where I left
him when a freight came along. He said, "I expect some nice pickings
here the next two or three days. Maybe I'll be seeing you in Rocky
Ford on Melon Day."

Thousands poured into Rocky Ford for the Melon Day celebra-
tion. Watermelon and cantaloupe were handed out free to every-
body. I rode a crowded passenger train that evening—sitting on a
small board over the rods of a truck between the wheels of the train.
I changed for a freight train where I had a boxcar sleep and got off
in the morning not knowing where I was. I didn't bother to go back
and read the station sign. I ate a sandwich as I walked west on the
railroad track. The day was sunny and cool. My eyes caught high
rises of tumbling land I had never met before. "Jesus," I said, "those
are the Rocky Mountains." I hadn't planned it but there they were,
rolling formations of rock and pine lifted away high. "There's the
Hand of God," I said. I couldn't think of anything before in my life
that had me using that phrase, "the Hand of God."

I walked on to Canyon City, took a look at the outside of the state
penitentiary and felt good that I wasn't inside. I picked pears, earned
meals and a few half-dollars, went on to Salida, where I spent two
days. Then I took a Colorado Midland train heading back east aiming
for Denver. It was night. There wasn't an empty boxcar on the
train, and for the first time I was riding the bumpers late at night. I
didn't know what a stupid reckless fool I was. My feet were on those
bumpers and there was no danger in that. My hands were on the
brake rod so in case my feet should slip I could hold on and not go
under the wheels. Suddenly I was saying to myself, "You damn fool,
you've been asleep." My numb brain was saying that when you go
to sleep on the bumpers you're in luck if your hands don't loosen
and topple you down under the moving train. I would watch myself
and not go to sleep again. We had been running along maybe an hour
when again I caught myself coming out of a sleep. From then on I
wouldn't trust myself to be still for even a second. I kept changing
my position. I kept moving my feet and hands. I beat the sides of my
head with my fists. I kicked one leg against the other. An hour of

that and the train stopped and I got off and thanked God and the everlasting stars over the Rockies. Many a time later I said that the Angel of Death hovered over that train that night and saw me standing and sleeping and brushed past me with soft wing tips saying, "Not yet for this boy. He's young yet. Let him live."

I saw Pikes Peak so I could say I saw it. At the Windsor, a first-class hotel in Denver, I washed dishes two weeks, collected a dollar and fifty cents a week, a cubbyhole for a room and meals as good as were served to the silk-hat guests. Then came the question whether I should head for the West coast or east to Galesburg. I admitted I was a little homesick for the faces and streets of Galesburg. Where a passenger train was on slow speed out of the yards I hopped on the steps of a Pullman vestibule. A conductor and porter ordered me off. I got off and saw the train slow to a stop. I climbed on top of a Pullman car, lay with my head toward the engine, swore a solemn oath I wouldn't go to sleep. The car rocked and shook going around curves and my hands held tight so I wouldn't slide off the roof of the car. It was a cool September night and the train speed made it cold. I still had no underwear. I buttoned my coat, turned the collar up and tied a handkerchief around my neck. I went to sleep twice and coming out of it kept hitting and kicking myself to stay awake.

Daybreak came. An early farmer waved to me and laughed. I saw we were pulling in to a division point, McCook, Nebraska. I climbed down and started to walk out of the yards. A one-eyed man in plain clothes with a club and a star stood in my way. "Where did you come from?" His tone was horstyle. "I just got off that train," I said. He gave me my orders in a more horstyle tone: "We don't want the likes of you in this town. You get back on that train." There were no trainmen in sight as I climbed back to where I had been riding. I had a daylight view of the Nebraska landscape from McCook for thirty miles to the next stop at Oxford. No one was waiting for me at Oxford. I went to a lunch counter, where they let me into the kitchen to wash the cinders and soot out of my head, hair, ears, and neck. Then I ordered a monster breakfast of ham and eggs, fried potatoes, bread, coffee, and two pieces of pie, paying thirty-five cents in cash.

Heading east I stopped three days in a jungle with five good fellows. Shirt, socks, and handkerchiefs got washed. We had several

meals of corn we picked from fields near by to roast or boil. One
fellow was short and slim with a stoop to his shoulders and thick
calluses on his hands. He could talk about hard work he had done,
husking corn ten hours a day, driving a coal wagon and unloading
the coal with a shovel, driving a team at spring plowing with the
leather reins scraping his hands. He said the police took him for
questioning in an Iowa city when there had been a burglary. They
asked where he had been, where he was going, and "What do you do
for a living?" He said, "Any hard work I can get," and showed them
the tough leathery insides of his hands. One policeman said, "You
can't be much of a thief with those hands," and they let him go.

He was in his middle thirties, had silky red hair, and a freckled
face that brightened with crinkles when he talked. He said, "My
mother had ten kids, six boys and four girls. The girls turned out
good, married and have big families, all the girls but one. She has
ways with men, went to Kansas City, paints her face, likes fancy
clothes on her back, and we've lost hope of her. The boys turned
out good steady workers, only one ever in jail and he broke out
and they haven't caught him yet. My mother's father had eight kids
and when his wife died at eighty-eight he waited till he was ninety
and then had three kids by a half-breed Indian woman he married."
The early September night stars were out and the six of us sat around
a fire talking after our roast-corn supper. I believed the talk of this
horny-handed, freckle-faced redhead. It seemed to me he was re-
membering the big main points of his family and folks and he talked
it as he remembered it. He did more talking about his brothers and
their jobs and troubles, about his sisters and their children. He went
on remembering and talking what he remembered but only part of it
stayed with me.

I was sorry to leave that friendly jungle. I caught a freight that
landed me in Nebraska City. I chopped wood and picked apples for
two sitdowns. At a large brick house where I chopped wood, the
man of the house, a lawyer, seeing my suit of clothes somewhat
ragged, asked me if I would like an old suit of his. He brought it out,
an iron-gray all-wool suit, better than any I had had in my life. I got
into it, thanked him, and offered to chop more wood but he laughed
and said I'd better be on my way home. I found myself that night in

a boxcar with four others. We spread our newspapers under us, threw our coats over our shoulders, and tried for sleep. The night was clear, cold and frosty. After two hours we were saying, "It's too cold to sleep here tonight." The five of us marched to the city calaboose and asked the marshal to let us in. The cells had the expected stink, but we spread our newspapers on the stone floor, slept warm, and on leaving were told to get out of town that same day.

I caught a freight for Omaha. For years I had been curious about Omaha. And of all interesting city names, is any more musical than Oh-mah-haw? I found Omaha merely smaller than Chicago and bigger than Galesburg. In Omaha, as in Kansas City and Denver, I stood before the United States Army recruiting office and lingered and read many times the pay and the conditions Uncle Sam offers his Regular Army boys. I was interested and came near enlisting. One year of service I could see, or maybe two years, but the required three years had me backing out. I would make my decision, walk away, and come back and read the pay and conditions again the next day and then make the same decision that three years was too long. I had met a Kansas harvest hand who had had three years of it and he said he spent most of his time in the Regular Army cleaning the same horse stables and mowing the same garrison lawns and it got monotonous. "I expected to get to travel," he said, "but about all the travelin I done was with a lawn mower." I thought of him too when I read on the boards the pay and conditions, and walked away.

The Hotel Mercer took me on as dishwasher at a dollar and fifty cents a week. It was a little queer how standard was the wage rate for a dishwasher. It never went as low as a dollar and twenty-five cents a week nor as high as a dollar and seventy-five cents a week. The pastry cook was a sweet Creole girl from New Orleans. The vegetable man, a fast potato-peeler, was John Whitney, and I hope he did well after what came to happen. The hotel was leased and run by a fancily dressed tall man who slid and slunk rather than walked around the place. He was known as Wink Taylor. I didn't notice him wink at any time but he probably had the name because he was quick as a wink. At the end of the first week I didn't get my standard pay of a dollar and fifty cents nor likewise at the end of the second week. Then came the word that the Hotel Mercer was closed, gone up the spout, foreclosed, and Wink Taylor vanished. He owed me three dollars that never got paid. He owed the chambermaids, the dining-room and kitchen hands, what they had coming, which they never got.

I had one last sleep in the Mercer, crossed over to Council Bluffs and had a breakfast of one pork chop, fried potatoes, and bread and coffee for five cents. Then I caught one freight train after another till I came in sight of Galesburg the afternoon of October fifteenth. I had timed it so that I wouldn't feel on my head the crashing club of the night policeman Richardson, known far and wide as "that goddam nigger bull in Galesburg."

I walked along Berrien Street till I came to the only house in the United States where I could open a door without knocking and walk in for a kiss from the woman of the house. They gave me a sitdown and as they had had only two or three letters from me, they asked me where I had been and I told them the half of it. When I showed my father fifteen dollars and a few nickels, he said the money would come in handy and I should watch it. The clean bed sheets that night were not so bad. Mart was suspicious of my fine suit of clothes the next day. "I'll bet you didn't buy it new. If you bought it, it was a hockshop." So I told him. Mart said that along in August he had read in a newspaper about a hobo riding the bumpers in western Kansas who fell off the bumpers and was mangled to death. The folks hadn't read it and he didn't tell them. "But I was afraid, Cully, that maybe it was you." Then I told him about how in Colorado it could have been me and I was a fool.

What had the trip done to me? I couldn't say. It had changed me. I was easier about looking people in the eye. When questions came I was quicker at answering them or turning them off. I had been a young stranger meeting many odd strangers and I had practiced at having answers. At home and among my old chums of the Dirty Dozen they knew I had changed but they could no more tell how than I. Away deep in my heart now I had hope as never before. Struggles lay ahead, I was sure, but whatever they were I would not be afraid of them.

I went to work on the Schwarz farm three miles east of Galesburg. I was up at four-thirty in the morning, curried two horses, and Mr.

Schwarz and I milked twenty-two cows. I milked eight while Mr. Schwarz, being an older and faster milker, squeezed the teats of fourteen cows. We put the milk into eight-gallon cans and threw them into a milk wagon. We went into the house and ate breakfast, Mrs. Schwarz favoring a hulled hominy I liked. I drove the milk into town, poured it out in pints and quarts, and drove back to the Schwarz farm. I bought a *Chicago Record* every day and read in the wagon going to the farm the two-column Home University series of lectures by University of Chicago professors on literature, history, politics, and government. The horses didn't mind. They liked going slow while I read.

After dinner I washed the cans by myself and again milked eight cows while Mr. Schwarz milked fourteen. Mr. Schwarz was tall, somewhat stoop-shouldered, with a black beard, a kindly and gracious man, his people Pennsylvania Dutch. Mrs. Schwarz was robust, matronly, and when her fourteen-year-old daughter one evening at the supper table used the word "spondulix" her mother said sternly, "Why, Ethel, I'm surprised at you using such language." They were Methodists, well read, devout but not pious. You might have said they were a *Youth's Companion* family come true. Mrs. Schwarz had noticed that I spent the hour or two after supper reading among their books and magazines. She said to me one day with a beautifully serious look, "Charlie, I think you're going to make something of yourself." Until then Mary had been the only one to hand me anything like that. I was in bed every night at eight-thirty. I had come back to Galesburg weighing one hundred and thirty-six pounds and on the Schwarz farm I gained sixteen pounds.

About the middle of February I was sorry to leave the Schwarz home. I hired out to a blank-faced Swede whose name I have forgotten. Under him I was going to learn the painter's trade. At last it had come my way, a chance to learn a trade. A few of the ten-hour working days I was trusted to put on the first coat of paint with a brush. Most of the time I scraped and sandpapered. I climbed ladders outside of houses and stepladders inside and pushed the sandpaper over the wood to make it smooth for the painter with his brush. The boss was a man spare of words. My "Good morning" would bring a grunt from him. He believed in work without talk and toil without laughter. Once when he caught me singing his face had the look of a pickle fresh out of vinegar. Toward the end of the afternoon I wished I was back at the Schwarz farm.

Yet each morning six days a week I was there at seven o'clock with my hands ready to wear out more sandpaper making more boards smooth for the boss and another painter to put on first the first coat and then the second coat. Not as much as a half-day a week did I swing a brush to put on a first coat. How long would this go on till I got where they would let me put on a second and last coat? I rolled that over in my head and said, "You're thinking like all apprentices think and that's what you are, one more apprentice." And as my hands went through the same thousands of the same simple sandpapering motions ten hours a day I said more than once, "Maybe they know best. Maybe you do learn the house painter's trade by wearing out sandpaper to make boards smooth for painters who learned painting by sandpapering."

★

TWENTY

★

Soldier

★

On the night of February 15, 1898, I went to bed at nine-thirty with my fingers aching a little from running sandpaper over wood ten hours that day. I was asleep at nine-forty and still asleep at two o'clock in the morning. Not until later did I know that at two o'clock that morning the Secretary of the Navy in Washington heard a knock at the door that woke him from sleep and he was handed a telegram that nearly keeled him over. He got a White House watchman on the phone and told him to wake the President. On the phone Mr. McKinley heard the telegram read to him: "MAINE BLOWN UP IN HAVANA HARBOR AT NINE-FORTY TONIGHT. MANY WOUNDED AND DOUBTLESS MORE KILLED OR DROWNED." The watchman could never forget as long as he lived how the President paced back and forth, shocked and trying to believe what he was saying as he paced back and forth, "The *Maine* blown up! The *Maine* blown up!" She was a first-class battleship and of her three hundred and fifty-two officers and men, two hundred and sixty were dead and the ship had settled to the harbor bottom.

As the days went by and I went on sandpapering wood to make it smooth for the painters with their brushes, I believed what I read and heard. I believed that the same Spanish government whose General Weyler had killed thousands of Cuban patriots who wanted independence and a republic, that same Spanish government had a hand in blowing up the battleship *Maine*. I learned later that nobody knows to this day how the *Maine* was exploded or whether some

man did it or it was an act of God. It became a mystery no more
cleared up than the name of the man who threw the Haymarket
bomb that killed eight policemen in Chicago. What I still believe to
be established fact is that Weyler herded more than one hundred
thousand people in concentration camps where more than half of
them died of starvation and fever. I was going along with millions of
other Americans who were about ready for a war to throw the
Spanish government out of Cuba and let the people of Cuba have
their republic. If a war did come and men were called to fight it, I
knew what I would do. Across March and early April while the
country roared with excitement, I went on sandpapering and think-
ing but I didn't tell my blank-faced boss what I was thinking.

President McKinley declared war and I was sworn into Company
C, Sixth Infantry Regiment of Illinois Volunteers, on April twenty-
sixth for two years of service. The regiment had been part of the
State Militia. Company C was a living part of Galesburg, had its
drill hall, marched in uniform with rifles and bayonets on public
occasions, went to Springfield once a year for regimental maneuvers.
The company needed a dozen recruits to fill its quota and I was
among the earliest. I knew most of the privates, had worked for Cor-
poral Cully Rose at the Auditorium and had gone to school with
the Q. boilermaker, Con Byloff, who was first lieutenant. About
three-fourths of the members were from Galesburg and the rest
from farms and country towns around Galesburg. They elected their
own officers and you could hear fellows, "No West Pointers in *this*
regiment."

When I quit my job and told the family I was going for to be a
soldier they were a little sad and somewhat puzzled. They knew
they couldn't stop me from going, as I was set on it. Mart spoke for
the family, "We'd like the honor of having a United States soldier
in the family but we don't want you to be killed." I said it might not
be a real war and if it was I might not get shot because some soldiers
always come back home. And besides, having seen the West I would
now see the East and maybe the Atlantic Ocean and Cuba.

The family were all there when the train carrying Company C
pulled out from the Q. depot, which had now become the "Burling-
ton station." There were hundreds of other families at the station.

The *Annals of Knox County* say: "The whole city was aroused as
it had not been before since the days of the Civil War. A great
throng, estimated at ten thousand or more of our citizens, gathered
first at the armory, where the men of Company C were assembled,
and again at the Burlington station where they were to entrain, to
give them last messages of farewell and God-speed." I saw my mother
crying and waved to her with a laugh and she laughed back through
her tears. The *Republican-Register* said, "The scene growing out of
their departure was one such as is witnessed but few times in the life
of a generation."

On the fair grounds at Springfield we were quartered in an im-
mense brick building used for livestock exhibits. Where prize milk
cows and blue-ribbon bulls had slept on straw we likewise had straw
under our blankets in late April and early May. We were not lacking
the lads who could moo like a Guernsey cow or bellow like a Hol-
stein bull. While still in civilian clothes I was handed a Springfield
rifle and put through the manual of arms and company drill. I was
certified as enlisting at "twenty-one years of age, five feet ten inches
high, ruddy complexion, grey eyes, brown hair and by occupation a
painter." It was the first I had heard that my complexion was ruddy.
And as I was ten months short of being twenty-one years of age I
think I may have told them I was twenty-one and therefore old
enough to be a soldier and full citizen.

In about ten days I slid into a uniform, a heavy blue-wool shirt, a
coat of dark blue with brass buttons that went to the throat, pants of
a light-blue wool cloth double as thick as the coat cloth. This was
the same uniform that the privates under Grant and Sherman had
worn thirty-five years before, intended for wear in those border
states of the South where snow fell and zero weather might come as
at Fort Donelson the night Grant attacked. The little cap was a cute
trick. It wouldn't shed rain from your ears and above the stiff black
visor it ran flat as though your head should be flat there. I felt hon-
ored to wear the uniform of famous Union armies and yet I had
mistrust of it. Now along with others like myself I could say
when asked my rank and position, "I'm a high private in the rear
rank."

In a big room of the state-capitol building a hundred of us stood

naked and one by one passed before an examining surgeon. He was
a German with a pronounced accent and a high falsetto voice. He
listened to our heartbeats. He had us open our mouths and hold
them open so we felt like horses to be auctioned. He called off his
findings to a recording clerk. His last call for the record came after
he had run his fingers over the right and left sides of the man's
scrotum. Then his high falsetto rang out and in nearly every case it
was either, "Slaihght vahrri-co-cele on duh raiahght saihde" or
"Slaihght vahrri-co-cele on duh lahft saihde." Every syllable of his
accent came clear-cut. He was pos-i-tive and ab-so-lute as to which
side had varicocele and in nearly every case it was "slaihght," mean-
ing "slight." He rolled the *r* in "varicocele" with a trill and you
couldn't mistake any of his vowels. After it was over the boys
mimicked him. For a thousand miles of journeying there were boys
and men of Company C crying their imitations of that honest and
well-meaning surgeon whose hands that day ran over the scrotums
of a thousand privates, corporals, and sergeants. He was no stickler
for regulations, this surgeon. When our little friend Joe Dunn came
along he was found to be an inch or two short of the required height.
The tears began running down Joe's face. The surgeon looked to-
ward officers near by, who gave him a nod. And he wrapped the
measuring tape around a finger, measured again and found that Joe
would pass.

We roamed around the capital, walked past the governor's house,
out past the home of Abraham Lincoln. We gawked at statues of
dead statesmen sitting and standing, dead generals riding horses, and
I think we found one statue of a private soldier in a cape overcoat,
standing with his musket at ease and ready for the order "Atten-
SHUN!"

On the train to Washington rumors ran thick and fast about how
soon we would be shooting Spaniards. On the day coaches we had
each a wicker-covered seat to sit in and to take our night's sleep in.
At some stations crowds met the train with cheers and smiles. Many
a boy cut off one brass button and then another because he couldn't
resist the pretty girls who asked him for something to remember
him by. Canned beans, canned salmon, bread and coffee, were the
rations. The train arrived in Washington and the night was dark

when it was shunted to Falls Church, Virginia. We marched two miles to level ground with underbrush and woods around it. We dipped our tin cups into a shallow creek, filled our canteens, and drank the murky water because we were thirsty. We put up tents and slept on the ground, two soldiers to a tent. The next morning we went to the woods, cut saplings with crotched sticks and branches and made bunks to lay our blankets on.

We drilled. Across late May and all of June we drilled. "Right forward, fours right, MARCH!" "Company, HALT!" "At EASE!" "Atten-SHUN!" "Eyes RIGHT!" "Eyes LEFT!" "Company, DRESS!" "Right shoulder, ARMS!" "Left shoulder. ARMS!" "Present, ARMS!" "Atten-SHUN!" "Break RANKS!"

We learned the bugle notes from reveille, mess call, sick call, assembly, to tattoo and taps. We filled our canteens from a piped water supply and washed our shirts, socks, undershirts, and full-length drawers at the murky creek in the woods. Most of the time we ate field rations as though we were in a campaign, bean soup and pork and beans more often than any other items. Our company cook was a prize—Arthur Metcalf, with his moon face and wide mouth having a smile that forgave you all your sins except murder. He did the best with what the War Department, through its quartermasters, let him have. I saw him one morning patiently cut away from a flitch of pork about a quarter of it that was alive with maggots. This was seven miles from the City of Washington where the Department of War had its office.

For the ritual relief of bowels or bladder we walked some two hundred yards to the "vaults." These were dug about six feet deep and three feet wide. At the sides were poles cut from the near-by woods and laid on crotched sticks with no overhead cover from the midday sun or a midnight rain. I saw no lime or sand thrown over the deposits to reduce the stench or the swarming flies. This likewise was seven miles from the City of Washington where the Department of War had its office. Along with many others I had my share of dysentery and endless quick trips to the vaults, which with many laughing others I took not as one of the horrors of war but as a mean and necessary nuisance. There were fellows who said they wished the stench could be wafted to the halls of Congress and the office of the Department of War seven miles away.

Evening parade was the high spot of the day. The twelve companies of the regiment assembled on the parade ground. The captains gave their sword salutes to the majors of the four company battalions. The majors with their swords passed it on to the adjutant who rode his bay horse to Colonel Jack Foster sitting his black horse, and with a salute of his sword spoke the words we could all hear, "Sir, the parade is formed." Then would come the clear ringing voice of Colonel Jack, tall, handsome, black-mustached, giving the orders of the day. The colors were hoisted as the band played "The Star-Spangled Banner" and the western sky gave out with a fine flaring sunset.

My tent mate was Andrew Tanning, as clean, scrupulous, and orderly a corporal as ever served Uncle Sam. What I didn't know or couldn't guess about army regulations he was there to tell me. He had been born in Sweden with near relatives in the Swedish army and could tell how the Swedes ran their army in good order, "right up to snuff, I tell you." When a Swede is asked "How are you?" or "How do you feel today?" he will often answer, *"Fint som snus,"* meaning "Fine as snuff." Andy Tanning twice a week wrote letters to his fine Swede girl in Galesburg whom he later married. Next to her he loved his Springfield rifle. The number of it was thirty-eight and he kept it spotless. He took for himself the number of his rifle and would enter the tent saying, "Here comes Old Thirty-eight," and I would ask him, "How goes it, Thirty-eight?" He had belonged to Company C for two years and was a member of the Monarch Dancing Club, so I had danced with his sweetheart, Amanda Hanson, and her sister Tillie who was slim and in a waltz light as a white feather in a blue wind. He had been houseman of the Union Hotel when I was its barbershop porter. So you can see we had plenty to talk about and we could talk it in either Swedish or American. I was in luck to have Old Thirty-eight for a tentmate. He was five feet eight inches high, weighed one hundred and forty pounds, had a prim face, a small mouth with a neat small mustache, and at no moment in our tent bunks at arm's length from each other did he ever let out one echo of a snore.

Our captain was Thomas Leslie McGirr, a second-rank Galesburg lawyer, a tall heavy man with a distinct paunch, heavy jaws, and a large mustache slightly graying. He kept by him a large yellow-haired St. Bernard dog named Smuggler, who in sight of the men was occasionally fed juicy sirloin steaks. Our first lieutenant was Conrad Byloff, my classmate in the Seventh Ward school grades. His father had been a captain in the Swedish army, and Con himself seemed to be a born commander. He had the voice, the posture, the eye. He had learned the boilermaker's trade working for the Q. The men had depths of affection for him or perhaps I should say they idolized him. He could be stern giving commands, but he never drilled us without at times giving us a smile that said we could get fun out of what we were doing. Once in a while before calling us to attention, he might recite the opening lines of Spartacus to the gladiators: "Ye call me chief and ye do well to call him chief who for ten long years has met every form of man or beast that the broad empire of Rome could furnish." He had the voice and smile for it and the men loved it. Our second lieutenant was Daniel K. Smyth, a scholar and a gentleman ever considerate of his men.

Ten of our company were Knox students and two were from Lombard. Some twenty or more were farm boys. At least twenty had had fathers, uncles, or near kinsmen in the Civil War. All had mixed motives in enlisting. Love of adventure, or a curiosity about facing dangers and standing hardships, was one and, I would judge, the outstanding one. A mystic love of country and the flag was there in degree among most of the men. Breaking away from a monotonous home environment to go where there was excitement could be read in the talk of some fellows. At least two of the older men had troublesome wives at home. The hope of pensions after service was sometimes definitely mentioned. Over all of us in 1898 was the shadow of the Civil War and the men who fought it to the end that had come only thirty-three years before our enlistment. Our motives were as mixed as theirs. I think many of Company C went along with my old chum Bohunk Calkins saying, "I want to find out whether I'll run when the shootin begins." The tall, thoughtful Charlie Winders hoped he wouldn't get shot, expected to come home and be a lawyer, though he couldn't have guessed at Camp Alger that he would end up in Seattle as general counsel of the Northern Pacific Railway.

On the lonely hours of guard duty you could study about why you had enlisted. Across twenty-four hours you had four hours off and two hours on, two hours walking a beat with your rifle on shoulder. You saw midnights of stars and you saw the red ball of sunrise come up. I walked back and forth rehearsing the lines of Gray's "Elegy" and "Oh Why Should the Spirit of Mortal Be Proud?"

How can you possibly forget a first sergeant who trains nis voice every day by six and eight times calling off a hundred names? And you answer "Here" when your name is called because if you don't it will be called louder a second time and front and rear ranks will know you are absent-minded or sleepy, and either is a disgrace to a soldier. After a few weeks some of the men without looking in a book could call the roll from Benjamin Anderson to Henry Clay Woodward as smoothly as F. Elmer Johnson, first sergeant, who kept records, read orders and was the hardest-worked man in the company.

Of the nine sergeants and eleven corporals I couldn't think of one that I hated and with the most of them I kept a lifelong friendship. Oscar S. Wilson, a Knox student, managed to be a true and devout Christian and an efficient corporal. Corporal Ed Peckenpaugh was up and down the company street and only the hard of hearing failed to get his baritone giving out "I Guess I'll Have to Telegraph My Baby." It was no surprise that later he led a choir and sang baritone anthems in a large church in Brooklyn, New York. Corporal James Switzer was the company bugler, a handsome boy of seventeen, nick-named "Mim." Years later I would walk into his office at the LaSalle Street station in Chicago where he was the passenger traffic manager of the New York Central Railway system. And on my saying, "How are you, Mim?" he would say, "Hello, Cully."

On a sweltering afternoon with rifles and blanket rolls we made a five-mile march from Camp Alger to a point on the Potomac River where we had a swim, slept on the ground with our blankets, and the next morning marched back. It was a "practice march." On leave for a day we walked two miles to Falls Church, took a trolley to Washington, saw the Capitol and wondered what Congress was doing, walked past the White House and tried to guess how President Mc-Kinley was feeling. I had my first look at the Ford Theatre outside and inside, the outside of the Peterson House across the street, and recited for Andy Tanning "Oh, Why Should the Spirit of Mortal Be Proud?" In Falls Church on returning we had a short talk with a pretty girl who asked, "You-all ah from Illinois?" It was the first Andy and I had heard from a Southern Belle. We had heard "you-all" but not with a Southern drawl.

For our State Militia caps we got felt hats with wide brims, and to replace our Springfield rifles we were issued Krag-Jörgensens. July sixth saw hustling and gabble. We began riding an Atlantic Coast Line train across Virginia and North Carolina to Charleston, South Carolina. We had our first look at tobacco and cotton growing, at the mansions, cabins, and hovels of the South, and at stations here and there men selling bottles of "cawn lickah" that had the color of rain water. We slept overnight in our coach seats and the next day quartered in big cotton warehouses on the wharf. We went swimming next to the wharf, and you could see the Illinois prairie boys taking mouthfuls of Atlantic Ocean water to taste it and calling to each other, "It *is* salt, isn't it?" As we strolled around Charleston in our Civil War uniforms, the people were warmhearted and cordial with shining faces. There were restaurants and saloons that refused to take our money for what they served us. Negroes stood quietly to one side and took off their hats to us. We had been issued hardtack, tough and flat biscuits that were good as money. In one case, on a dare, a Southern Belle gave one of our boys a big resounding kiss for his handing her one hardtack.

We saw lying at anchor the *Rita*, a lumber-hauling freighter, the first ship our navy had captured from the Spanish. Six companies of the Sixth Illinois boarded her on July eleventh, each man given a bunk made of new rough lumber. Running your bare arm or leg over it you met splinters. The air below was heavy, warm and humid. On clear nights several hundred men brought their blankets up and covered the upper deck as they slept. The first day out one man said, "This tub rolls like a raw egg in a glass of whisky." One of the seasick said to another, "Why is your face so lemon-green?" Another reported an Irishman leaning over the deck rail and saying, "I'm not sick. I'm trowin it as far as anny of thim." The rations were mostly cold canned beans and canned salmon. The day or two when canned tomatoes were issued we called holidays. The band played every day and men were thankful. A waterspout was sighted for a while one day, one shark and a few flying fish another day, and the landlubbers felt this was part of what they had come for. I lay on the deck and read a best-seller of the time, *Called Back* by Hugh Conway. I might as well have looked at the ocean.

The *Rita* arrived in Guantánamo Bay, Cuba, on the evening of July 17, our band playing and cheers coming to us from the decks of famous battleships, the *Oregon*, the *Indiana*, the *Iowa*, and more cheers from cruisers and torpedo boats. In the morning Colonel Jack Foster and staff officers went ashore to come back soon with word of Santiago taken and we wouldn't be put ashore to fight in Cuba. Some men were disappointed. Others were satisfied. Also, it was reported, there were ashore some four hundred troop cases of yellow fever and Colonel Jack had been ordered to get back to the *Rita* at once.

We lay at anchor a few days. We were landsmen from the Midwest Corn Belt, yet we spoke of lying at anchor and being fore and aft instead of front and rear and going below decks instead of going downstairs. We sailed out of Guantánamo Bay, three thousand troops on the transports. Rumors ran that we were going to Porto Rico. If we had been reading United States newspapers, we would have believed we were going to land at Cape Fajardo near San Juan, the capital of Porto Rico. If we had asked the Secretary of War in Washington where we were going on the ship *Rita*, he would have said we were going to land at Cape Fajardo on the north coast of Porto Rico and march on San Juan. The War Department so believed and expected and therefore was sending transport fleets from Charleston and Tampa to be of help when we landed at Cape Fajardo and moved to attack San Juan. Of this we, the men and officers of the Sixth Illinois, knew no more than the nakedest Zulu in the African jungles. Even the commander of the three thousand men on this expedition to Porto Rico, General Nelson A. Miles, who had commanded a brigade in Grant's army in 1864, didn't know where we were going. When we sailed out of Guantánamo Bay he believed like those who read the United States newspapers and like the Secretary of War that we would land on the north coast of Porto Rico at Cape Fajardo.

Then about halfway, about mid-passage of our cruise to Porto Rico, General Miles changed his mind. After he changed his mind he was sure of where we were going. Instead of landing on the north coast we would land on the south coast of Porto Rico and he had picked the spot. We could see his ship but we couldn't read his mind. It seemed that as his ship sailed the idea came to him that since the War Department had told the newspapers and the newspapers had told the world where his expedition was going to land and march and fight it might be safer and easier to land somewhere else where he wasn't expected. There were those who said afterward that to attack the fortified harbor of San Juan would have required the navy and the guns of the fleet and General Miles as an army man preferred to land on the south coast and have the army take over the island from the south so that in time San Juan wouldn't have much of an island to govern.

Soon after daylight on July twenty-fifth we sighted a harbor and moved into it. Ahead we saw gunfire from a ship and landing boats filled with bluejackets moving toward shore. We were ordered to put on our cartridge belts and with rifles get into full marching outfits. We heard shooting, glanced toward shore once in a while and saw white puffs of smoke while we stood waiting our turns to climb down rope ladders into long boats called lighters. We were rowed to a shallow beach where we dropped into water above our hips. Holding rifles over our heads, we waded ashore. We were in Guánica, a one-street town with palm and coconut trees new to us. We expected to be ordered into action against Spanish troops somewhere in the town or near-by hills. So our talk ran. We were marched to a field near the town where we waited over noon and afternoon. We ate our supper of cold canned beans and hardtack and soon after were ordered to march.

When we came to a halt we waited in the dark and heard shots that seemed not far away. This was the one time on that island when most of us expected to go into battle, to shoot and be shot at. And it didn't happen. We waited and marched back to our fields near Guánica. A story arose that Sixth Illinois troops that night did some wild firing, some of their bullets hitting the transport on which General Miles was sleeping, others of their bullets hitting a ship carrying Red Cross nurses. I can merely testify that neither Company C nor the companies on our flanks did any firing that night. It could have been that the shots we heard sounding to us like enemy fire were from the Krag-Jörgensens of Sixth Illinois boys aiming at random at an unseen enemy. Some of us had been "shaking in our boots" and it would have been a relief to shoot at anything in any direction. We heard in the morning that bluejackets from the ship *Gloucester* and regulars with artillery had killed four Spanish soldiers, driven a troop of cavalry to the hills, and there was no enemy in sight or hearing. We heard later too that the Secretary of War and many others in the United States were stupefied to learn that General Miles had changed his mind and begun operations on the south coast.

We marched to Yauco and on to Ponce, finding those towns surrendered. We had camped in a wooded ravine two nights. After the first two or three hours of mosquito bites, sleeping in our underwear and barefoot, we put on our pants, wool shirts, and socks, for all of the moist heat. They were mosquitoes of the type you say "One could kill a dog, two could kill a man." They were large, ravenous, pitiless. "They came with bugles sounding mess call," said one man with a swollen face. At mess, at roll call, whatever was doing, you kept slapping your hands and face. I had one eye closed by the swellings around it. There were fellows had both eyes closed. On the second night I followed others in wrapping my rubber poncho around my head. After an hour I would wake with an aching head from foul air breathed over too many times. I would throw the poncho off, beat away the mosquitoes, wrap the poncho around my head again, then sleep till awaking with a headache—and repeat.

On roads and streets as we marched were barefooted men and women smiling and calling to us "*Puerto Rico Americano*." For four hundred years this island had been run by a Spanish government at Madrid. Now it was to be American and it was plain that the island common people liked the idea and had more hope of it. More than once we saw on the roadside a barefoot man wearing only pants, shirt, and hat, eating away at an ear of parched corn. We saw knee-high children wearing only a ragged shirt and their little swollen bellies told of something wrong with their food, not enough food and not the right kind.

We picked up Spanish *buenas dias* for "good morning," *buenas noches* for "good evening," *muchacho* and *muchacha* for "boy" and "girl," *hombre* for "man," and very important, *Quanto vale?* meaning "How much?" or "What's the price?" My favorite was *cinco centavos*, meaning "five cents," a nickel. Yet then and now *cinco centavos* sounds to me like more than a nickel. If a Spanish scholar should tell me that *Señorita, cinco centavos*, has an ancient meaning, "Lady, I love you ever and ever," I might believe him.

We camped at Ponce a few days and then began a march up mountain roads. The August tropic heat was on. We carried cartridge belt, rifle, bayonet, blanket roll, half a canvas pup tent, haversack with rations, a coat. We still wore the heavy blue-wool pants of the Army of the Potomac in '65 and thick canvas leggings laced from ankles to knees. On one halt after another there were men tearing their blankets in two so as to lessen weight to carry. I tore a third of mine away. Some let the whole blanket go. Men fell out, worn-out, and there were sunstroke cases. We passed more than one on the ground raving about the heat. It was an eight-mile march upgrade. We halted for the night on a slope above the road. We were sleeping and all was quiet about midnight. Suddenly came a shriek. Then a series of yells and shrieks and several companies of men rushing headlong down the slope to the road. Men sleeping or just awakened were trampled and bruised. It was found that one of the bullocks hauling carts loaded with supplies and ammunition had got loose and hunting for grass had tramped on a sleeper who gave the first piercing shriek that was taken up by others. We went up the slope and back to our sleep calling it the "First Battle of Bull Run."

On one steep grade the day before as we plodded up wondering how long we would last, saying little because it would be a waste of needed breath, I remembered an old Salvation Army song. And I couldn't help giving out with it. I remember Mim Switzer, Ed Reed, Wiz Brown, and others in the line ahead turning their heads for a look back with smiles at the tune and the words:

> Oh, I'm glad I'm in the army,
> I'm glad I'm in today,
>   And I mean to keep on fighting
>   In this hallelujah way.

We camped on a slope on the edge of Adjuntas, where we saw the American flag run up. Cook Metcalf over a long afternoon had boiled a tinned beef we named "Red Horse." For all the boiling it was stringy and tasteless, "like boiled shoestrings flavored with wallpaper." We had set up our pup tents, laid our ponchos and blankets on the ground, and gone to sleep in a slow drizzle of rain. About three o'clock in the morning a heavy downpour of rain kept coming. We were on a slope and the downhill water soaked our blankets. We got out of our tents, wrung our blankets as dry as we could and threw them with ponchos over our shoulders. Then a thousand men stood around waiting for daylight and hoping the rain would let down. Daylight did come. Metcalf did manage some hot pork and beans with coffee. Midmorning the sun did come out and we dried and marched on to Utuado.

There at Utuado came news, "The protocol has been signed and peace is declared and we are ordered back to Ponce." Marching down the mountain roads we had climbed came easy along with rumors that we would take transports home from Ponce and replacements were on the way. Rains beat down and we were lighthearted and cried, "Hurrah for the protocol!" It was a new funny word we liked. Instead of "Good morning," we said, "How's your old protocol?" We slept a night in a building used for drying coffee. Each man fitted nicely into a dry bin enclosure rich with a coffee smell.

At Ponce many of us weighed to see what he had sweated and groaned out. All but a half-dozen men had lost weight. The scales said Andy Tanning had lost twelve pounds and Wiz Brown sixteen pounds. My one hundred and fifty-two pounds in April had gone down to one hundred and thirty pounds in August. Many were gaunt and thin, with a slightly yellow tint on the skin of hands and

faces. Uniforms were fading, here and there ragged and torn. Hats
had holes in them. On some hats the fellows had written in purple
with indelible pencils the names of places we'd been.

We had a prize chaplain in Jack Ferris, a short, trim, well-muscled
man with a close-trimmed black beard. To a ship-deck crowd or a
hillside of men he could preach—"and they heard him gladly" and
went away feeling renewal.

Our transport with the whole Sixth Illinois sailed for New York.
We were divided into messes of eight men for rations. A tin of "Red
Horse" would be handed to one man who opened it. He put it to his
nose, smelled of it, wrinkled up his face, and took a spit. The next
man did the same and the next till the eight men of the mess had
smelled, grimaced, and spit. Then that tin of "Red Horse" was
thrown overboard for any of the fishes of the Atlantic Ocean who
might like it. Somehow we got along on cold canned beans, occa-
sional salmon, and the reliable hardtack. What we called "Red
Horse" soon had all of our country scandalized with its new name of
"Embalmed Beef." It *was* embalmed. We buried it at sea because it
was so duly embalmed with all flavor of life and every suck of nour-
ishment gone from it though having nevertheless a putridity of odor
more pungent than ever reaches the nostrils from a properly em-
balmed cadaver.

On the transport we went through a ceremonial we had gone
through many times before. A circle of men might be sitting on deck
talking and jollying when one would call out "Shirts off! Time for
inspection!" Then each man ran his eyes over all parts of the shirt,
especially the seams, picking the graybacks and crushing them.
Underwear and pants were more of a problem. In camp we boiled
them occasionally when there was time and a big kettle of water. But
only a bath all over with sizzling hot water would get those in arm-
pits and other hideouts where they were dug in. This I had learned
the year before in hobo jungles.

When Finley Peter Dunne had Mr. Dooley referring to "Gin'ral
Miles' gran' picnic and moonlight excursion to Porther Ricky," he
had probably had a tenderloin steak garnished with onions before he
took up his writing for the day. When Richard Harding Davis wrote
that for the troops under General Miles "Porto Rico was a picnic"

he was remembering the dry corners he slept in, the roads where he never walked carrying fifty pounds in a baking sun, the mosquitoes that never bled him nor closed an eye for him, the graybacks he never picked from an inhabited shirt, the rains he never stood in waiting for the rain to let down. And we can be sure that if the elegant straight nose of his handsome face had ever had a sniff of "Red Horse" he would have put a few lines about it in what he wrote and added that as picnics go, the war in Porto Rico, while not bloody, was a dirty and lousy affair while it lasted.

Dicky Davis, the shining star in the firmament of war correspondents, wrote, "In comparison to the Santiago nightmare, the Porto Rican expedition was a *fête des fleurs*." If you look it up in a French dictionary you will find a *fête des fleurs* is a feast of flowers and Dicky Davis was the kind of a fine-haired dandy who would rather write *fête des fleurs* than "feast of flowers" because though it means the same it sounds more classy. He was writing sober and awful historical fact in saying that Santiago was a nightmare, but only by comparison with that nightmare of blood, fever, and blunders was our campaign a feast of flowers. Mud and mosquitoes are not roses and poinsettias. Nor is sleeping in rain and marching in a baking sun carrying fifty pounds a feast. Few are the picnics where they eat from baskets holding canned beans, hardtack, and "Red Horse" and then take off their shirts and pluck out "seam squirrels." Dicky Davis lived with the high commanding officers, unlike the later Ernie Pyle who lived with the rank and file.

As for history, Theodore Roosevelt summed it up in a speech at the Stockyards Pavilion in Chicago which I covered for a newspaper. He happened to mention the Spanish-American War and added with a chuckle and a flash of his teeth, "It wasn't much of a war but it was all the war there was." There was history with a light extravagant touch in John Hay, Ambassador at London, writing to Theodore Roosevelt: "It has been a splendid little war; begun with the highest motives, carried on with magnificent intelligence and spirit, favored by that fortune which loves the brave." And the mayor of Yauco, Francisco Megia, whom we saw on a balcony, wasn't all wrong in his proclamation words: "Porto Ricans, we are, by the miraculous intervention of the God of the just, given back to the bosom of our mother America, in whose waters nature placed us as people of America."

The war, though a small one, was the first in which the United States sent troops on ocean transports to fight on foreign soil and acquire island possessions. At a banquet in Paris American citizens celebrated and offered toasts, the first one, "Here's to the United States, bounded on the north by Canada, on the south by Mexico, on the east by the Atlantic Ocean, on the west by the Pacific." The second speaker: "In view of what President McKinley has termed manifest destiny and in consideration of the vast new responsibilities that loom before our country, I offer the toast: To the United States, bounded on the north by the North Pole, on the south by the South Pole, on the east by the rising sun, on the west by the setting sun." The third speaker: "With all due humility in view of the staggering tasks our country faces across the future, I would offer the toast: To the United States, bounded on the north by the Aurora Borealis, on the south by the Precession of the Equinoxes, on the east by Primeval Chaos, on the west by the Day of Judgment." It was a small war edging toward immense consequences.

We sailed into the port of New York at night, docked at Weehawken, and in the morning saw a small crowd looking up at us and waving hands and hats. On the dock I bought a loaf of white bread for a nickel and a quart of milk for another nickel. As I ate that bread and milk I felt that I had been an animal and was now a human being—it was so clean, tasty, delicious. We were in the newspapers. We roamed around New York City and people saw we looked lean, somewhat faded and ragged, tanned by sun and sea, with perhaps a touch of malaria, hard-bitten by circumstance and insects. Men and women stopped us to ask where we had been, some to ask if we had news of regiments their boys were in, others to ask what we might want in the way of food or drink. There was hospitality that made us feel good about the country. They acted like we were heroes. We had our doubts about that but we did know we could use more fresh victuals and boiling hot water with strong soap. At moments you just had to reach in a hand to scratch at an armpit.

Again on a train of coaches with wicker seats we rode and slept, reached Springfield, Illinois, and camped there while our muster-out papers were arranged. I went to a dancing party given by Springfield people for the troops. A blue-eyed blonde with a pert walk had signed my card for a waltz with her. I had put my arms around her as the music started and made the remark, "You remind me of a girl I used to dance with in Galesburg." She slipped out of my arms and walked away pert as you please. After that I was slow about telling any girl she reminded me of another.

When our train pulled into the Burlington station at Galesburg on September twenty-first we had been gone only five months but we looked like we had been somewhere. The station platform swarmed with a crowd that overran Seminary Street for a block to the north, and from there on to Main Street the sidewalks were lined thick with people. I caught my mother's face and others of the family laughing and waving their hands high. The *Annals of Knox County* say: "Although the Company suffered no loss in killed or wounded, all of them returned emaciated and worn, bearing the marks of great hardships and suffering. . . . They arrived amidst the rejoicing and acclamations of thousands of citizens who had gathered at the Burlington station and lined the streets for blocks, to express to them their welcome home."

A mother would rush out to put arms around a boy. There were sweethearts who had to plant a kiss they knew where. We made a company formation and marched to the Company C drill hall while sidewalk crowds yelled hello to fellows they knew, called out jokes to old friends, though most of them stood with solemn faces and curious eyes peering and puzzled.

I went that evening with Mary to a farmhouse near Dahinda where she was teaching a country school. They put me in a room with a four-poster feather bed. I climbed up on the mattress, laid my head on a pillow, and sank into the feathers for a sleep. I tossed around a half-hour, then got out of the bed and in thirty seconds went to sleep on the rag carpet on the floor.

The next day I went to home and mother. Mart said, "Well, you didn't get killed, did you?" "No, they didn't give me a chance." "Well, what did you learn?" Mart went on. "I learnt more than I can use." "Well," said Mart, "last year you was a hobo and this year a soldier. What's next with you?" "Maybe I'll go to college." "College! Jesus, that'll be something!" came from Mart.

My father gave me a rich smile that spread out and around his mouth and went up into his twinkling eyes. He gave me a handshake that wilted me. He said he stayed on the job the day before and when shopmen asked him why he didn't take the day off and go join the big cheering crowds, he said, "I will see my boy at home and he will tell me everything." Mother said it had been a big summer for him, with the shopmen and neighbors often asking him, "How's the boy, Gus?" or, "Company C is getting a long ways from home, Gus. We hope your boy comes through all right," or, "We hope your boy has good luck if they get into fighting." Mart told me such talk hit our Old Man deep and it seemed that now he was sure he was an Americanized citizen. He liked it where it said in my muster-out papers, "A good soldier, service honest and faithful," and said we should frame it to hang on the Front Room wall. I gave him fifty dollars of my muster-out money, which amounted to one hundred and three dollars and seventy-three cents. He was walking slower, moving around slower, his shoulders more bony so that the hump of muscle on the right shoulder stood out more.

We were in the newspapers that week. The Army and Navy League gave us a banquet at the Universalist Church and the Ladies' Society of the First Presbyterian Church another big dinner where the main speaker was Mrs. George A. Lawrence of the eighty-thousand-dollar stone house on North Prairie Street. I shook hands with her but kept it a secret from her that for a year I delivered the *Republican-Register* to her house and always tried to throw it in a dry place when there was rain or snow. The *Annals of Knox County* say: "Mrs. Lawrence made an address to the men which was replete with patriotic fervor, and with serious and convincing argument and utterance regarding the obligations and the privileges of American Citizenship she warmly commended the part which they had so nobly played in fulfilling such obligations and rising to such privileges. After referring to the military maps, charts and tactics which had guided them in their recent campaign, she spoke of the Bible as embodying in its teachings the only sure and safe chart and rule of practice, which if loyally followed would successfully guide one

through the great battle of life." I could see Joe Knutson listening
and I think he got part of it. He was a silent man, the hardest-drink-
ing man in Company C, and he never failed on a march or an assigned
duty. He was one of the few men I had picked who in a real battle
would likely have won a medal for valor.

The biggest affair was an oyster supper in the basement of the
First Methodist Church where ex-Mayor Forrest F. Cooke, Con-
gressman George W. Prince, and the Reverend W. H. Geistweit
spoke. President Finley of Knox read a poem about our exploits. It
was a freegoing poem with nice touches of humor and a printed copy
of it in a little book with red covers was presented to each member
of Company C. President Finley was followed by our Captain
Thomas Leslie McGirr, who assumed nothing less than that we were
heroes who had been to war. "Having marched to Yauco we were
weary and lay down and got some slumber," ran one of his sentences.
We believed we had *slept* but he had us *slumbering*. I could see one
private restless during the captain's speech. At least half the company
knew this private had sworn that if we got into real action he would
shoot our captain before he aimed his rifle at any Spaniard. It reached
Captain McGirr and in the muster-out he gave the private a dishon-
orable discharge.

The captain had given Wiz Brown an honorable discharge which
Wiz didn't expect. It was Wiz who that week broke into the *Eve-
ning Mail* with a signed column of bitter remarks very uncompli-
mentary to Captain McGirr and his ways as a company officer. It
was Wiz who was the keenest wit and the best public speaker in
Company C. He became a lawyer and went West to become mayor
of Bellingham, Washington, and a judge of circuit court. At meet-
ings of the Henry W. Lawton Camp of the Spanish-American War
Veterans organized in Galesburg Wiz Brown made speeches that had
the men splitting their sides over what kind of heroes they had been.
He was the equal of Bill Nye when he got into his monologue on
"Red Horse." He was a stubby, deep-chested, red-haired Irish Cath-
olic, a total abstainer and one of the most independent Americans I
have ever known. He belonged to the Holy Name Society, yet he
could spit out the equivalent of fiery curses without violating any
sanctities.

In nearly every life come sudden little events not expected that change its course. A Negro spiritual sings the line, "We walk by faith and not by sight." I had the faith but not the sight to expect two actions that came. Private George R. Longbrake of Company C, whose back yard on Brooks Street touched our back yard on Berrien, had spoken to me on the transport about my going to Lombard, now a university, where he had been a student for a year. He asked whether I would enter as a student if, as he believed, they would give me free tuition for a year. I said yes. So after all the cheering and the church banquets were over, he came to me saying the arrangement had been cheerfully made at Lombard. Private Lewis W. Kay, one of the two Lombard students in Company C, had died of fever about the time of our muster-out.

Then came Wiz Brown saying there was a fire-department job vacant. The department had two "call men." They slept at the department at night and in the daytime listened when the fire whistle blew and was heard over the town. They went to a telephone and if it was a big fire they bicycled to it as fast as their pedals would take them. A call man was paid ten dollars a month. "That's nice money, Cully, and I'm sure if I speak to Mayor Carney he'll appoint you," said Wiz. He appointed me. I bought a bicycle and a blue shirt with a big collar that buttoned far down the chest and two rows of pearl buttons of silver-dollar size. I began sleeping on the second floor of the Prairie Street station house. We were sixteen men sleeping in one room. Alongside each iron frame bed was a pair of rubber boots with pants and when the alarm bell rang we stepped out of bed, pulled up the pants, ran to slide down a brass pole and hop on the chemical wagon or the hose cart. Chief Jim O'Brien gave me a glad hand and said, "Considering where you been, Charlie, I think you'll make a good fireman."

I enrolled at Lombard for classes in Latin, English, inorganic chemistry, and elocution, drama, and public speaking. That was what I elected. They had an "elective system." I had to leave class when the fire whistle blew but that wasn't often enough to bother either the class or the professor. I was going to get an education. I remembered Lottie Goldquist saying you could never get enough of it. In a few days I would report at eight o'clock in the morning for a class in Latin under Professor Jon W. Grubb. Years back I had seen him milk a cow and drive her to pasture. I thought it would be interesting to study Caesar's *Commentaries* with a professor who could wear overalls and milk a cow.

Prairie Sunsets

*

Outstanding among all these crowded memories are the father and
mother and the Kranses. There were no mountains in or near Gales-
burg. There was no sea, no river. The sunsets they saw were all on
the prairie. The passing of the father and the mother and the passing
of the Kranses had sunset quality.

I don't see it as strange that the father and mother told us so little
about the Old Country. For all that was unjust in living conditions
in Sweden that had sent them to America, they kept a warmth of
feeling, a genuine affection, for Swedish people and the language of
gamla hemlandet (the old country). It stayed deep in their hearts.
Why then did they talk so little about how they lived, what their
folks were like, who their neighbors were and what kind of interest-
ing men, women, and children they played, worked, and talked with?
If I had been brighter of mind, with a healthy curiosity about the
early lives of my father and mother, I would have asked them many
questions and had them talking about those meager years of their
childhoods.

My mother did refer to her mother dying early and her father
marrying again. She once told Mary, going into few particulars, that
her mother was a gooseherd in Apuna. She helped her mother in
working with geese and ducks in two ponds on their place. When
the new woman came, her stepmother, "We didn't get along so good.
I left Sweden because she was so different from my mother. And
letters came from Swedes in America about how things were better

425

there and I managed to save the money to come over and do my best. There was a chum, like you say, a good friend of mine, came with me and I wasn't lonely."

But of the father's early years we know less than that. In their first years in America they had their minds set on making a go of it in the New Country, and perhaps it was a help to forget the Old Country. Then as the years passed they spoke the language of the new land, made many friends and acquaintances who spoke no Swedish, and saw their own later children speaking only English. They became part of the new land.

My father was a careful man. He went up ladders slow, reaching a hand up to test each rung overhead before he set foot on it. He could step fast out of the way of a falling plank or two-by-four. When he would say to me, "Take your time, Sholly," he had it in mind partly that accidents can happen when you go too fast. Late in the year 1909 I'm sure he was a little more careful than any year before in his life. He probably had tested by pushing and pulling the branch of a tree he was trimming in the back yard of the second Berrien Street house where the family lived. But the branch went crashing down with him. His good right arm was broken. Dr. Maley was called and put it in splints. At the age of sixty-four he had to take to his bed, to lie for days horizontal with his head on a pillow— in the daytime! To be in bed at nighttime was natural for him but to be in a bed seeing daylight come and then to stay in bed morning, noon, and afternoon, this wasn't easy for him. The days came when he was up and around the house for an hour or so and then back to his bed. But for that sudden unlucky fall from a tree he would have been good for several more active years, said Dr. Maley.

"He read his Swedish Bible a good deal and he never had seemed so kindly and thoughtful about all of us," Esther said. Then pneumonia set in, with some heart complication, and on March 22, 1910, "he died sort of sinking away and not afraid to go."

Mother's radiance grew as her hair silvered, her face kept on giving brightness. An inner grace ripened and flourished. Her interest in her children and in neighbors and friends, her unchanging Swedish accent quaint and lovable to those of us familiar with her face and voice, are shown in two letters. The first was written to Mary, then teaching music in the public schools of Rockville, Indiana.

Galesburg March 29 1902

Dearest Marie

Enyoed your letter so much think you are a pretty good musician by this time neednt tell you any more just now tried to tell Martin about it he yoked me so and laughed at me likes to hear it allright I have been out a few times lately

Mrs Brown told me at the systermöte [Swedish for sister meeting] that Mrs. Sallsberg has a new babe boy I think I shall call on her some afternoon Wednesday evening me and Martha were at the Knox street church a surprice party for the pastor had been planned he received a purse of 50$ Mrs. van Brunt was there on crutches her knee is so bad she asked for you if you remembered the consert you and her practise for years ago. Thanks for the box you sent ve vere so glad to received it The Nelson Co. has sent there bill of the dry goods. Sunday afternoon albert Krans called and also Mr. Elsen vi vere in the sittingroom while the Willits girls and alvira Nelson & our two roomers were with Esther in the parlor I was a little bit surprise when two fellows from the college came to the door paid the rent to April 1 for the two the are baseball sports Alfred Bloomgren died Monday noon is to be buried this Wednesday afternoon Harry Palmer is maried so is Robert Samuelson and vi have cleane the two frontroom and the sittingroom and think to finish our downstears this week vi are all well here and things are as usually hope you are the same will close with much love from home

Mother

The second letter to Esther, nicely married and living in Gibson City, Illinois, is undated and is probably some ten years later:

Monday

Esther dear

I am allways glad to hear from you especially at this time midsummer time when nature has brought everything to its hight so buetifully of course the storm is nature too and so general too all over the country the people are stormy everywhere too so what can we do. out north of us was more fierce the Drury greenhouse homes around roofs windows were destroyed churches windows down town boards are hanging across from the waitingroom every window were out but are gradually restored again

Yes Mary came to my birthday too we rode to Wataga came back made icream and cake from the store with Mrs. Johnson and Esther. She was so glad to hear of your coming to see us and we all are how much it would add to the summers enjoyment and the Children

Mary is yet I gass at the hospital her diningroom in the cellar pieces of glass muss everywhere a beautiful white lylack bush vint all to pieces she said repair to be done when she is tru at the hospital

How we all loved little Yanes letter and it is hard to wait so long until the time when we will se you both when we shall hear Yane play piano and recite something too as there is so much to do to learn in this great world of ours

I hope that everything may well go nothing interfere with the planed viset untill than I am as ever yours

mother

These letters were news budgets. They give nothing of the talk that flowed from her at times in smooth cadence. In December of 1926 while in bed with pneumonia and a heart complication she took a lead pencil and wrote on a cheap tablet of blue-lined paper, on two sheets, a prayer and a meditation. Some of it had the sound of her talk and her affirmations of many years back. Much of it had the quality of a psalm and a final testament. She seemed to know the end of her earthly road was not far off. It came December 30, 1926. She titled her paper "Souvenir," spelled that French word correctly and seemed to know it meant a keepsake or memento to be a reminder out of the past. We can so regard it:

SOUVENIR

My heart is so full of thoughts and feelings, so great, so much to be greatfull for, my heart at times overflow. Therefore help me to be strong and patient now in present struggles for I am yet on the climbing upward path but soon I shall go down in the silence and the deep peace underground. Life is short if early days are lost. I think a bible verse each day, so deep so sweet so many of them rich in contents and wisdom for those who apply or have desire, hunger, thirst after righteousness. Sacred, mighty as ocean, the gem is called Patience. With thought and love in the home so much can be overcome. I suffered last summer and yet too, my shock, I feel it yet. Sometimes I think how long it will last, thank goodness it is better now. When will we learn to love, to sacrefice, when will we learn to overcome our own selfish ways, to bow down, to meditate? Wishes is good for the soul and strength to the mind. O yes, I am yet strong and filled with the desire to live and when I think of the past, the old home and fireside when we were yet altogether, O so many pleasant memories, enough I say a thousand times enough to make me happy. All good gifts all perfect deliverance comes from above. I do look above to my deliverance, everything comes from above my complicated life to the last full measure of error. I look to my redeemer who has come as an excempel for us to follow, who has been preached and upheld for centuries for those who wants to obey and follow the christian rules and follow his footsteps. So help me to be patient, take my cross and follow on to the last step. Lift me up high above those low and simple, ugly black waves that only torment, chafe upon the spirit and troubled mind. I find so much comfort in sayings of wise men, the bible is full of it. Am I wrong in saying the larger wisdom that can see the use of earthly pain and sorrow and not abuse the Hand behind the veil is yet strong and able to uplift the crushed. Crushed I   am   many   times but   not   yet   to   death. The aprons of silence is with me. Silence   is   a   gift.   Be   silent.   Forget   it.

Tired and stifled, she had called once from her deathbed, "Give me liberty or give me death—I don't want to stay here." Two or three times she murmured, "That old man up in the sky, I am going to join him." She looked from her bed to see the sun of a warm winter day slanting into her room and gave out with the words, "It is a beautiful spring morning." Soon after her eyes closed in a peace that was perfect and on her face composure and majesty.

I was in Santa Fe when a telegram came from Mart: "Mother passed away today." I caught the next Santa Fe train and Mart met me at three o'clock in the morning of the day of burial. We went to the house at Main and Farnham where she had lived her last years and died. We saw her body and we smiled to each other. She seemed to be saying, "I had seventy-six years of life and I had more glad years than sad and I've gone on a flight you will also take and I hope you will like it." On the third finger of her right hand was the gold wedding ring that her husband gave her as a token that matrimony might be holy. She had spoken this wish more than once. "Put my ring where I have worn it all these years."

Mart and I opened a couple of bottles of beer and sat two hours talking memories of her. We talked of tender, solemn, and beautiful things we remembered about her. We brought up comical affairs at which she would have laughed with us. We laughed there before her silent presence, Mart saying, "She'd want us to laugh rather than cry." I said, "The Swedes can hold a wake as well as the Irish."

There was always a bond of understanding with the mother. With the father it was different. In these memories, in this endeavor at portrayal of my father, I would stress one point. It would be wrong to pity him. It would be a serious mistake to feel sorry for him. There is a load of pathos in what I have written of him. He was never elected to any office, never made chairman or even a member of any committee, never any kind of a delegate or spokesman, never chosen for any special duty except once for two weeks' jury duty. He never sought honors and had none pinned on him. He was that simple or careless or shrinking that it was clear he didn't want office or honors and it seemed never to enter his mind that it would be worth while to try to be anything other than a plain and honest workingman, living decently and paying his own way. Does this amount to saying he lacked ambition? Yes, if ambition is a feverish and quenchless thirst for money and property or leadership and power. No, if it is correct to say that his eagerness to do a good day's work for enough wages to stay off want and misery, his aim to constantly improve and to do any piece of work a little better than he did it the last time, his never-forgotten purpose to see that his name was good and his family kept from poverty—if we allow him these motives and objectives, he had some definite and clean ambitions.

No glory of any kind ever came to him. I am quite sure his name was never printed till he died and there was a brief obituary—and in the paragraph about his funeral his name was spelled "Andrew" instead of "August." Yet there is an affirmative view that can be taken of his life, not merely affirmative but somewhat triumphant. The days of his life had little of sickness. He did the work of a strong and healthy man nearly all of his sixty-four years. When he quit the railroad blacksmith shop, he worked as a handyman for whoever wanted some repair job, having a reputation so that more work was offered him than he had time for and he took home better pay than from the railroad. His muscles, digestion, nerves, and mind never suffered a break. He was more kindly and thoughtful in the later than in the earlier years. He looked on life here as good, in the main, and his fears of the hereafter didn't run deep.

He was never haunted by the mean and low rivalries that run through so many chapters of politics and business. He never took a dirty dollar or nickel out of dealing with other men. He never put a competitor out of business. He was never a candidate or a henchman working a double-cross on the opposition. He went without the company of rowdies, gamblers, pimps, whoremongers, forgers, embezzlers, drunkards, dudes, didn't understand them and couldn't have fraternized with them if they had asked him, and he never seemed enough of any of their kind for them to have a dim dawning that he might be worth taking for a ride. He had no jealousy of the rich and affluent. If he could see his way to board, lodging, and a roof for family and himself, that was about all he wanted. He had a hankering after thrift that was born in his peasant blood and intensified by training and pressures of need. His instinct said that if he could make an old thing do he wouldn't have to buy a new thing and there was that much laid by "for a rainy day." One of his best Sunday go-to-meeting suits of clothes I saw him wear I don't know how many years. I know he cast it off and got another suit only when the old one was worn threadbare from his thorough and earnest brushing of it.

There are humble lives that have their treasures. There are lives of men aflame with driving ambitions and they get offices or they sack away the wherewithal and in the end it is only a few butts on an ashtray and an epitaph that stinks for lack of accuracy. I remember when James G. Blaine was a national hero and my father's hero. And he was one time the hero of James Ford Rhodes, the historian, but you may go read Rhodes and what he made of the case of James G. Blaine. You will find Blaine shrinks. He was an imitation hero, so many of his words diminishing as the wind from a punctured bladder. I heard marching men of a rally in 1884, their voices beating time to five steps they took, "Blaine, Blaine, James G. Blaine!" I heard the hoarse and ringing cries, "Three cheers for Blaine!" From coast to coast a million men marched with those cries.

And when I look back at the record of the ambitions, pretenses, shifts, falsifications, and petty greeds of the life of James G. Blaine,

I'm not sure but I would rather have the life of a score of working-men I could name who lived plain lives, managed to get a lot of fun or quiet pleasure in their work and play, never went around reforming other people, never ran for office, never fell for get-rich-quick schemes for the reason that they didn't have the itch to be rich, in complete understanding of Tom Edison asking whether any man should want more out of life than just "board and clothes." Only by comparison with the strutting fools and sinister schemers in high places, victims of nameless thirsts that will never be quenched, strumpets of fame and fortune, can I look at the days and deeds of August Sandburg and say he was a somebody rather than a nobody even though he was never a committee chairman or even a member of a committee, even though his name never got into a newspaper till he died and at last something had to be printed about him.

Peace be to your ashes, Old Man, where you were laid there in Linwood Cemetery out a ways from Main Street, to be followed later by the Old Woman who said so often, "There are so many interesting things in life—wonders made by God for us to think about." Yes, peace to your dust and clods of earth. You were givers of life and did no wrong by any you met on your mortal pilgrimage.

John Krans is a rich memory with me. When he came to our house in town or I met him on his farm, his greeting came from a deep, well-rounded voice, "*Hur mår du, Kalle?*" ("How are you, Carl?" or more strictly, "How do you feel?"). His eyes had gleam and his lips had a smile you could see through and behind the beard. He was a landsman, belonged to the country. I never knew him to stay more than a day in town. His thoughts were never far from his land, the animals, the crops, and how they were doing.

Swedish words came from him so strongly shaped by his tongue that they seemed to say more than the same words spoken by other Swedes. I think he loved all the simpler words of the Swedish language better than any other Swede I have known. *Havre*, meaning "oats" (pronounced "hawvre") seemed to mean more than "oats" when he said it. He could talk about *hästarna*, meaning "horses," so to my mind he seemed part horse.

He was a medium-sized man but he had a loose easy way of carrying his shoulders with his head flung back so he gave an impression of being a big man and one who could take care of himself and others in a pinch or a crash. Even amid the four walls of a room his head, hair, and beard seemed to be in a high wind and proud of it. When I sat on his knee and ran my five-year-old hand around in his beard and he called me *min lille gosse* ("my little boy") there was a ripple of laughter and love in it that still stays with me. He read his Bible and sometimes a newspaper, though most often he liked to read the land and the sky, the ways of horses and corn. He was a loyal Republican voter and a devout Lutheran churchman while he gave a fine and decent respect to the opinions and beliefs of others. Politics would take time he didn't have to spare from his farm work and he couldn't see any fun in arguments. He wasn't an arguing man unless we should say that with a plow he could argue against stubborn land and with strong hands on leather reins he could argue with runaway horses. I saw him once coming into Galesburg when he had walked seven miles from his farm leading a cow he was going to sell in town.

Not often on a Sunday did he miss hitching a horse to a light wagon and taking the family to the country church a mile or two away. I doubt whether he ever listened to a preacher who had less fear and more faith than he had. I have sometimes thought that John Krans pictured God as a Farmer whose chores were endless and inconceivable, that in this world and in worlds beyond ours God planted and tended and reaped His crops in mysterious ways past human understanding. When I spoke of this once to my mother, she said, "That might be, Charlie. I see you are talking like a preacher. I wish you could be a preacher." When I told her that Mr. Krans with his head and beard reminded me somewhat of Elijah riding his chariot of fire in the mural painting in the First Lutheran Church, she said, "You are thinking up things. Elijah was a prophet in the Holy Land. Mr. Krans is a farmer in Knox County, Illinois." And to that I couldn't think up anything to say that might help. She had a reverence for John Krans and could understand her cousin Lena who for fifty years and more loved, cherished, and obeyed her husband in weal or woe.

When John and Lena Krans bought their thirty-acre farm seven miles from Galesburg in the early 1870's, they worked hard from daylight till dark eight or nine months of the year till at last the mortgages were paid off. Then the land was their own and their two growing sons helped them work it. They had help from neighbors in getting in their own crops and in turn helped the neighbors. To me it seemed that the Kranses became part of the land they owned and the land could say it had a hold on them. They never moved to another place. Their feet had worn paths that didn't change over the years. The cow pasture with a small creek winding over it, the corn and oat fields, the vegetable garden and potato patch, their shoes traveled every foot of it.

John Krans lived long. Mary once told him he looked older than the last time she saw him. He sighed in a Swedish song tone, *"Tiden går—och vi går med den"* ("Time goes and we go with it"). One of his eyes failed him in his later years, his son Charlie saying, "He couldn't tell daylight from dark with it." He kept on doing some farm work as long as he lived. Charlie was standing by the coal stove in the front room, a sofa four feet away, when I asked him about his father's last day. "Paw was eighty-eight years old and he was sittin here by this stove right where I am now and he was talkin just as natural and he got up from his chair and came over here on the sofa and laid down and that was all. He didn't say a word and we soon saw he was gone."

As Charlie told that, it seemed to me the passing of John Krans was like one of those prairie sunsets when the red ball of fire drops under the horizon rim and you think it should have taken a little longer and yet there was a loveliness, even a majesty, in the way it happened. The barn, the corncribs, the fields, would miss him. The winds would miss him, the winds he listened to in the corn leaves, the rusty brown curls of cornsilk and tassels, the wind that rustled soft in his red beard on zero mornings when the snow lay white on the yellow ears in the bushel basket at the corncrib. It could be that in the grave his hands might dream of Illinois corn and the seasons he had spent with it from plowing and sowing till falltime and the harvest wagons.

In the first three years of John and Lena Krans on the farm a girl baby was born and died within a year and a second girl baby came and likewise passed away. I am sure they told my father and mother about it but no word of that deep double grief came to us children. Not until forty years later, when looking through the Krans Family Bible, did I learn of those two baby girls who came and went so soon.

Their third girl-child lived into her early twenties and died of consumption. The older son Albert was the only one who did a little straying from the farm, working sometimes a year or two as a sawmill mechanic at different places in the Midwest. Albert had sick spells and died at fifty-two.

The one living child of John and Lena Krans, my cousin Charlie, was in Galesburg about the year 1934 and Mart and I met him on Main Street. I hadn't seen him in ten or fifteen years and it was good to look into his bronzed and rugged face and to hear his deep, husky voice with a corn-wind tang to it. Mart and I exchanged the news with him and talked about old times. Just before parting I asked him, "That old barn on your place, Charlie, was nearly falling the last time I saw it, how is it now?" His eyes twinkled and his face had a slow rich smile: "I got some poles to hold it on the east side and the wind holds it up on the west."

Then in October of 1951, Alan Jenkins, minister of the Central Congregational Church in Galesburg, an old and valued friend, drove me in his car out to the Krans farm. On those seven miles I didn't see a horse nor a zigzag rail fence. The roads were concrete till the last mile, which was gravel. Not a wagon wheel nor a galloping horse did I see kicking up the dust on a dirt road. Charlie Krans saw us getting out of the car and came from the house to say hello. We hadn't seen each other in seventeen years. He still had a bronzed and rugged face with no furrows of age, though this month he had his seventy-fourth birthday. At the core of him he still has a boy heart. We went into the house and met Mrs. Krans. I saw the rooms, chairs, tables, stoves, much the same as I saw them over sixty years back when John Krans dandled me on his knee and laughed, "*min lille gosse.*"

Charlie was working the farm and helping neighbors who helped him. During hay harvest on a neighbor's farm some piece of machinery slipped and Charlie had a fall of fifteen feet, lighting on a shoulder and hip. He was carried home and put to bed and stayed in bed thirty days. He wouldn't call a doctor. He was going to die or get well and he got well, though the shoulder was still lame. He said four words with a fine slow smile and in a tone of voice I can't forget, "My time ain't long." I said, "My time ain't long either, Charlie," and told him the Chinese have a saying, "At seventy man is a candle in the wind." Charlie's wife spoke with a solemn face, "One of us will go first but only God knows which." She mentioned how Charlie loves the old place. When she made a trip to Sweden some years ago to see relatives and the old country, he refused to go. He stayed home and kept house for himself. When they go to town he wants the shopping finished as soon as can be so he can get back to the old place. "If I go to the Five and Ten," she said, "when I get back he says where you been so long, I want to go home."

We talked about the old folks gone years ago. Charlie told of his mother when she was a young woman in Sweden getting letters from Soperville, a crossroads with a post office a mile from the Krans farm. All the news of America she got was from Soperville. In her mind Soperville became the liveliest and most wonderful place in America. So when she got off the sailing ship in New York and saw the crowded streets and tall buildings she said, "If this is New York, then what will Soperville be like?" She told this to her children and they joked her about it. I like to think of a cousin of my mother telling such a thing about herself.

Charlie's wife set us a table of meat, vegetables, milk and butter, all from their own farm as in the old days. As I shook hands with Charlie before getting in the car I said, "I think we'll meet again, Charlie. We're too ornery to die soon." And his slow smile came, "Maybe you're right, Charlie." If or when he should go he will not go afraid. His sunset and evening star will be like that of his majestic father. I know that from the calm and half-laughing way he can say, "My time ain't long." If it can be done it is not a bad practice for a man of many years to die with a boy heart.

★

INDEX

★

Names preceded by an asterisk (*) are fictitious.

437